P9-DBL-344

Victims, Authority, and Terror

Victims, Authority, and Terror

The Parallel Deaths of d'Orléans,

Custine, Bailly, and Malesherbes

by George Armstrong Kelly

The University of North Carolina Press

Chapel Hill

Library of Congress Cataloging in Publication Data

Kelly, George Armstrong, 1932–
    Victims, authority, and terror.

    Bibliography: p.
    Includes index.
    1. France—History—Revolution, 1789–1799—
Causes and character.   2. Orléans, Louis Philippe
Joseph, duc d', 1747–1793.   3. Custine, Adam
Philippe, comte de, 1740–1793.   4. Bailly, Jean
Sylvain, 1736–1793.   5. Malesherbes, Chrétien
Guillaume de Lamoignon de, 1721–1794.   6. France—
History—Revolution, 1793–1794—Biography.
I. Title.
DC138.K35   944.04   81-10298
ISBN 0-8078-1495-4   AACR2

FOR JOEY

Contents

VI. Aristocracy and the Republic of Virtue

Acknowledgments

This book was eight or nine years in the making. In that time it has been conceived, misconceived, reconceived, researched, researched anew, thought, rethought, written, rewritten extensively. It is not intended to be my last word on the subject, but it is long enough for now.

I am indebted to many people. Students at Brandeis University suffered patiently through the first course I offered in the political doctrines of the French Revolution and helped me confront my subject in a setting of dialogue. The John Simon Guggenheim Foundation generously granted me a fellowship to pursue my work in France in 1974–75. In 1979–80 I enjoyed the hospitality and facilities of the School of Social Science at the Institute for Advanced Study in Princeton: its ambiance and its scholars aided me greatly. The same should be said for my current association with the New York Institute for the Humanities and for that supremely civilized institution in Baltimore, the Johns Hopkins University, which honored me with a visiting professorship in the humanities in 1980–81. While doing my work in France I received valuable help from François Furet and Daniel Roche. Precious research assistance was provided by Jeanne Pryor and Marilyn Gillet. I am grateful to the personnel of the Archives Nationales, the Bibliothèque Nationale, the Bibliothèque Historique de la Ville de Paris, the Bibliothèque de l'Institut de France, and the Bibliothèque de l'Armée de Terre (Vincennes) for their retrieval of the papers and materials I wished to study. I also had a useful communication of documents from the Conservateur de la Bibliothèque Municipale de Nancy. The insights and criticism of an old friend, Judith N. Shklar, and a new one, Keith Michael Baker, were both sobering and inspiring. Dale Van Kley and Orest Ranum reviewed the entire manuscript, urging me away from a number of pitfalls, and gave handsomely of their learning and talent in helping me to produce a better and fairer study than I could have done without their aid. My thanks go also to Sandra Eisdorfer and the staff of the University of North Carolina Press.

I thank the following publishers and publications for permission to use and adapt writings for this volume:

"The Political Thought of Lamoignon de Malesherbes," *Political Theory* 7 (November 1979). (Sage Publications)

"The Machine of the Duc d'Orléans and the New Politics," *Journal of Modern History* 51 (December 1979). (The University of Chicago)

"Bailly and the Champ de Mars Massacre," *Journal of Modern History*, supplement to 51 (March 1980).

"War, Revolution and Terror: A Public Biography of Adam-Philippe de Custine," *Studies on Voltaire and the Eighteenth Century* 205 (1982). (The Voltaire Foundation, Oxford, England)

The portraits of Bailly and Malesherbes are reproduced through the courtesy of the Prints Division, The New York Public Library, Astor, Lenox, and Tilden Foundations.

This book is dedicated to my wife. According to best recollection, I wrote the first pages of what was to become this study in the early spring of 1975 with her two cats trying to sit on my yellow pad or bite the end of my pen. Somehow I prevailed against those cats. Prevailing was one thing; Joanne had a lot to do with surviving.

G. A. K.
December 1980

Titles are like circles drawn by the magician's wand, to contract the sphere of man's felicity. He lives immured within the Bastille of a word, and surveys at a distance the envied life of man.

—Thomas Paine, *The Rights of Man*

PART I.
The Terror *Per Differentiam*

1. Introduction

Rethinking the French Revolution

Jacobinism is most often considered the doctrine of a centralizing and authoritarian political regime with a large component of populist and egalitarian appeal. How it comes to define itself in this way is less clear. The many thousands of pages written about the Jacobin regime of 1793–94 and its famous instrument of internal control, the Terror, still leave us dissatisfied and confused. This is especially true of the Terror. Was it a logical internal development or a prudential burst of fanaticism, a politics consummating morality or suspending it? Was it conceivably, as Merleau-Ponty writes, "the Terror of History" itself, history being terror and culminating in revolution "because there is contingency"?[1] Both partisanship and deficiencies of historical recitation have been at fault in creating confusions of these concepts. I shall attempt here a new departure that will at several points clash with the received wisdom of French historiography. Since I can, for the time being, make only a partial offering, my interpretation will be vulnerable as such. What I shall do in this volume is examine the Terror *per differentiam* in its roots and sources: I shall be showing, in the context of both Old Regime and Revolution, what Jacobinism *was not*; *what* and *whom* it could not stomach in its transitory "republic of virtue." Gaining a theoretical and historical grasp of these issues and their anchorage in the French authority crisis of the eighteenth century will place us in a far better position to understand the texts, acts, and legacy of Jacobinism itself.

Not only do I regard this indirect route as the preferred approach to a vexing subject, but I have chosen to examine the cases of significant victims of the Jacobin Terror, rather than compose a synthetic account of the currents of reason and passion that converged on the Year II. The persons I have selected are: Louis-Philippe-Joseph, Duc d'Orléans; General Adam-Philippe de Custine; Jean-Sylvain Bailly; and Chrétien-Guillaume Lamoignon de Malesherbes—all of them executed by the Jacobin regime. This exploration should of course be accompanied eventually by a direct and searching appraisal of the positive doctrines of Jacobinism, a project I hope to conclude at some later date. For present purposes this chapter must assume the burdens of anticipating how such an account might proceed as well as introducing the framework for my treatment of Jacobinism *per differentiam*.

A pervasive mood of ferment and revisionism in French Revolutionary studies admittedly affects my vision. The following appear to be the major issues involved in that ferment. In the first place, we witness a constant shifting of our sense of the French Revolution within the total revolutionary history of modernity; we struggle to establish its specificity in a bicentennial experience of global unrest. Secondly, intellectual crises within both the liberal and Marxist world views have promoted efforts to reduce the celebratory or teleological proportions of this event. Thirdly, there has been a gradual reaction against socioeconomic explanations of the Revolution, sometimes waged by proponents of "superstructure" against "base," sometimes more directly indebted to the current rage for theories of semiotics, language, and symbolization. Fourthly, there have been controversies pitting structural and depersonalized interpretations against more explicitly psychological or *événementiel* modes of treatment. Finally, owing to new departures within the history of political thought, there has emerged a tendency to recover the French Revolution as, par excellence, a sequence of political action represented by styles or traditions of political rhetoric. These overlapping controversies of method and and meaning supply the background against which the contemporary historian makes his way.

François Furet's collection of essays *Penser la Révolution française* (Paris, 1978) became an important stimulus, both positively and negatively, in the final organization of this work. It would be digressive here to deal with that book in detail, but a few observations about it will help to clarify my own scheme of reference.[2] I concur entirely with Furet in his distemper against "commemorative" or "teleological" Revolutionary history, although his special form of polemic is appropriate only to French academic circles.[3] I also agree broadly with his account of the genesis of French revolutionary thought, which amalgamates and goes beyond the theses of Alexis de Tocqueville (the historian of *continuité*) and Augustin Cochin (the historian of *rupture*). Briefly put, Furet argues that the intellectual debate of political ideas (from about 1750 on) in a vacuum of politics imposed by the closure of the Old Regime (Cochin's model of the *société de pensée*) engendered habits of a *sociabilité politique*— the phantom of a *société réelle* coming into being—which would be translated into the ideology of 1789 and reach their apogee (a *sociabilité démocratique*) in the Jacobin mentality.[4] Thus a theme of continuity prepares us for the eventuality of rupture. This type of explanation has the advantage of restoring political ideas to a role of causal efficacy and of stressing that the diffusion of the *lumières* provided something far more complex than a mere philosophical pendant to the aspirations of a rising bourgeoisie. It also connects the eventual implementation of Terror to

the internal developments of the Revolution without exaggerated recourse to the "circumstantial" features of patriotic defense, the war with
the dynasties, hoarders, speculators, and "the gold of Pitt and Cobourg."
"The truth is," Furet writes, "that the Terror was part of the revolutionary ideology, which, creating the action and the politics of that period,
exaggerated the meaning of 'circumstances' which it did so much to
bring to birth. There weren't any revolutionary circumstances; there was
a Revolution that fed on circumstances" (p. 90).

Furet properly insists on the Revolution as a political event. He writes
of "the double advantage of restoring to the French Revolution its most
obvious dimension, which is of a political nature, and of focusing our
reflection on the real solution of continuity permitting us to separate the
before and after, a continuity of legitimation and representations of
historical action" (p. 45). (The reader will discover that I take partial issue
with Furet's view of continuity, but this difference may be deferred for
the moment.) Furet's position on the political primacy of the Revolution
is complex, for he regards the political rhetoric of the period as "transparent," revealing depths unknown to itself, and all historical recitations
of the *vécu* (day-to-day events) as superficial; Michelet is for him the
perpetrator of an "histoire sans concepts" (p. 28). He has every respect
for the "live forces" that act beneath political ideologies. His point is not
to dismiss the explanatory power of "society"—the "God" of the new
order (p. 60)—but rather to assert its temporary suppression in a wave of
politics, in a situation where the political *parole* for at least six years
(1788–94) founded transient legitimacies through its pretense to speak
for an abstract people or nation. A void in the social coherence of the Old
Regime created the opportunity for an overdetermined political ideology,
a politics that could be presented directly as truth and falsehood. Here
Furet takes pleasure in agreeing with Karl Marx (p. 84). Jacobinism, he
writes, was "based on the immanent realization of the values in and
through political action, implying further that its values would be the
object of personal conflicts, incarnate in persons, precisely located, know-
able like truth itself" (p. 48). He places, as shall I, great stress on the
dichotomy "aristocratic plot/popular vigilance" in exploring the Revolutionary dynamic (p. 88f.). On 9 Thermidor, an II, according to Furet,
society reclaimed its rights (p. 101).

I distance myself from Furet's account in three major respects that bear
on the structure and content of this book. In the first place, I am less
confident than he is that the Revolutionary historian is today in a position
to overcome both ideology and transparency and to create, in Lévi-
Strauss's term, a *refroidissement* of the object. Furet writes of the present

availability of "conditions" and "elements," of the separation of "revolutionary myths" from "revolutionary societies," and of the "mutations of historical knowledge." "I do not say," he cautions, "that these conditions and elements will finally constitute historical *objectivity*; but I think they are beginning to produce a fundamental change in the relationship between the historian of the French Revolution and his object of study: they make identification with the actors or execration of the deviants less spontaneous, and therefore less compelling" (p. 24). Insofar as this means a sublimation of prejudice and a rectification of reason, I have no quarrel. But Furet also suggests that we must totally penetrate the *vécu* to frame our structures of argument, thereby abandoning the meaning *for* the participants as the meaning *of* the events. Such a position is quite consistent with his Tocquevillian heritage. And, on the face of it—to refer only to Jacobinism—it would seem quite logical to excavate beneath a rhetoric and an action that believes itself "transparent to knowledge and morality" and a "politics [that] traces the partition between the virtuous and the wicked" (p. 43). For that is indeed ideological self-delusion and not historical *savoir*.

However, if one's task is to understand Jacobinism, in the French form or perhaps some other, rather than try explaining the Revolution in *longue durée*, one must conjure with the psychic and literal reality of the Jacobin ideology. The revolutionary ideologies are in themselves closed discourses of explanation and justification that not only stimulate the *vécu* but endow it with permanence in the larger wholes we are trying to fathom. Grasping the internal logic and the boundaries and clashings of these fields of ideological discourse is a part of the problem of seeing beyond them. This is nowhere more true than in dealing with the theme of the *complot aristocratique*, to which we shall be referring frequently. It may be that such ideological points of concentration dwindle within the explanatory features of the capital structures—continuity and rupture— but our present errand cannot be to dismiss as illusions beliefs that contributed not only to distorted self-perception but to political consequences in their full categorical reality. Beyond this doubt that we can discard "understanding" (*Verstehen*), I would also argue that, as historians, we can scarcely avoid "ideologizing" our materials by imposing patterns that represent the rationale of others in ways intelligible to ourselves. Human beings with a difference must translate for one another. I am perhaps only saying, in vagrant deference to Hayden White, that the historian submits his work to an emplotment and a rhetoric consistent with his art and the demands of contemporary communication.[5] That may not be an ideology in the sense that others would use the concept.

But it is a sense in which, *pace* Furet, the French Revolution, and little else, is ever really over.[6]

A second dispute with Furet's approach implicates the manner in which my own work is presented. Furet absolutely rejects psychological explanations, which he holds to characterize the methods of, among others, Taine, Michelet, Aulard, and Mathiez.[7] I share the bias. However, the scope of Furet's indictment would seem to deny the importance of biographical treatment. We may grant that there are many instances where mindless biography of the heroic or defamatory sort has clouded our understanding of Revolutionary processes.[8] We should never want to read history as a set of biographies, much less psychobiographies. Yet history must deal with persons and their strategies; they cannot be eternally incarnations of something else. In particular, opportunities arise for the judicious mediation of lives with large historical structures by way of the analysis of roles and institutions. The exploration of public careers can serve as an indicator of the coherence of practices embodied in social groups and corporations. There are check points from the bottom as well as the top of every historical construction.[9] A life, even while transcending the structure or institutional abstraction in which it is embedded, can also illuminate a *persona*, constituting a problem of limits and recurrences, without signifying any vacuous return to the moralism and romance of the old historical biography. The present work elaborates such a method.

Finally, my interpretation takes exception to Furet's conviction that, despite its segmentary character (noble, bourgeois, peasant, *sans-culotte*), the Revolution is in fact a bloc: as a continuity, a tendency, a structure of thought, speech, and action.[10] For Furet there is no basic disparity between 1789 and 1793, between "liberal" and "Jacobin" revolutions, or between constitutional monarchy and republic. With the collapse of the Old Regime, the country was plunged into an increasingly intensified experiment of egalitarian democracy promoted by the rhetoric of its passing oligarchs. To argue otherwise would be to regress to an attribution of reality to the ideologies of the participants—royalist, liberal-constitutionalist, or Jacobin—and their historical friends in court. Furet's Terror begins with the murders of Foulon and Berthier in 1789. For him the language of "plot" does not essentially change from the summoning of the Estates-General to the fall of Robespierre. This follows from the thesis of continuity and the allegation of transparency. It also undermines the adversary supposition that the factions of the Revolution had determinate and determining social bases.

A rigid acceptance of Cochin's *société de pensée* model, leavened by

Tocqueville's interpretation of the role of Enlightenment intellectuals, will lead toward such a conclusion: a straight line can be theoretically traced from the formation of opinion in a *sociabilité politique* to the abstract excesses of Jacobinism. However, it seems to me that the intellectual, and oppositional, structure of the late Bourbon monarchy is far more complicated than that simple model would suggest. In part, the Old Regime killed itself with its own intellectual materials; in part, the diversity is to be explained in terms of competing authority models that I shall presently examine. If the catch-basin term *société de pensée* is held to cover indifferently the proliferation of academies, salons, and lodges in the last forty years of the Old Regime, we shall have no trouble in perceiving the existence within them of cultures and countercultures in which variant conceptions of revolutionary change could germinate. It is, for example, significant that Jacobinism relentlessly pursued both intellectuals and Freemasons in 1793–94. When we use the unanalyzed concept *société de pensée*, "alien elements," to follow Quentin Skinner's observation, "are dissolved into an apparent but misleading familiarity."[11]

If this observation is correct, it would be susceptible to modifying Furet's shape of the Revolution. Although I would agree with Furet that we discover in 1789 the dichotomization *royaliste/patriote*, which will furnish the foundation for the much more savage couplet *complot aristocratique/vigilance populaire*, I argue in this work for a break in the Revolution. There is not an unproblematic ascent to Jacobinism. Indeed a distinction needs to be made, in rhetoric and in ideology, between a Lafayette and those who called for his assassination, Marat and Fréron. We do not have to go back to playing the old game of royalist, liberal, and Jacobin historians in order to revalue a Revolution in parts. Just as the political overdetermination of the new order was created in the womb of the old, so there was an aristocracy, or several aristocracies, of the Old Regime that stood with a foot in the new. This work will illuminate their failure. My aforementioned aristocrats, with their internal contradictions of new rhetoric and old habits, did not have the "transparency" of 1793 or its utter conflation of morals and politics, virtue and vindictiveness. Their sociabilité politique had not ripened, nor could it, into a sociabilité démocratique. Finally, despite those moments when Mirabeau and Barnave were at their best, the aristocrats had limited communicative competence in a radicalizing atmosphere. The center could not hold.

Patterns of Authority

Since I have suggested that we must begin rethinking the Revolution in terms of its political theories and its translations of political structures, I will begin by concentrating on that specific problem that accompanies the degeneration of an older political order and the legitimation of its successor: the question of authority. By authority I mean the presence and the rationalized justification of a system of order by which men extend, condition, or refuse their civic allegiance and cooperation. There were five basic models of authority in conflict in the period leading up to the Revolution. I take my models to approximate relatively coherent clusters of doctrine professed in eighteenth-century France and not as merely retrospective constructs. It goes without saying, however, that they were neither totally transparent to the political class or to emergent political actors nor descriptive of a great number of doctrine-straddlers (after all, theorists themselves straddled doctrine or produced combinations to serve various needs). The models lean toward ideal-type employments, for they should not be hypostatized, but they are intended to situate both commitments and deviations. In the motion of French history they may shade toward or into one another, but their rationales remain discrete. Although these models were loosely associated with "real" elements of French society, they were not merely rationalizations of interest but also functional schemes of the body politic expressing values that lay deep in French history and in French legal and political discourse.

The first model is the *absolute royalist*, the ideology of the kings of France. It maintains that France is by nature a monarchy, and that the monarch is the viceregent of God on earth. This ideology asserts that the king is to his subjects like a father to his children, and that both parental concern and filial loyalty are owing. The king incorporates the will of the nation and, as such, is supreme lawmaker and judge within his domains: in the words of Bishop Bossuet, "the state is in the person of the prince."[12] All public offices are the king's creation, endowed with their functions as a benefaction to the commonwealth. Without this divinely ordained supreme power (*summa potestas*), government would dissolve and public happiness and tranquillity would be menaced. To be sure, seigneurial elements linked *absolute royalism* to other doctrines. But this is the model that was the special target for attack by all the others up to about 1787.

The second model I call *Aristocratic I*. It is essentially the ideological expression of that part of the nobility of the sword (*épée*) that had not been co-opted to the royal administration. According to this doctrine, France is a kingdom established by the Frankish conquest, with the putative descendants of the original nobles sharing rights and liberties with the monarch. The monarch is therefore owed fealty as *primus inter pares*, the top of a pyramid. Reciprocity of service, sometimes described as a "contract," is emphasized. Because legal forms issued from the conditions of the conquest, sovereignty is conditional and authority is, to that degree, dispersed. The nobility have indefeasible rights: they wage war, administer lesser justice, enjoy special privileges of inheritance and relief from taxation, and are the king's natural agents and counselors. This spirit of the *thèse nobiliaire*, announced in Boulainvilliers's *Essais sur la noblesse de France* (1729), whetted by the Regent's brief experience with the *polysynodie* and encouraged by the later books of Montesquieu's *De l'esprit des lois*, remained a fundamental element of opinion and pamphleteering during the 1780s.

Aristocratic II depends on some of the previous ideology but places special weight on the independent role of justice in the French kingdom. Emanating from the spokesmen of the *robe*, it spills over more widely into public opinion by the 1750s, since the sovereign courts (*cours souveraines*) are now regarded as the principal opponents of royal despotism. This model concedes a radiation of national authority from the monarch but makes monarchy in some sense coeval with its subordinate parts owing to an original procedure of election. The monarch authorizes justice but is restrained by fundamental laws guarded by parlements that were of ancient and indivisible origin. Separately or in unison these courts possess the right of registering the laws or remonstrating against them: they are sorts of republics within the monarchy. In the absence of Estates-General, the sovereign courts speak for the nation, that is, the people. If the free exercise of these rights, established by ancient precedent and consent, are infringed (as between 1673 and 1715, when the parlements were deprived of their right of preliminary remonstrance), royal authority is "despotic." This type of brief was argued with skill and force against Louis XV by Adrien Le Paige, a prominent Jansenist *robe* controversialist and advisor to the Prince de Conti, and it continued to have wide echo until 1788.[13]

I label the fourth model *usufructory*. In its specifics it enlists the support of the a considerable part of the royal administration, *économistes*, and many of the intellectuals. It is therefore of special importance to the revolutionary tracery of the Tocqueville-Cochin-Furet thesis. We shall later encounter an instance of it in Turgot. The usufructory ideology runs somewhat as follows. Monarchy is the legitimate and proper form of government for France, but this is established neither by divine command nor by historical contract: it depends on more pragmatic considerations, such as the thesis voiced by Montesquieu, Rousseau, and others that large countries require a government of the One. Therefore, the justification of monarchy is in its public utility. Although no writer said it publicly, it follows from this principle that a monarch who undermines public happiness should be replaced with another, according to proper forms. The king is, therefore, "the first servant of the state" and the representative hereditary magistrate of the nation.[14] There exists a "natural order" in the political economy: royal policies (war and taxation, for example) should conform to its laws. Although the phrase "legal despotism" was used by Mercier de la Rivière and a few other Physiocrats, it would be more appropriate to say that the king is constitutionalized by the natural order. It follows from this that the king should depend closely on the advice of a philosophical and enlightened administration, selected according to talent and *lumières*. It also follows that public opinion and public assemblies should be sufficiently articulated to permit the measure of public happiness. Real sovereignty is placed not in the prescriptions of the Salic law, but in the judgment of reason and its executants. This conception of authority desacralizes kingship, demythifies ascription, and is basically negligent of the independent values of justice and liberty.

The fifth and final model is the *consensualist*. Without it there can be no real *peuple* and no political transparency. The consensualist model, above all others, requires genetic explanation because of the dynamism it suddenly displayed in 1789. At the strict level of political theory it does not seem to have had the prominence in France that it enjoyed in the Anglo-American world. Contractual theory, except the kind associated with the Frankish conquest, was not the French forte. To be sure, the leaven of natural rights philosophy was generated by way of Barbeyrac's translations, Burlamaqui, and later editions of Locke. The *Encyclopedia* treats it, especially Diderot's article "Droit naturel"; Mably promotes it in some of his incarnations; and there is indisputably Rousseau's *Social Contract*, which, according to modern scholarly consensus, was little read before 1788. Recently, however, other currents have been identified and researched. The tendency often referred to as "Richerism," which a recent historian has described as a "peculiar mix of Gallicanism, Jansenism, and parlementary constitutionalism—or perhaps distortion of all three,"[15] played an undoubted role in the gestation of the consensualist model. With roots reaching back into the conciliar controversies of the fifteenth century, elements of the French clergy, following upon the expulsion of the Jesuits in 1764, ambiguously transferred their claims for representative forms in the ecclesiastical polity to notions of a civil polity. More-over, they had operated with the collaboration of parlementarians in the 1750s and 1760s. Throughout the century, such currents as those con-tained in texts cited by Taveneaux and traced in research by Dale Van Kley,[16] drove the opinion of both the lower clergy and certain members of the robe toward consensualism, especially as implicated in the phrase "the rights of the nation." A shared interest in the primacy of judicial remedy also brought these lawyers toward new ideas of common right and common cause. This mutation still requires further study. What is of interest here is some notion of fusion between Aristocratic II and consen-sualism. Although the fusion, such as it was, helps to explain the shape of the Revolution (especially the Civil Constitution of the Clergy and the later passion of certain *robe* Jansenists for quasi-republican institutions), it does not undermine the integrity of the models. For it really required Sieyès's *Qu'est-ce que le Tiers Etat?* and the climate of opinion accompany-ing the collapse of faith in Aristocratic II to galvanize the French around a doctrine far more radical than Barbeyrac, Burlamaqui, or these other intimations.[17]

The details of the consensualist model are these. The rights of society are prior to the authority of government. Society itself is created by consenting, presumably sociable and moral, individuals: it forms a na-tion. That nation, composed democratically in assemblies, has the right to determine the form of the regime, its constitution, and its laws. The law-making power ascends from the people: they remain the formal possessors of sovereignty. The legal rights of persons are grounded in nature: therefore all must be formally equal in rights, of which a vital portion is reserved to society. For the protection of these rights, the powers of government should be limited and divided (this from Montes-quieu). The form of regime is a convenience based on the will of the people, and on traditions and geography, so far as these are presumed. The notion of an "ancient constitution" is false or trivial or both: either it is not legitimate or it never could have happened. Freedom of shaping the body politic is totally detemporalized. The consensualist model is not only rigorously agnostic about monarchy; it also leaves little comfortable place for it. In practice, however, the legislators of 1789 did not feel totally bound by this model.

It may be asked, in view of previous remarks, where my model of Jacobin authority is. First, there is strictly speaking no Jacobin model in the period before 1789. That model, in the first instance, will be the progressive creation of the radical journalists and the Cordeliers.[18] But, in the second place, the principal elements of such a model are already prefigured in the suppression, inversion, or intensification of some of the doctrines already presented. We shall return, below, to this alchemy.

Much of the history of France from the Regency on is a record of the moral and intellectual subversion of the absolute royalist model. Constantly it is attacked in its main particulars: the king does not hold his sovereignty from God, but, according to various formulas, from the will of the nation, which he represents instead; his so-called paternal power is at best a nice biblical fantasy and at worst a deceit, for the French people have a public opinion and are not minors; the king has not guaranteed the public happiness but, rather, has sunk the people in misery and debt by despotic techniques. Moreover, the king is surrounded by evil and frivolous counselors and an aura of immorality. In these charges we witness the combined assault of all the other models of authority. By 1787, according to Furet, the magic of the royal doctrine is played out.[19]

However, this is not quite the case. To begin with, emotional attachment to the person and splendor of the king did not go bankrupt like the French treasury: it had far wider popular spread than the other learned formulas. Moreover, many careers in the administration depended on precisely these principles and the etiquette they had instilled. While the sacral-paternal ideology could neither resist too many *lumières* nor suffer too many Du Barrys, eighteenth-century France remained to a considerable degree a seigneurial society.[20] Do we not, as Furet reminds us, perceive this still forcefully in many of the *cahiers*, which, as even Aulard concedes, were written with "nulle flagornerie"?[21] Witness the following, from Saint-Jean-de-Caugessac (Tarn-et-Garonne): "That paternal love which is deeply engraved in your works . . . and that goodness which illuminates your other fine qualities. . . ."[22] Or from Sèvres: "Father of the people and regenerator of France. . . ."[23]

Still, there had been progressive diminishments of the king's aura of majesty throughout the century causing the Crown loss of a "prestige which had so far enabled it to reconcile traditional values with the demands of an increasingly bureaucratic state" (a combat in which both the absolute royalist and Aristocratic I models were assaulted by the usufructory).[24] With the summoning of the Estates and their transformation into a Constituent Assembly, the pertinence of the usufructory and the consensualist models began even among the more conservative deputies to transfigure and debase the old ideology. J.-J. Mounier, for example, writes: "The organization of a monarchical government should be such that the Monarch can enjoy all necessary authority to insure the execution of the laws, maintain internal safety and tranquillity, and protect the state against its enemies."[25] Yet even Mounier knows that the sacral has vanished and that the utilitarian is uppermost: because the king is, among other things, "the representative of the majesty of the French people . . . great brilliance should accompany his eminent dignity."[26] J.-D. Lanjuinais, the Breton deputy who swiftly tempered his Revolutionary enthusiasm, declares: "A king is a magistrate, but the primary and most necessary of magistrates, especially in a widespread country (*empire*) like France; he is the head of the family holding it together, a center of unity without which there would be only a disorderly heap of uncoordinated tribes. . . . He is the vital support of the people, the cornerstone of our social edifice."[27] For these constitutional monarchists it is clear that the king's majesty has become reflected light and his fatherhood a kind of geographical fix.

Much of the majesty of kingship had been lost over a span of years by the scandal surrounding the treatment of the Jansenists and the seizure of the powerful talisman of Gallicanism (i.e., proto-nationalism) from the crown by the parlements during the reign of Louis XV, culminating in the period of the Seven Years' War.[28] This gave enormous impetus to the Aristocratic II model of authority, reinforced in part by its victorious, though possibly Pyrrhic, clash with the usufructory model in the disgrace of Maupeou in 1774. Yet, although the demolition of the absolute royalist model was awesome, there remained potent residual elements that could be refabricated for other purposes.

How should Aristocratic I, a patently mythological doctrine advanced on behalf of just a part of a thoroughly quarrelsome estate of not more than four hundred thousand persons, have stayed seriously in the running? There was a decided fragility to what the controversialists of the *épée* were arguing.[29] Their claims by right of conquest in France's shrouded past could be accepted as facts and then castigated as mere barbarian practices, as they were by Mably.[30] Moreover, they had no natural rallying point, as the *robe* had in the *cours souveraines*, unless it was in the royal army, and as we shall see, that too was shot through with bickering over status, even after the *règlement Ségur* of 1781. Yet the *antique noblesse* (as all but the very poor and the upstart *anoblis* were pleased to style themselves) had a conceivable capacity to govern France in collaboration with a tempered monarch. A considerable number of these nobles were patriotic and intellectually well endowed; they could carry their ideas into the arena of opinion and perhaps make common cause with other *notables*. Finally, there was a powerful instrument of action looming behind the model: the enforced summoning of an Estates-General. Judging from past experiences of the kind, the nobility might well be able to dominate such an assembly, assisted by the noble prelates and by junior emulators in the Third Estate (*Tiers*). No doubt the appeal of Aristocratic I was narrower than many contemporaries believed. Yet it was against the "triple *aristocratie* d'Eglise, d'Epée, et de Robe"—with special animus toward this theory—that Sieyès composed the *Tiers Etat*.[31] The deepest hatred of the Jacobins, nourished by the "tiersianism" of 1789, would be against *perfidie aristocratique*, the ur-model of the *complot* legend; their enmity toward monarchy (*tyrannie*) was less intense, except when it and aristocratic treachery were perceived as the same.

The Aristocratic II model had moments of great prominence during much of the century, for it was under its aegis that all the major battles against rapacious royal administration, court profligacy, arbitrary arrest, unjust taxation, ultramontanism, and Jesuit hegemony were fought. The records of the sovereign courts, as we shall see, are a minefield of combats against the absolute royalist position. The problems of this view of authority were, however, threefold. In the first place, while the criticism it elicited received a wide audience, its constructive side was less formidable. The *parlementaires* were at most a couple of thousand persons, some upright, others corrupt, who formed an aristocratic network of their own. Many of them were line crossers, if they saw advantages on the royal side, although some would embrace consensualism in the 1780s. Secondly, despite their guardianship of the law, the parlements were often desultory or biased in their own administration of justice, as befitted their caste pretensions. And finally, the whole substructure of assumptions behind this model clashed with the usufructory view of what has sometimes been called the "modernizing monarchy." In that view there was scarcely more room for the moss-covered institutions of the *robe*, with their hereditary anchorage, than there was for any other breach of political rationality. If Turgot and Malesherbes were able to remain fast friends and collaborators in the early reign of Louis XVI, it was because they were each enlightened examples of the two positions and knew how to split their differences. We might describe the complex relationship between these two models in the latter half of the eighteenth century as hostile, but infinitely nuanced: some of the opacity of the Enlightenment is related to this fact.

The exile of the Parlement of Paris in 1788 by Louis XVI made it publicly popular, and its return occasioned wild rejoicing. But the Parlement's ideology was out of sorts with these expectations. By a succession of acts in 1790 and the inauguration in 1791 of an entirely new system of justice, largely consensualist, the Constituent Assembly swept away the premises and institutions of a once-powerful model of authority. In so doing, it achieved a considerable degree of transparency in its actions, hastening the advent of the Jacobin system of organized "popular" justice by the decentralizing void it had created.[32]

Although highly subversive to the absolute royalist position, the usufructory model was not notably a seedbed of political liberty in the manner of Montesquieu, nor was it a precursor of consensualism. Justice followed, rather than created, this model's premises of the *ordre naturel*. It was an ideology of taste as well as of government: when d'Alembert, in his eulogy of the prolific Abbé de Saint-Pierre, writes: "He composed many works where, totally absorbed in the substance, which infatuated him, he showed a complete neglect of the form," he is carrying this ideal into matters of literary judgment.[33] Furet accurately notes that, unlike the English, who tended to believe in a finality of collective interest begotten from the individual inputs of self-interest (hence no human planner at the top), "French thought . . . even when directed toward economics, and a liberal economy . . . needed to incarnate the social in a unified image, which was the rational authority of legal despotism."[34] I have already disputed the phrase "legal despotism," but the point still holds. We find echoes of the same technique in the far more radical writings of Helvétius.

The happiness of the nation was undoubtedly the supreme value in the usufructory model. But it was essentially to be achieved by a substitution of the radiance of reason for the radiation of the monarch's arbitrary will, not constructed from any aggregate of the wills of Parisians, Bas-Bretons, and Dauphinois. It was, if one likes, "revolution from above," still requiring a throne and a unified power of command. Even if the *sociétés de pensée* created habits of *sociabilité politique* that were unavailable within the traditional corps of the French monarchy, they were also infected with features of the usufructory model. The "republic of letters" was free and sociable internally, but it was also at the service of a highly integrating ideology that tended to totalize its vagrant empiricisms.

It is perhaps an irony that the king, to whom the usufructory model was by definition highly offensive, especially in matters of etiquette and religion, depended in part on its rationale both before and after the deluge. Beforehand, the intellectual achievements of the usufructory model glorified the monarchy, and its applied knowledge improved the health and welfare of the nation; afterwards, especially through the voice of Mirabeau, it favored the monarch's executive autonomy. It is less of an irony that in the early stages of the Revolution the usufructory and consensualist impulses coalesced to deal the final blows to the Aristocratic II model. In the last analysis, however, the usufructory theory lacked rooted legitimation in the unchained nation; it had to work subterraneously beneath the new rhetoric and transparency of consensualism.

To give a similar précis of the consensualist model would be, in large measure, to write the history of the first three years of the Revolution from the point of view of transparency and the *vécu*. I do not mean that the voices of the National Constituent Assembly were concordant, for it took them until September 1791 to hammer out a constitution whose existence they somehow, in the meantime, had assumed and constantly referred to. Rather, this was, as Furet notes, the heyday of the word, spoken and written, and consensualism dominated this rhetoric.

It was a consensualism of many voices, often honored in the breach. In the first place, the National Assembly was faction-ridden from its earliest beginnings. Even within the somewhat truncated spectrum of opinion that the Constituent provided, significant cleavages occurred, especially a major, though shifting, separation between aristocrats and others. Second, beyond the Assembly itself, in the clubs, cafés, and printing shops, there were those for whom, to say the very least, *sociabilité politique* required an immediate and heavy dose of another watchword, *sociabilité démocratique*: Robert, Danton, Loustalot, Desmoulins, Marat, to name some. Third, the agnostic premises of consensualism regarding the form of regime were consistently breached by the natural assumptions of an assembly whose members had been summoned by a king. Although on 19 September 1789 Brissot argued that "the rights of the Nation are abused if, before declaring the Crown hereditary and indivisible, it is not stated that the power of the Crown derives from the People, which has the right to withdraw it as well as to confer it, and which it grants only . . . of its free consent," this was not the way the legislators saw the matter.[35] The Constitution of 1791 was sanctioned by the king but not submitted to the primary assemblies of France. Finally, the consensualist model was infringed by the National Assembly's pretense of representing the newly defined "nation." The Assembly had been drawn from a mingling of the estates, not from a transparent society and had given itself delegated sovereign power without regard for the true processes by which consensualism defined sovereignty. Yet a motion by Volney to elect a new constitutional assembly from the nation at large, without reference to orders, was rejected.[36] Residues of the aristocratic and usufructory models subsisted; it was they, paradoxically, that made this assembly revolutionary.

These issues illustrate the practical shortcomings of consensualism's ideological coherence. Leading spokesmen of the Constituent Assembly attempted to refract this contradiction through a few implicitly aristocratic borrowings detached from their Old Regime mythologies, as well as through more perceptible assertions of the usufructory view. Indeed the Declaration of Rights itself mentions the phrase "public utility" and, in spots, borders on an exaltation of the *citoyen propriétaire*. In the transparency of politics, fissures beneath the surface of the *vécu* could be identified.

The Ideology of Combat

Out of the clash of models I have abstractly described, chaos was more to be expected than any stabilizing pattern of authority. In real society, not only were there innumerable recalcitrants and pockets of resistance to the "transparent" claims of politics, but there were grave difficulties of historical transition. The rationality of the usufructory model was often hard to reconcile with the voluntarism of the contractualist one, even though, according to the root metaphor of the century, "aristocracy" could be pursued as being *contre nature*. Both of these, while favorable to eliminating the "dead hand of the past," needed sometimes to appeal to nature and sometimes to convention. It was not difficult to find evil in the empirical world if one's rhetoric was generated by absolute political convictions issuing from notions previously attributed only to the public person of the monarch: "will," "reason," "justice."[37] This was especially true if *sociabilité politique*, now called *fraternité*, failed to convert the miscreants.

The obstacle was how to move from a vague ideology of nature to a practical exercise of community. Sieyès had proclaimed "the nation," but he had constructed it out of materials bequeathed from an individualist and contractualist philosophy. The single will of France required citizens as well as a social ambiance. To change a man into a citizen, according to Rousseau, one had to "denature" him, that is, empty his *amour-propre* (a human quality that had gnawed on French moral discourse since Pascal and La Rochefoucauld) into the well of the common good.[38] There was, to be sure, a different solution, more in the line of Helvétius, and with usufructory overtones: government might cause individual interests, knowledgeably manipulated, to appear with "transparency" in the laws of the state.[39] In the present case, most of the rhetoric went to Rousseau and some of the reality to Helvétius. Both remedies can be summarized in a single porous word: education. But beyond education the Revolutionary ideology of community looked something like this:

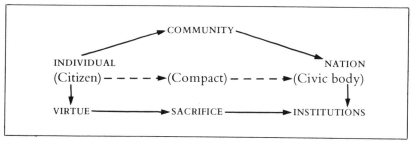

Figure 1

Here we are approximating the Jacobin transformation of the constitutionalist (impure, besides) ideology of nature. The formal mechanism of creating a nation, or a republic, is the same, but the mythology is fundamentally altered in an important particular. If Furet represents the political ideology of the Revolution as "transparente au savoir et à la morale," the emphasis here is rather on creating a new *savoir* out of *morale* through the constraint of institutions (as illustrated, for example in Lepeletier's plan for national education and Saint-Just's posthumous fragments) and through the internalized practice of civic virtue by the citizen-patriot. I do not think that this represents a palpable continuity with the dominating features of the "constitutionalist" phase of the Revolution, where the *morale* was largely a negative indictment of impediments to the new regime. Here, instead, the *morale* is mediated through the populist image of *nature*, which rebuffs as "aristocratic" many of the elements of the previous *savoir*, including things very dear to the Enlightenment. It is true that some of the voices that were to enunciate Jacobinism were already heard in 1789 and that the Revolution was never a complete pitched battle between two opposing rhetorics or dramatis personae. Nevertheless, such symbols as the Revolutionary calendar and such practices as the collapse of public and private in an atmosphere of virtuous surveillance, not to mention corruptions of the legal machinery to suit the new *morale*, are symptomatic of a rupture.

That rupture requires a fuller explanation than I can furnish at this point. For the present, our summary will need to be of the following sort: to a great extent, the Revolution was made with aristocrats and waged against aristocracies. Part of the Jacobin perplexity was how to solve this contradiction once and for all. Could the new wine be carried in old wine-skins? Jacobinism, inspired no doubt by literary and historical precedents of the past, but existing in a timeless zone of moral rectification, contrived a resoundingly negative answer. At the ideological level, this meant reducing the space between the citizen and the state by a ruthless demolition of the traditional buffering agencies. Morally, it meant a citizenship that could achieve itself only in republican virtue, and a virtue that demanded the presence of an enemy in its own midst.[40] Sociologically, it meant a hot pursuit of the privileged who had inhabited the buffering zones. Emotionally, it provided for a wide and sometimes indiscriminate sphere of revenge, based nonetheless on a decipherable political rationality. All this was enacted within the linguistic conventions of a moral dualism—patriots and traitors—with the terms subject to precipitous modification. At the same time the Jacobins were embarked on the frantic construction of a nation purged and purified. Those born to the ancient ways were not safe unless camouflaged by their obscurity or exemplary cleverness. Those who stood with a foot planted on each slope of France's perilous political divide, its chasm of rebirth, were suspected of guilt by aristocracy. Though there were many false, fellow-traveling, or expedient patriots—yes-men, moneylenders, facile orators, survivors—the core of Jacobin doctrine and its radical instrument of surgery, the Terror, could not have existed without authentic commitment to an obsessive goal of political regeneration.

Thus we arrive at the ideology of combat. Here Furet has put his finger on the centerpiece of Revolutionary discourse: even before the fall of the Bastille the French had discovered their essential binary rhetoric that would pass from voice to voice as the orators of the Revolution succeeded one another and were themselves submitted to the relentless vilification of moral transparency. The vocabulary of good and evil remained constant, even though the combatants changed and linguistic chastisement was seconded by the blade of the law. The phenomenon looks something like this:

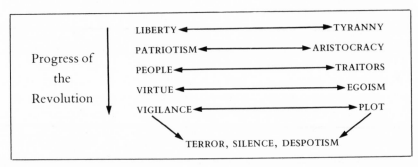

Figure 2

Within this sweep of epithets there is a certain progress in the style of vilification as well as in its inclusiveness: for example, "undesirables" are eventually seen as "traitors," and all plots are suddenly believed to coexist in a single overwhelming plot, usually described as the "complot aristocratique." In the final analysis, both series lead to an analogous result.

The key term is "aristocrat," later linked to "moderate"; its career suffuses the entire Revolutionary experience up to Thermidor. Already, in 1789, it was recognized by some that "aristocracy" had a broader reach than "Eglise, Epée, Robe" and their dependents: "The word aristocrat, as accepted today, applies rather indistinctly to all those who by privilege of birth, of fortune, of ministerial influence [etc.], stand out a bit above the numerous mass that lives only by constant and indefatigable labor. It thus applies to all classes enjoying some abundance, some ease, and especially possessing a great fortune. . . ."[41] For a time, though, the main hostility of the patriots was vented against uncivic nobles and clergy, especially the entourage of the Court. After Varennes, a total war against the traditional aristocracy was declared by the democrats. Finally, the scandal of the aristocracy was transferred to the bourgeoisie. As Brissot put it: "Besides the aristocracy with feudal titles, there was also the bourgeois aristocracy, and that aristocracy has not yet been destroyed."[42] "Citizens," Billaud-Varenne declared to the Jacobins on 9 June 1793, "do you sincerely want liberty? Do you want to end this struggle between aristocracy and patriotism? Remove the exercise of the right of the citizen from all those antisocial persons who despise or usurp that right; cast out of the political sanctuary all who profane it."[43] J. K. Lavater, who had flatteringly analyzed the physiognomy of Hérault de Séchelles,[44] wrote his quondam friend from Zurich on 21 November 1793:

> You tyrannize men ten thousand times more than your tyrants did; raising yourself above your trophies, you exclaim "Farewell, tyranny! Away with despotism!" . . . Since [under your regime] men no longer dare to say and write what they dared to say and write under the most despotic kings, I AM HORRIFIED TO HEAR YOU SPEAK OF LIBERTY. . . . You wish to destroy despotism.
>
> I speak in vain; you will destroy me with a word . . . you will call me an aristocrat, and reduce me instantly to nothing. . . . But in six months, or in a year, spare one of your idle moments to cast a glance at this wretched sheet of paper.[45]

Hérault de Séchelles did not have even that space of time to ponder Lavater's charge. His own aristocracy weighed heavily against him. Found guilty of counterrevolutionary treason with the *Indulgents*, he was stripped of his mandate and executed on 16 Germinal, an II (5 April 1794), the single member of the Committee of Public Safety to fall before 9 Thermidor.

In the language of the more humble, an aristocrat was "one who through wickedness will not wear a *cocarde* three fists in circumference; one who has bought clothing that is not national; and especially one who refuses the glory of the title and headdress of the sans-culotte."[46] According to Varlet, addressing the Cordeliers, only the sans-culottes were virtuous: "*eux seuls composent le peuple. . . .*"[47] Hébert declared simply: "whoever has sucked the milk of aristocracy is a traitor, or will be."[48] Finally, at the virtual climax of the Terror, Robespierre would continue to insist: "The revolutionary government has two objects, the protection of patriotism and the annihilation of aristocracy."[49] This recitation could go on endlessly, but the point is made: the hatred of the Jacobins for aristocracy was insatiable, and the category was expanded to include virtually any sort of enemy suspected of connections with that vast single plot against the republic. This dynamic, in turn, called forth the stern instruments of vigilance and terror. At the apogee, "aristocrat" became even more a moral than a social category, although it had certainly been constructed from social outrage.

The Jacobin mastery of political power and discourse lasted only fourteen months, but it has left a long and confused legacy. Its fragility can be measured by its assumptions. Its strengths can, in part, be explained by its compression of disparate sorts of authority within a mixed model of theory and expediency. It used the resources of the consensualist model, carried to their logical limits, to put a formal leveling of the citizen body into practice and to draw legitimacy from the will of an elected, though purged, Convention from whose jurisdiction even the "great committees" were never detached. It also owed something to the usufructory model through its aspiration to unify and coordinate, to run France effectively, if savagely, and to strive for the "public happiness" by waging unlimited warfare on its enemies. It flagellated the aristocratic models. But it performed a very different operation on the royalist model: despite fundamental recriminations against *tyrannie*, it took the will of the *république une et indivisible* and turned it into something very much like a royal will; in its feasts, celebrations, and patriotic rhetoric, it gave the French a mother, a *mère-patrie*, to substitute for the father they had lost; and, finally, it restored a Gallican religion to the French, primarily under the sponsorship of the god of battle, with or without the transcendental appurtenances of the Etre Suprême. That was no mean manipulation of traditions.

We have, then, some intimations of how the Jacobin model acquired authority in society—a society marked by upheaval and *sauve qui peut*. That authority was refused by others who objected to its potent mixtures and inversions, those who had much to lose by it, or those who took at least parts of the predecessor models seriously and who began to reflect, as their classical training easily prompted them to, that despotism was the function of a cycle, not the stigma of a single type of political regime.

The Victims

This is all that I shall say for now about the context for understanding the Terror. What follows is a work about the Terror *per differentiam*, a book about victims rather than executioners. These are victims of a special sort: they accepted revolutionary political change up to a point, and they embodied in their persons hereditary and institutional mentalities and visions of a political outcome offensive to the Republic of Virtue. It is not my concern whether these victims were noble or enlightened or right. My sole interest is in what they appear to have stood for, the sources of their discomfort in old and new regimes alike. Their biographies are also intended to serve as an indicator for determining the crisis of institutions, the impact of intellectual patterns and ways of life on the breakdown of the monarchy, the rise of new elites, and the nature of the republican rupture.

Although all four subjects share certain Old Regime mentalities and the fateful stigma of aristocracy (even though one of them is formally a bourgeois), their births are spread over an entire generation and they represent very distinct careers. Philippe, Duc d'Orléans (later Philippe-Egalité), latest to be born and first to be arrested, though not killed, was the king's cousin, father of a future king, first Prince of the Blood, and an instinctive *frondeur*, who assiduously cultivated the revolutionary enterprise but soon found himself out of his depth. His was the mock radicalism of a bored and jealous man, wealthy beyond description and impotently powerful. General Adam-Philippe de Custine was a leading military noble, eventually the commander of republican armies, but too haughty and ambitious to please his Jacobin masters. Jean-Sylvain Bailly, a noted scientist and academician, rushed into politics in 1789 and, as mayor of Paris, was the executor of a conservative repression that ultimately cost him his life. Finally there is Lamoignon de Malesherbes, a great noble of the robe, whose public career spanned forty years and was marked by the high drama of his appearance as one of the public defenders of Louis XVI before the Convention. These persons will be studied against the background of their corporate social roles; their destinies will be shaped in a preponderate sense by the perception of their roles by the Jacobin revolutionaries. This assertion is given plausibility by the fact that each of the victims was more progressive than his caste experience would lead us to predict, although none could efface the stigma from his political image. There were specific reasons for the deaths of d'Orléans, Custine, Bailly, and Malesherbes; but they do not, in my judgment, overshadow these men's symbolic representation of what was obnoxious by definition in the Jacobin model of society and government. The Jacobins, unlike the Marxists after them, did not have any historical philosophy for distinguishing between the baseness of the person and the corruption of the institutional network that shaped his habits; thus the issues of specific crime and universal plot were easily conflated.

One great—and obnoxious—institution will not be treated in this study: the church. This omission is both lamentable and logical. It is lamentable because, if one subtracts the church, one dismisses an estate and a major corporation of the Old Regime. It is logical, however, on two grounds, In the first place, a proper investigation of the social, doctrinal, and territorial tangle called the French Catholic Church is beyond the scope of these pages—and perhaps beyond the scope of current French historiography.[50] Secondly, the shape of that problem has different aspects from the one we will be examining. The floodgates opened on the cohesion of the French church, not so much with the alienation of elites as with the political debates leading to the downfall of the Jesuits in the early 1760s. In the reign of Louis XVI, abetted by trans-European currents, the fate of established religion was buffeted by factions, by currents of "civil religion," by the spread of incredulity, by faithlessness in the high reaches of the church, and by social protests from the humble levels. Despite the devout bearing of the king, the historic faith accompanying sacral majesty was shaken. While religion could not in the end be so shattered as other customary allegiances in France, it did not require the Terror to disorganize French Catholicism. To a considerable degree that was a result of the consensus of more conservative elites. The civil constitution of the clergy was acted on with dispatch in the Constituent Assembly in 1790 by legislators who do not fit our description of Jacobin. The zealots fled or hid. There is a comparative paucity of religious martyrs to the Terror, although throughout France the symbols of "fanaticism" were visited by vengeance.[51]

D'Orléans, Custine, Bailly, and Malesherbes advanced along distinct life-trajectories, but they all inhabited a rather exclusive world accessible only to the few. In this glittering but fatally fractured world they were affiliated, though distant, members of what may be called a "politics of connections." Neither particularly well acquainted nor allied in political judgment, they were conjoint actors in the early stages of the Revolution. We may take their quality of contact to be rather typical of the relationships of the French political class of that time. In the politics of connections, access and communication were generally to be obtained through mutual friends, go-betweens, patron-client relations, or corporate bodies that might or might not be called civic. Although after 1789 the public space of parliament, clubs, and press was greatly enlarged and furnished many contacts, the old ways were not dispelled until France had experienced the explosive populist hatreds of 1792.[52] Thus it can be truly said that while our subjects pursued convergent lives, they experienced parallel deaths. It will be helpful here to furnish some specifics about the lives.

D'Orléans, prince, magnate, and consummate libertine, cultivated numerous literati, parlementarians, and aspirant statesmen in his surges of political intrigue; but none of our subjects falls within that category. As Grand Master of the French Freemasons, d'Orléans shared membership in that influential society with Custine and perhaps Bailly. While still very young, he appeared (as Duc de Chartres) to register a royal edict before Malesherbes's Cour des Aides, where he received a stern message to carry back to Louis XV. Custine and Bailly were among his colleagues in the Constituent Assembly.

Custine does not seem to have known the Duc d'Orléans well, but through his wife, who died tragically in 1774, he was well acquainted with Philippe's mistress and confidante Madame de Genlis, who recounts several interesting anecdotes about the Custine family in her memoirs.[53] Custine's "Orleanism"—by 1793 it was a convenient brush with which to tar one's enemies—probably has no basis in fact. Custine of course knew well, and was jealous of, d'Orléans's bosom companion, the Duc de Lauzun (later Biron). Custine and Bailly probably knew each other only at a distance. However, there was a closer contact with the Malesherbes family. In 1763, as a young man, Custine addressed a routine letter to Malesherbes, then director of the Librairie, requesting a publishing privilege for some priests who wished to start a journal.[54] More significantly, Custine's son and daughter-in-law were good friends of the Rosanbos (Malesherbes's daughter and her husband) and the Chateaubriands (Malesherbes's granddaughter and her husband): after the September Massacres of 1792 they passed a peaceful sojourn at the chateau of Malesherbes.[55]

Bailly had no intimate connections with any of the others. Shortly after the formation of the National Assembly he consulted with the Duc d'Orléans on a political matter (their first real meeting); later he came to despise the machinations of the *parti d'Orléans*. As a fellow member of the three premier academies of France (Sciences, Inscriptions et Belles-Lettres, Académie Française), he must have been acquainted with Malesherbes over a considerable time, but I have located no correspondence between them.

Malesherbes, it seems, knew virtually everyone in the academic and political milieux, but none of our other subjects can be classed among his intimates. There is evidence that he, too, came to despise the d'Orléans faction and the man who voted for the death of a monarch he cherished.

What we are especially involved with in this study is the matter of symbolization and personification and the linkage of our subjects with the authority patterns traced earlier. Four lives, however rich and interesting, do not in themselves provide more than a coincidence of victimization. But much of the institutional and mental structure of the Old Regime, and hence many of the incoherencies of the new, are entangled in the careers and commitments of these four persons. They were, by definition and standing, "aristocrats." "Democratic communities," Tocqueville writes, ". . . will endure poverty, servitude, barbarism, but they will not endure aristocracy."[56] The Jacobins aspired to create, at least for the future, a democratic community where no semblance of aristocracy would remain. The statistics of the Terror do not lead us to conclude directly that it was an unproblematic episode of aristocratic slaughter, nor do the mechanisms of revolutionary government allow us to suppose that the French had inaugurated a democracy; nevertheless, the tendency observed by Tocqueville will be clear in the acts and rhetoric we are about to witness.

PART II.
Louis-Philippe-Joseph, Duc d'Orléans 1747–1793

F. Bonneville del Sculp.

2. The Institution of Orléans

Louis-Philippe-Joseph, Duc d'Orléans, later Philippe-Egalité,* is still a riddle wrapped inside an enigma. The contours, or even the persistency, of an "Orleanist conspiracy" have never been effectively defined. D'Orléans has been more or less buried by the social-quantitative concerns of modern historiography. Yet contemporaries of the French Revolution took him much more seriously than we do, because they understood the making of politics differently and because the presence of this colossal prince-plutocrat could not be avoided. His 7.5 million *livres* of annual rent staggered the imagination; his territorial *apanage* was huge; he was the nominal leader of French Freemasonry; his Palais-Royal dominated Paris as Versailles dominated France; he had the temperament and intermittent talents of a *frondeur*; and his ostentatious separation from the politics of the court gave credibility to the notion of a "revolution from above" where certain shrewd political bankers were investing.

Like so many privileged figures of the Old Regime, Philippe d'Orléans was essentially a creature of his milieu and the lessons of recalcitrance and opposition it taught. He stepped into the "new politics" of 1789 with seeming willingness, but without psychological preparation. Where he had conjured *fronde* (i.e., aristocratic rebellion), he encountered revolution; where he coyly disdained leadership, he found it seized by persons with whom he might connive in his antechambers or hire at a distance—

*A NOTE ON NOMENCLATURE: The senior male member of the younger branch of the Bourbon dynasty was invariably called the Duc d'Orléans. This was Louis "le Gros" until his death in 1785; the later Philippe-Egalité until his execution in 1793 (he had in fact renounced his title in 1792); and his son, Louis-Philippe, from 1793 until he ascended the throne in 1830. Before 1785, Egalité was Duc de Chartres and Louis-Philippe was Duc de Valois; in 1785 the latter became Duc de Chartres.

The Comte Charles-Alexis Brulart de Genlis, husband of Félicité Ducrest de Saint-Aubin, inherited a fief and a title, the Marquis de Sillery, from his uncle in 1786. Thereafter, until his death in 1793, he was called Sillery; his wife continued to call herself the Comtesse de Genlis.

Louis-Armand Gontaud, the Duc de Lauzun, became Duc de Biron on the death of his uncle, the Maréchal de Biron, commander of the Gardes Françaises, in 1788. He was "Général Biron" during the Revolutionary war and until his execution in 1794.

I have preferred here the traditional English language spelling of Lafayette, instead of La Fayette.

slum with but not sup with. Yet this immensely rich prince and accomplished sensualist instinctively gave his total blessing to the value of liberty, which for him basically meant liberty of the person and lack of constraint. D'Orléans was an Anglomaniac, with a passion for horses, jockeys, and northern forms of debauchery; he was an intimate of the Prince of Wales and admired Charles James Fox and Whiggery.[1] Later, in 1790, when in unofficial exile in London, he would write: "My taste for liberty had, for a long time, caused me to circulate among different classes of society in Paris; there, my opinions were changed or strengthened by healthy debate (*le choc des opinions contraires*). The same impulse caused me to travel abroad . . . several times to England, that womb of liberty. . . ."[2] What he wanted from 1789 and the events leading up to it was precisely this: no longer would any king, any church, any code of manners tell him, or kindred spirits, how or where they must pass their time. As a contemporary memoir quotes him: "When I wanted to go to England, several times I was stopped [the first Prince of the Blood needed the permission of his cousin the king to travel abroad]. I don't give a damn what the Estates-General accomplish, but I wanted to be there at the moment when they took up the matter of individual liberty, so as to give my vote to a law that would assure me . . . that whenever I wanted to leave for London, Rome, or Peking, nothing could get in my way. I couldn't care less about the rest."[3] This is not elegant political theory on a par with the Rights of Man, but it is important to grasp where d'Orléans's model of liberalism lay and what were some of the motivations that led him to chart a course in antiregime politics. Yet the psychology goes somewhat deeper. D'Orléans sensed that his own life had been largely squandered; he placed great hopes in his posterity. For this reason he took the wise precaution of having his children educated to the new principles by the remarkable Madame de Genlis, his former mistress. As Louis-Philippe, later King of the French (1830–48), recounts: "Madame de Genlis made us into honest and virtuous republicans; nonetheless, her vanity made her wish us to continue to be princes. It was hard to be both at the same time."[4] To his credit, d'Orléans was determined to turn his sons into statesmen. A *règlement de vie pour le Palais-Royal*, dated 20 February 1789, states that he wishes to reserve one evening a week between All Saints' Day and Easter to invite twenty-five or thirty interesting men and women to supper in order to enlighten his children with their conversation and views.[5]

We have already some notion of the idiosyncratic traits of Orleanism, and the special placement of the *maison d'Orléans* within the sphere of the French princely institution. This chapter will explore both the nature of that institution and the flavor of the family as they affected our subject. Orleanism was to become one of the great political forces of France. In Marx's writings it emerges as the faction of the *grande bourgeoisie*, self-made men, individualists, bulldozers of legitimacy and enemies of democracy—conservative liberals agnostic about regimes, advocates of formal constitutionalism and "bourgeois" liberties, oppressors of the proletariat. Yet Orleanism lies submerged in the Old Regime and is filtered through the Revolutionary experience. In the eighteenth century, there was no "social question" as Marx and others would later raise it, but there was the rivalry of families and connections, as well as alternative views of royal power, such as were described in the preceding chapter.

Louis XII (1462–1515) was a d'Orléans. For our purposes, however, the story begins with Philippe, Duc d'Orléans (1674–1723), who became Regent of France in the minority of Louis XV. This prince was dissolute and ambitious, but brave and capable.[6] In Voltaire's words: "Of all the descendants of Henri IV, Philippe d'Orléans was the one who most resembled him; he had his valor, his goodness, his indulgence, his light-heartedness, his ease, and his frankness, together with a cultivated mind. His features, incomparably more winsome, were still those of Henri IV."[7] D'Orléans's ambition led him into a plot for the Spanish throne against the weak Philip V. Though angered by these machinations, Louis XIV showed clemency to his dangerous relative and gave his disgrace little publicity. Shortly thereafter, between 1712 and 1714, the French royal family endured a series of tragedies: the death of the king's only son, of his grandson the Duc de Bourgogne and his wife, and of their eldest son. Rumors began circulating. Again in Voltaire's words: "Philippe had a laboratory and studied chemistry, as well as other things: this seemed proof positive. The public outcry was frightful; you had to be there to believe it. Several writings and a few ill-composed histories of Louis XIV would perpetuate these suspicions if the better-advised did not take care to remove them."[8] At his death in 1715, Louis XIV could not keep d'Orléans from the regency during his grandson's minority, but he made every effort, by will, to reduce that title to a nominal role. The Duc fought back: he asserted his constitutional prerogative and negotiated with the Parlement of Paris (restoring their right to remonstrance) to nullify the will and confer the plenitude of royal agency on him. It was above all a victory for Paris against Versailles, the real against the false capital.

The Regent, who governed until 1723, was fundamentally talented. One of his wiser policies was to seek accommodation with England. But he had to weather the financial scandal created by John Law, and his administration was compromised by squabbles with the Paris Parlement and with *les grands*. Above all, d'Orléans was licentious. As a biographer writes: "His reprehensible morals spilled over from the Court to the City, producing an evil climate that went from bad to worse during the reign of Louis XV."[9] In a discussion of his ancestors, Louis-Philippe confirms that this debasement of morals "destroyed the prestige of the upper classes . . . in the eyes of the lower classes. Thus, more than ever, a levelling set in."[10] This was another facet of the Orleanist image.

In an alternation expressive of the versatile genes of the family, the next Duc d'Orléans, Louis "le Pieux" (1703–52), was an austere person, a humanitarian and a scholar, converted from libertinism by a profound sense of sorrow at the death of his father. Then followed Louis-Philippe, nicknamed "le Gros" (1725–85). This Duc was a good soldier and high liver, who fought the campaigns of Louis XV in Germany. As a typical example of Bourbon endogamy, he married Louise-Henriette de Conti in 1743. For two years of matrimony their public ardor for each other was so blatant that a court wit asserted that they had "managed to make marriage indecent." But the Duchesse, tiring of the first Prince of the Blood, went on to numerous affairs with the nobility of the household and finally the servants.[11] She died at the age of thirty-three, when her son, the future Philippe-Egalité, was twelve. Louis le Gros eventually had a long relationship, ending in a morganatic marriage, with Madame de Montesson, sponsor of the Ducrests, who will figure importantly in our account. Louis was not notably learned, but he loved the theatre: there was much miming and acting at the Palais-Royal and the château of Villers-Cotterêts (we think of Madame de Staël's Coppet). The Duc had a philanthropic nature and generously supported the arts. He also saw that his heir was duly initiated at fifteen to the delights of the flesh by the most experienced and least diseased of the young Paris professionals. Although Louis "les Gros" was not a political figure and preferred to stay in the background, he signed the princes' petition against the coup of Chancellor Maupeou in 1771, an example, incidentally, of the princes' intermittent common cause with the *robe* in support of an Aristocratic II model of authority.

The princes, axiomatically, together with other *notables* (court nobles, royal officers, *gens de robe*, higher clergy, territorial magnates, *intendants*, and municipal administrators), were part of the ruling class of the time. They could not, nor had they since the days of the Valois, run France, but they could interfere with the process. Indeed, during the first four years of the regency, with a council of princes and high peers known as the *polysynodie*, there was an intimation that such a situation could be resurrected, but the royalist instincts of Philippe d'Orléans soon dissipated this illusion. At the accession of Louis XVI the royal princes included the king's two brothers, the Comte de Provence (later Louis XVIII) and the Comte d'Artois (later Charles X), his aging cousins the princes of Condé and Conti, the Duc d'Orléans (Philippe's father), Philippe himself (then Duc de Chartres), the Duc de Bourbon, and, finally, the Duc de Pen-thièvre, of bastard descent and hence entitled to all the privileges of the previous except succession to the throne. The princes had the right to sit with the Parlement of Paris in the Cour des Pairs, and they performed various ceremonial functions.[12] The Duc d'Orléans, by tradition, was accorded the title *premier prince du sang*: he was descended directly from Henri IV, the founder of the Bourbon line. All the royal princes were persons of considerable wealth, but only three of them (Provence, d'Artois, d'Orléans) held *apanages*, an *apanage* being "lands which the sovereigns give to their younger relatives for their division, which are revertible to the Crown in case there are no male children in the branch that received these lands."[13] The recipients of apanages could live in a style corresponding to their birth.[14] The d'Orléans apanage was the most ancient, dating from 1661, and the most splendid.

The traditional role of a royal prince, if he was politically inclined, was that of a *frondeur*. He would be disposed to plot: to fish in foreign waters or in the politics of courtsmanship, or to cultivate coalitions with other *notables*, especially in our period the parlementaires, who were the most substantial political opposition to the crown. The Prince de Conti played this part in the waning years of the reign of Louis XV.[15] It is quite arguable that princely plotting, as a habit practiced since time out of mind, created the moral and political category of aristocracy in which dedicated Jacobins were later able to conceive all their enemies: French history made it easy for the Jacobins to call their antagonists "aristocrats." The private feelings of the princes were variable, but they were encouraged, as agents of the peerage, to become "defenders of the nation." It has been remarked, with some exaggeration, that a monarch had no more dangerous enemies than the Princes of the Blood, not because they schemed for the throne, but because, short of *fronde*, they had no outlet for their political appetites in a centralized administration run far more reliably by ministers and intendants than by brothers and cousins. The best strategy, then, was to debauch and neutralize them, beginning at a very young age. Philippe d'Orléans-Egalité was certainly subjected to debauchery, but other ancestral instincts and personal tastes collided with his pronounced absorption in the senses.

Egalité was first of all a prince. From his lineage he appears to have inherited the sensuality of the Regent (and his mother); the individualism and *esprit frondeur* distributed throughout the family; the respect for new ideas far more solidly founded in the *maison d'Orléans* than in the elder branch of the Bourbons; and, from his father, a certain wish for military glory. He was not well brought up; no one discouraged his corruption. His tutor, Monsieur Pons, declared: "I have finished the education of a young prince who will make a noise; but he must not be offended—he does not pardon."[16] We shall sift other evidence of his character. However, there can be no doubt that he was devoted to his children and servants.[17] Moreover, he was beloved by women of taste, Agnès de Buffon, Grace Dalrymple Elliott, and probably even his pathetically unhappy wife, who, in one of the most moving letters of the d'Orléans collection, wrote him at the time of their separation in 1791: "If you don't listen to the voice of friendship, which is the voice of nature, you will cast away your happiness, and all happiness will cease for me. Think of this. Think it over and don't rush to decide the destiny of our whole life."[18] D'Orléans had learned how to charm and wound women. At times he also knew how to charm men or even, at a distance, the masses. He craved popularity, but his contempt for the public forbade that he should change his train of life.

He had a boundless appetite for self-indulgence, of all possible varieties except intellectual. He lacked *lumières*: others filled his inkwell, transcribed his thoughts, and packed words into his mouth for the necessary occasions. As Louis-Philippe tells us: "My father never cared for the *gens de lettres*, something very curious for his time. His staunch mind had no taste for the false brilliance which often flabbergasted the uneducated masses; and since he had read little, really not at all, he knew scarcely anything of literature but the ridicule, the self-satisfaction and cutting tone of certain writers, and this always repelled him."[19] But perhaps this description does d'Orléans something of an injustice. Blind to philosophy and belles-lettres, and preferring the indolent or manly sports, he was in part receptive to forces swirling in the new age. He knew that his position as a *grand seigneur* depended on a coalition with learning. That was not new in the history of court cabals; in the reign of Louis XV, Madame de Pompadour had posed as the protector of the *parti des lumières*. D'Orléans cast blessings on the Age of Reason without understanding it. He received Voltaire and introduced him to his children, whereupon that obliging old despot of the Republic of Letters had the courtesy to remark that the young Duc de Valois (Louis-Philippe) had the features of the Regent.[20]

From 1775 on, d'Orléans had been engaged in a withering combat with the queen, whose own brand of self-indulgence knew more mannered limits.[21] This family wound, which was never healed, had its influence in the Revolution. At the same time that d'Orléans, shunned by the court, felt deprived of his patrimonial rights, he was also, after the monarch himself, the richest person in the kingdom. The d'Orléans apanage was equal to three or four of today's *départements*.[22] These lands were increased considerably by Philippe's marriage to Louise-Adélaïde de Bourbon-Penthièvre, daughter of the Duc de Penthièvre, who owned large tracts of Brittany.[23] This family was wealthier than most of the ruling houses of Europe, and the children of the unhappy union were doubly descended from Henri IV. Given his political values and his riches, Philippe could well afford to welcome the "bourgeoisification" of the aristocracy, while other members of his order, impoverished, saw it as their ruin. Moreover, as Walzer has succinctly observed: "What has often been called bourgeois political thought was first of all the work of aristocrats and of writers in their pay. The notion that a man's home was his castle, protected even against royal invasion, was first put forward by men whose castles were their homes."[24] However, before Philippe d'Orléans took that bourgeois turn, his *fronde* was waged over etiquette and manners. He contributed to the debauchery of the Comte d'Artois. His Anglomania was offensive to the Austrian alliance. But there was already a deeper issue: Paris against Versailles; isolation versus exposure (Philippe travelled; Louis XVI could not be persuaded to, except between royal residences).

His honor was soiled at sea. In 1778 Louis XVI sanctioned a naval *guerre de course* against the British.[25] Philippe, Duc de Chartres, thirty-one years old and restive against idleness, obtained with some difficulty the commission of lieutenant-general of the fleet. He "travelled and sailed, at Toulon, Cadiz, and Brest" and "became an accomplished pupil of Bougainville in sighting and steering by the compass."[26] On 27 July 1778, under the command of Admiral Louis-Jacques-Honoré de Guillouet, Comte d'Orvilliers, with Philippe in charge of one of the three squadrons, the French Atlantic fleet gave battle at Ouessant to a slightly superior English force under Admiral Keppel. Maneuvers caused Philippe's ships to engage with the enemy first. The indecisive battle lasted for about a half-hour with no ships lost; the French held the field, but due to a confusion of signals, had failed to destroy five English vessels. The British sustained three times as many casualties as the French.[27] The Duc de Chartres had weathered his first combat well; d'Orvilliers appointed him to carry the news to Versailles. There, however, he was received icily, for a separate dispatch had already accused him of costing France the victory. Calumnies against Philippe were distributed. Avid for approval, he sought revenge in Paris, especially at the Opera, where he received a hero's welcome. The applause of Paris irked Versailles and provoked cannonades of pamphlets. Philippe, who had been neither hero nor fool in the engagement, lost his naval career. Though he was later commissioned an army colonel, he never again commanded Frenchmen on land or sea.[28]

By 1780 the Ducrest family had moved into the Palais-Royal: the Marquis Ducrest, as superintendent of finance and political advisor; Félicité Ducrest de Saint-Aubin de Genlis, his sister and Philippe's mistress, who would play a capital role in succeeding events; and the Marquis de Sillery, captain of the guard of the Maison d'Orléans and husband of Madame de Genlis, forever the faithful second of the Duc. Madame de Genlis, a petty noblewoman from Autun, was a gifted bluestocking and social climber: she danced, sang, and played the harp miraculously (once even for the queen, whom she came to despise); she had literary talent and political skill; and she not only retained the confidence of Philippe after love had fled, but she contrived to educate a king of the French, which is more than Rousseau, or, for that matter, Bossuet or Fénelon, had ever managed to do.[29]

The Duc's life-style ran him into enormous debts; with Ducrest's advice, this prompted him to make a commercial enterprise of the Palais-Royal. That traditional residence in Paris was of course, not his, but his father's. However, the generous Louis le Gros was persuaded to give his son the palace in 1780 without furnishings or art objects.[30] Egalité turned the remodelling project over to one Victor Louis, architect of the theater at Bordeaux. Neighborhood proprietors protested vigorously, but the Conseil du Roi approved Louis's plan on 17 June 1781. The Duc assured his neighbors that he was creating "a spectacle and strolling garden for all moments and all seasons . . . a kind of beauty unrivalled in Paris."[31] This did not allay the environmentalists' fears. One pamphlet charged that "sacrilegious hands, armed with saws, have in a few days destroyed a work [i.e. trees] that it took nature a century to create," and accused the entrepreneur of despotism worse than that of the Great Turk.[32] It was also argued that Philippe had no legal right to receive the property, which had been originally testated by Cardinal Richelieu to Louis XIII. But the Palais-Royal seems to have been an undisputed part of the d'Orléans apanage.[33]

Finished in 1784, this new creation received the plaudits of the public: "The marionette show, the museum of Pilâtre de Rozier, the cannon that fired at noon for the amusement of idlers, contributed to its reputation."[34]

Soon, "the Palais-Royal drank in all the substance and life of Paris. The other neighborhoods, especially the Left Bank, abandoned like provinces, shrank and dried up."[35] The boutiques beneath the colonnades were rented out in advance for sums ranging from fifty thousand to seventy-five thousand livres for life possession. Crowds mingled in the gardens or in the galleries, where especially in the evening there was a wide choice of cafés, restaurants, shows, billiard rooms, private clubs, and brothels. When Louis le Gros died in 1785, his heir—now Duc d'Orléans —was able to complete this vast construction. He had captured the vitality of the city, as well as its unrest, within his own precincts. For it was from this swirl of carnival and agitation that crowds later poured forth to march on the Bastille, the Hôtel de Ville, and Versailles. With the onset of the Revolution, the Palais-Royal, teeming with excitement and ambition, contrasted strangely with the Tuileries, deserted by France's kings for over a century, and with the fairyland of Versailles. The royal, and later the municipal, police were constantly frustrated by this enclosure.[36] It was pure expression and pure pleasure, Philippe-Egalité's most original and enduring work. But the power of his own palace escaped him, seething from within and flowing outward along the streets of Paris, the routes of France.

Thus had the first Prince of the Blood turned "bourgeois"—gone into trade, as the king remarked. His later radicalism was somehow connected with this exploit. The Revolution could not mean for Philippe d'Orléans that one returned to the "state of nature." It meant rather that one buried feudal privileges within the greater good of the nation, receiving praise for the sacrifice and resuming life with most of the amenities intact. Despite occasional rhetoric, d'Orléans scarcely expected to begin again as a common citizen.[37] Once having regulated affairs with his creditors, he did hope to emerge as one of the dignitaries of a commonwealth where personal fortunes would be protected. The minuet of the Old Regime was cloying. If France adopted the kind of regime that d'Orléans cherished, then his private rights and life would be his alone, whether in England, or in the Palais-Royal, or at Raincy, or at Monceau: his castle would be his home.

As it turned out, extravagance and defeudalization cost d'Orléans far more in revenues than he could ever have expected. In the midst of the Revolution, a document declared: "The Revolution came and reduced the Prince's fortune a great deal through the suppression, without indemnity, of numerous feudal rights which had formed a considerable part of his income, and thereafter by the abolition of apanages. . . . His annual income has diminished by about 3,200,000 livres [from est.

1787, 7.5 million livres]. . . ."[38] The document breaks down capital (117,976,946 livres) and debts (67,611,946 livres).[39] Obviously, in such an immense estate the capital was not liquid, being mostly in land, and a method was needed for the systematic payment of debts to d'Orléans's creditors. This was arranged by a contract between the Duc and the numerous merchants, furnishers, and private lenders who had claims against him. What he was forced to sign with his creditors in 1791 was essentially a constitution rivaling that of France. It consisted of fifty-seven articles, within ten long pages of text.[40] In effect, a joint corporation of creditors sitting with councilors of the Maison d'Orléans were instructed under articles XVIII and XIX to "henceforth and successively during the following years . . . offer for sale investments and real estate until the price of the debts is obtained." Conditions and objects of sale would be mutually agreed on.[41] At the bottom of the document are the names of some 427 creditors forming the "union," including members of the Duc's own family.[42] B. F. Hyslop has studied the administration of the d'Orléans apanage in the period of Philippe with remarkable thoroughness: there is no need to repeat her information.[43] The ducal holdings were not managed by crooks or imbeciles: under chancellors Ducrest and Latouche-Tréville and their staffs, the Duc may have received sounder advice than the Maison de France. But when his house fell into disorder, it could not be financed by the *taille* and *vingtièmes*.

A pendant to the prestige and, as some claimed, intrigue of the Duc d'Orléans was his long-standing connection with Freemasonry. Since 1773, then as Duc de Chartres, he had been Grand Master of the Grand Orient of France. French Freemasonry, undergoing a period of reconstruction guided by the Duc de Luxembourg-Montmorency, erstwhile patron of Rousseau and later a political conservative, sought support in high places and was only too eager to offer its most eminent title to a Prince of the Blood (the Comte de Clermont had been Philippe's predecessor). Philippe accepted the honor in 1772, but he was still exiled from the court for his participation in the protest against Maupeou. Thus he could not take office until he had made his peace with Louis XV and Madame Du Barry.[44] Though the lodges became widespread and influential (thirty thousand Masons in France in 1785, distributed among 505 lodges, not counting those in the colonies or attached to military units),[45] d'Orléans's part in their operation was perfunctory, more for diversion than by premeditated political design. According to one historian, what Philippe appreciated about Masonic life was its intimacy and lack of constraint.[46] He created his own lodge at "Mousseaux" (Monceau) in 1774, where members of both sexes were freely admitted. This addition of "ladies' auxiliaries" was a singular characteristic of French Freemasonry: "in the eighteenth century, when women played such an important intellectual and social role, it was hard to keep them out."[47] D'Orléans also had a small, richly decorated temple constructed in the Palais-Royal, and he browbeat his father into being initiated.[48]

As Grand Master, d'Orléans no doubt presided over many grave ceremonies, such as the reception to the brotherhood of the Comte d'Artois on 15 July 1778 and the famous initiation of the elderly Voltaire the year previous.[49] He himself is supposed to have passed through the sinister rite of becoming a "Chevalier Kadosh," approximate to the thirtieth degree of Masonry, which included fearful oaths and the mimed slaying of a king—a point made much of by royalist biographers.[50] For the most part, though, Masonry seems to have meant for d'Orléans free expression, drinking, women, and a general air of Anglomania; his sidekick, the Duc de Lauzun, was also a brother of the Grand Orient. Indeed, lodges became à la mode at Versailles. As Marie-Antoinette wrote to one of her sisters: "Everybody belongs; everything that goes on is known—what can be the danger?"

The danger was of a distant ideological kind, the encouragement of new habits of social mixing (*sociabilité politique*) and vulgarized refractions of the *lumières* that would prove incompatible with the old order. Commenting on the constitution of the Grand Orient, Martin writes: "Everything calls attention to the will for creating a body where the majority will rule instead of just a few."[51] Yet both the grand master and the director-general were irremovable. A powerful and restricted executive committee, elected by the "brothers," shared power with these officers. The Freemasons were not a democracy; they were a kind of elective aristocracy. They had advanced part of the way to 1789, for the estates mixed freely; the *plebs* alone was excluded. Out of the 505 lodges listed by Martin, only 111 were presided over by nobles or clergy.[52] Moreover, the spirit of criticism and free examination had penetrated deeply into the Freemasons as well as the learned societies. The lodges acquired the parliamentary habit of initiating discussions, debates, inquiries, and reports on matters of substance.[53] Finally, "Masonry gave its members not only intellectual tastes, but the habit of unity. In the lodges there were no longer nobles or bourgeois, Bretons or Dauphinois. Philosophical ideas traversed the kingdom."[54]

The lodges have been seen as the substantial shadow of the agitation of 1789: the Club Breton (ancestor of the Jacobins) and the Comité des Trente. According to Martin, "it is not exaggerated to say that almost half the deputies to the Estates-General were active members of the

Grand Orient."[55] If this is true, it means that out of a total French population in which the proportion of Mason to non-Mason was about 1:70, the representatives at Versailles achieved a proportion of 1:2. Sieyès might more properly have complained about the Masons than about the nobles and clergy. In my own research, I have checked the names of the electors of Paris *intra-muros* in 1789 (407 in number) against Le Bihan's list of Parisian Freemasons;[56] admitting all questionable cases, my finding is that twenty-eight percent of the electoral assembly of the Tiers alone could be identified as Masons. Moreover, when we approach politics, it must be remembered that the Grand Orient could include a Comte d'Artois, a Mirabeau-Tonneau, a Duc de Guines, as well as a Dr. Guillotin, a Barère, or a Couthon. And we must not confuse Freemasonry with what later became known as a *parti d'Orléans*, despite the Duc's eminence in the Grand Orient.

When in 1793 the Jacobins, countenancing no "partial societies" that might interfere with citizenship, brought Terror upon the lodges, the prudent grand master had already made his exit. A letter of 22 February 1793 states: "In a time when nobody at all foresaw our revolution, I became attached to Freemasonry because it offered me a sort of image of equality; since then, I have left the illusion for the reality."[57] Another letter, dated 25 March 1793, informs us: "Surely . . . it is best for me not to belong to any gathering that is not entirely public."[58] Two weeks afterward d'Orléans was placed under arrest by the Convention; his retreat from the Grand Orient no doubt involved fear as well as civic conviction.

D'Orléans had a character both transparent and enigmatic. How shall we best approach it? We shall, in the first place, have trouble finding disinterested witnesses. For early royalist historians, d'Orléans had "an extraordinarily fierce, hate-ridden, and vindictive soul"[59] and offered "the most astonishing contrast of ambition and cowardice, daring and weakness, avarice and prodigality."[60] The tendency of later Orleanist writers is to concede his baseness, but to exonerate him from charges of conspiring at regicide: "ever wanting in character, hypocritical and evil, he could only trail in the wake of the revolutionary actions taking place around him."[61] More modern interpreters tend to attribute a lack of *sérieux* to d'Orléans and to stress the vulnerability of his private qualities to the mercenary ambitions of his friends and advisors.[62]

From contemporaries, most having reasons of their own to condemn him, we do not receive a more favorable impression. Among his circle of intimates, Laclos, Biron, and Sillery have left no clues. Only Charles Voidel, who defended him to the last, was moved to comment: "He was dangerous because his name was used. Well, what name will evil designs not stoop to using in order to mask their criminal projects? The 'd'Orléans faction' was a fantasy, behind which every agent of intrigue, every aristocrat and conspirator, took shelter to undermine the building of liberty."[63]

The enemies are legion. To Talleyrand we owe the most sustained profile of d'Orléans by a political associate: "Unbridled in his tastes, using his pleasures as a rampart against love, he began with every abuse and his only constancy was in his excesses."[64] The Comte de la Marck wrote: "The Duc d'Orléans had a very weak character: he never shed the humor of his childhood, and I have often seen him dissolve in silliness. He couldn't even control his attention span for a quarter of an hour, not in a serious discussion."[65] Regarding the judgments of Mirabeau and Lafayette, we shall reserve comment for later. Barnave, who passed for a radical in 1789, was unimpressed with Philippe. "Did there exist a man," he asked himself, "who, if Louis XVI were removed, could claim the throne by his position, his great deeds, or his great virtues?" It was "absurd" to think so.[66] Brissot, who had worked for Ducrest in the Maison d'Orléans, found the Duc frivolous and inconsequential.[67] Dumouriez, sometimes accused of being an Orleanist agent,[68] had every reason after his treasonable conduct of April 1793, to write that "Philippe-Egalité is totally unworthy to bear the name of Duc d'Orléans."[69] Mounier declared: "No, M. de duc d'Orléans is not a defender of liberty, but of license. . . . It is not the people who do him the honor of their affection, but the vilest rabble."[70] Mounier's political friend Malouet, equally scathing, denied d'Orléans a central role in the revolutionary turbulence: "The Duc d'Orléans had his own separate intrigue. His personal goal was vengeance; and that of his *petit conseil* was not democracy, but profit."[71] Madame Roland claims to have shunned d'Orléans like the plague and would not even receive Sillery, supposedly "good and kind," because of their close relations.[72]

In proper perspective we shall see how Philippe d'Orléans's earlier advocates deserted and vilified him when they could no longer use him. Barère's extended reflections are more noteworthy, for they describe the reactions of a trimmer, a *dérogé* noble on the make, who, newly arrived at Versailles in 1789 as a deputy of the Tiers from Pau, found a warm welcome in the Palais-Royal, becoming the private tutor of Pamela, an English ward of the d'Orléans household.[73] Eventually Barère would be presiding officer of the Convention when Louis XVI was questioned. Barère was at first overwhelmed by his reception: "What delicious days I passed in that elegant society! . . . I was continually flattered by Madame de Genlis and the young princes [Louis-Philippe later gave the aged regicide a small pension], a memory that I shall always cherish."[74] According to Barère, the Duc d'Orléans "expressed strong thoughts and just opinions. People thought him made for society, not for the political arena, but he was misunderstood. He was shy, though a great lord; he was a citizen, though a prince; and if he could have conquered his natural hesitation and political shyness, which were taken for faults of character, he would have shown that he could reign."[75]

After this commendation it is unsettling to read Barère's tortuous speech to the Convention of 16 December 1792 on the subject of his quondam patron: "he was truly an ambitious man, disturbing to liberty . . . who stirred up the events of 5–6 October at Versailles . . . who had himself elected the twenty-fourth and last deputy of Paris [to the Convention] in the midst of knives and daggers pointed by him and his henchmen . . . who had such close relations in London and so many confederates in Paris. . . ."[76] Delicious evenings at "Mousseaux" and grave conversations with a citizen prince had evaporated in the heat of opportunism.

Perhaps the last words of this discussion, which poses a problem it cannot solve, should go to the most intimate chronicler of d'Orléans: his son, who saw his father, lovingly, as a weak human being who neither wanted nor could have launched a campaign for the throne. During their last meeting of 4 December 1792, Louis-Philippe recorded the Duc's melancholy words: "Really, I sometimes think that, without being aware of it, I must have a contagious disease; for certainly there is a general dread of being in contact with me or coming near me. This isn't the first time I've noticed it. I saw the first signs in the Chamber of the Nobility of the Estates-General of 1789."[77] These were pathetic thoughts to come bursting out, even in private, from the first Prince of the Blood, whose great-great grandfather had had the following proud epitaph composed by the poet Malherbe: "Apprenez, âmes vulgaires, à mourir sans murmurer."[78] Just as the old politics had lost its relevance, the old sentences had lost their savor.

3. Preparing for the New Politics

In 1774 the Prince de Conti, the leading defender of the parlements, soon to be restored by Louis XVI, had been acclaimed at the Opera.[1] Philippe, then the young Duc de Chartres, would aspire to the same kind of popularity. He had joined his father in Conti's protest and had suffered temporary exile from the court of Louis XV, even though he was "by conviction and by duty of birth . . . the most zealous defender of royal authority. . . ."[2] Retrospectively from London in 1790, he justified his politics in the following terms:

> Three times [i.e. 1771, 1787, and 1789] I was the victim [of a lack of liberty], and each of these three passing occasions increased my taste for it, although they were intended to destroy it.
>
> The first time, without really seeking reasons, I followed my impulses, those of trust in public opinion and example. . . . I cannot say that conduct was entirely *my* conduct. . . .
>
> The second time, my motive was in not wanting to contradict by a public act positions that I had previously supported publicly.
>
> But the third time, my behavior was entirely the result of my ideas and the effect of my will.[3]

This account of the self-education of a prince, probably drafted by Choderlos de Laclos, speaks of the existence of a dominant taste (*goût dominant*) in every person, which in the case of the author has always been liberty.[4] Despite the learned reference to the "will," we may take this to mean the liberty of the physical person.

In 1785, when Philippe d'Orléans acquired his father's titles and fortune, it was just becoming clear that France was running to its ruin. The ambitious Necker first made the country aware of its fiscal plight.[5] He and his successor Calonne blamed each other for the damage. But that was not precisely the point. Over more than half a century the court's prodigality had dissipated the resources of the nation, and new taxation could no longer staunch the wound. Calonne suggested mild reforms on 20 August 1786. There were three possible ways to navigate. As had not been done since 1614, the king could summon an Estates-General of the realm: this threatened to hand the power of the purse over to the estates, especially the nobility. Or the king could try to rule by arbitrary *lits de justice*: but incessant quarrels with the parlements, now heavily backed by public opinion, might easily lead to a breakdown of order and authority.

The king and Calonne, not the easiest of bedfellows, chose a third method. They would summon an *Assemblée des Notables* (a mixture of prelates, high-ranking nobles, parlementarians, and royal and municipal officers) to deal with the predicaments of the floundering kingdom; the last of these gatherings had been held in 1626.

An *Assemblée des Notables* had no resemblance to the Estates-General. It was appointed by the king directly and not elected; its members served as individuals and not by orders (though the two privileged estates were vastly overrepresented); and there were no *cahiers de doléances*.[6] But the individuals represented functions: "The King did not choose the notables *intuitu personae* . . . but according to their function or situation in the state. . . . Certain personalities summoned in 1787 were not called [to the second Assembly] in 1788 because they had ceased to hold these positions."[7] After assembling in plenary session, the notables were distributed into committees (*bureaux*), each presided over by a prince and peer of the realm. The sitting of 1787 was opened in great ceremony in the royal capital on 22 February: in the company of the princes, the king attended a mass, followed at noon by a convocation of the Assembly.[8] The Assembly then divided into its seven bureaux to consider the reforms.[9] The Duc d'Orléans presided over the Third Bureau. Each committee of 1787 debated the same problem: how to restore national solvency.

From the outset Calonne struck a belligerent posture, angering many of the high magnates, who were seeking an aristocratic quid pro quo; his doom was sealed by his own strategy as well as by the connivance of such rivals as Lamoignon, the Garde des Sceaux, and Loménie de Brienne, Archbishop of Sens, a favorite of the queen.[10] On 8 April the king dismissed Calonne, and his enemies drove him into exile in England. The titular leader of this opposition was the Comte de Provence, president of the First Bureau; he was seconded by d'Orléans.[11] The Duc d'Orléans had no love for the Brienne faction, nor they for him, but he was then allied with the parlementarians and had many reasons for wishing to embarrass the government.[12] There was no evident dynamism in any of his maneuvers: he attended only six of the fifteen meetings of the Court of Peers held between 22 June and 13 August 1787.[13] But other events were moving swiftly. The king and Brienne entered into a series of classic collisions with the Parlement of Paris.

At the peak of this crisis a memoir written in the Duc's name by Ducrest, chancellor of the Maison d'Orléans, was submitted to the king. It envisaged a reform of government along lines that might have won Turgot's approval. Ducrest attacked the present ministers as "guilty of the greatest crime, that is, of compromising the King's authority so as to satisfy their personal resentments with useless *coups d'autorité*."[14] The king was momentarily impressed, but the document withered beneath the queen's scorn. Its authorship was unmasked, and Chancellor Ducrest resigned. Probably it was the Duc's trial balloon, disowned as a tactical mistake. Afterward, on 13 January 1788, d'Orléans awarded Ducrest a generous annuity of twenty thousand livres.[15] In leaving the Maison d'Orléans Ducrest did not completely forsake political theory. He wrote another tract in 1789, showing pronounced conservative tendencies, championing the value of liberty against that of equality.[16]

Thus it may have been Ducrest's political ideas as well as his contacts that cemented d'Orléans's links to the *robe* at this time. On 19 November 1787, Louis XVI, at the behest of Brienne and Lamoignon, summoned a so-called *séance royale* of the Court of Peers, where the crown proposed to register an edict imposing 120 million livres of new taxation over the next five years in exchange for an Estates-General of 1792. The ministry sought to frustrate the rights of debate and remonstrance. Hereupon, d'Orléans rose to his feet and mouthed the words, "Sire, c'est illégal."[17] France had reached a turning point. As Talleyrand later wrote of the event: "The whole history of the monarchy had offered nothing like it. With weapons in their hands, Princes of the Blood had resisted royal authority; but no one before this had tried to place constitutional limits on that authority."[18] The episode made Philippe d'Orléans wildly popular. The assembly interpreted the occasion as a registration, entailing right of remonstrance; the king, angered by the proceedings, turned it into a *lit de justice*, exiling the Duc and two parlementary *conseillers* the next day. The banishment of the Duc to his estate of Villers-Cotterêts elicited immediate parlementary protest. "Sire," declared the Parlement of Paris, "if M. le duc d'Orléans is guilty, so are we all." Other parlements chimed in, for example, Toulouse: "Sire, your Parlement of Toulouse adds its voice to that of the whole magistracy. The chief Prince of the Blood has been exiled from your person. The astonished nation cannot see what his crime is. . . ."[19] As for d'Orléans, his punishment was somewhat sweetened by an eventual permission to visit Raincy, halfway to Paris, where Agnès de Buffon could join him. On 3 May 1788, secretly warned that force was to be used against it, the Parlement of Paris protested against all taxation without approval by an Estates-General and all arbitrary justice. Lamoignon had already lashed out on 16 April against an "aristocracy of magistrates."[20] The exile of the Parlement to Troyes, its triumphal return in September, the recall of Necker, and the convocation of an Estates-General followed swiftly.

The second Assemblée des Notables was not a high point in this drama. It was summoned by the king to meet on 7 November 1788 to consider the form and functions of the Estates-General, which would convene in May 1789. In this instance, the committees had different questions for deliberation. The Duc d'Orléans, reprieved from exile on 23 September, was once again allotted the presidency of the Third Bureau. Its object was the critical matter of how to elect the Estates.[21]

At the outset, d'Orléans expressed the intention of refusing to preside. The Comte de Provence advised on 10 November that in the absence of his cousin the sessions would be chaired by the Marshal de Broglie.[22] Besides d'Orléans, there were twenty-three members of the Third Bureau. It held twenty-five sessions; the Duc d'Orléans attended ten of these and kept the chair when he was present. The Bureau's spiny problem was Question Five: "What should be the respective number of deputies of each order? Should it be equal for each deputation?"[23] The committee explored numerous criteria: historical tradition, possession of landed wealth, contribution to the national welfare, and population. When it came to population, the *procès-verbal* noted that the Third Estate "is infinitely larger than the two preceding orders," but warned that if those orders were diminished, the commons "would deprive themselves of protectors, who, in supporting the duly constituted privileges of the nation, defend those of the Tiers as well. . . ."[24] Equal representation was decided by a vote of sixteen to six (two of the majority recommending that the king voluntarily add more members to the Tiers).[25] On the important Question Six, the Bureau advised that "in view of constant usage . . . it thinks that initially each order should deliberate separately . . . [but] it does not think it should propose to the Estates-General the normal manner of deliberation to be followed during the tenure of its sessions."[26]

Almost exclusively, the Duc d'Orléans refused to sign this document. Once again, he was accused of indifference, but later on he commented: "I judged that, especially in questions as important as those we debated, I could not and should not take the responsibility of certifying any majority, when I was convinced that it was [often] really a minority. . . . I demurred from presiding."[27] This is disingenuous: d'Orléans had gone to only ten sessions and had by now forged links with the elements of ferment. Exiled with the parlementarian Duval d'Eprémesnil, he had returned with very different ideas about the Estates-General; his break at this point with the basic ideology of the *robe* deserves to be stressed. Yet, in another sense, his rejoinder is honest: the nation demanded at least the doubling of the Tiers. The age of the Tiers Etat was beginning; modern Orleanism was emerging in its shadows.

D'Orléans and his cohorts had already invented something novel in the history of French politics: the massive use of wealth, research, and propaganda for the purpose of forming public opinion and swaying public policy. If we are to judge by the evidence, d'Orléans never used his money or ideas with consummate creativity, but the fault does not defeat the model. Philippe could buy consultants and scribblers as well as volatile and suggestible crowds, with orators to influence them and rouse them. The crowds became concentrated in the Duc's newly refurbished enterprise, the Palais-Royal, with its promenades and fountains, boutiques and cafés, gaming tables and bordellos. Through his vast landholdings and his agents in Valois, Chartrais, Beaujolais, and elsewhere, the Duc could also influence opinion and local administration in the provinces.

As for the "idea men" they moved in steady succession through the Palais-Royal and the more secret plotting sessions (*conciliabules*) sometimes held in the Duc de Lauzun's cottage in Montrouge. Already the Ducrest entourage had been aiming high. The Marquis Ducrest had, according to his chief lieutenant, "une tête d'où les projets débordaient de toutes parts."[28] It was also from the Palais-Royal, no doubt under the spiteful influence of Madame de Genlis, that many of the libels against Marie-Antoinette emanated, especially following the "affair of the necklace"; little sophistry on her part was needed to animate d'Orléans's hatred for his Austrian cousin. It did take some exhortation from the Ducrests, however, to rouse the Duc to sustained political action. They wanted power, he wanted intermittent revenge, in the spirit of his ancestors. Brissot, who was at the time political secretary to Ducrest in the Maison d'Orléans, described the Duc's attitude: "The prince was rather fond of conspiracies that lasted only twenty-four hours—any longer and he grew frightened. 'He will never take the leadership of a party,' Ducrest said to me one day, 'because he is afraid that he won't have the Opera and the girls on his side.' "[29] Regarding the Duc's widely imputed murderous designs on the throne, Mirabeau is later reported to have said in his salty language: "He wants to, but he can't; he is a eunuch when it comes to crime."[30]

In October 1788 the supremacy of Marquis Ducrest was over: Choderlos de Laclos, the author of the *Liaisons dangereuses*, had entered the Palais-Royal.[31] Madame de Genlis was not so easily expendable as tutor of the princes; she struggled with the new intruder for the soul of Philippe d'Orléans, but for the time being she was forced to retreat step by step. Her career was not helped by the circulation of libelous poems. One of these, anonymous, refers to her supervision of the d'Orléans children at Belle-Chasse:

> Yesterday's mistress, chaste today,
> Savage lover, then professor:
> Genlis, hide your charms away
> And become a strict assessor.
> Yet always this lovely creature
> Will use the gifts she had before;
> One can take up as a preacher
> Without resigning as a whore.[32]

Another stanza, authentically by Laclos, ordinarily a prose artist, runs thus:

> Get rid of your pen, my beauty:
> The needle is your duty;
> Set your papers burning,
> For now you must know
> How to spin and to sew
> For the pay you are earning.[33]

The notorious Laclos (in reality, a mild and compassionate family man) moved into the d'Orléans web of intrigue. Shortly, it was he alone who was planning the political campaign on an unprecedented scale. As La Luzerne, the French ambassador to London, somewhat later observed, Laclos, as private secretary, had d'Orléans in his grip "as much as one can possibly dominate such a fickle man."[34] Was it Laclos or "la Genlis" who really created this phase of Orleanism? The preliminary findings are that they tilted against each other for the soul of the movement and must share the credit: Madame de Genlis educated the future King of the French with that peculiar combination of republican sincerity and princely habits, and Choderlos de Laclos vastly developed the ideological and electoral machine that served the Duc in his ambiguous combats on the steps of the throne.

The political machinery used by Laclos anteceded his own arrival in the Duc's employ. For as Brissot, who departed before Ducrest, writes: "My work consisted of examining all the projects that the prince could carry through with his immense fortune. We wanted to attach the intellectuals to us, to patronize the arts and the learned societies. Thus, we gave pensions to the farmer and provided aid for new research. We created a load of philanthropic societies in the apanage of the prince." "But," Brissot laments, "this good start was not sustained. To prepare the Revolution, one needed good morals, energetic pamphlets, everything that could tie the prince to a people weary of despotism. And

nothing more ever happened than making plans in the middle of profligate dinners, served by lackeys who were, for the most part, spies [of the
court]."[35] Obviously, the fashionable aristocratic liberals of the Duc's
entourage—Lauzun, Noailles, Sillery, d'Aiguillon—who raced horses,
gamed, and wenched were not cut of the same cloth as the austere
Brissot; for him the ideas of the d'Orléans circle owed more to the
memoirs of the Cardinal de Retz than to the philosophy of the century.[36]
This frivolity also unnerved Ducrest and was perhaps instrumental in the
contretemps that caused his disgrace.

Laclos never had anything to do with the administrative side of the
Maison d'Orléans; he was strictly a political mentor and confidant. When
Chancellor Ducrest resigned on 5 December 1787, he was replaced by an
obscure naval officer, Admiral de Latouche-Tréville, who had gained
Philippe's admiration during a visit to Rochefort, where Latouche's
father commanded the garrison.[37] Loyal and modest, Latouche directed
the Conseil de la Maison and acquitted himself well in such difficult
straits as Philippe's immense debts and the loss of feudal dues after 1789
and the apanage in 1791. He was also frequently scalded by the anti-
d'Orléans libelists and was prosecuted thereafter in 1793, when in
fact he had only performed his professional duty. Needless to say,
his political ideas were also liberal. The records of the Maison
d'Orléans that he and his council have left reflect the financial
tribulations already mentioned, but they reveal no evidence of the
Duc's political uses of his fortune. A later story tells us that Napoleon, on being presented with a bundle of this evidence, a part
of the secret documentation of the trial of d'Orléans in late 1793, ordered
his minister of the interior, the Duc de Rovigo, to burn it.[38]

Enlarging on the work of Ducrest and Brissot, Laclos and his adjutants
drew up plans of government and reform, devised philanthropic works,
issued libels, and prepared the campaign for the Estates-General. If we
add together the many, often unreliable, accounts of the period, we learn
that not only Brissot, but Barère, Mirabeau, Sieyès, Desmoulins, Danton,
Duport, Dumouriez, and Marat all passed through the Orleanist receiving line. Later, the Gironde and the Montagne would mutually accuse
each other of being bought. We will always, however, find the names of
Mounier, Lafayette, and Robespierre conspicuously absent: these men
were bitter enemies and not for hire. We may confine ourselves to
observing that Laclos sat in the Palais-Royal, turning the Duc's great
resources to his profit; he scorned the liberal amateurs who could play at
conspiracy but not revolution. "His energy," a biographer writes, "was
like a charge of powder placed amid fragile and inflammable material."[39]

What is most intriguing about this sequence is not its dark, conspiratorial character at all, but its revelation of a new politics that we would judge normal. When Louis XVI invited all the educated people of the realm to submit ideas for reform either personally or corporately through the *cahiers de doléances* and summoned the primary assemblies to choose electors, it little occurred to him that the court should form a party or attempt to manage these elections.[40] At the king's behest, his brother the Comte d'Artois, who had toyed with the idea of becoming a deputy of the nobility, withdrew. Not so d'Orléans. From its harried perspective, the court regarded all parties, all organized electioneering as seditious. The suborning of the intelligentsia, the hiring of propagandists, the investment in philanthropy, ideas, and votes were disloyal acts. They breathed of an English license that was offensive to Louis XVI (one of the few judgments he shared with Lafayette). But Laclos, and behind him d'Orléans, did not particularly care what Versailles thought; they were going to have their organized plutocratic fling at national politics. The prince did it for popularity and revenge; the valet did it for power and the joy of the game: each, in his way, did it in the spirit of "liberalism." The French game, as Laclos foresaw, would be on a new playing field and would unleash massive frustrations bottled up for well over a century.

Did d'Orléans set his sights on the throne or the regency at this moment? Louis-Philippe presents the whole notion of an Orleanist conspiracy as a red herring. He sees his father as a weak man who neither wanted nor could have launched such an operation. All Philippe wanted was "a shelter against the caprices and evil designs of the court, and later against its prosecution and vengeance."[41] He maintains further that nobody else wanted Orleanism either: "It is precisely because no one wanted to place the Duc d'Orléans on the throne that everyone was afraid of being accused of it and that the accusation disturbed everyone's views and plans."[42] This touching annal has a ring of honesty. But many others in 1789 thought differently. And nowhere, in all of his eight hundred pages, does Louis-Philippe once introduce the name of Choderlos de Laclos. This is a striking omission that renders a partial flavor to all his other evidence.

The unmasking of the conservative character of the *révolte nobiliaire* did as much as anything to drive the strategists of the Tiers Etat toward thorough revolution. And after the second Assemblée des Notables, a *Mémoire des princes du sang*, warning the king against serious constitutional change, failed to receive the signature not only of the Duc d'Orléans, but also of the Comte de Provence, who had his own ideas of fronde.[43] But unlike Provence, d'Orléans was mobilized for a try at "modern" politics;

he had his machinery and brain trust ready. The idea of Brissot and Ducrest would be consummated by Laclos. Concerning the winter of 1788–89, there is a congeries of royalist charges against d'Orléans. Allegedly, with the aid of Brienne's edict for the free exportation of grain (1787), he captured the grain market, causing famine and unrest in France; he distributed vast amounts of charity for seditious purposes; he bought up the lumpen-intellectuals and had their tracts and libels widely distributed; and, in a later stage, his agents created panic in the countryside, leading to looting, burning, and anarchy, and they subverted the royal troops with bribes and flattery. The reality seems less picturesque.

So far as the evidence can be reassembled, the charges against d'Orléans are a tissue of half-truths. The Maison d'Orléans undoubtedly did speculate in both land and commodities for the purpose of maintaining the Duc's fortune and paying his extravagances, but he did not instigate the French people to rebellion by depriving them of bread: the harsh winter, crop failures, and an alarming ascent of prices from 1785 on accounted for that. As for the charity, it may have served the Duc's political interests, but it was also the natural bent of many rich aristocrats in a time of misery: Philippe's father, Louis le Gros, had also been philanthropic; so was his conservative father-in-law, the Duc de Penthièvre. In any case, on 20 December 1788, the *Journal de Paris* published a letter written by the Marquis de Limon to the parish priest of the Church of Saint-Eustache announcing that the Duc d'Orléans would provide every day a thousand livres of bread for the poor of the parish, that women in childbirth would have free medical assistance, and that help and shelter for the indigent would be furnished while the freezing weather lasted.[44] An extraordinary kind of seditious act, unless one grants that he had caused their hunger—or pregnancy—in the first place!

Pamphleteers and writers were certainly subsidized by d'Orléans. Libels were no new practice, either for the Maison d'Orléans or for the court and its competing cliques—or for other powerful sources of ambition. Printing and disseminating the remonstrances of the sovereign courts at the end of Louis XV's reign seemed more scandalous than the aggressive language used in the tracts. Shortly after the convocation of the Estates-General at Versailles, Mirabeau, Barère, and others would successfully challenge press censorship and usher in a period of unrestricted license and fertility that lasted until 10 August 1792.[45] Yet the king, in summoning the Estates with their inevitable *cahiers*, had expressed the wish for a communication of public problems. In the aftermath of the Revolution, the Duc d'Orléans's foray into publishing and propaganda would seem like a vile conspiracy to royalists, but he was not alone in contributing to the multiplication of brochures. If he bought talents, he did not need to invent their ideas for them: he also bought the ideas.

The charge that the Duc d'Orléans, either in concert or in parallel with Mirabeau, Duport, Sieyès, to name some, personally plotted and caused insurrections in the countryside—the so-called Grande Peur of 1789—has long been disproved. No doubt rumor played its part in the wave of regional panics that produced brigandage and arson; no doubt the arms that the peasants acquired were taken from somewhere: but no single personage, operating through his own agents, could have substantially created these brushfires. Georges Lefebvre has the decisive word on this subject.[46] On another affair of 1789, the question of undermining the loyalty of the troops (especially the Gardes Françaises), the evidence is much more complicated and probably impossible to settle.

D'Orléans's main ambition at this point seems to have been to influence the *cahiers* and the representation of the nobility in as liberal a direction as possible. By November 1788 he had broken his coalition with the backsliding parlementary forces, whose view of French constitutionalism had been overtaken by events. In this estimation he was joined by other powerful nobles, including some of the *gens de robe* themselves. The agitation that the Duc promoted, either by the dispersion of agents throughout his apanage or by printed matter, was a serious business, especially as conceived by Laclos.

Much of the literature upholding the thesis of Orleanist conspiracy is right in affirming that, with some notion of strategy, d'Orléans attempted to organize for the elections and the meeting of the Estates. But what is condemned as treasonable proceeds from the refusal of these writers to acknowledge that the form and substance of politics in France were changing from closed to open. The Duc wanted to influence the composition of the Estates-General and the trend of their demands and policies. So did a number of other aspirants. But the Duc was extraordinarily well placed in rank, visibility, and wealth to do this. Already Sieyès's influential pamphlet had made the rights of the Tiers Etat those of the nation, demanded a constitution in the image and interests of a nation that was not "ancient" but timeless, and established (through natural rights arguments) the virtually unlimited powers of a constituent assembly with its delegated primordial strength.[47]

There are various accounts of how the Duc's *Instructions à ses bailliages* came into being; this pamphlet, presently to be analyzed, passed through four editions, the first three being accompanied by a separate document called *Délibérations à prendre dans les Assemblées de bailliages*. In his apologia, written later from London, the Duc d'Orléans cites these pamphlets as proof of his personal concern for individual liberties and his determination to see them made a basis for the *cahiers*.[48] Louis-Philippe, in his memoirs, is silent about the activity of the period, except for mentioning the convocation of the Estates-General on 24 December 1788. Our most detailed source is Talleyrand, who informs us that Laclos persuaded the Duc to entrust him with the authorship of this document, intended as a political manual for the agents of d'Orléans acting in the primary assemblies of all the bailiwicks of his apanage. According to Talleyrand, the philosophical ideas advanced by Laclos were too transparently radical to satisfy his master; d'Orléans felt obliged to seek a second editor. Sieyès was recommended to him; they met at Lauzun's cottage at Montrouge, where, as the account continues, the peremptory Sieyès redid the whole thing in a form that d'Orléans accepted and had printed. Apparently this was the only meeting between d'Orléans and Sieyès before the National Assembly.[49]

Given the form of the work and the difference between its first and second editions, it seems more likely that Laclos was largely responsible for the *Instructions* and Sieyès for the *Délibérations*. At least, this is what d'Orléans appears to be implying when he writes: "In attaching [to my *Instructions*] a work of our most powerful publicist, I had two motives in mind: first, to express, in my different *bailliages*, a uniform resolution that was my own; and second, to give my agents definite guidance for unanticipated cases."[50] Laclos's biographer surmises that the "excessiveness" referred to by Talleyrand centers mainly around the article on divorce contained in the *Instructions*, uniquely advanced for its time and wounding to the Duchesse d'Orléans and obliquely humiliating to the queen.[51] It is also possible that Madame de Genlis saw some need for tempering the tract and was instrumental in getting Sieyès.[52] Whatever the authorship or editorship of these pamphlets,[53] they were advertised as the Duc's contribution to the political thought and strategy of his time. I shall comment only on the *Instructions*,[54] for the *Délibérations* bear more on tactics than on doctrine.

This document is cast in the form of seventeen articles, of which the first, a kind of preamble about liberty, is divided under five heads, mentioning conspicuously at the outset "the liberty to live where one wishes, to go, to come, to stay where one wants, with no impediment": the vital center of the Duc's liberalism. The other liberties are the right to fair arrest and trial; the right to regular justice within twenty-four hours following exceptional cases of arrest; the illegality of any interference with a citizen's liberty by anyone but a duly appointed magistrate; and the legal punishment of any violation of this precept. Article two demands complete liberty of the press; article three, the complete confidentiality of correspondence; article four, the absolute right of property; article five, the illegality of taxation except by consent of the Estates-General. Article six provides for brevity of term and regular summoning of the Estates-General and for their meeting in emergencies. Article seven states that royal ministers will be accountable to the Estates-General for their official conduct; article eight foresees the consolidation and single reckoning of the national debt; article nine declares that the Estates-General will not grant new taxes without proper public accounting; article ten envisages a general and just form of public taxation. In article eleven, the Estates-General is charged with a profound reform of civil and criminal proceedings. Article twelve demands the institution of civil divorce, "to avoid the unhappiness and scandal of incompatible unions." Article thirteen demands better and prompter execution of the laws; article fourteen enjoins the Estates-General not to act until proper guarantees of liberty have been established and the constitutional laws of the state fixed. The remainder of the *Instructions* is more personal: article fifteen directs the agents of d'Orléans not to raise unnecessary obstacles in defense of his privileges in the editing of the *cahiers*, especially those of the Tiers; article sixteen promotes the abolition of certain historic privileges of the nobility but argues for their hunting rights (not just for sport, but as a matter of agriculture and conservation); and article seventeen directs the agents to particulars further developed in the annexed *Délibérations*.

As compared with most of the general *cahiers*, the tone of the *Instructions* is quite progressive, though not deliberately provocative. It is monarchical, but it speaks of the "nation" and never of royal majesty; its objectives are not to be "granted" but rightfully obtained. The emphasis on personal physical liberty and the right to act as one desires remains contemporary. "Society" is almost absent from the document. The divorce demand, though not unique in the writings of the period, is bold nonetheless: while most of the liberals were combating the church with religious toleration (granted to the Protestants in 1787 by Louis XVI after a long campaign by Malesherbes) and a weakening of the temporal-spiritual connection, the Duc was desacralizing marriage. Whoever wrote them, the *Instructions* are stamped with d'Orléans's personality. Their concerns were the issues closest to his political conviction and understanding.

The intention of the *Instructions* was not only to serve as a theoretical guide for the agents of d'Orléans but also to focus a propaganda effort to influence the fledgling political community. In short, these principles formed a model *cahier* that could be adapted to local conditions by unimaginative or inexperienced assemblies. It is estimated that at least a hundred thousand copies of this piece of literature were circulated, usually with the attached *Délibérations*.[55] It was by no means the only model *cahier* in the field. The leading emergent politicians of the commons were also very active in putting across their views by this means: the effectiveness of Thouret's model *cahier* in Normandy is often cited. The explicit results achieved by the Duc's propaganda are somewhat nebulous; the extraordinary circulation is, nevertheless, striking. It was widely distributed, not only throughout the Duc's apanage and Paris, but in other regions as well: in his research Henri Sée discovered copies of it in the *Sénéchaussée* of Rennes.[56] One writer tells us that "it was one of the 'models' most widely adopted in the editing of the *cahiers*;"[57] but this judgment may be excessive, since many of d'Orléans's demands were a part of the general program of the Tiers.[58] Hyslop, who has studied closely the genesis and content of *cahiers*, concedes the immense circulation of the *Instructions* but is more skeptical about its direct influence. Indeed, the demand for civil divorce and one or two of the less important issues of the *Instructions* are rarely encountered in the general *cahiers*. But, with this document, the Duc specifically defined his political distance from his royal cousin.[59]

There was not just the matter of the *cahiers* but also of elections. The royal convocation permitted each noble to participate in the assembly of his order wherever he held a property: d'Orléans could therefore appear, or be represented, in twenty-nine assemblies. He sent agents to all of them, but only four of these men were elected deputies of the Second Estate. D'Orléans personally attended the assembly of Paris *intra-muros* and weighed heavily on the *bailliages* of Villers-Cotterêts and Crépy-en-Valois, where he owned vast properties: all three of these constituencies elected him.[60]

The Paris elections produced an almost complete representation of nine constitutionalist nobles, the exception being the Marquis de Mirepoix. D'Orléans was close to the bottom of the elected list here; with sixty-seven votes he tied Duport and Lepeletier de Saint-Fargeau, both eminent parlementarians, and he had less than half the votes of Clermont-Tonnerre, the front runner.[61] He chose to represent Crépy, because its *cahier* was most in conformity with his own views. Other political friends of the Duc were elected: Mazancourt at Villers-Cotterêts, Sillery at Rheims, Lauzun at Cahors, Latouche at Montargis. To speak of the success of a party, however, would be totally false. Far from all liberal nobles were friends of d'Orléans (some, like Lafayette, would be his bitterest enemies), and the liberals were still very much a minority in their order. As for mobilizing the membership of the Tiers or the lesser clergy, it was a task beyond d'Orléans's means.

The Duc d'Orléans seems to have made no great political splash between the elections and the plenary meeting of the Estates-General on 4 May 1789. No doubt his advisors and clique were active in secret plots, or to use the word of that day, *conciliabules*. But we see no plot; we have only veiled glimpses of ambitious designs. In the ceremony at Versailles, the Duc abandoned the train of the king, taking his place among the other elected members of the nobility; this occasioned popular admiration. We have only disordered records of the Chamber of Nobles before the National Assembly was formed. It is doubtful that the tongue-tied Duc had much to say, when there were liberal orators in abundance: Lafayette, Clermont-Tonnerre, Lally-Tollendal. On 17 June 1789, the Tiers declared itself, together with the absent orders which were invited to join it, a "National Assembly," by a vote of 491 to 89. The resistance of the Jeu de Paume occurred on 20 June. On 25 June, the Duc d'Orléans accompanied forty-six other liberal members of the nobility to receive their credentials as representatives of the nation. Two days later the principle of the reunion of the three orders (minus dissidents) was fait accompli.

The National Assembly adopted a kind of rotating procedure for naming its presiding officer; the first had been Bailly, leading deputy from Paris and *doyen* of the Tiers. By 3 July it seemed conciliatory to pass the temporary presidency to another estate. The logical candidate was d'Orléans, Prince of the Blood and ranking noble of the assembly, who by conviction and example had shown his willingness to follow the wishes of the nation. He was overwhelmingly elected, with 553 votes out of 660. But he declined the day after, and the Archbishop of Vienne was chosen in his place.[62] Royalist historians considered the size of the vote as evidence of the depth of the Orleanist plot.[63] This is nonsense: d'Orléans did not win the election because his colleagues wanted to place him on the throne, or even admired him; they were simply performing deferentially, while cautioning the court at the same time. Having had his *succès d'estime*, d'Orléans refused because, in his words: "If I thought I could do justice to the position . . . I would take it with the greatest joy; but,

messieurs, I would be unworthy of your kindness if I accepted it, knowing how little fit for it I am."[64] Ruse, false modesty, humility, or avoidance of a diplomatically demanding chore? Probably all these elements
figure in the Duc's self-effacement. They would predict his reaction in
later episodes. Instead of directing traffic from the *fauteuil du Président*,
d'Orléans went to sit with the founders of the Jacobin Club, soon to be
the "Left," where he would remain, often in silence, until his fate removed him from politics.

4. The October Days

If the royal head of the national household wavered, a surrogate of royal blood had to be found. D'Orléans, most in tune with the new ideas, stood next in line after the Dauphin, Monsieur (the king's oldest brother), and d'Artois and his male descent (d'Artois had pointedly exiled himself after the fall of the Bastille). Louis-Philippe writes: "My father was so highly placed that his ambition could have no other goal than royal power, whether he exercised it as lieutenant-general of the realm or dethroned the elder branch and sat on the throne."[1] Any allegation of "Orleanist conspiracy" could not help being a potent psychological factor.

Louis XVI had received public acclamations on 17 July, and it was still felt, even by Marat, that he could be brought under control if the evil influences surrounding him were removed, if he could have "patriot" advisors and dwell amidst a "patriot" people. The notion of a mass movement on Versailles culminating in the forced return of the court to Paris had been in the wind for some time, bruited in the gardens of the Palais-Royal. On 30 August the radical déclassé noble Saint-Hururge had attempted to lead an unarmed crowd of fifteen hundred to Versailles but had been turned back by Lafayette and his troops.[2] If not involved in that event, d'Orléans's agents had surely been watching.

On 5 October, drained of patience by the bread shortage and inflamed by oratory, a large gathering, mostly women, set out for the Grand Palais on a miserably rainy day. It was not the first time that the housekeepers of Paris had marched on Versailles to confront the monarch directly. This had happened during the famine of 1709, when the mob had been turned back by soldiers at the Pont de Sèvres; in October 1789 both the ministry and Lafayette neglected this elementary precaution. In 1775, during the *guerre des farines*, there had been bread riots within Versailles itself, but a suddenly militaristic Turgot had stilled the panic with force. Tradition lent its cachet to the *journées d'Octobre*. Yet, a new political epiphany agitated the crowds (Louis-Philippe estimates 100,000 Parisians) who poured into Versailles by the morning of 6 October. In their confused way, they wanted bread *and* liberty, and counted on their presence to make the king grant these things. Liberty, in the form of the tricolored cockade, had been tramped underfoot at a recent banquet attended by the royal family to celebrate the arrival of the Flanders Regiment. The angry petitioners trudged off in the late morning. After much confusion, a reluctant but coerced Lafayette, at the head of twenty thousand National Guardsmen, set out after the mob at about five o'clock in the afternoon.

Upon receiving the news, Saint-Priest, the Minister of the Maison du Roi, retrieved the king, who had gone hunting, for a meeting of the Conseil at about three in the afternoon.[3] The ministers debated leaving Versailles and appealing to the loyalty of the nation; the practical Necker pointed out that there was no money. At about five-thirty the king received and apparently appeased a delegation of the exhausted women. Two messengers from Lafayette arrived a little past nine. The night was chaotic, as more and more civilians and guardsmen arrived needing provision. Complicated diplomacy averted clashes of jurisdiction between the king's troops and the Paris militia. At six the next morning a crowd managed to force a palace gate and break into the living quarters of the royal family, possibly intending to murder the queen, who sought refuge in the king's apartment. There was fatal bloodshed.

Finally, Lafayette reconciled the quarreling soldiers, persuaded the crowds to withdraw, and appeared with the royal family on the balcony. The crowd applauded and shouted: "To Paris!" The king consulted briefly, but his decision was forced. At one in the afternoon, amid rain and gloom, the royal carriage set out for Paris, accompanied by the Guard, the regular soldiers, and a horde of Parisians with loaves of bread and a few more ominous souvenirs on the points of their pikes. Lafayette trotted beside it on his famous white horse. At the gates of the city the king was harangued by the oratorical Bailly, then taken to the Hôtel de Ville to endure more patriotic speeches. Not until ten at night did the unhappy Bourbons reach the Tuileries, with its cobwebs and draperies of more than a century of royal absence. The Assembly, declaring itself inseparable from the king's person, moved to Paris on 19 October, installing itself in the Manège.[4] Many royalists began to flee the kingdom.

What was the political structure of the situation? How did it implicate or involve Philippe d'Orléans and his political mercenaries? By 5 October many forces were in presence. The court faction of intransigents for the most part simply refused to recognize the Assembly. Slightly less extreme was a large group of royalists whose major spokesmen were the Abbé Maury and the petty noble Cazalès. Then there were the constitutional monarchists à l'anglaise, like Mounier, Virieu, Bergasse, and Lally-Tollendal: October abolished their designs. In the center were the Fayettists, who accepted the idea of a reformed monarchy but were more interested in the shape of liberal institutions; to them we may add other single individuals of note, like Sieyès, Le Chapelier, and Thouret. Mirabeau was a lone wolf: also a monarchist, he favored a more powerful executive regime, which he worked to fortify beneath his revolutionary rhetoric. The Orleanists, as we have noted, privately envisaged a regency or a change of dynasty. The Left of the time (Pétion, Buzot, Grégoire, Reubell, and Robespierre, the "new Left" of 1791, may be included) was led by the future Feuillants Barnave, Duport, and the Lameth brothers: sometimes operating in parallel with the Orleanists, it was indifferent to the person of the monarch but wanted a pronounced legislative supremacy. However, the National Assembly scarcely voted along such rigid factional lines.

Louis-Philippe simplified this constellation into three parties: "the aristocrats or blacks" so-called because of "the large number of clergy in it," the largest but least able group; the centrists, whom I have called Fayettists, who would found the Club of 1789; and the "Jacobins" (Barnave, Pétion, Duport, et al.). "My father and the Duc de Biron," the Duc de Chartres specified, "almost always voted with this party . . . least numerous . . . but [having] the best sense of tactics." He denied the existence of any "parti d'Orléans."[5] Mounier, writing from exile in 1790, also contended that there were three parties in the Assembly: one (of his own kind) solicitous of the public welfare and resolved to make orderly changes in the government of France; the other two bent on license and destruction. "The ones," he charged, "believed that, amid convulsions of anarchy, they could take possession of the supreme power, and grab the favors and privileges that it had formerly been able to bestow. The others worked out a simpler plan, that of destroying all the distinctions to which they could not aspire, of levelling everything that caused their jealousy . . . ruling through the fury of the multitude, which would become the instrument of their power."[6] Fayettists, Jacobins, and Orleanists all fell within the scope of this censure.

For the unconditional royalists, the best strategy of 1789 would have been a coup d'état, challenging the Assembly with a superior force, dissolving it, and governing by moderated principles of the Old Regime. The fallback position was to remove the king from proximity to Paris and the Assembly. Mounier, and much later Mirabeau, tended to favor the less stringent plan.[7] The centrist "patriots," on the other hand, had a great interest in bringing the monarch back to Paris, where Lafayette and Bailly were dominant; the Jacobins especially wanted the king exposed to a maximum of popular pressure. But for the Orleanists a Louis XVI in the Tuileries was worth little more than a Louis XVI at Versailles. Either they required a bloodbath at Versailles or the monarch's improvident defection to another part of the kingdom. On the morning of 6 October these conditions came perilously close to fulfillment.

The reluctant Lafayette was the apparent victor of the day. He rode like a constable of France beside the vehicle that returned Louis XVI to Paris. He had marched his troops in response to the will of the people. He had perhaps saved the king's life and certainly his popularity. And Lafayette still ruled Paris: while the capital was his, the king was his. He would waste no time in disposing of d'Orléans. But this young nobleman, the "hero of two worlds," was not a Parisian. He did not quite know what to do with the king, and he had a dedicated enemy in the queen.

History will perhaps never shed total light on d'Orléans's actual role in the events of 5–6 October. The charges are like those discussed in the last chapter: he stirred up sedition in the Palais-Royal; he subverted the troops; he infiltrated the Versailles marchers with agents disguised as women; he distributed secret funds; he had a network of messengers (some made up as jockeys) along the route to Versailles and had rented the Boulainvilliers house in Passy so as better to observe events; he was physically present in Versailles, in the corridors of the Assembly and even within the palace on the morning of 6 October.[8] The Duc d'Orléans categorically denied all these charges. From London in 1790 he wrote, or had written for him, his view of the events.[9] He affirmed that he had no interest in the throne, only in "liberty," and could not imagine himself climbing over the bodies of his cousins to seize the crown. As for the furious libels disgorged against him: "These calumnies cause one to shudder! . . . Let us for a moment rise above our indignation at the horrors [of Versailles]; that will be enough to show the absurdity [of the accusations]."[10] To the end of his days, Philippe-Egalité continued to assert his innocence. When questioned in Marseilles in 1793 on the episode and relations with Mirabeau, he replied: "No, citizen, I never sponsored any kind of party. I always had an aversion to the throne; I never thought about it, and I was never particularly close to Mirabeau."[11]

Public opinion attributed a much more active role to the Duc than his disclaimer would suggest. Of course the swell of protest owed much to the orchestration of libels by his enemies, royalists or Fayettists. Yet, while the French nation approved the transfer of the king to Paris, it was shocked by the bloodshed of 6 October, which was widely blamed on d'Orléans. "Still bolder than his ancestor the Regent," said one pamphlet, "he would have pushed Monsieur out of the way; d'Artois, in emigration and hated by the people, could not have interfered with his criminal designs; he would have taken responsibility for the upbringing of the Dauphin, who would not have lived long. By these accursed steps, he hoped to be proclaimed King of France by the nation itself. . . ."[12] Another tract traced the Duc's plot in depraved colors, up to the murder of Louis XVI, concluding: "our *abbés* in bourgeois clothes will say: 'We have no more king, we must proclaim another . . . Monseigneur le duc d'Orléans.' And surely this will win approval."[13] For a year after the events of Versailles such broadsides poured forth, the vast majority against the Duc.

In the early period of the Revolution d'Orléans was part of a parallelogram of forces representing the aspirations and tensions that met in the October *journées* and in subsequent political struggle. For the sake of brevity, the remaining forces can be incarnated in three other individuals: Lafayette, Mirabeau, and Marat.

Gilbert du Motier, Marquis de Lafayette, and the Duc d'Orléans were fated to despise each other. One's wealth was immense, the other's considerable; both were noble, and liberal, but there the resemblance stops. Lafayette had won the popularity and glory that the Duc coveted. He had crossed an ocean and fought for the liberty that the Duc only mused on in his *garçonnière* at "Mousseaux." Lafayette was also rather starchy and moralistic, neither a good courtier nor a jolly playfellow. A later writer remarked "he always had his touch of Grandisson."[14] Anglomania did not tempt him in the slightest: he had named his son George Washington and sent him to North America to be educated. Lafayette's brain teemed with unoriginal political theory; in deference to his great services the Assembly ruled that he should be the first to present a Declaration of Rights.[15] A native of Auvergne, Lafayette had taken on the job of policing Paris: the Palais-Royal was his bane, not his blessing. He could use words and especially gestures with good effect; d'Orléans, while occasionally witty, had none of this public gift. Never a military genius, Lafayette knew how to command and march men, and win their loyalty; the Duc gained his applause for flimsier reasons. Lafayette took his Freemasonry seriously, as a kind of substitute Protestantism; for the Grand Master d'Orléans the lodges were playthings. Lafayette modestly abstained from running the kingdom when it could have been virtually his in late 1789. Instead, having shaken the steps to the throne, he then stood at the base and barred the way to d'Orléans.[16]

In his memoirs Lafayette claims that Mirabeau and others proposed, on 10 July 1789, that he and d'Orléans should unite their efforts against the court.[17] Similar testimony, relative to 7 July, is given by Mounier.[18] Lafayette's description of the proposition is: "he would be my captain of the guards and I his."[19] His response was of course negative, but he determined to keep an eye on d'Orléans. In the meantime he became commander of the Paris National Guard, setting the stage for collisions with the Duc, who, he feared, was subverting the Gardes Françaises and scheming to become chief of a national militia.[20] As the events of October approached, it seemed to Lafayette that the constitutionalists were being caught between extremes, threatened by "three intrigues . . . the Court, the *parti d'Orléans*, and the one later called Jacobin [meaning here the followers of Duport and Barnave; Lafayette considered Danton and Marat Orleanists]."[21] It was at this moment that Montmorin, the Foreign Minister, offered Lafayette the position of Constable of France, which the general refused, fearing a trap.

Lafayette lacked substantive proof of an Orleanist plot, or he would have had the force to act against it. This did not diminish his suspicions.[22] In his deposition to the Châtelet after the march on Versailles, he claimed that in the confusion in front of the Hôtel de Ville on 5 October before the National Guard marched off, he had heard the term "council of regency" bruited about, which suggested to him the character of a plot.[23] Yet in his memoirs, probably written down years later, he was not sure whether the regency was intended for him or for d'Orléans.[24] In any case, he resolved to put d'Orléans out of harm's way: "After 6 October, the dangers of an Orleanist plot were scotched, but the spirit of that faction was not destroyed, and through his fortune, his connections, and his immorality its chief had means of influence that needed to be cut off."[25]

The court shared this desire to squelch Philippe d'Orléans. Lafayette apparently obtained the king's permission to deal with the task immediately after the return to Paris. He summoned the Duc to the house of a mutual friend, the Marquise de Coigny (the "politics of connections"), where he bullied d'Orléans so (Mirabeau said that the conversation was "very haughty on the one hand and very resigned on the other")[26] that the latter agreed to leave for England on the pretext of a diplomatic mission. Lafayette wrote on 23 October to Mounier: "I planted a little worry in him, and that was enough to encourage his natural bent for travel."[27] The Duc's official story was this: "Monsieur de Lafayette told me that it was the king's wish to charge me with a mission abroad, and he added that my absence would remove all pretext for using my name improperly, thus making it easier, he believed, to maintain calm in the capital. . . . He added finally that he personally thought that I could be of great usefulness to the nation in England."[28] Of course d'Orléans's "usefulness" was in his absence, but Lafayette erred in believing that this would remove the problem.

Perhaps d'Orléans had succumbed to Lafayette from lassitude or had even wanted the Revolution halted. But the same evening Biron and some other friends stiffened his back, pointing out that he, a member of the National Assembly, would be accusing himself by leaving under a cloud.[29] Mirabeau is said to have promised a damaging speech against Lafayette in the Assembly.[30] However, the government, perhaps mixing cajolery with warning, persuaded d'Orléans to make a prudent departure. This sent Mirabeau into his best bad language: he would now turn to other channels for his advancement.[31]

D'Orléans was apparently given the notion that if England and France could agree on the question of the Austrian Netherlands, then inflamed by revolt, there might be a future for him as Duc de Brabant.[32] He wrote most correctly to his monarch: "this mark of confidence, in present circumstances, is the most flattering witness of his [Majesty's] kindnesses toward me."[33] At Boulogne the Duc was detained by admiring crowds, but he proceeded onward to his cherished London. Soon Laclos, Agnès de Buffon, and members of the ducal household joined him there. On 29 October he attempted to play host to William Pitt, but the invitation was declined.[34] Montmorin ignored his frequent missives and allowed his "diplomacy" to collide embarrassingly with the initiatives of the French ambassador La Luzerne. Meanwhile at home he was being prosecuted by the Châtelet and roasted by the pamphleteers.

We turn to Mirabeau. Both Mirabeau and d'Orléans were ardent protagonists of "negative," physical liberty, as a result of their careers and tastes. That liberty, Mirabeau had declared, in his indictment of the *lettres de cachet* in 1777, was "an inalienable right of the human race."[35] But Mirabeau had pounded on the stones of prisons many times; d'Orléans had known only the enclosures of frustration. Both were notorious womanizers; but for Mirabeau this was life itself, for d'Orléans a princely form of escape. While d'Orléans had immense debts and an even greater fortune, Mirabeau had only debts: the one could buy, the other could be bought. In his desultory way, d'Orléans was orderly: he ran a household equivalent to a kingdom. There was never a scrap of order in Mirabeau's whole existence. Mirabeau's gift for speech could carry him aloft and wring compliments from his bitterest enemies; d'Orléans was usually afraid to open his mouth except in self-defense. Both were wise and jaundiced about the habits and values of the Old Regime. Mirabeau, like d'Orléans, cultivated the "new politics"; he had his researchers and speechwriters (among them, the Swiss exile Clavière, later Minister of Finance) as far as he could afford them. Mirabeau was also a Freemason, and among the "brothers" had passed some of his dreary hours of exile in Holland, when he was escaping from the arms of Sophie. He was the closest thing to a political realist in the first wave of patriots. Like d'Orléans, he came to Revolutionary politics from a long experience of playing family politics.

Mirabeau and d'Orléans seem to have met for the first time, and a few times thereafter, at the house of the Comte de La Marck in 1788. La Marck, an aristocratic cosmopolite (his family name was Arenberg and his title was Austrian), knew virtually everyone and was one of the indispensable "contact men" of the confused early period of the Revolution. He became Mirabeau's close friend and, after his death, the executor of his papers; but his more traditional politics allowed him to serve as intermediary in the arrangements between Mirabeau and the court.[36] According to La Marck, d'Orléans inspired no confidence in Mirabeau. When they met at his table on 1 October 1789, he "saw clearly that there was a reserve between them that excluded any suspicion of a secret understanding."[37]

Why then is such a collusion imputed in the period between July and October 1789? In the first place, Mirabeau's policies were two-sided: he wanted to destroy *féodalité* root and branch, but he also desired a strong executive for France and ridiculed the "metaphysical" theorizing of the vest-pocket *philosophes* of the National Assembly. For a time he may have felt that he could work toward this goal behind d'Orléans. In the second place, he aspired to being more than "quelque chose" and to turning the tables on those who had muffled him, imprisoned him in dungeons, chased him abroad. Many of the elites shunned him because of his bohemian and unsavory life. However, d'Orléans himself was no model of virtue, and Laclos swept such people as Mirabeau up in his wide net. Mirabeau believed in keeping doors open; more than a few were shut on him.[38] His road to power was thorny: after the eclipse of d'Orléans he seems to have cultivated a brief political understanding with Monsieur in January 1790 before finally becoming a paid advisor of the court. In the third place, Mirabeau and Lafayette shared a bottomless contempt for each other. Lafayette was not displeased to see Mirabeau accused before the Châtelet of conspiracy in the October *journées*, and he apparently reneged on a promise to defend Mirabeau's innocence when that case was debated by the National Assembly.[39] On his part, Mirabeau made it clear in one of his two important letters to Lafayette regarding possible grounds for collaboration (3 May and 1 June 1790) that he believed Lafayette to be surrounded by mediocrities.[40] Shortly afterward, Mirabeau became caustic. In his "first note to the Court," written at just the same time as the second letter to Lafayette, he belittled the general, referring to "the inertia of his thinking and the nullity of his talent."[41]

D'Orléans was both a power and a pawn in this jealous competition. By assisting d'Orléans or paralleling his efforts, especially with regard to the troops, the clubs, and the crowds, Mirabeau could weaken Lafayette. To be sure, after October 1789, Mirabeau also despised d'Orléans: this facilitated the later rapprochement with the court. Yet, for a period of time, d'Orléans and Mirabeau were tarred with the same brush, the inquiry by the Châtelet into the October violence, which lasted almost a year and produced two volumes of testimony. From that angle, the court and Lafayette had a common interest. Mirabeau was of course aware of, and touched by, the venomous libels between the royalist/Fayettist and the Orleanist/Jacobin pamphleteers during the Duc's involuntary exile. His fortunes were to that extent bound up with those of his alleged coconspirator. He found it increasingly difficult to act as tribune of the people and secret advisor to the court at the same time, even after his exculpation. The more he spoke out of both sides of his mouth, the more unwelcome he was at the Jacobins and the more suspect in the Tuileries. Sick and propelled only by his sheer animal energy, he died a hero's death, just in the nick of time.

"Mirabeau," La Marck writes, "wanted a revolutionary monarchy (*la monarchie par la révolution*), but freed of its anarchic shackles . . . [by pursuing the logical consequences of the Revolution] he wanted the King really to rule. In his view, unless the King took this tack, he would surely lose both the throne and his life."[42] This policy is beneath the surface in several of Mirabeau's great speeches (on the right to make war and peace, the right of the veto, and the nature of the division of powers); it comes out clearly in the notes to the court, some of which are astonishingly clairvoyant. As Chateaubriand quoted Mirabeau: "I wanted to cure the French of the superstition of the monarchy and make it into their ordinary form of worship (*culte*)."[43] Mirabeau was engaged in desacralizing the most ancient and ceremonious of consecrated offices and turning it into a functional magistracy, what we have called a *usufructory* authority. Beside it, but not suffocating it, would stand a strong national legislature. Privileged intermediary bodies would have been swept away. It is not clear (at least in 1789 and early 1790) on whom Mirabeau counted as his agent. As the Duc de Castries writes, "it has been asked if Mirabeau was not a part of a plot to transfer power by violence to a regent designated in advance. Sometimes the name of the Comte de Provence has come up and, much more often, with more serious arguments, that of the Duc d'Orléans. It is a good guess that this was so, but there are no documents to prove it."[44] A usufructory monarchy does not require the same aura of legitimacy as a paternalistic one. It merely requires a royal person who accepts the new definition of his charge. The leaders of the Constituent successively tried to persuade Louis XVI to follow their counsels. In the end his obstinacy confounded them all.

Marat's particular traits are not the issue here: we take him as the symbol of a far greater and anonymous force swelling outside the walls of the Assembly. The man himself was neither a plebeian nor a young hothead. Like Brissot, but with more venom and no compromise, he was the image of the frustrated intellectual.[45] He had Newtonian aspirations. Before he called down the blade on the aristocrats, he had called down thunder on the academicians who blocked his way to scientific eminence. The *ami du peuple* was not an *ami des hommes*. The Revolution would be invoked to right personal affronts that had become inseparable from political evil. Marat worked for lowly wages; he was a gifted and indefatigable reporter, specializing in self-fulfilling prophecy.[46] Of the revolutionary journals of its time, the *Ami du Peuple* is most interesting, aside from its savagery, for uncanny revelations and predictions.

In October 1789 Marat was only an enthusiastic but obscure advocate of the march on Versailles; still, he was prosecuted by the Châtelet and forced into hiding.[47] He attacked Necker; he attacked Lafayette; in January 1790 he was forced to flee to England, and was not back in France until the following April.[48] If he did not encounter the Duc d'Orléans in London, he at least had conversations with Laclos. In any case, he returned to edit the *Ami du Peuple* with vigor, launching a devastating series of attacks on Lafayette in the issues of 26–28 April 1790. His onslaughts against "le divin Mottié" (a vulgarization of Lafayette's family name) never ceased until the desertion of the general in August 1792. Bailly, the mayor of Paris, and finally Mirabeau also felt his lash. Marat and his radical associates were playing for control of the municipality and, consequently, of the Revolution itself.

A connivance with d'Orléans? Both were in London at the same time. Both hated Lafayette and the court. Never before had Marat's journalism paid d'Orléans any special attention. But scarcely had Marat returned to Paris when he began to use the Duc as a club against Lafayette. He lengthily described the persecution that Lafayette visited upon d'Orléans: shadowing him with spies in London and hindering his return to France, when Philippe wished to be present with the National Assembly to swear loyalty to the nation at the great festival of 14 July 1790. Marat's leading biographer does not qualify this affiliation as a conspiracy: "Marat's campaign against Lafayette was a necessary part of his program of revolutionary propaganda. Certain persons very highly placed may have found it to their own advantage to ease his task financially."[49] Probably, then, d'Orléans subsidized Marat and others at this time: Laclos knew the meaning of quid pro quo. Marat was often short of money. The Interior Ministries of Louis XVI had budgets for selective press propaganda, but even the Girondin Roland would not give Marat a sou. Even after the collapse of the monarchy Marat addressed the following *placard* to his erstwhile supporter, the Duc: "You are the model, but be the benefactor, in the name of the country, contribute now. . . . The modest sum of 15,000 livres would be enough for paper and labor costs. . . . The *ami du peuple* only asks this as a loan, and he counts on your civic virtue."[50]

After the October *journées*, the monarchy's judicial arm in Paris, the Châtelet, a court of ancient standing with more than sixty *conseillers* and several *présidents*, opened an inquest into the causes of the march and the disturbances.[51] This venerable institution took copious testimony from 388 witnesses. Its investigations were conducted between 11 December 1789 and 10 June 1790; the National Assembly received the full report, running to 570 pages, on 7 August 1790 and ordered its printing on 19 September. The work of the Châtelet was approved by a Comité des Recherches of the city of Paris; one of the signatories was Brissot.[52]

The range of testimony would have been more complete if it had included statements by d'Orléans and Mirabeau themselves, Sillery, Latouche, Laclos, Duport, Barnave, Madame de Genlis, and others.[53] The documentation was full of suggestive nuances, but its mass of evidence was neither sifted, nor crosschecked, nor carefully analyzed. An atmosphere of conspiracy was created, but no conspiracy was proved. Yet the Châtelet returned a guilty verdict against both d'Orléans and Mirabeau. Even Lafayette, who had an obvious interest in the outcome, was quoted only indirectly as recalling miscellaneous rumors of a regency in the Place de la Grève.[54] Indeed, as he wrote to George Washington on 28 August 1790, while the Assembly was still considering the report of the Châtelet: "The report [still in committee] . . . should be presented to the Assembly next week. I don't believe that there is sufficient evidence to inculpate the Duc d'Orléans and I am sure there is not enough against Mirabeau. There is something hidden in the present relations of these two men, though they don't seem to have an alliance."[55] We can scarcely wonder, then, that the Assembly took a dim view of the Châtelet proceedings.

The Duc d'Orléans was chafing to return to Paris.[56] On 13 February 1790 he wrote to the president of the National Assembly expressing his desire to be included among those who had sworn an oath to the nation on the fourth of the month, and he so notified the king the next day.[57] By

March he wanted either the dismissal of La Luzerne or the termination of his own mission.[58] Lafayette sent an emissary to London to delay the Duc's return;[59] d'Orléans signed an agreement with him on 3 July, stating that he had "consented to defer his departure for a few days."[60] But he had written to the king on 25 June that "my disposition is to return instantly to Paris to resume my place as deputy to the National Assembly, where my duty calls me."[61] On 3 July he complained to Latouche-Tréville about the calumnies spread against him, and announced his arrival.[62]

On 1 July 1790 Mirabeau argued in his seventh note to the court that it would be unwise to make d'Orléans seem a victim of persecution. If he were welcomed, his utility to the Jacobins would be minimized; but if he were encouraged to rally his faction, the court would need the help of Lafayette, making "any return to a better order of conditions impossible." As for d'Orléans, "the only precaution is not to furnish him with strength that he doesn't have. To meet his wishes is to weaken him; to manipulate him is to destroy both him and his party."[63] D'Orléans arrived in Paris. He and the king seem to have had a gracious, cousinly conversation. But the courtiers could not be controlled. The Duc was treated to abuse and even spat upon as he descended the grand staircase: "The first time that M. le duc d'Orléans appeared at the Tuileries, he was brutally insulted by the most faithful servants of the King. . . . From that moment on, [he] was once again the most relentless enemy of the court."[64] Not only politics, but princely honor was at stake.

The radical press was convinced that the venerable Châtelet was under the thumb of the court. Fréron's *Orateur du Peuple* exulted at the prospect of Philippe's return "in greater glory."[65] "When," it asked, "will the Châtelet cease its acts of proscription against patriot writers" and not "vomit on the citizens to whom we owe the Revolution?"[66] On the release of the *Procédure* it howled: "Châtelet, Châtelet, this affair crowns your wickedness . . . you will not escape public outrage or the horror of posterity!"[67] The *Ami du Peuple* concurred: "Although full of errors, inconsistencies, contradictions, and impostures, the *Procédure criminelle instruite au Châtelet* concerning the events of 5 and 6 October is nonetheless an important piece in the justification of the accused, a precious document for history, because the lies with which it is spangled contradict and destroy one another."[68] Marat pressed his conclusion home against "l'infâme Mottié": "His criminal views are now well known; in imputing to Louis-Philippe d'Orléans these ambitious schemes and in designating the elder Mirabeau as his accomplice, his own design was to destroy the patriot party . . . and return absolute power to the King."[69] (Marat, usually well informed, had not yet gotten wind of Mirabeau's excursion into court politics.)

Prudhomme, in the *Révolutions de Paris*, also scourged the Châtelet as "aristocratic" and "anti-patriotic," expressing gloom and "the shame of the nation."[70] When the Assembly found its two members innocent, the journalist was only somewhat assuaged, demanding justice for those without parliamentary protection.[71] Hébert declared that "Philippe d'Orléans and the elder Mirabeau have an incontestable right to the gratitude of good Frenchmen." D'Orléans had not been "a *jean-foutre* like the other former [sic] princes. . . ."[72]

With the pride of an uncorrupted legislature, the National Assembly demanded to judge its own members. Earlier, an obscure deputy, the Abbé Barmond, had been arrested; the Châtelet had been called to account for this malpractice in August 1790. Now Mirabeau rose to affirm the precedent and to defend himself, passionately and persuasively.[73] D'Orléans left his oratorical chores to Biron, who assured the Assembly that the Duc would presently offer a patriotic account of his actions.[74]

The Assembly's report was made by a committee chaired by Charles Chabroud, a legal expert who later passed by way of Jacobinism to a quiet but illustrious career. The document is in striking contrast to the *Procédure instruite au Châtelet*: it is analytical and only 116 pages long.[75] Admittedly it is a political treatise written against "judges . . . abandoned to themselves, to the caprice of their suspicions." I find nothing less here," Chabroud wrote, "than a conspiracy hatched against the constitution. A league has been formed on the debris of the Old Regime to attempt the overthrow of the new regime."[76] Chabroud was not swaddled in impartiality. However, the political thrust of the report is not its most original feature.

What Chabroud does skillfully is to pose a conundrum in political explanation: "Here is a sketch, and you want a picture; you would like to be shown the causes that produced this sudden convulsion, to go backward as far as possible, to the first spark that lit this frightful fire. . . ."[77] Ideology and interest are both involved: "A great insurrection may have been premeditated, but it may also be due to natural causes. It has been said that the people rose because of their needs and because they saw their rights threatened by a new affront [i.e., the Flanders Regiment banquet]."[78] Chabroud proposes to examine both elements. As for the plot, he concludes: "no witness has shown the linkage of a concerted intrigue. . . . See if you can finally put [these pieces of evidence] together to form a coherent whole. . . ."[79] What the *rapporteur* sees is "a multitude of chips that do not form a setting."[80]

For Chabroud the socioeconomic explanation is basic: "It is quite clear that the lack of bread was extreme in Paris. The people could hardly get enough to live on day by day. . . . The most pressing of needs creates enough energy by itself. . . ."[81] This contention that fear and hunger provided a sufficient cause lies at the heart of Michelet's later interpretation, which finds no stigma attached to the Duc d'Orléans.[82] The account of d'Orléans's former mistress Grace Dalrymple Elliott regarding his comings and goings also insists on his innocence.[83] However, other views, such as Mounier's lengthy dissection of the Châtelet testimony, are not to be dismissed out of hand.[84]

The extreme Right, mainly through the oratory of the Abbé Maury, led the attack on d'Orléans (though not Mirabeau) in the debate on the *rapport Chabroud*. Biron defended his friend, "un des premiers sectateurs de la liberté," with energy. It was Barnave, leader of what were then the Jacobins, who moved that the Assembly sustain the opinion of its committee.[85] The charges were declared dismissed. Following the exculpation, a document labeling the decision infamous was signed by 117 deputies (plus twenty-five others, who took exception to certain conclusions of the Châtelet, mostly relative to the guilt of Mirabeau).[86] Thirty-nine other deputies who had given depositions to the Châtelet did not participate in the manifesto. The day after the verdict, d'Orléans appeared in the Assembly and said: "It is time to prove that those who have supported the cause of the people and of liberty . . . were impelled by feelings of justice and not by vile and odious motives of ambition and revenge."[87] To which the *Orateur du Peuple* responded: "Bravo, Monsieur d'Orléans, your frank and courageous conduct is the best reply you could make to those atrocious slanders hurled against you!"[88] The royalists turned to poetry:

> Thanks to our Assembly's will
> Virtue has its triumph still.
> To be powerful, you see,
> All one needs is its decree.
> Now that this brave soul collects
> Constitutional respects,
> Tell the world that you are sure
> He's the purest of the pure.[89]

And the rage of polemics, for and against d'Orléans, peaking in the summer and autumn of 1790, knew little abatement in 1791.

The first high noon of the Jacobin Club was at hand. The more conservative "patriots"—Lafayette, Sieyès, Talleyrand, Mirabeau, Le Chapelier —had withdrawn and formed the Club of 1789, which failed to have much public repercussion. In 1790 the Duc d'Orléans belonged to no club, but his sympathizers were with the Jacobins. In October 1790, his eldest son, the Duc de Chartres, turned seventeen. Bred for politics, Chartres was dragged to patriotic events and meetings, including the Jacobins, by Madame de Genlis, much to his mother's distaste (d'Orléans used this as one of his reasons for separating from his wife).[90] On 2 November 1790 the young man was presented as a member of the club by the Marquis de Sillery;[91] subsequently he served on its admissions committee.[92] Louis-Philippe later regretted the Jacobins. But his republican reputation and patriotism were established here, even before he went off to the army. On 21 November the ambitious Laclos became the editor of the Jacobin circular and an influential figure in regulating the correspondence of the society.[93] Would the chance again arise for him to persuade d'Orléans to grasp for the throne? Could the sybarite of "Mousseaux" and lover of liberty rise to that occasion?

5. Nightmares of a Royal Republican

Found innocent of complicity in the events of 5–6 October 1789, d'Orléans took little further part in the proceedings of the National Assembly. Polemics continued to rage around him. "I will take you on in your own palace as soon as I manage to assemble complete proof of your abominable conspiracies," one of them declared.[1] Radicals who hated Lafayette answered in kind: "That traitor wishes to rule alone like a despot; he is afraid that M. d'Orléans, who is jealous of neither him nor his place, will topple him under his white horse."[2] After the king's ill-advised flight to Varennes on 21 June 1791, his subsequent recapture, and temporary suspension from the throne, a new possibility for the Orleanist regency arose: few were yet vowed to the adventure of republicanism. Philippe's opponents fought back venomously against "le petit Cromwel [sic] de Monceaux."[3] "Monster that hell has vomited forth for the sorrow of the human race . . . no, you shall not reign; no, France is not yet debased to that excess of evil and shame."[4]

Was there a chance of d'Orléans reigning in 1791? Not much: for the Fayettists and Old Left (soon to be called the Feuillants), making common cause, determined to rehabilitate their humiliated monarch by proclaiming the fiction that he had been kidnapped by the ultra-Right and by winning his approval of their constitution. Rather than run the risk of d'Orléans on the throne, moderates like Lafayette and La Rochefoucauld even began contemplating as a last resort the inauguration of a conservative *république à l'américaine* in France.[5] The revolutionary Left, vocal but not yet sure of its mass of maneuver, was divided on the question of regimes. Though there was Roman-style republican sentiment in the Cordeliers Club and the radical press, as well as a profound desire to eliminate Louis XVI and judge him for treason, the more polite and powerful Jacobins could not reach a settled position. Eventually the repression of 17 July (the "massacre of the Champ de Mars") threw the democrats on the defensive.

There had been a certain swell in the Revolutionary press in favor of d'Orléans. He had two particular supporters in Fréron, who typically called attention to such things as the applause the Duc had received at the funeral of Mirabeau on 4 April 1791,[6] and Marat, who wrote in the wake of Varennes: "Louis XVI is unworthy to recover his throne. . . . He is a fearful monster who should be strangled if public liberty and public safety are to be assured. . . . The conscripted fathers [i.e., the Assembly], together with their slaves and accomplices, would have the nation's cruel indignation to fear if they did not name a regent. . . ."[7] That regent, of course, could only be d'Orléans; Provence had fled abroad.

The year 1791 was a difficult one in the Duc's life. Not only had his creditors pinned him down, but he was having the worst sort of family quarrels with the Duchesse, especially over the children's education, which touched directly on politics. As we saw in the preceding chapter, the Duchesse deplored her eldest son's "republican" initiation. The episode caused not only a violent altercation with d'Orléans, but a temporary split with Louis-Philippe. In a letter redolent with pain, she wrote her son on 26 April: "I can't hide from you how much your latest behavior has hurt me. . . ."[8] Even the mild-mannered Duc de Penthièvre had felt constrained to admonish d'Orléans: "You know that I have never wished to meddle in the affairs of your family, since it's none of my business, but you can well believe how pained I have been by the education that your children have been receiving."[9] The reference is of course to Madame de Genlis's curriculum. We can sympathize with the unfortunate Duchesse. Of Madame de Genlis she wrote: "I know her well, and nobody but your wife would put up with all she has had to take [from her]."[10] "Just think," she lamented to d'Orléans, "you are taking away my most precious rights and forbidding me my most sacred duties."[11]

Louis-Philippe was rather more generous about his father's part in the "painful memory" of events that resulted in his mother's quitting the Palais-Royal for the consolation of her father's company at the Château d'Eu.[12] By June he was off to join his hereditary regiment (now called the 14th Dragoons), of which he was titular colonel. He described his leave-taking of the king and queen as "extremely chilly."[13] Almost every day he received affectionate and newsy letters from Madame de Genlis, addressing him as "cher fils." Owing to the political rupture in the family, the substitute mother had, to all intents, become the real one: shades of Emile and his tutor, in Rousseau's work. What Madame de Genlis did not control at this point was the political strategy of the Duc, which had passed to Laclos.

Laclos, too, had been exposed to a rash of pamphlets. "Machiavelli," said one, "would not have succeeded better in hoodwinking a people which, just beginning to emerge from slavery, was barely glimpsing the dawn of liberty."[14] Another, allegedly addressed by the Duc to his secretary, ran in part: "You alone made me ambitious, and you figured me out wrong. You were always talking to me about *Guise* and *Cromwell*; I am not born to their role . . . [but] I must conceal my plans; I must succeed."[15] The libel had a grain of truth. Try as he might, Laclos could not make the Duc lunge for the crown, even after Varennes. Thus Madame de Genlis was to have an immortal triumph over her avowed enemy, whose novel she later declared "execrable in principles . . . and very bad, too, as a literary work."[16] Her "cher fils" would sit on the throne as the last King of the French; as if to underscore the irony, the aging General Lafayette would hand him the crown, forty years after so staunchly denying it to his father.

At first Laclos seemed to have the advantage. On the day after the king's arrest became known in Paris, 24 June 1791, Philippe d'Orléans made a conspicuous entry to the Jacobin Club, where he was proposed for membership by his second son, the Duc de Montpensier. Some thought this arrogant; but Dubois-Crancé reminded the audience that deputies, if duly presented, had an automatic right to join. Laclos quickly took the floor. He wondered out loud what action the Assembly should take when the humiliated king was brought back. Then the Jacobins gave themselves over to their favorite pastime of heated patriotic debate. Danton—sometimes accused of Orleanism—demanded the destitution of Louis XVI, "either a traitor or an imbecile," but hesitated over regency or republic, preferring to temporize with an executive council chosen by the departments.[17]

Laclos intended to sell d'Orléans to the people and receive back their petitions and encouragements. The Duc was no doubt subject to the customary vibrations of his wavering spirit. Laclos peddled the English model of 1688; Paris and the Jacobins debated it. But on 28 June his plans were struck by lightning. Rumor had it that d'Orléans had renounced all claims to a regency; this would appear in public print the next day. But why had the Duc gone so ostentatiously to the Jacobins, and what had happened in the interval?

Very likely Laclos had persuaded his master that at such a grave moment he should appear among his supporters and lend weight to thwarting the designs of Lafayette. Probably, too, the Duc was not entirely reassured by what he found at the Jacobins. Their habits of vituperative controversy, so easily turned on new victims, may have unsettled his instinct of privacy. On the other hand, he was deeply concerned for the prestige of his posterity in a changing world. He could grasp the sentiment for a republic. He probably also knew that the institution of monarchy in France ran deeper than the person of Louis XVI, and that the future might offer many surprises. Marie-Antoinette based her private hopes on the Dauphin; Philippe d'Orléans must have harbored similar presentiments about the Duc de Chartres, who had had a systematic, if unorthodox, education fit for the times and was embarked on a military career that invited public admiration. Moreover, at this particular moment, Madame de Genlis was there to remind him of all these things.

"It's a very well known fact," she writes in an innocent tone, "that since the Revolution [d'Orléans] had asked advice only from M. de Laclos, and that he had confidence in no one else."[18] However, she goes on, "since the Revolution he asked my advice on one thing: that was relative to the regency, at the time when people spoke of deposing the King, after his return from Varennes." According to Madame de Genlis, "[the Duc] begged me to compose [his renunciation] for publication. I immediately wrote a half-page, which announced this very formally."[19] The text is dated 26 June 1791: "If there is a question of a regency, I renounce hereby and forever the rights to it that the Constitution gives me. I shall dare to say that after having made so many sacrifices for the people and the cause of liberty, I am no longer permitted to leave the class of ordinary citizens, where I placed myself with the firm resolve of remaining always. For me, ambition would be an unpardonable inconsistency."[20] Evidently the d'Orléans-Genlis conversations had proceeded over several hours' time, at a distance from Laclos; for here is what she wrote to Louis-Philippe, dated midnight, 24 June: "Oh, *mon fils* . . . your glory is mine; it is my wealth, my happiness, it is mine as well as yours; if only I could share your dangers! [*sic*: France was not at war]. . . . There is much talk here of a Regency: in that case it will certainly be offered to M. d'Orléans, who is irrevocably determined to refuse it, as well as any kind of position that would show ambition." Her rhapsody concludes: "You will agree, *cher ami*, you who, I know very well, would refuse the throne if it was offered to you and you could not have it without injustice; you, who have the morals and soul of a Spartan. . . ."[21] Pure casuistry lurks in that sentence.

With the publication of the renunciation, interest did shift, at least spasmodically, to the Duc de Chartres, whose patriotism, courage, and talents were applauded by the papers. It seems that a trial balloon was floated. Barnave, who had no reason to lie, writes of a gathering at which he was present: "[M. Sillery, Madame de Genlis's husband] said that, in all truth, M. d'Orléans had publicly announced that if the regency were offered to him, he would not accept it, and that it was no longer possible to consider him. However, M. de Chartres had refused nothing; although he was still quite young [18], his sterling qualities could compensate. The fifty or sixty deputies present seemed, for the most part, so struck by this observation that it is hard to believe that several do not still remember it."[22] Louis-Philippe is mute on the topic.

Laclos would persist. He had influence in the Jacobins, and conceivable allies in Danton and Marat. He intrigued for a common policy of the Left behind the notion of a regency. To this end, on 12 July 1791, he published side by side in the *Journal des Jacobins* an essay by Brissot demanding a republic for France and his own rebuttal entitled "De la monarchie et du républicanisme." Brissot had preached a "new republicanism" relieved from the anarchic fears of antiquity and indebted to the American experiment in representative government for much of its appeal, a republic preserved from the mobs by the buffer of a legislative elite, but with a relatively weak, nonhereditary executive.[23] This was not exactly the democratic republic of the Cordeliers.[24] Laclos hoped to boost the regency by exposing the defects of conservative republicanism: he proposed "a monarchy that can maintain equality among the different departments, that will assure the national sovereignty is not parcelled out . . . especially in a monarchy in which the department of Paris will not become . . . what in antiquity Rome was with regard to the empire. . . ."[25] If this seems an odd doctrine to feed to future Montagnards, it must be remembered that in the summer of 1791 Paris was in the hands of Lafayette and Bailly. Laclos wished to provoke agitation from below: the country itself would demand the deposition of Louis XVI, while retaining monarchy and bearing Philippe d'Orléans to power—in spite of himself and Madame de Genlis! In the midst of a populist temper he told the Jacobins: "I propose that we draw up a sensible but firm petition, not in the name of the Society, for societies don't have that right, but in the name of all the good citizens of the Society. . . . I ask that all citizens be permitted to sign it without distinction—active, nonactive, women, minors, taking care only to classify these three kinds of signatures. I cannot doubt that our petition will come back to the National Assembly with ten million signatures."[26]

As Laclos finished his proposal, demonstrators invaded the Jacobins, armed with texts of their own. In the ensuing turbulence, Laclos's motion was brushed aside, and a committee consisting of Brissot, Danton, Lanthenas, Sergent, and Ducancel was appointed to edit a new petition for the following day. Brissot recounts that he was charged to write the draft: "It was done in less than half an hour. I read it to my colleagues; they approved it. Laclos invited me to read it to the Jacobins, who were to meet at eleven. I declined . . . he said he would do it. . . . I never saw him again until 1793."[27] D'Orléans's enterprising secretary added a small phrase at the end which "seemed to the Jacobins to invite d'Orléans to the throne, and thus it caused ripples of discussion. Laclos thought he would calm them by saying that I was the author of the petition; nobody thought me a member of the *parti d'Orléans*. . . ."[28] The text that Laclos read to the Society was as follows: "[We] . . . formally and especially ask that the National Assembly should receive, in the name of the nation, the abdication, made as of 29 June, by Louis XVI of the crown delegated to him, and should provide for his replacement *by every constitutional means* [my italics]. . . ."[29] The last phrase indicated the customary facilities of a regency for the minority of Louis XVII. The fate of the petition, questioned by the Jacobins, rejected by the Cordeliers, and never circulated publicly, need not occupy us. However, Madame de Genlis became extremely agitated when she learned of these maneuvers. Foreseeing the voyage of the petition to the Champ de Mars, she dispatched her husband Sillery as fast as he could go to the Hôtel de Ville to denounce Laclos's plot against law and order to Bailly, who speedily warned Lafayette.[30] The idea of Sillery's saving the Fayettists from the designs of the Jacobins is not without humor, but this was actually a case of Orleanist civil war. Yet it was the Cordeliers, not Félicité de Genlis, who delivered the fatal blow to Laclos's design: they wanted nothing but the democratic republic. With this episode Laclos's political role was finished, as Sillery would soon announce for the edification of the Assembly.[31] As a precaution, Laclos was later arrested with other Orleanists in early April 1793, following the desertion of General Dumouriez and "cher fils."

War was on the horizon; Philippe d'Orléans failed to receive a command and was consoled only by the reflected glory of his two older sons.[32] A letter of his to Chartres, written on 18 September 1791, coolly describes his reaction to the acceptance of the Constitution by Louis XVI. Again, on 30 September, he writes his son about the closing business of the Assembly and the persecution of the clubs by the Feuillants. This he sees strictly from a family perspective: "Take all the precautions you can, because surely you will be closely watched. Be carefully on your guard . . . they will try to use [the decree] to cause us discomfort."[33] Chartres was posted first to Rochambeau's command, based on Valenciennes; in December 1791 he joined the staff of his father's old friend, the Duc de Biron. In October 1791 Madame de Genlis left for England with d'Orléans's daughter Adèle: education, not emigration. They would stay a long time. Finally, in April 1792, war was declared.

Four months later, popular turbulence, royal recalcitrance, and military setbacks toppled the monarchy. D'Orléans followed the sequence of events with keen interest, but from a distance. Receptive to the radical drift of French politics, he seems to have had little influence over it, in spite of a police report of 8 August 1792, signed Charles Goret, but a composite of different handwritings, that states, "we are more and more aware of the evil designs of the *parti des factieux*; there is no longer any doubt that the Duc d'Orléans is the leader" (corrupting the clubs and the "federated" troops in the precincts of the Palais-Royal).[34] The scenario seems rather fanciful. For months, d'Orléans had kept up a lively correspondence, especially with Chartres. In a letter of 3 May 1792 he wrote: "it is not possible to stay here [Paris] and to tolerate the joy of the aristocrats and the lamentations of the false patriots."[35] By 15 May he was reporting: "People think there will be bad trouble in Paris within several weeks or that the King will get out. . . ."[36] Louis XVI survived the *journée* of 20 June, but fell on 10 August, when the people, with loss of life, stormed the Tuileries. D'Orléans was not in the least disturbed. He wrote twice to his daughter in England shortly afterward (15 and 23 August) without mentioning the fate of the king, reassuring her in the second letter that "everything is quiet here."[37] During the horror of the September Massacres, it is reported that a group of admiring citizens carried to Monceau on a pike the head of his kinswoman, the Princesse de Lamballe. D'Orléans blanched; his dinner companion, Madame de Buffon, fainted.[38]

The Duc accommodated himself to the rhythm of events. Already, before 10 August, he had written to his elder sons: "I would not be at all surprised to see a new constituent assembly within a short time. If so, I think you should want to be a part of it. Let me know your ideas, because neither your age [Chartres was eighteen and Montpensier seventeen] nor your status as French princes counts against it."[39] This became a repetitive theme; on 4 August he laid out a detailed strategy for Chartres's election: "Voidel [later the defender at his trial] thinks it would be best if you were chosen elsewhere than in Paris and that if you agreed, he would be delighted to get you elected in Sarreguemines, which is in his area . . . you have only to drop him a line." Would Antoine [Montpensier] also like to be a candidate?[40] On 18 August, no word of the conquest of the Tuileries, but still the same obsession: "Voidel . . . is sure you can be elected at Sarreguemines. . . . We'll just have to see once the Convention meets whether it will certify you, or demand its age requirement [i.e., twenty-five]."[41] Voidel wrote to Chartres on 26 August: apparently it was to be Metz, and not Sarreguemines. Evidently willing to seek election, Louis-Philippe was prevented only by the age barrier. Voidel praised the idea of "a member of the stricken dynasty supporting a form of government contrary to his private interests and giving an example of absolute devotion to those of his country."[42]

Philippe d'Orléans wanted to pass his credentials to the next generation: his own life was a shambles. Probably he would have preferred not to stand for the Convention if his sons had qualified. Following his election to that assembly, his laments were recorded by Louis-Philippe in a conversation held toward the end of September 1792: "today they are no longer satisfied to have brought us [the family] down to the common level; we have to pay the price for our former rank, by being placed lowest, at the end of the list [d'Orléans was the last of twenty-four deputies chosen from Paris]. That's why they put me where they did. . . ." "And yet they wanted you," said Louis-Philippe. "Yes, either you or me, they didn't care who, just as long as they had a prince sitting in the midst of their faction, but without any influence."[43] It may be that Louis-Philippe garnished the story to show his father in a more favorable light, for, in a letter, written only a few days earlier, d'Orléans had expressed more optimism: "If, as I'm beginning to think, I won't be in the National Convention, for there are only three deputies left to name, Sillery has at least been chosen by the Somme, and everything looks just fine. The Assembly will be excellent."[44] We cannot know whether the forthcoming task of judging the king weighed in the slightest on d'Orléans at this time.

There was simultaneously another whisper of the throne, dispatched from strange quarters. During gentlemanly consultations over the exchange of prisoners, the Prussian general Heyman had taken Louis-Philippe aside and asked him to convey to d'Orléans a message stating that in the interest of saving France from anarchy the allies would be reassured if he "were at the head of the French government." Chartres patriotically refused the errand. Nevertheless, with the consent of generals Dumouriez and Kellermann, he brought back a note of greeting and an invitation to communicate. D'Orléans refused to open it, handing the envelope to the officers of the Convention. Brissot burned it.[45] D'Orléans was not only being civic but prudent. There is little likelihood that the allies would have sought him as sovereign under any conditions, and the émigrés would have been outraged. On that very day, in fact, 22 September 1792, Collot d'Herbois moved the abolition of the monarchy in the Convention. It evaporated in bewilderment, without debate, and by the unanimous consent of an assembly that would shortly begin to cannibalize itself.

To sit "at the peak of the Montagne," d'Orléans had to renounce his name. The story has been told many times, usually with derogation.[46]

But the simple fact is that "d'Orléans" was a feudal title and no more a name than "de Bourbon"; by a law of 19 June 1790 the Constituent Assembly had abolished such titles, without, to be sure, much effect on customary nomenclature. When the Duc presented himself on 10 or 11 September 1792, to vote as an active citizen of the Saint-Roch district, he was refused a ballot and directed to the Hôtel de Ville. An average French prince would have strangled the clerk. But the republican Louis-Philippe-Joseph d'Orléans marched off dutifully to the municipal offices, where, it will be recalled, the Revolutionary Commune of 10 August was still implanted. Somebody of genius there suggested the name of Egalité. Louis-Philippe recounts that his father smirked at the silliness of the idea. Well, would he prefer Publicola? "'No, of course not,' my father replied, and the name of Egalité was awarded to him."[47] And, naturally, to his family as well. The Palais-Royal, "henceforth [to be] called the 'Garden of the Revolution'," became popularly known as the Maison-Egalité.[48] D'Orléans expressed "extreme gratitude" to the Commune.[49] The name seemed only slightly less absurd in that time than in our own. There was still some confusion: the *Almanach National* carried him, on its electoral lists of 1793, as d'Orléans. By then he had taken his place with the Montagne (the Republican Left) in the Convention, while leading his disorderly bachelor life in the Maison-Egalité.

Philippe d'Orléans had to confront the moral issue of the trial and punishment of his cousin the king. According to a long conversation held between Louis-Philippe and his father at the beginning of December 1792, Egalité was torn. He did not accept the thesis that Louis XVI was non-justiciable as the Constitution of 1791 implied, "especially when public opinion felt that this prince had violated his sworn oath and had conspired with the foreign powers and the émigrés. . . ."[50] He hoped for a finding of guilt and a mitigation of the sentence of capital punishment. But he could do nothing. He wished to be spared from the burden of voting, but feared what it might cost in reprisals. He authorized Louis-Philippe to seek an interview with Pétion (with whom he was not on speaking terms) to find out if this other enemy of the king would take the lead in softening the sentence. Pétion demurred.[51]

The overture to the king's trial brought forward the play of factions. Members of the so-called Gironde (whose special mouthpieces were Buzot, Louvet, and Boyer-Fonfrède) sought at once to embarrass the patriotism of the Montagne and show the purity of their own. On 16 December 1792 Buzot rose to place a motion, whose gist was that whatever was done with Louis XVI, the Republic would remain in peril unless his entire family was banished. The intention was to distress the Montagne for harboring a prince. Following a review of Orleanist perturbations, Buzot concluded: "I ask that Philippe and his sons . . . should carry elsewhere than in the Republic the sorrow of having been born near the throne, having known its maxims and received its examples; the sorrow of bearing a name which might rally the seditious or the emissaries of foreign powers, but which can only offend the ear of a free man!"[52] The Montagne was thrown into disarray; Buzot's allies pressed for an immediate vote on the motion to expel all the Bourbons. Saint-Just argued for an adjournment of the question. It was Barère, however, who saved the day by pointing out that "one of the members of the Bourbon-Capet branch happens also to be a *representative of the people*. . . . I ask for a debate on this question."[53] Finally, the Convention decided that all of the royal family, except those in detention, "will leave the Department of Paris within three days and, within eight days, the territory of the Republic and the territory occupied by its armies." But with regard to Philippe-Egalité the application was deferred two days.

This gave the Jacobins and sections time to recoup. That evening, Camille Desmoulins went to the tribune at the Jacobins to describe the tactical dilemma: the "Brissotins" were hoping that "a sincere friend of liberty" would be assassinated at Koblenz and were trying to "make the Montagne look like a faction."[54] Robespierre, who had always recoiled from Egalité's breeding and morals, argued that to sacrifice Egalité would unmask the Gironde: "I have for a long time thought of insisting on the exile of Egalité and all the Bourbons, and the demand is not inhuman, as you may think, because they can go to London [France did not declare war on England until 1 February 1793], and the nation can provide an honorable stipend for the exiled family."[55] This brought Marat to his feet: "I am far from agreeing with Robespierre; Egalité must remain because he is a representative of the people. . . . The patriots must not abandon the battlefield. If we do that, liberty is lost forever."[56] The debate raged for several sessions.

It found its echo in the press. Marat backslid in his double-edged article called "Profession de foi de l'Ami du Peuple sur Philippe d'Orléans, dit l'Egalité. . . ." Accusing Roland's faction of fomenting the trouble, he asserted: "as representative of the nation, d'Orléans cannot in any way be punished by such a decree." But, he added: "I declare that I have always [*sic*] regarded d'Orléans as an unworthy man favored with fortune, without virtues, without soul, without guts, having as his only merit the language of the gutter. . . . I have never believed in his civic qualities; the proofs he has given all seem to hinge on his ambitions, which he has neither the boldness nor the courage to succeed in, . . . despite the numerous supporters that his birth, his wealth, and his enormous prodigality procured." "If I were still among the living," Marat declared, "I would suffer martyrdom rather than support him."[57] Dogs, it has been said, bite hands that feed them.

Robespierre, who could not be accused of any *volte-face*, devoted an entire number of his *Lettres à ses commetans* to exposing the nefarious designs of the Gironde; he even dishonestly accused the friends of Roland and Brissot of influencing d'Orléans's election.[58] He regarded exile as "a politic and necessary measure."[59] Hébert was more colorful; he searched his soul rather than his previous writings: "At the bottom of my heart I have always detested Philippe d'Orléans: I looked on him as a hypocrite who, sooner or later, would play turncoat; but since that ugly villain served our cause by spreading his gold to trip up the traitor, I thought, like all the patriots, that we should wear him like a shirt you shed once it gets dirty."[60]

Despite these fulminations and the hostility of the Gironde there were two reasons why d'Orléans continued to be tolerated. The first is that his case would have become a diversion from the main point, the king's trial, which had begun on 11 December; the second is that d'Orléans seems to have retained some popularity in Paris that was useful to the strategy of the Montagne. "In the evening [of 19 December] there were mobs gathering at various points; groups of Cordeliers ran through the streets crying *Vive Egalité!* and swearing to shed the last drop of their blood for d'Orléans."[61] And on 24 December the Section du Mail of Paris addressed the Convention: "To banish one of your number, a deputy of the people! Ah! Most likely, citizen legislators, you would not want in these trying circumstances to violate the principles you swore to protect forever!"[62] The sections, through the voice of their mayor Chambon, forced the Convention to adjourn the decree. In the meantime, the patriots could have the pleasure of watching d'Orléans squirm as the fate of his cousin approached.

D'Orléans went toward the candle of regicide like a moth. Did hatred drive him to this pass, as royalist historians assert? The Duc could be unforgiving. But Louis-Philippe writes that "implacable hatred" was foreign to his nature.[63] Probably there was a confused mixture of fear, prudence, and fatality, reinforced by moral misjudgment. Montpensier, his second son, had urged him on the evening before the balloting to remain absent from the Convention, but he had later been convinced by two deputies, Merlin de Douai and Treilhard, that abstention would be cowardly. So he went and did his perplexed duty. We may doubt that he was simply craven. Though his whole being was involved in physical sensation and he had no religious or moral convictions about the inter-penetration of life and death, he faced his own death with courage almost a year later. He was scheming for survival, not prestige, for the protec-tion of the fortunes of his descendants, especially Chartres.[64] His political and moral perceptions were now swamped in a wash of regret, even panic, which he masked with the slogans of his suspect patriotism.

He did not really think about the king at all. He did not attend the Convention and listen to the arguments. His mind was engaged with the fate of his own posterity; the struggle over banishment unsettled him far more than the straits of Louis XVI. Only five days before the execution he drafted this document:

> Several newspapers have the gall to publish that I have ambi-tious designs contrary to the liberty of my country, that in the case that Louis XVI would cease to exist (*ne serait plus*), *I stand behind the curtain to place my son or myself at the head of government.* . . .
>
> I come to the conclusion . . . that you regret, purely and sim-ply, the judgment that your committee adopted [i.e., the Buzot motion]; but if you were to sustain this motion, I hereby declare that I will hand your officers my formal renunciation to the rights of the royal dynasty in order to keep those of a French citizen.
>
> My children are ready to sign in blood that they share my opinion.[65]

We do not know if the children were consulted in this matter; it seems unlikely, since none but the Comte de Beaujolais was in constant prox-imity. What is more striking is that d'Orléans was so obsessed with his own political status that he seemed oblivious to the main issue. In re-nouncing the regency in 1791, the Duc had made exactly the same pro-fession of faith. He now repeated himself needlessly in a panic-ridden defense of his family.

The early months of 1793 were a time of military reverses, public hysteria, and character assassination. The patriots saw treason every-where. The external war became, more and more implacably, an internal war also. Paradoxically, the Maison-Egalité, once the source of revolu-tion, had become, according to police reports, a hotbed of royalism and sedition. In this endless warren of arcades, clubs, shops, and private rooms pictures of the dead king were peddled, forbidden gambling raged unchecked, royalist whores entertained aristocrats or fellow patriots, and political slogans were whispered in the dark.[66] The Jacobin prince could not control his monster. On 20 April 1793 a police agent reported tersely to the Ministry of the Interior: "il faudrait établir une grande surveillance sur la maison Egalité."[67] In four years much had changed in Paris and in men's minds, but not this.

Shortly before, the decisive episode in the eclipse of the d'Orléans family had intervened: General Dumouriez's treason. In late March, Dumouriez, propelled by events and ambitions, had been negotiating with the Austrians for a cease-fire in view of marching on Paris with his army, dispersing the Convention, placing Louis XVII on the throne, probably with the Duc de Chartres as regent, and restoring the Constitution of 1791. This seemingly staunch republican had made a ringing patriotic speech to the Jacobins on 14 October 1792, wearing the red bonnet of liberty. Collot d'Herbois had responded handsomely. But three days later, in the same setting, Marat had growled: "Dumouriez is a villain just like Lafayette."[68] Dumouriez fulfilled Marat's prediction, but he could not march his army. On 5 April, together with Louis-Philippe and General Valence, Madame de Genlis's son-in-law, he escaped to the Austrians. Dumouriez had despised Lafayette and schemed for his place; now fortune made their actions parallel. Dumouriez acknowledged this similarity in his memoirs, when he wrote that "both [the Fayettist and his own "classes" of émigrés] upheld with constancy the noble cause of humanity, and if they differed over the means, it was only a variation that did not assault the principle."[69]

Louis-Philippe accompanied Dumouriez, not because he was in any plot, but for personal safety. He had lamented the death of Louis XVI, but never made himself available to politics.[70] He sensed what was happening but repudiated the charge that "any sort of political connection or solidarity ever existed. . . . [Dumouriez] constantly denied this in all his writings. . . ."[71] Egalité would immediately have denounced Dumouriez before the Convention in a splash of patriotism; but this Chartres would not do. Laclos's principal biographer writes: "It was the Duc de Chartres who destroyed his father by following Dumouriez in his treason. He took the risk also of sending his mother and all his relatives to the guillotine."[72] But Louis-Philippe had little choice; moreover, he had already shared his premonitions with his father and had warned him.

A half-compromised Danton finally denounced Dumouriez at the Jacobins on 31 March.[73] In a reprise of December 1792, the Gironde, sorely pressed, now demanded the imprisonment of the whole royal family, as well as all close associates of Egalité and all in proximity to Dumouriez, notably Valence. Moreover, "the fathers and mothers of the officers of the army commanded by Dumouriez . . . will be kept in custody as hostages by the municipality where they live, until the commissioners of the National Convention and the Minister of War [four deputies and General Beurnonville, sent to arrest Dumouriez, had been handed over summarily to the Austrians] are set free and the Army of Belgium is placed under the orders of a new commander."[74] Philippe-Egalité, stricken by the edict, wrote his son in anguish: "Is it possible that you have been led so far astray (*aveuglé à ce point*)? No, I can't believe it. I will still see you come before the bar of justice to prove your innocence. If you do not, I will be the most wretched of fathers."[75]

The d'Orléans family had become a pawn of forces outside of its control. Heretofore, in the millennial history of the French monarchy, princes had been in a position to command clientage. Now a hydra-headed clientage had unexpectedly become the master of the prince; yet, due to the suddenness of Revolutionary change, the clients were unable to free themselves of all deferential habits, often acting like servants in the kitchen, and the prince scarcely questioned that his status depended on clients. Whatever their departures from the orthodox or official position, the d'Orléans had never lacked the loyal support of a retainer-ship. Now naive republicans, so recently proud princes, they were dismayed and deceived by the hostile rhetoric. The narrow maneuverability of the ideology of *Aristocratic I* was eclipsed. The Girondin flights of Boyer-Fonfrède, who declared, "the Egalités, it is said, have served liberty . . . [but] I want to owe nothing to these men in whose veins there flows the blood of kings," could not match the Montagne in denunciation.[76] When Louvet spoke of "Cordeliers in the pay of d'Orléans," he was fighting a rear-guard action.[77] Dumouriez had climbed to power with Girondin connections; he had, it was said, become the political guiding spirit (*âme directrice*) of the Duc de Chartres and had met with Madame de Genlis, now in Belgium with Adèle. The proscriptions of December were flung in the face of the Gironde. Robespierre had royalty barred from the popular societies on 1 April.[78] Marat demanded that a price be set on the head of all Bourbons who had fled abroad.[79] On 10 April Robespierre wanted the whole d'Orléans entourage criminally prosecuted.[80] A circular of the Jacobin Club, dated 19 April, explained the case:

> D'Orléans was never connected with true patriots. Robespierre, whom the subversives accused of being chief of his faction, had always opposed the nomination of d'Orléans to the National Convention . . . penetrating their plots, [he] voted for the expulsion of the Bourbons. . . .
>
> The apparent behavior of d'Orléans since the Revolution, his insignificance, the nullity of his talents and character, all seem

sufficient to refute the danger of the ambitions imputed to him; but the emigration of his eldest son, the emigration of Valence, all these intrigues uncovered by the knowledge of their complicity with the royalist Dumouriez, and especially their intimate contact with his friends seated in the National Convention, are certain proofs of the assaults of the house of Orléans on the Republic.[81]

Together with his remaining kinsmen, Egalité was arrested on 6 April. He begged the Convention to suspend execution of the decree until his case had been examined, arguing that otherwise "I might compromise my dignity as a representative of the people."[82] This did him little good. While the factional quarrel swelled, the Convention decided that d'Orléans, his son Beaujolais, the Prince de Conti, and the Princesse de Bourbon-Condé, the remaining members of the royal family, would be transferred to prison in Marseilles.[83] Egalité's estranged wife, also scheduled for the trip, wrote the Convention on 9 April: "I would have expected that since I am guilty only of the name I bear, the Assembly might consider my state of health, which is very bad at the moment. I have a terrible cold and a migraine that doesn't allow me to get out of bed."[84] Fortunately she was spared the journey; it would not have been a lovers' meeting. Why Marseilles? Marat suspected a sinister design, but it was probably so as to get the troublesome crew as far as possible from Paris.[85] The Marseillais were certainly not enchanted: they, too, were deeply factionalized. Moïse Bayle blamed the Convention "for sending into our midst a *pomme de discorde*."[86] The Montagnards regarded Egalité as part of a Rolandist plot; the moderates claimed that the transfer of the Bourbons to Marseilles was "a Montagnard ruse . . . to 'preserve' them in order to make Egalité king."[87] Thus Egalité spread dispute in his wake wherever he went, hindered or unhindered.

The Convention appointed several commissioners to accompany the wretched Bourbons to their destination. The prisoners were to be decently treated, but denied all access to the public; their chaperones were to keep a diary.[88] The journey was slow, taking about two weeks, with some difficulties along the way. Though Egalité displayed model comportment, Madame de Bourbon-Condé made life hard for her escorts: "[She] threatens us with divine wrath and eternal damnation; but that does not frighten us terribly. . . ."[89] Nogent-sur-Vernisson was unfriendly and royalist; in Moulins "the patriots hunt down the aristocrats and thwart their intrigues"; but in Vienne "greedy and fawning innkeepers with exaggerated memories treat the princes as one would have done in the old days."[90] Finally, on 23 April, the relieved commissioners could report a safe arrival in Marseilles, "where our travelers are watched by the citizens under the supervision of the public authority."[91] Egalité's second son Montpensier was sent under guard from Nice to join them.

In the midst of the journey, on 16 April, the Convention authorized the legal authorities in Marseilles to question the Bourbons regarding "the conspiracy plotted against French liberty" and to forward their findings; the prisoners, much to Egalité's distaste, were to be held incommunicado.[92] Their possessions were sequestered;[93] however, the apartments of the Palais-Royal and the properties of Monceau and Raincy were not searched and inventoried until after the execution, between 8 and 21 Messidor, an II.[94] Egalité's interrogation took place on 10 May. He put up a stiff case for his patriotism and republicanism, denying all affiliation with Mirabeau, Dumouriez, and others. He had undertaken no plots with the English. He believed in the "république une et indivisible." He had no personal ambitions.[95] When his youngest son, the Comte de Beaujolais, was questioned in his turn, we have the following exchange: "Q—Did your papa ever tell you he was going to be king? A—Never. Q—Did he tell you good things about the Revolution? A—Yes, always."[96]

Matters appeared to slumber, although Marat raised his voice in June when the Gironde fell. He connected d'Orléans with the "machinations of the *faction infernale*."[97] "D'Orléans, called Egalité," he wrote, "who had secret communications with Brissot, Gensonné, Lasource, Vergniaud, Guadet, and Pétion and held secret meetings with them, was politically guileful enough to sit with the Montagne."[98] By autumn the Montagne was strong enough to proceed to arbitrary justice against the imprisoned Girondins. It was very convenient, if not quite plausible, to link their political crimes with those of d'Orléans in a comprehensive plot. Thus, on 3 October 1793, when the Convention voted to send the Girondins before the Revolutionary Tribunal, Billaud-Varenne added: "I demand that we should not leave in silence a man almost forgotten, despite the imposing evidence against him. I ask that d'Orléans be sent to the Revolutionary Tribunal together with the other conspirators."[99] Amid loud applause this was voted. And so d'Orléans was brought back from Marseilles, this time alone.

His friend Voidel defended him vigorously and even wrote a pamphlet that later cost him his life.[100] The trial was cursory and its outcome foreordained. As Sanson writes: "Fouquier didn't even do him the courtesy of drawing up an act of accusation."[101] The dossier is very sparse: certain parties may have wished the evidence to vanish. Or perhaps, as the story goes, it came into the hands of Napoleon, who caused it to be destroyed. Egalité's servant Gamache, who attended him through these assembly-line proceedings, has left a touching account.[102] Found guilty, d'Orléans demanded to be executed without delay, and his request was granted. This was on 6 November 1793 (16 Brumaire, an II), just a week after the beheading of his friend Sillery and the Girondins. An apocryphal story tells us that d'Orléans, hearing himself hooted as the wagon bearing him to the scaffold passed the Palais-Egalité, remarked: "Only a short while ago they applauded me." When one of the executioners tried to help him out of his boots, he protested: "They will be easier to pull off after I am dead." He made confession and received the sacrament from the Abbé Lothringer (who had consoled Generals Miaczynski and Custine), one of the few recorded religious acts of his life.[103] Then he died, "proudly and haughtily," before a hostile crowd.[104]

If d'Orléans had once had a *parti*, it was a fair-weather faction. Previous adulators now lined up to vilify him. The *Révolutions de Paris* set the tone: "Never has a more despicable man soiled society, and his eldest son gave promise of even greater villainy. . . . Justice has finally delivered us from this monster."[105] Well-rehearsed popular societies chimed in. On 17 Brumaire, unaware of his death, the Society of Egalité-sur-Marne (formerly Château-Thierry) wrote: "Hasten, legislators, to destroy that corruptor and villain beneath the blade of the law. . . . All France has long judged him guilty."[106] From Lure, there was applause for the death of the "infamous Philippe";[107] from Roanne, "witness of joy" at the execution of this "monster of nature."[108] For the patriots of Nogent-sur-Seine, "d'Orléans . . . suffered a punishment too brief and mild for the crimes he trailed behind him on the way to the scaffold."[109] In his own phrase, he attracted hatred like a contagion.

D'Orléans was both a creation of the Old Regime that his "new politics" could not efface and a plaything of the republican factions. In 1793, France was still trapped in the memory and habit of old structures. The Republic was not just created *ex nihilo* like its calendar. The structural position of the d'Orléans family in French politics, however renovated, was an ancestral hurdle for the Jacobins to demolish. The more that d'Orléans pleaded his attachment to the new order and cultivated the Left, the more he evoked suspicion in the new men. He could not be a Girondin or a Montagnard, for his real interests were fixed on the placid political values of security, privacy, property, material enjoyment. If there was also a touch of glory mixed in, it came from his royal and princely descent. Aside from this, his caprice touched a nerve of modernity.

D'Orléans is, in fact, the apotheosis or caricature of Kenneth Minogue's notion of liberalism as a "philosophy of desiring."[110] In this case, it was a riotous, if ultimately pathetic, instrumentalism on behalf of the private choices that blood and money have procured. Such a visage of man is far older than the French Revolution. But d'Orléans is specifically the empiricist construction of man run amok: his "ideas," in the formula of Hume, are truly "decaying impressions"; he is the statue of Condillac, activated by its senses to the dignity of cognition and yet finally sculpted as the prince it had been in the first place. We study Robespierre and Saint-Just as if they were Plutarchian figures; but d'Orléans, head of the younger branch of the most presumptuous dynasty of Europe and sire of a king, is truly our ancestor.

PART III.
Adam-Philippe,
Comte de Custine 1740–1793

6. Royal War and
Political Rebirth

Adam-Philippe, by descendance Comte de Custine, chevalier and Baron de Sarreck, was born on 4 February 1740 in Metz to a well-placed family of the military nobility. This region and condition of birth powerfully affected traits of his public character and career. His vocation was prefigured: commissioned when only a small boy, he was at the siege of Maastricht in 1747 with Marshal de Saxe,[1] an example of what Carré calls "an unhealthy fantasy of aristocratic vanity"—child colonels and the like.[2] He would always be supremely vain about his "military seniority." Custine was also a provincial, an important territorial magnate coming from the Germanized East, one of the *quatre grands chevaux* of Lorraine. "His personal fortune was considerable," a biographer tells us;[3] accounts pertaining to his estates verify this.[4] Not only was Lorraine a highly militarized province; its frontier atmosphere subjected Custine to a psychological pull in the direction of the Rhine. In due course this aspect of his personality somewhat chilled the winds of liberty blowing from the West.

Schooling gave him a certain polish and a pompous eloquence. His official military record furnishes the major benchmarks of his advancement. Beginning his mature soldierly career as second lieutenant with the Ducroy regiment on 6 June 1758, he was promoted to full lieutenant on 22 May 1759.[5] By 7 March 1761 he was captain and company commander with the Schomberg regiment, experiencing combat in Germany until 1762. Then, on 5 June 1763, he became headquarters commandant of some dragoons; according to Chuquet, his career was under the protection of the War Minister Choiseul.[6] Afterward, there seems to have been little activity. Finally, on 1 March 1780, Custine received promotion to brigadier, commanding the regiment of Saintonge. He had married in 1767, but in 1774 a fatal disease claimed his young wife, described in angelic terms by Madame de Genlis.[7] This was a cruel blow to the fond husband, who remained from then on a widower.

In 1780 war with England was at hand. For over four years the fledgling confederation of North America had been in arms, and France's pride still smarted from defeat in the Seven Years' War, when she had not only lost an overseas empire (Voltaire's "quelques arpents de neige") but had even been unable to defeat tiny Prussia. Together with the most ardent and liberal part of the military aristocracy, Custine requested and received posting to Rochambeau's Expeditionary Force.[8] After a voyage by way of Caracas he finally disembarked in Newport, Rhode Island, with his Saintonge regiment in July 1780. His notice recounts: "he was at the siege of Yorck [sic] in Virginia, where he mounted the trenches. . . ."[9] Verger's journal records that Custine pressed an infantry charge at Yorktown recklessly and "lost a lot of men."[10] Von Closen portrays the action as a fiasco: Custine was drunk and an hour late, but "got off with 24 hours' arrest and many jests."[11] Intoxication and lack of punctuality were charges that would be made against him years later. Custine must have done better than this in America, for Rochambeau endorsed his request for promotion to *maréchal de camp* (major-general). The promotion was confirmed on 5 December 1781, and Custine assumed command of the Fourth Division.[12] He remained in America long enough to present General Washington's wife with a set of porcelain from his factory at Niederviller.[13] According to Blanchard's diary, Custine made a "journey into the interior of America" and recorded his observations in a journal, "which seemed to me most judicious. . . ."[14] Unfortunately that document has been lost.

With Virginia behind him, Custine received the undemanding post of military governor of Toulon on 19 April 1782, remaining there for six years until appointed inspector of cavalry troops in Flanders. By then both nation and army were in full effervescence. Custine shared these tensions, which had been building for over a generation.

The French military exploits in America had been costly, but a source of pride. As the grandson of the great Montesquieu wrote: "I am enchanted with our generals, with their conduct, their affability, their justice, their humanity, and the care they take of a small army, which is the most disciplined in Europe."[15] Bluche asserts: "Rarely has France had a better army than Rochambeau's expeditionary corps in America."[16] But this *was* a small army—5034 officers and men[17]—mostly commanded by the enlightened part of the officer corps: Noailles, Ségur, La Rochefoucauld-Liancourt, Broglie, Lauzun, Custine, Beurnonville, not to mention the meteoric Lafayette, officially major-general of the American Continental Army. The American experience did much to hasten the consolidation of a liberal nobility that would precipitate the political crisis six years later. America was, however, an exception to the rule. In reality the French army was swollen with generals, most of them having no postings or practical functions. During the reign of Louis XVI, 1322 general officers were appointed in eighteen years as compared with the

1106 promotions during the seventy-two-year reign of Louis XIV, thirty-five of which had been spent at war; moreover, the total of military effectives was smaller.[18]

The royal army was not exactly centralized, although the policies of Le Tellier and his successors had consolidated the army into a national military force at the beck of Bourbon dynastic pretensions. This course followed a rhythm experienced by all the major European continental states, whose power was measured "not only by the quantity of troops they could raise, but could maintain under arms."[19] No doubt the Bourbons had mastered the feudal aristocracy and monopolized the means of coercion. The king controlled the powers of peace and war. But, in counterpart, he depended far more completely on the nobility for these functions than for the parallel employments of administration and justice. This dependence was progressively exacted from the end of the reign of Louis XV on as the centerpiece of the aristocratic revolt.

The army was also plagued by venality and the hereditary acquisition of commissions and commands. Entire regiments, both French and mercenary, were bought or inherited. Some commands were ludicrously exercised by inexperienced *anoblis* or by immature scions of the court aristocracy. Coherence was warped by family vanity or aspiration. Orderly promotion practices could sometimes be reestablished only by arbitrary acts of the monarchy. These features, abolished by the Constituent Assembly on 28 February 1790, nevertheless persisted into the Revolutionary War. In 1789 Servan, a bourgeois engineer officer and later Minister of War, complained bitterly: "France has no army. Out of fifteen or sixteen hundred generals, there are thirty-seven to forty-one capable of commanding a division with success, ten to twelve able to direct the campaign of an army corps."[20] Many of these generals were the uninspired products of a mixed system of neo-feudalism and venal preferment.

Heredity meant the occasional appearance of a child colonel, but it had its compensation in encouraging military professionalism, as in the case of Custine. Venality, which mixed social classes and strata in disregard of merit, intensified the hatred of the petty military aristocracy for the newcomers. Up to mid-century the practice had been dictated by the monarch's policy of somewhat balancing social power, by the need for revenue, and by military necessity. In 1750 a decree of the War Ministry granted hereditary nobility to all general officers and to all other officers whose father and grandfather had also served as officers; all were exempted from the *taille*, and this exemption was made hereditary for those decorated with the Cross of Saint-Louis. That aroused the fury of the old nobility. Even the liberal Marquis d'Argenson, whose younger brother had implemented the policy, fretted: "There will soon be as many nobles as there are inhabitants."[21]

In 1758, under the impulse of the Marshal de Belle-Isle, a concerted attempt was made to reform the officer corps by limiting access to it to the nobility; although arrangements continued to be made, this was a prefiguration of pressures to come.[22] In the 1760s and 1770s there was still a considerable bourgeois component in the officer grades—the commoners often occupied the desk jobs with real distinction—and it was not unusual in many regiments for one or two lieutenants to be promoted from the ranks each year.[23] But by 1781, in the midst of the American excursion, the old and often penurious nobility of the sword (*noblesse d'épée*) raised a cry for solitary preferment. That was one factor behind the *règlement Ségur* of 22 May 1781, which forbade further access to commissions to anyone not possessing four quarterings of validated nobility. The règlement Ségur persisted until 29 July 1790, allowing for a whole decade of aristocratic retrenchment. Its intentions are still in dispute: recently D. D. Bien has argued, with a careful marshaling of evidence, that the motive was not so much to blockade the commoner (*roture*) as to deny advancement to the recently ennobled (*anoblis*), on whose incompetence the "true" aristocracy glowered with contempt.[24] Bien has especially insisted on the goal of professionalization in Ségur's reforms: "The minister wanted . . . a structure that would absorb and make useful as officers nobles of all kinds, the rich as well as the poor. . . . The trick was to create the right military 'constitution'. . . ."[25] Be that as it may, it was intrinsic to the defensive ideology of the nobles (according to the authority pattern of *Aristocratic I*) to regard themselves as "protectors of the people, who give the example of patriotism, virtue, and honor; who, exalted by the memory of the distinction of their ancestors and by the delicate pride embodied in their name, guide our legions on the field of glory and inspire the French soldier with the lessons of conquering or dying for the fatherland."[26] The règlement Ségur was at once the agency of purity and preferment.

Reforms notwithstanding, by 1787 France's army seemed irreparably sunk beneath its own dead weight. It cost the state almost as dearly as the Prussian and Austrian armies combined; it was badly equipped and trained; it was top-heavy with 1250 generals (more than in all the other European armies put together, although the Austrians alone had more foot soldiers); and of this plethora of generals, most were continually unemployed.[27] Out of the total officer corps of thirty-five thousand, only about ninety-five hundred were effectively serving with fighting units in 1787.[28] Baron de Besenval wrote of "a country where the officers are, so to speak, only like temporary sojourners in their regiments."[29] Of those officers, at the time of the summoning of the Estates-General, approximately 1845 were *roturiers* who had escaped the règlement Ségur by antecedence or default.[30]

Existing jealousies were profound: the army was "divided into classes as distinct from each other as different races of men."[31] At the top of the social structure one found the prestigious high nobility of the court; beneath them the masses of provincial nobles, jealous of their four quarterings and ancient profession, further subdivided by their fortunes (the poorer sorts were doomed to infantry commands). This second category supplied the great majority of officers. Beneath them, in two distinct layers, were the *anoblis* and the commoners, most of whose commissions preceded 1781. The last echelon was the smallest: officers of fortune who had risen through the ranks.[32] Embedded in a society where "*politesse* played a great role in the upper strata . . . [and] an infinite value was attached to forms and formulas," the different classes quarreled formulaically but in deadly earnest.[33] Ségur's "equality inside, inequality outside" may have been the norm, but it was not achieved in practice.[34]

Another important question was drill and discipline. By the mid-eighteenth century the military establishment of Frederician Prussia had begun to influence all other nations except England, which maintained no standing army: "it was imitated even in its worst faults."[35] But here the French were divided. The French garrison soldier enjoyed an enviable degree of freedom compared to the Prussian. His chastisements were less harsh, he was less servile, and he ate better. Opponents of the Frederician system saw in it a kind of soldierly humiliation that clashed with the military value of *honneur*.[36] They prized spirit and independence: "Initiative, spontaneity of attack, quick comprehension (*le coup d'oeil prompt*) are the masterful French qualities. Who cares if they are lax in drill, so long as they are superior on the field of battle?"[37] However, these qualities, believed natively French, were waning by the end of the reign of Louis XV; correspondingly, the Prussian model gained support, especially after the defeat of Rossbach. Of course there was a heavy dependence on mercenaries (useful in a peasant society, where the importance of a harvest could outweigh a campaign)—Irish, German, and, in our period, mainly Swiss.[38] As yet the ideal of the politicized citizen-soldier had not been glimpsed, except in literature.

There is a parallel between the officers and the troops. Both were considered professionals, the ones by hereditary calling, the others by career and seasoning. Wars created a community of danger and relations of esteem and attachment between the best leaders and the best soldiers. The officers frequently shielded their men from civil prosecution for crimes like pillaging, rape, and assault, having a haughty disdain for ordinary justice and a proprietary interest in their commands.[39] The officers fought the enemy and one another, wenched, ate, and drank like their men, but in a much more opulent and refined way.[40] Nothing was Prussian about their style of life if they could afford it. The luxury of the generals was notorious: "foreigners claimed that a French general on campaign took with him thirty or forty cooks."[41] In its much-resented reforms of 1788, the Conseil de Guerre forbade divisional commanders to serve more than sixteen dishes at a meal, and major-generals more than twelve.[42]

A factor working somewhat at cross-purposes with luxury and aristo-cratic caste consciousness was the prodigious growth of Freemasonry in the army, especially after the experience of the American war. The number of lodges and adherents multiplied in the reign of Louis XVI: 13 *ateliers* in 1777, already 40 in 1779, and 68, according to the annual list of the Grand Orient, in 1787.[43] In these gatherings nobles and bourgeois, officers and non-coms, fraternized. By the end of the Old Regime, it may be calculated that one military regiment out of three possessed its own atelier.[44] These lodges communicated a certain revivalism, a certain elitist democracy, which would help to prepare the ground for the army's conspicuous part in the pre-Revolution of 1787–88.[45]

The Comte de Guibert, in a minutious report prepared for the Con-seil de Guerre in October 1787, attempted to bring about some badly needed reforms, subsequently embodied in an ordinance of 17 March 1788. Many superfluous positions (especially government-generalcies and lieutenant-generalcies of regions and their staffs) were suppressed; the regiments were reorganized territorially and in twenty-one divisions; pay increases were granted; new regulations for training and maneuvers were issued; certain exceptions to the règlement Ségur were allowed. However, the grip of the *noblesse de Cour* on the highest grades was tightened, infuriating the petty nobility, while no real prospects for advancement were extended to the lower strata (officers of fortune could still not command a company).[46] The officer corps fell into a state of rebellion. Unit after unit declared against Guibert, his ordinance, and the authorities. This was unjust to Guibert, who was later praised by Napo-leon, for he had been responsible for the technical, not the social, portions of the ordinance.[47] As Hartmann comments: "This is not one of the least remarkable episodes of the Revolution: the participation of noble officers in the weakening of loyalty in the army and the preparation of near-anarchy among the soldiers, things they would lament so bitterly later on, when they became the victims."[48] The army's insurgency stimulated disobedience in all ranks and served as a dress rehearsal for a later fracturing of fealty. The *noblesse d'épée* shuddered with provocation at the precise moment when the ramparts of the Old Regime were tottering against the weight of the nation's newly gathered forces. But of course the royal army could not contain the power of that explosion. And the bourgeoisie would soon be clamoring to be let in: "it is we who fill the army quotas, who pay for the food and the upkeep of our children that, according to their will or not, serve the king and the country. . . . It is we also who bear the burden of lodging the soldiers during troop movements, without any hope of seeing our children reach high military rank. The door is shut upon them and they are told that they are not skilled enough to command."[49] Yet an army in the image of the nation would not be forged, as easily as a parliament, in a short time. Aristocratic generals would continue to lead republican citizens into battle five years after the Guibert mutinies.

Custine was a military noble who adopted the new slogans. His melange of ideology came from vulgarized *lumières*, the fraternal tendencies of Freemasonry, the *esprit frondeur* of the pre-Revolution, and a certain noblesse oblige. Madame de Genlis, who is the source of much of our personal and anecdotal material about the Custine family before the Revolution, mentions that the Comte de Custine formed part of a *société particulière* of about twenty-five persons who pursued topics of intellectual curiosity and dined often at the Palais-Royal.[50] The widower seems to have parceled his life between his regimental duties, the oversight of his properties in Lorraine, and the attractions of Paris, where he lodged with his younger brother in the rue du Bac.[51] He had also caught Masonic fever; we find him duly recorded among the brothers of the regiment of Saintonge upon his arrival on 8 March 1780 as garrison commander.[52] I have found two imputations of "Orleanism," which might be hinted at by Masonry and the connection with Madame de Genlis. Both are from 1793: one an extract from the minutes of the trial of General Miaczynski, guillotined for conspiracy with Dumouriez, alleging that Custine would support the aspirations of the Duc de Chartres;[53] the other (dated 4 August, when Custine was already imprisoned) from a Jacobin agent named Bouvard, referring to events of 1792.[54] Neither seems reliable: Custine's political ambitions could be satisfied only by his own amour-propre.

Custine's background permitted him to navigate effectively in a highly mannered and socially conscious professional corps, but it also bred in him a rancor toward certain court officers, younger in service and experience, who were given choicer commands. He persistently quarreled with his fellow officers. As the amiable General de Biron (Lauzun) wrote to Lebrun, the Minister of Foreign Affairs, on 22 November 1792: "I cannot conceal from you, Citizen Minister, that I am disturbed by the rift that exists between General Beurnonville and General Custine and which will perhaps always exist between General Custine and his collaborators, for—and I say this without modesty—all men are not so courageously patient as I am."[55]

Custine had his century's veneer of charm: Madame de Genlis describes him touchingly in the aftermath of his wife's death and calls him a man of "excellent heart."[56] His military notice credits him with being "a sensitive man, honest in his thoughts."[57] But "General Moustache" (as he was nicknamed) could be brash and vindictive in the discipline of soldiers, when required, and in his verbal treatment of brother officers and political associates. Sometimes he played for popularity: "The commanding general cajoled the men whenever he could, and affected harshness, even crudity, toward the officers."[58] An obviously hostile writer described him as "vainglorious, tough, trouble-making, overbearing, choleric, and grudging."[59] In 1787, when Custine was desultory in negotiating the marriage of his son François to Delphine de Sabran, the prospective bride's mother, soon to emigrate, lamented: "This father-in-law is a curse sent down from heaven to finish me off."[60] To balance the portrait, Gay de Vernon, though not concealing Custine's faults, presents him as "sober, robust, generous with his pocket money, severe, active, careful for the well-being of his soldiers," and impressive in his vigor and capacity.[61] Finally, however, anyone reading for very long through Custine's prolific and bellicose correspondence gets a heady whiff of megalomania, a vanity that was, in Chuquet's words, "furious, ferocious, implacable."[62]

Stubborn and abrasively egoistic, Custine nevertheless held interesting views on politics and military operations that are worth examining, for they help us to understand in what ways he was typical of his caste and in what ways distinct. We have seen something of the former; the German connection is a significant particularity. During the Seven Years' War, Custine became a convert to Prussian drill and discipline, superior, he thought, to the effete disorder of the French army.[63] He sent his son to be educated at the Military Academy of Berlin, and he himself caught the eye of Frederick the Great.[64] A thirst for order and authority tempered his patriotic reception of the Revolution, as countless small details of his politics will reveal. More than most of the military liberals, he was inclined to place professional discipline and civil liberty in separate compartments. His admiration for Prussian ways made him the enthusiastic proponent of an *Ostpolitik* that would debase the House of Austria (like most of the French military Custine deplored the reversal of alliances of 1756 and shared a general contempt for Marie-Antoinette) by detaching Prussia from its embrace. He would seek to cultivate pro-French feeling in the German states during the Revolution: both he and his son had the intermittent opportunity, costly to both of them, as we shall see, to dabble in high politics.

Custine, no less than Marat, later his sworn enemy, believed himself endowed with prophetic genius. In August 1791 he wrote: "From the beginning of the revolution up to the present I have not erred in any of my predictions."[65] Moreover, he vaunted his skill not only as a military organizer and leader, but as an economist, diplomat, civil administrator, and grand strategist as well. Often, when his views were sound, he proclaimed them overbearingly and offended mortally the allies he needed.

He made his début in Revolutionary politics as a provincial *grand seigneur*. Presiding over a common session of the electors of Lorraine and the Three Bishoprics at the Hôtel de Ville of Nancy in early 1789, he deftly complimented each of the orders, but reserved special praise for the Tiers, "that order which not only represents the nation, but constitutes it." "All of us have today the benefit of knowing one another," he added. "That union will survive forever."[66] This felicitation was perhaps the first of Custine's untimely predictions. The inflated language of fraternity was in store for future shock. Avid like so many others to sketch out his vision of the new politics, Custine presented at this time a "consultative plan" (model *cahier*) to the notables of Lorraine, to "facilitate the composition of the *cahiers* of the representatives of these provinces."[67] Through it and later documents of Custine that have survived we can trace the political evolution of an important figure of the military aristocracy and cast some light on that career.

In this first effort at constitutional theory, several items stand out. There is a typical emphasis on individual liberties and on the permanence of the Estates-General to guard them.[68] The idea of a national assembly, circulating since 1787, is absent: France will have an active legislature, but it will remain feudally stratified, with membership dependent on considerable wealth.[69] Taxation, much equalized, will be the prerogative of the Estates; they will exercise judicial power against arbitrary acts of the ministry.[70] Court and ministry will be curtailed by fiscal control and oversight. But the state is to remain thoroughly monarchical; all laws will require the monarch's consent.[71] It is interesting in this regard to note that in late 1791 Custine could write of "the wise Washington, who now fulfills the functions of a king."[72] Custine believed in a liberty tempered by authority. As much as the next patriot, he could be lyrical about liberty. But he would recall, when his legislative mandate was expiring, that "in the National Assembly I often fought the prevailing opinions, and I always showed myself to be the opponent of those who would provoke the license of the people or tolerate that of the soldier. I never ceased to declare myself the enemy of those kinds of people."[73] In the "Plan à consulter," Custine's enthusiasm for the Tiers was tempered by a warning: "If the Tiers has its own best interests at heart, it will support the principles of the [monarchical] government, as opposed to those of democracy, which the equal admission of the Tiers, accompanied by the joint deliberation of the three orders voting by head in all cases, could not fail to make preponderate, necessarily bringing about the destruction (anéantissement) of royalty." "These reflections," he cautions, "should convince the Tiers of this province to maintain the instructions of their deputies within proper boundaries (justes bornes)."[74] A firm sense of order is visible.

The 1789 Chamber of Nobles included 154 military officers: 11 lieutenant-generals, 74 major-generals, 4 brigadiers, 43 colonels, and 22 of subaltern rank. Of these, more than fifty shared liberal ideas. At Versailles Custine was not among the forty-seven liberal nobles who, on 25 June 1789, united with the Tiers; like Lafayette he had briefly to await the mandate of his constituency. But from 10 July on he was taking an active part in the affairs of the newborn National Assembly. Like so many proponents of national renovation, Custine composed and published his own Declaration of Rights of the French Citizen, where he changed some of the views of his "plan." That document, in thirty-seven articles, is considerably longer and less pithy than the Assembly's own famous declaration; it goes far beyond "rights" and might permissibly be called the sketch for a bourgeois constitution.[75] Indeed, Custine warned his colleagues against too much prefatory philosophical material that could lead only to arid disputes of interpretation. At this moment he still envisaged an unproblematic monarchy in France and rejected the notion of the dissolution of estates within a more egalitarian legislative body. In the first article of his Déclaration," Custine wrote: "A political society can have no other object than the greatest good of all." His subsequent presentation links the usufructory concern for strong government with the consensualist motto of legitimacy (for example, article XXVII: "All public powers emanate from the Nation; their sole object is the Nation's interest").

Custine's *Déclaration* deals with four major areas: the rights of individuals; the form of the state; the conduct of officials; and the formal administration of the law. As opposed to the "Plan à consulter," there is a move toward a society of capacity and talent, although some of this is ambiguous. While there is greater liberal latitude, there is a certain regress of specificity. Strict legal equality and personal security are emphasized. Venality and corruption are attacked. Relief for the poor, although not in the positive form of the "right to work," is stressed. The status of the monarch is, interestingly, not included; Custine would later regret this omission from the Assembly's Declaration. Reflecting perhaps his distaste for "metaphysics," the document mostly shuns the language of natural rights, asserting the priority of society or nation. Custine's views in his *Déclaration* are, on the whole, consistent with his later positions in the Constituent Assembly. Accused of playing the maverick, he once replied pompously: "I have made it my principle to join no faction, no more that of the Jacobin Club than that of the monarchists. . . . My opinions are those of a French citizen whose free soul can never be put in chains."[76] Custine voted for the Declaration of Rights of Man and the Citizen on 26 August 1789. But he expressed certain regrets that his own "enchaînement des principes" had not been followed. A special disappointment was that religious freedom had not been more forcefully inscribed in the Declaration, for, as he put it, it was crucial for "the rights of man in the state . . . of organized society" and would have made the "agents of public power responsible for abuses of their authority."[77]

Between 4 August 1789 and 9 January 1790, Custine issued five lengthy *comptes rendus* to report his views and actions to his constitutents.[78] With regard to the abolition of feudal privilege, he partook of the enthusiasm of the night of 4–5 August. The Grande Peur had just licked at Lorraine. Custine regarded the suppression of *féodalité* as a measure of noble generosity and national strength: "I was struck by the degree of preponderance that the adoption of this measure could give to France, if, without convulsion and by the exclusive will of the nobility, it destroyed the hydra of feudalism."[79] He imagined a contagious effect in neighboring states and increased prosperity for France: others would be encouraged to "strike down the monster" and France, in its "solitude of calm," would reap the commercial benefits.[80] Later, as a military commander, he would enforce these "spontaneous" imitations on foreign soil.

Custine was concerned about the privileges of the church. Though a Freemason and a proponent of complete toleration, he came from a traditionally religious province. He opposed the relinquishment of the *dîme* as a general capitation tax: "I cannot ever believe that a just nation would ratify [the abolition], for [such an act] goes beyond the mandated powers of the electoral assemblies."[81] Later he argued with conviction that this measure would disorganize the relief of the poor, which the church, after due deductions of salaries, the building of places of worship, and the maintenance and propagation of the faith, had traditionally provided.[82] Though Custine wanted a reorganization of the administration and finance of the Catholic clergy, he regarded the church as a historically specific intermediary body of society; thus he could not accept Talleyrand's flippant sacrifice of its privileges and vocation. "All goes to show," he wrote, "that the clergy cannot give its possessions to the nation; it cannot even alienate a portion of them." If Catholicism did not succor the paupers of France, who could be expected to do the job?[83] Custine foresaw that the rich would profit from the dispossession. Later, the Jacobins would use Custine's position on the *dime* to tar him as an unregenerate reactionary.

Like most of the Constituents, Custine decried the censorship of opinion (covered in articles IV and V of his draft of the Declaration). His bravado, however, went even further: "My contempt for libels and for their authors convinced me to oppose their suppression with all my strength, in the belief that, however well they are written, they are only effective if plausible."[84] But two years later, after experiencing the radicalization of the "patriot press," he would come to deplore the writings of "those overheated and turbulent idlers . . . who would like to lead [the French people] into a revolution that is really a subversion bent on destroying everything."[85] He became the victim of such libels as commander of the Army of the North in 1793.

In his first *compte rendu* Custine acknowledged that the provinces (incoherently administered as *pays d'état* or *pays d'élection*) should be equalized in privilege. However, as a Lorrainer, he argued that certain frontier areas, potentially exposed to the shock of war, the garrisoning of troops, and maneuvers, should receive special indemnification.[86] When the issue of abolishing the provinces in favor of eighty approximately equal departments came up, Custine was hesitantly favorable. But he was not an admirer of Sieyesian geometry, and he granted that the measure, when first proposed, "had encountered among a great number [of deputies] that feeling of resistance so natural to those whose every prejudice one had the desire to destroy instantly."[87] He promised his constituents earnest and critical attention.

Custine imagined himself a gifted economic theorist; numerous pages of his reports are given over to the subject. Deeply influenced by the Physiocrats, he described agriculture as "the true source of riches."[88] But, like Barnave,[89] he also had a lively appreciation of manufactures and colonial commerce. "Not only," he wrote, "should the government encourage and protect all branches of commerce, but especially those directly involved with its colonies, which are the sources of its wealth."[90] Like most liberals, Custine believed in the free trade of grain, which he desired to implement unexceptionally within France and, as for foreign sales, leave to the discretion of the administration.[91] His particular nemesis was the Finance Minister Jacques Necker; he disapproved of the Genevan's prodigious loans and pragmatic recourses.[92] Custine was indignant that "the nation must prostrate itself before its idol and await his oracles in silence."[93]

Custine had no romantic feelings for the House of Bourbon; indeed he was contemptuous of the extravagances of the royal household and the impact of court manners on military discipline. Yet, convinced of France's natural vocation for monarchy, he saw the king as the necessary counterweight to an oppressive aristocracy which might one day capture the National Assembly.[94] Thus he favored the monarch's constitutional inviolability, his right to veto legislation for six years, and—beyond the coverage of the comptes rendus—his right to declare war and make peace.[95] Because France is "a society organized as a monarchy," Custine even proposed to incorporate the king's inviolability into the Declaration of Rights itself.[96] The executive should also have the power of martial law "in order to protect the liberty and property of the citizens, to disperse gatherings and seditious crowds, and to prevent the seduction [of the ignorant] by persons of evil intention."[97] Custine's wish for a strong state and his fear of anarchy thread their way through his correspondence and public writings. In counterpart, he felt that "it is indispensable for a National Assembly, meeting yearly, to impose a holy terror on the agents of [the executive] power, whoever they are, if they are tempted to abuse it."[98]

As might be expected, Custine also interested himself in military matters. On 1 October 1789 he opposed a motion by Baron de Wimpffen for the formation of a legislative military committee on the grounds that it usurped too much power from both the executive and the Assembly as a whole.[99] Later on, he called for a permanent and ready peacetime army of one hundred fifty thousand men, composed of recruits and, only in case of necessity, of militias.[100] He was then generally opposed to national conscription, which would be implemented (largely from National Guard sources) in 1791 by the Narbonne War Ministry.[101]

Custine showed a perverse originality regarding voting qualifications and elections. He reversed the supposition that service in the National Assembly should require greater wealth (and taxability) than service in the electoral assemblies. The latter rate was not, in his judgment, high enough: he wanted to raise it to a *demi-marc d'argent*.[102] This elite, however, should be able to send to the national legislature anyone whom they pleased on the basis of his "qualities, talents, and virtues."[103] Moreover, the privileged atmosphere of the Assembly should disappear. On 18 September 1789 Custine was coauthor of a letter (associated with Volney's proposal) favoring the election of a new Constituent by a common franchise, a measure that did not carry.[104]

The émigré issue had not become significant during the period of the comptes rendus, but it may usefully be included here. Custine, like other 1789ers, had been repelled by the royal power in the Old Regime to hinder arbitrarily the free movement of individuals. In 1791 he was consistent in opposing interference with the emigrations from France or the reentry of previous emigrants, and he published a short memoir justifying his position. Custine believed that emigration and foreign travel could be dealt with by a covering law that would simply double the taxation on both the land and movable property of those persons remaining abroad or leaving France after the promulgation of the legislation.[105] Otherwise, there should be "no wounding of the sacred rights of individual liberty" or interference with "the faculty that should motivate every citizen, especially every merchant, to leave the kingdom in pursuit of his interests."[106] This argument might be thought disingenuous: Custine's son had married the daughter of an émigrée, who repeatedly urged the young couple to join her in Berlin.[107] Yet his views were perfectly justified by the arch-liberal principle of the "freedom of locomotion" so dear to the Duc d'Orléans.

Custine, as we have seen, was inspired chiefly by the conventional ideology of 1789. But we discern four distinct special inflections. Three of these have been mentioned: the defense of the *dîme*, the defense of émigré rights, and an intermittent support of the powers of the royal executive. In addition, Custine had a rather more conservative view of the constitutional project and process. He wished to uproot the Old Regime while still managing to preserve a good deal of continuity in the social order. In this respect he agreed with most of the Constituents. However, in contrast with Sieyès and some of the lawyers, whose tendency was to reason and write in the abstract, he saw dangers in going off the metaphysical edge. The separate and preambulatory nature of the Declaration of the Rights of Man and the Citizen implied that it was intended for socialized man unaccompanied by any fixed regime or institutions. Custine, however, accepted the apriority of the French monarchical regime, wishing the institutions of freedom to be shaped to that reality. Although the future course of events would cause him to change his mind, his was more of a realist's position than that of many of his colleagues. As early as 1789, Custine wanted the Constitution more supple than it was later to become. "Experience," he wrote, "[often has] effects contrary to those foreseen by reasoning, and their natural cause is in the habit patterns (*caractère moral*) of men for whom constitutions and laws instituting them are made."[108] The forms and purposes of a political society were not eternal. This belief may have made Custine somewhat more pragmatic in accepting the Republic of 1792, although his own ambitions obviously counted for the most.

Custine grew disturbed by the plebeian turn that the Revolution appeared to be taking after October 1789. Yet he felt no temptation to join the military emigration, which accelerated with the final abolition of nobility on 19 June 1790. Changes in army organization, especially the law of 25 February 1791, stimulated emigration and resignation. The radical press began to insist on wholesale purges of the remaining officer corps; in June, the *Révolutions de Paris* proclaimed: "Citizens . . . make your demand heard for the cashiering of officers; if this is refused, raise a cry so terrible that it will reverberate in the soul of the traitors and freeze them with panic."[109] On 28 May previous, Custine, anxious for activity, had requested to be employed in Alsace, "having always been where there is action, and in the most military provinces."[110]

Hastily, on 15 June 1791, the Assembly passed a law requiring all army officers to swear an oath "to the nation, to the law, and to the king," denying the traditional supremacy of the commander-in-chief. Five days later Louis XVI fled to Varennes and was returned to Paris a prisoner. In these circumstances, according to Baudot, "the first to speak of a Republic was General Custine after the departure of the King. He said at the tribune: 'All I can see is the Republic.' But he was hooted from the right side of the Constituent Assembly."[111] Two days later, Condorcet, Thomas Paine, and Achille Duchâtelet began some real republican agitation. It is remarkable that Custine's voice should have been heard first, given what we know of his politics.

The archives furnish Custine's own clarification of the matter in the form of a draft address.[112] The reasoning is not that of Condorcet:

> The day the King left Paris it was I who proposed at the tribune
> of the National Assembly the concentration of executive power in
> the hand of the ministers in proximity to that assembly, I who urged
> a decree that no order would bind any citizen unless countersigned

by them. I did not then wish to see a king, abused by trouble-makers (*factieux*), against the wishes of his own heart, place a part of the citizens of this land (*empire*) in combat against the other, nor let a faction usurp an illegal authority; what I did then, *I would do again*.

By the time this explanation was composed, the royal restoration and acceptance of the Constitution of 1791 were accomplished facts. Custine was clearly disposed to march with the Feuillants. Earlier in the document he comments critically on the first acts of the Legislative Assembly and its tendency to encourage "quelques folliculaires" who seem to aspire "to a republican government, which cannot suit a great nation, and still less the French nation. . . ." Custine continues: "For the good administration of a great country one needs a unique center, a supreme chief, whose [mode of] existence preserves him from the bribery, intrigue, and shocks that elections to places of supreme executive power will always entail. . . ." Washington had overcome this defect by becoming a de facto American monarch; the supreme executive head should be, in Custine's words, "un colosse majestueux." When Louis XVI fell on 10 August 1792, Custine was leading troops in Alsace, far from Paris, but no doubt he had lost faith in the colossal proportions of his monarch.

After Varennes the Assembly required a new oath of its officers. Custine "refused to believe that a single one of his brother officers could, in these circumstances, evade his duties as a citizen"[113]—another untimely prediction. On 21 June the Assembly decreed an oath as follows: "I swear to use the weapons placed in my hands for the defense of the country and to maintain, against all its internal and external enemies, the Constitution as decreed by the National Assembly, to die rather than permit the invasion of French territory by foreign troops, and to obey only those orders given as a result of decrees of the National Assembly." Patriot officer-deputies of the Assembly were dispatched to the border and garrison departments to exhort and receive the allegiance of the units. Custine was among them: his mission was to secure the oaths of officers in the departments of the Haut-Rhin, the Bas-Rhin, and the Vosges. There his rhetoric helped obtain a good result: 822 officers swore the oath, 213 were absent for legitimate reasons, 52 were absent without permission, and 56 refused the oath and were stripped of their commissions.[114] In other areas about one-sixth (fifteen hundred) of all active officers replied negatively.[115] The military needed both replenishment and a new standard of loyalty. From 12 June 1791, steps had been taken to create a bicephalous army composed of volunteers (often from the National Guard) and traditional line units. The volunteers, more highly paid and empowered to elect their officers, represented the first great infusion of bourgeois values into an impeccable citadel of aristocracy.[116] Here were the first stirrings of a citizen army. Custine felt a certain discomfort about the transitional solution. In a pamphlet dated 26 August 1791 he wrote that "discipline will be restored when the troops are led by truly patriotic chiefs; they will deserve the confidence of the soldier."[117] He opposed the Chabroud report of 28 August on the reform of military discipline, holding that it made the officers inadequately responsible for the conduct of their troops.[118] He predicted, rashly but justly, of public opinion that "it will forgive misguided soldiers, but the chiefs, from the general of the army on down to the non-coms, will never be able to escape death."[119] Custine's last bow in the Assembly in September was to propose the following decree: "The king will be authorized and invited with the shortest delay possible to raise the line army to a full war footing."[120]

On 6 October 1791 he was promoted to lieutenant-general. He was eager for the fray, especially against Austria; he was convinced that the English, "knowing the price of liberty," would remain uninvolved.[121] "O King of the French," he apostrophized, "you have given liberty to America; you have agreed that the French shall have it. Do not reverse your steps; enter upon your career and dare to pursue it. . . ."[122] He would now pursue politics by other means on the eastern frontier.

7. Revolutionary War in the East

In late 1791 France prepared hesitantly for war. Conflicting ambitions brought a solution by arms closer as the year turned: royalists who hoped for coup d'état, patriots who dreamed of the expansion of liberty.[1] Despite propagandistic impulses, all parties hoped that in some sense the conflict would remain limited. Both the radicals and the ultras agreed on Austria as the preferred target of hostility, although the famous Declaration of Pillnitz of 27 August 1791 had already suggested the outlines of coalition and had further served to inflame public opinion against all the dynasties. The isolation of France was not a new theme; it had preoccupied Montmorin, the Minister of Foreign Affairs, at the beginning of 1789: "Holland has escaped us. Denmark is in Russia's pocket. Sweden no longer deserves our confidence; besides, she could be of only limited ability on the main continent. Prussia has joined forces with England and become our enemy. The empire is only a puzzle of unrelated pieces (*un composé sans rapports*); besides, its principal members are allied to Prussia. . . ."[2] But this gloomy view was thrust aside by the "Brissotins," who accepted the opinions and blandishments of radical refugees from abroad with little discernment. As Isnard proclaimed: "The French people will issue a great summons and all the other peoples will reply to its voice."[3]

The aristocracy wavered: by the end of the Revolution almost nine-tenths of the military nobility would pass to the Coalition.[4] This was not an instantaneous, but a steady drainage, especially from a once-swollen reservoir of general officers. Biron, assuming command of the Army of the Rhine in the late summer of 1792, wrote to his minister: "I haven't any lieutenant-generals; M. de Custine and myself are almost the only ones."[5] Still, in the words of Carré, "the Revolution retained under arms enough capacity (*éléments vivaces*) to assemble a military force that could withstand an attack from abroad."[6]

The War Ministry of Louis de Narbonne attempted not only to staunch the wounds of attrition but to create, reluctantly, a new model of military service. Paths of reform had already been more radically traced, as early as 1789, by Dubois-Crancé, who declared, "I establish as an axiom that in a free country every citizen should be a soldier and every soldier a citizen"; and by Servan, a bourgeois officer and future War Minister, in his scathing polemic *La Seconde aux grands*.[7] Narbonne created new volunteer units in parallel with the professionals, and allowed senior noncommissioned officers to fill vacancies in the officer corps.[8] These changes were accepted unenthusiastically by the conditionally loyal royalists. As early as 8 June 1791, Robespierre was asking for the destitution of all noble officers, well in advance of Marat's more concentrated campaign.[9]

Most of the fighting forces were regrouped in three armies stretching from Flanders to Switzerland. The northernmost one was given to the aging commander of the American expedition, Rochambeau, promoted to marshal, who had offered lukewarm assent to the Constitution of 1791. Lafayette had the central, and smallest, army: his politics were constitutionalist and sour on the court, but also fiercely anti-Jacobin. The southern command went to Luckner (also promoted to marshal), a rough-and-ready Bavarian mercenary who had served French kings for forty years and was widely believed to be the country's most able soldier: Luckner's political views could be swayed by Lafayette. None of their destinies was brilliant: Rochambeau resigned on 18 May 1792; Lafayette's coup d'état of 28 June 1792 failed, and he later surrendered himself to the Austrians; Luckner, implicated in Lafayette's maneuvers, was guillotined. French officers were riven by mixed feelings. Even among those who had not resigned in June and July 1791, many accepted the Constitution as a ruse so as better to serve the monarch. In Paris a small but vocal radical element cast constant doubt on the loyalty of the nobles, raising the prospect of a Fayettist version of Caesarism so repetitively that Brissot, in order to sustain his pro-war thesis, wrote that even if a few officers proved treasonable, "we will be rid of them . . . we will purify the army . . . we will regenerate the civic spirit of their units if it has faltered."[10] The career of one vociferous patriot, Dumouriez, was at this same time in swift ascent: he used his political skill to obtain promotion to the Girondin ministry as head of Foreign Affairs, and finally succeeded to Lafayette's command.

On 20 April 1792 Louis XVI proposed to the Legislative Assembly a declaration of war against the "King of Bohemia and Hungary" (a subtle formula intending, though without result, to limit the Hapsburg mobilization). Prussia and the client states of Austria came into the war. France, divided and ill prepared, faced a formidable challenge. It was a challenge which the Feuillant diplomacy of Delessart and Narbonne had already attempted to blunt. At the end of December 1791 they had secretly dispatched François de Custine to sound out Ferdinand, Duke of Brunswick, on becoming generalissimo of the combined French armies, thereby guaranteeing the experienced leadership that France lacked, as well as driving a wedge between Austria and the Germanies. Brunswick was to be the new version of Maurice de Saxe.

Custine *fils* arrived at Brunswick on 13 January 1792 and gingerly pursued his overtures with the duke, whom he found Voltairean and cultivated, anticlerical but profoundly contemptuous of the "vile multitude."[11] In his letter to Delessart of 21 January, Custine reports Brunswick's answer: ". . . I see too many problems to conquer. I know enough about your country's troubles to sense how difficult it is there to keep up one's credit and reputation. You have too many *gens d'esprit*. . . . Public opinion is too nimble. . . ."[12] While leaving young Custine with the impression that "he has not said yes; but he has not said no," this was in effect the last word of the warrior who might never have delivered his "manifesto" and might have been on the opposite side at Valmy. After the refusal it was, ironically, Dumouriez (Delessart's successor and one of the victors at Valmy) who wrote to François de Custine on 13 March: "We can only hope that M. le duc de Brunswick will become field marshal of the Empire. His wisdom, his prudence, his love of peace and order guarantee us that he will not be led astray by vainglorious desires. . . ."[13] Meanwhile French diplomacy conducted at Berlin by Ségur had also failed; on 7 February 1792, Prussia and Austria signed their alliance.

Custine *père* was probably not long a stranger to these events. By royal order of 19 February 1792, he was posted to the fifth and sixth divisions of the southern army under Luckner.[14] Finally, on 23 April, Luckner gave him a command at Belfort and the mission of leading a detachment through the Gap of Porrentruy to intercept some Austrians in a local engagement. Under extenuating circumstances, Custine arrived three days late.[15] Luckner exploded: "I have reason to be most astonished, Monsieur, by your inexactitude in executing the orders I had so clearly and positively conveyed to you. . . ."[16] Again, on 6 May, Luckner rebuked Custine for perverting his orders.[17] The imbroglio became so severe that, in the kind of gesture he would repeat so often, Custine wrote to the Minister of War on 19 May, with a copy to Luckner, requesting to be judged by a court-martial. The old Bavarian replied sardonically: "I cannot doubt, Monsieur, that if you have a few objections to make . . . the Minister will act with all speed to render you the justice that is your due."[18]

By now Luckner had been sent to replace Rochambeau in the north. Victor de Broglie, his chief of staff, pleaded with the quarrelsome subordinates to cooperate: "It is only by establishing concert among the generals commanding each of its parts that [the army] can act in concert toward a single goal."[19] The eighty-five-year-old General La Morlière replaced Luckner: he favored Custine on 7 June with command of the Fifth Division. Biron was the other divisional commander. Finally, on 20 July, the octogenarian, completely in thrall to his subordinates, retired. Biron was made the chief of the Army of the Rhine, with Alexandre de Beauharnais as chief of staff. Only a few weeks later Dumouriez replaced the fugitive Lafayette, and Kellermann received an army of his own.

These developments made Custine furious. Was he not senior to these generals, and more meritorious? He treated Biron's directives with contempt, prompting another warning from Luckner.[20] Custine was not merely negligent about orders; he bombarded the War Ministry with his distemper, accusing Biron of cowardice and expostulating that "Washington and Rochambeau judged . . . that Biron should take orders from me, and now you have just proposed the opposite!"[21] He wrote Servan again on 24 August to protest the nomination of Dumouriez, and on 2 September he attacked Biron, Dumouriez, and Kellermann all together.[22] Then he made Biron his confidant: "What madness can we expect from Dumouriez? Brave, I suppose, but incapable of drawing up or following a plan; he is no more accustomed to handling troops than Kellermann. And Kellermann! A man of that incompetence! What plan could he squeeze from his brain? I can already see him back in Burgundy if the enemies march against him."[23] As the occasion demanded, Custine could write polite letters to Dumouriez, Biron, Beauharnais, or Beurnonville (never Kellermann); but they were constantly belied by the venom he spouted behind their backs.

On 10 August the French monarchy fell and a National Convention was summoned. Four days later Lafayette's countercoup in the north failed. In parallel with royalist disturbances in the interior, France's unsure armies retreated before the forces of Brunswick. The major penetration was made through Luxembourg: on 23 August the Prussians took the fortress of Longwy, and, on 2 September, as the primary assemblies were meeting to select a Convention, Verdun fell. With the path to Paris seemingly open, panic reigned in the capital. The bloody September Massacres, abetted by Marat's savage rhetoric, began. This was the moment Custine had chosen for firing off his defamatory broadsides. To be sure, the southern front was relatively quiet. But the destinies of the new, de-Bourbonized France lay athwart the road from Verdun to Paris; a victory was desperately needed, perhaps a miracle.

On 30 August, Custine had proposed to Biron "to cover Paris by threatening the hereditary states of the House of Austria."[24] His division

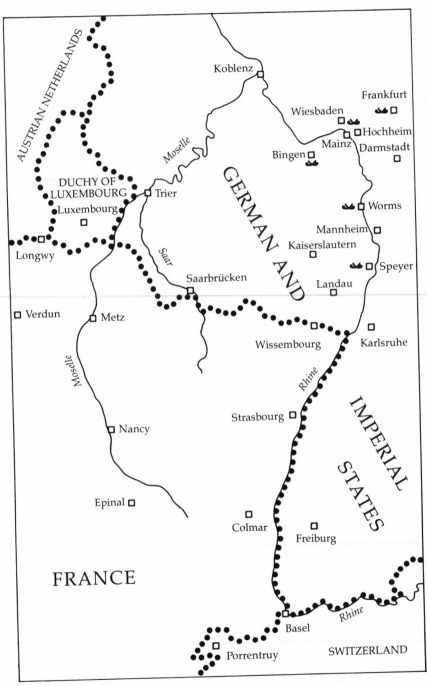

Front of the Armies of the Rhine and the Moselle, 1792–93.

was based on Landau, north of Strasbourg; the penetration he envisaged was along a south-north axis parallel to the Rhine, menacing Brunswick's stores and staging areas in the Palatinate and prince-bishoprics. Biron, an extremely cautious commander, continually advised Custine to take no unnecessary risks and "to keep his forces always within reach of the nearest supply depot."[25] Custine prudently mended his fences after the fall of the monarchy: on 17 August the Municipal Council of Landau had written to Servan, the War Minister, praising "our loyal General Custine, who is the terror of the enemies of liberty."[26] The former monarchist was little moved by the commotions in Paris; all he required was victory against the hated Austrians. "He knew," according to Gay de Vernon, "that, for the French, success at the beginning counts for much, because at the beginning of any operation our soldiers will put forth their best efforts."[27] On 16 September Servan granted his request to march on Speyer; three days later he was made commander of the Army of the Vosges, but on the express condition that he remain Biron's subordinate.[28]

On 29 September, nine days after the Convention assembled and Kellermann and Dumouriez threw Brunswick into retreat at Valmy, Speyer surrendered to Custine. It appears to have been a handsome feat of arms, "a brilliant success," according to Chuquet, and in Gay de Vernon's words, "in the moments when [Custine] needed to display the personal bravery of a soldier, he went to it in praiseworthy fashion."[29] He was able to follow up his victory and seize Worms on 6 October. Here he halted momentarily, for he needed a chance to requisition stores, levy harsh indemnities—eight hundred thousand livres in Worms alone—and provide for an occupation politics.[30] Custine carried out these tasks with republican relentlessness, replacing the aristocratic authorities and broadcasting sonorous decrees. "The war we are waging today," he told Worms on 7 October, ". . . so different from earlier ones, is directed against all who have made bad use of their powers (*ont prévariqué dans l'usage des pouvoirs confiés*), and not against the peoples. . . . War on the palaces . . . peace for the peaceful cottages and for the friends of justice."[31] When French looting broke out in Speyer, Custine quelled the disorder with summary executions, a "discipline of blood and iron."[32] Paris was ecstatic at the victories; Custine celebrated by firing off a barrage of self-laudatory dispatches to the Ministry and the National Convention. It was said that even in the midst of demanding military operations he could dictate to three secretaries at a time and still pay heed to the business at hand.[33] He banked the publicity value of his successes.

Expressly against Biron's orders and after a brilliant and exacting forced march, Custine deployed his army before the prince-bishopric of

Mainz on 20 October and summoned its garrison to surrender. He made his triumphal entry into the city two days later, having achieved not so much a feat of arms as of daring. The riches of Mainz were at the disposal of the French, who had reached the Rhine intact. Mainz was also the crucial pivot for an enduring triumph. Custine had only to wheel his forces downstream about forty kilometers to fall on a scantily protected Koblenz, thereby cutting off Brunswick's Prussians, now desultorily pursued by Kellermann, from important stores of food, equipment, and munitions. Brunswick would have been severely harried, perhaps decimated in minor engagements, and forced back behind the Rhine to regroup. Dumouriez, following his important victory at Jemappes on 6 November, which had permitted the temporary occupation of Belgium, could then have advanced on Cologne and Düsseldorf. Republican France would have fulfilled ancient ambitions of obtaining natural frontiers and could have demanded peace and foreign recognition from a position of strength. Instead, Custine launched his troops across the Rhine to gain the rich prize of Frankfurt on 23 October. He "wanted not only to tax Germany, raise immense contributions and gather abundant provisions. . . . He wanted to deal a mortal blow to Austria."[34] Indeed, his campaign had captured immense amounts of ammunition and "sown terror in the Empire."[35] Custine insisted that Kellermann mop up Trier and Koblenz.

No doubt Custine's decision was a costly error. However, there are extenuations. Though engorged with spoils, his army was fatigued and overextended, and diminished by garrison duties. Kellermann's was not: it had moved at a slow crawl, without further engagement, to follow up Brunswick's retreat. Moreover, as Custine himself argued, Kellermann's advance units were closer to Koblenz than his own, by a whisker. Finally, although Custine might have begun the semblance of an enveloping movement, he would have greatly lengthened and exposed his flank to Austrian forces that had been repulsed but not, as yet, badly mauled. In any case, Custine was not the hierarchical culprit. An official directive of the War Ministry ordered Kellermann to "hasten to attack Trier and Koblenz; the people await you, your success will cost you little; it is indispensable that you back up Custine and leave no rest to the enemies who might reunite to crush him."[36] "Kellermann's obstinacy," Chuquet writes, "was the equal of his vanity."[37] He balked, demanded a marshal's baton for his victory at Valmy, and embarked on secret negotiations with the Prussians that furnished them a breathing space. In brief, he was disobedient. However, his panache and his famous cry of "Vive la Nation!" at Valmy have powerfully secured the reputation of this commoner who was finally made a noble of the Empire.

Custine exploded in anger. An incredible tangle of correspondence of some 108 items composed by Custine, Kellermann, Biron, Dumouriez, Beurnonville, the War Minister Pache, and other writers was compiled in the period 2 October through 9 November.[38] It breathes the toxic quarrelsome spirit of the French officer corps. Especially notable is a sizzling letter from Custine to the President of the Convention calumniating Kellermann and demanding that he be cashiered and tried for treason.[39] It concludes most dangerously: "even past services cannot justify the avoidance of a just punishment; if I were so fortunate as to raise the glory of my country to the point I desire . . . an instant of forgetfulness should carry my head to the scaffold." Kellermann rejoined that "Custine could only have fathered this irrational composition in a fit of insanity, or more likely a moment of drunkenness."[40] "General Moustache" did have a fondness for the bottle; one of his detractors later wrote that "sometimes even immoderately, he savored a liqueur that he had always adored."[41] However, Chuquet asserts that drink never in any way affected his reason.[42] The other generals were scandalized by Custine's extravagant ranting. But the main point is that a golden opportunity to turn the war around was lost: on 27 October the Hessians managed to fortify Koblenz, followed by the retreating Prussians.

Neither general was disciplined by the weak French executive. Kellermann passed shortly into mediocre roles; by 9 November Custine, whose reputation for victory excused his temperamental follies, replaced Biron as chief of the Army of the Rhine. Biron, more ardent in the boudoir than on the field of battle and becoming world-weary, sought to resign. Though Custine attempted to keep him,[43] he could not resist a parting shot of malice: "You came here to command me; I had always commanded you up to then; now I recover my rightful place (*je reprends mon rôle*)."[44] Biron was posted to the Var and later to the cruel war in the Vendée, before his own appointment with the guillotine. Custine requested Félix Wimpffen to replace him, but was instead given Desprez-Crassier, whose demotion the terrible chief would be demanding within five months.[45]

French victories from Belgium to Savoy in the autumn of 1792 thinly veiled chronic weaknesses. Capacities were overextended, supplies were niggardly, and communications were strained and garbled. Between December 1791 (Narbonne) and April 1793 (Bouchotte) France had seven different War Ministers, all ambitious or incompetent, or both, all frustrated by the complaints and vendettas of the generals. The aristocratic habits of the military chiefs clashed with the republican politics of the Convention and the rags-and-tatters government of 10 August.

Royalist sentiment threatened the nation from within, especially in the
Vendée, Normandy, the Midi, and the Lyonnais. Moreover, the ruling
republicans were falling into lethal factionalism as the ex-king awaited
his fate. It was almost as if authority itself were suspended. Most of the
remaining noble generals could expect no benefit from desertion. What
they wanted, usually vying with one another, was to halt the plebeian
drift of the Revolution, gain an indispensable influence over war and
diplomacy, and obtain glory. In their hearts they of course favored the
moderates, who were more accommodating to ancient ways and were a
barrier against unruly populism. But they despised most of the civilians,
not least the ministers.

Custine trumpeted republican policies in the conquered lands. On
23 October he proclaimed at Mainz: "May [this city] become the boule-
vard of liberty of all the peoples of the German Empire. May the
principles of eternal truth burst from its breast; may their witness strike
all men who are bowed beneath the yoke of servitude!"[46] In Frankfurt,
through his subordinate General Neuwinger, he demanded an obligatory
contribution of a million florins "according to the principles of justice."[47]
The Jacobinism and "clubism" of the Rhineland went only skin deep;
but, as Custine well knew, this propaganda fortified his reputation in a
radicalized Paris. Still he had overreached: spoliation did not provide the
best rear-guard security. When his campaign turned sour, his many
enemies would charge him with voluptuous living and the theft of many
precious objects in Frankfurt and Mainz.[48] Gay de Vernon attests, however, that all seizures from the princely residences were scrupulously
inventoried and turned over to members of the Convention on mission
in January 1793.[49] As for voluptuousness, Custine, "without priding
myself on being as chaste as Joseph," later denied the charge of an
infamous liaison.[50] What is undoubtedly true is that this conqueror
conducted himself with aristocratic airs while purporting to spread the
republican and Jacobin gospel of fraternity in the cities of Mainz and
Frankfurt.

There was soon a bloody reckoning. Custine's original military strength
of about forty-five thousand officers and men had suffered considerable
attrition and dispersion. After the regrouping of the Prussians, his blitz-
krieg sputtered to a halt; from mid-November he was thrown on the
defensive, and skill and luck seemed to desert him. On 2 December,
aided by a civil insurrection, the Prussians overran a detachment of about
twenty-five hundred men left at Frankfurt under General Van Helden. A
carnage of nearly one thousand French troops followed. Custine cravenly
covered this disaster by accusing Van Helden of incompetence, the Frank-

furt authorities of treachery, and the Prussians of barbarism.[51] As yet he held his positions on the right bank of the Rhine, mistaking the capacities of the Prussians for winter war. He incessantly demanded resupply from Pache, the War Minister. He also had a "plan" for the preservation of the French position in the Rhineland, which Pache accepted.[52] General Beurnonville (then styled as "Ajax" and esteemed by Biron and Dumouriez), with his Army of the Moselle, was to clear the path toward Trier where Kellermann had earlier failed, thereby correcting the French front. But in the month of December Ajax achieved no gains.[53] Beurnonville, admittedly ill supplied, took it out on Custine, praising his own skill in extracting himself from a "monstrous mistake in military principles."[54] Custine, of course, passed the blame back. The failure had jeopardized his forward position at Mainz. But, already, constant pressure by the Prussians had caused Custine to declare Mainz in a state of siege on 14 December, accompanied by rosy promises to the population. Custine would henceforth make the preservation of Mainz his leading obsession. As late as 28 April 1793, with his own remaining forces back at Landau and Wissembourg, whence they had begun the campaign, he could still declare: "I believe I am able to predict that Mainz will be the tomb of the Prussian armies."[55]

Custine and Beurnonville had not yet lost the confidence of the civilian authorities or kindled a high degree of radical suspicion. In that month all attention was riveted on the trial of the deposed Louis XVI. Few were aware that Dumouriez had mixed mysteriously in these proceedings. New Year's Day 1793 saw the first dispatch of political commissioners, "representatives of the people," from the Convention to the armies, though not yet endowed with their later dictatorial powers. Custine treated these emissaries—Reubell, Haussmann and Merlin de Thionville —with feigned deference; but when he wished to gratify them with a feat of arms, his best field commander Houchard was thrown back from Hochheim with loss of artillery. The "expedition of Custine" was effectively over.[56] Custine used bold republican language to the ministers on 14 January.[57] But the news of the king's death, received on 26 January, left him "aghast." Deploring both the vindictiveness and the impracticality of the execution, he believed that if Louis XVI had remained a hostage, France's enemies would have been better prepared to negotiate a reasonable peace.[58] In the Army of the Rhine there was mixed emotion: desolation among the regulars, jubilation among the volunteers.

From 18 October 1792 to 4 February 1793 the Minister of War was Jean-Nicolas Pache, a minor *commis* initially indebted to the moderates for his advancement but prescient enough to move speedily leftward.

Pache stocked his offices with Cordeliers, savage democrats, no doubt, but incompetent clerks, including the notorious François-Nicolas Vincent. Everyone virtuously practiced the familiar form of address, and disorganization reached its peak; "ineptitude" and "treachery" were Madame Roland's words of rebuke.[59] At first Custine cultivated a correct relationship with Pache, hoping to dominate him. But by January when Beurnonville's castigation was smarting, Custine showed his teeth: "How have I behaved to you? . . . You had no knowledge of details; you admitted as much. . . ."[60] Dumouriez now stepped into the situation: having decided to risk all for a political objective, he would sweep back from an advanced position in Holland and place either the child Louis XVII or the Duc de Chartres on the throne.[61] On 1 February the French Republic declared war on Holland and England. Dumouriez's plan evidently required the displacement of Pache; but the appointment of Beurnonville on 4 February could surely not have been to Custine's liking. On 8 February Lebrun wrote an apologetic letter to Custine on the subject.[62] Was Beurnonville then in Dumouriez's pocket? It would not seem so from the documentation we have. On 10 February, Dumouriez wrote to the War Minister (presumably Beurnonville) demanding further supplies and criticizing Custine's position at Mainz, which "paralyzes the movements of the other armies, leaving the Moselle, the Saar, and the Bas-Rhin unprotected. . . ."[63] Three days before, Custine (no doubt ignorant of the change of ministers) had written that he considered Mainz as "being in many respects the most important of our conquests."[64] Custine was having a bad time: he was now forced to warn the citizens of Mainz that indefensible buildings and outworks would be destroyed and that no inhabitants could remain after 1 April unless provided with seven months' stores.[65] Then he announced a forthcoming trip to Paris and complained against the scheming of those "who would make us abandon our conquests." It is appropriate here to record that Pache obtained revenge: on 14 February the Parisians elected him mayor, together with a full slate of other radicals.

For the following days the documentation is confusing. On 14 February Dumouriez heard from the War Ministry that although Custine's position was too advanced, "he should nevertheless remain at Mainz. . . ."[66] Yet on 16 February Beurnonville testified to the Convention that he disapproved of all of Custine's operations, especially Mainz.[67] To add more mystery, we have two further documents dated 19 February. One is to Dumouriez, "[announcing] that Custine will hold his position to keep the Prussians in check."[68] The other is to Custine (apparently in answer to his letter of 9 February), acknowledging his impending trip to Paris: "I look forward to it with impatience so that we can concert our plan of operations. . . ."[69] This reference may be to the long sketch entitled "Réflexions sur le plan de campagne des armées de la République française, tant sur le continent qu'au delà de la mer," found in the same liasse, a fine example of Custine as putative generalissimo. Beurnonville also commented with respect to Pache: "The disorder that I found in all parts of the War administration singularly multiplies [our] obstacles and difficulties. . . ."[70] Unfriendly as they were, Custine and Beurnonville could easily have made common cause over the deradicalization of the War Office. François de Custine, sent as an advance man for his father's trip, counseled: "[Beurnonville] has had it in for you till now, but he is rather courageously, if a little clumsily, attacking the abuses and Jacobinism of his offices."[71] On 23 February François hoped that Custine would "be able to establish good relations with the Minister. . . . In showing him your esteem, your willingness to back him up, and the importance . . . of a loyal forgetfulness of past quarrels, you must . . . bring him around to views that he ought always to have held."[72] Custine's popularity remained untarnished in Paris, where he arrived on 26 February. "Received with enthusiasm," he delivered a long exposé of his military thinking to the Convention and conferred with the Executive Council.[73] But he would not relinquish the leading role to the War Minister. For on 1 April he was writing to the President of the Convention: "Beurnonville may have military talents, but I declare that he is far from having the virtues of a republican. . . . I do not judge him; France and posterity will make the point."[74]

France's two most powerful generals, Dumouriez and Custine, both had plans of total political and military scope, working everywhere at cross-purposes, squandering troops in indefensible salients, north and south. Dumouriez was strongly convinced that Custine's thrust to Frankfurt had been instrumental in keeping Prussia in the war; he deplored his colleague's want of diplomacy and military sense.[75] But by now Dumouriez had decided on a solution which, in the words of Louis-Philippe, "would be neither the triumph of the émigrés and the Counterrevolution nor that of the perpetrators of revolutionary excess. . . ."[76] Custine was not bent on treason, if by that we mean the restoration of a monarch. But he, too, was entangled, in fact and fantasy, in the tortuous diplomatic game of splitting the coalition. Given his altitudinous self-esteem, we can surmise that he coveted the combined jobs of War Minister and generalissimo: he would not dismiss the Convention, merely bend it to his wishes. Prussia would be offered a reasonable peace and Austria a crippling setback. His "Plan pour la campagne de 1793" reiterates this:

"Without [destroying the House of Austria], the sovereigns of the coalition will surround us with intrigues and destroy us through internal agitation."[77] Custine had a phantom image of Prussian susceptibilities. In the Kellermann documentation of late 1792 there is the long draft of a memorandum suggesting a negotiation with the King of Prussia, to be conducted by François with Custine's personal supervision. "As for the Prussian army and Prussia," he wrote, "the philosophical spirit of the late king has prepared that of the whole nation, and no army is as likely to become revolutionary as the Prussian army. Our relations, even indirect, will increase this tendency, and I pledge to make the revolution break out coincidentally with the annihilation of the strength and power of all the other states. . . ."[78] The sovereign, the court, and the army of Prussia were to consent dreamily to revolution, and an honorable peace was to be secured in Europe by the diplomatic genius of the Custines: a figment of ancient memories of Berlin.

However, as early as December 1792 Custine was empowered by the Foreign Minister Lebrun to pursue conversations about an armistice. Military manners were still those of the Old Regime: "Any pretext for a meeting was valid, especially the exchange of prisoners of war."[79] Thus Custine had intermittent communications with the enemy commanders Brunswick and Würmser. A letter of special interest from Lebrun to Custine on the same day as Dumouriez's desertion and the formation of the first (Dantonist) Committee of Public Safety counsels the general to take advantage of conversations with the enemy to develop the subject of an eventual peace.[80] Modern historians with pro-Jacobin leanings have regarded these peace feelers as treasonable, indeed as justification for Custine's execution.[81] This is incredible. Custine might have acted foolishly; but he did so according to the orders of his government, whose policy, like that of its predecessors, was to split the coalition and seek a negotiated peace. The only guidelines constraining Custine were that no French territory could be surrendered and that the Republic must be recognized. However, April's actions would make him a traitor in the eyes of France's July masters.

A new order of politics was coming into being. The world of the ci-devants had been accepted by the moderates as a world of military skill and valor, laced with quaint and overbearing etiquette; soon it would give way to an austere patriotism that regarded all commerce with the enemy as part of a treasonable plot, placing the noble, the priest, and the foreigner in the same sack of villainy. All military power would be suspect unless held within a vise-like patriotic grip. "For it is in wartime," Robespierre declared, "that the habit of passive obedience and the

all too natural enthusiasm for victorious chiefs makes the soldiers of the
patrie into the soldiers of the monarch or of his generals. In times of
trouble and faction, the heads of armies become the arbiters of the
destiny of their country and tilt the balance in favor of the party they
have embraced. If they are Caesars or Cromwells, they themselves usurp
authority."[82] Dictatorship lurked in this collision between purity and
professionalism. In June 1793, when Jacobinism had all but triumphed,
Beauharnais wrote to Custine: "The deliberations of the Jacobins and the
Paris Commune seem to presage that some day you and I and all the ex-
nobles will be stripped of our high commands. If this unjust measure
only takes the top posts away from us I won't complain, but I confess
that nothing will console me if I lose the right and duty of defending the
liberty of my country at the peril of my life."[83] Custine and Beauharnais lost not only top posts, but their heads. They went down in true
aristocratic fashion, squabbling like little puppies over war plans and
jurisdictions.

On 23 March, a week after being crushed by the Imperial army at
Neerwinden, Dumouriez opened secret negotiations with Cobourg. On
29 March the government decided to remove him: Beurnonville and four
members of the Convention were sent to Belgium to bring him back
under guard. Dumouriez arrested these emissaries and handed them over
to the Austrians. On 5 April he sought refuge behind Austrian lines,
leaving his troops in disarray. He was not the first French army commander to pass to the enemy: Bouillé, Lafayette, and Montesquiou-
Fésenzac had also done this. But, in patriot eyes, Dumouriez's
was the ultimate case of *perfidie* and *scélératesse*. Only a month before, in
the Convention, Robespierre had given Dumouriez his confidence. But,
he had warned, "however powerful a general might be, his crime would
not go unpunished."[84] On the same day as Dumouriez's desertion, Marat
thundered against the "traitorous generals." He demanded the arrest of
Dumouriez and added: "[This fate] is also reserved for Beurnonville and
Custine if they are taken. . . . Thus my sad predictions are completely
verified by event. How could we have placed at the head of our soldiers
of liberty infamous aristocrats (*privilégiés*), old slaves of the Court?"[85]
Hatred against the ci-devant generals quickly spread through the clubs
and cafés of Paris, as police reports witness: "General Custine is beginning to appear suspect to public opinion. Some say he is in the coalition
of traitors. Others maintain that he is falsely accused."[86] Custine was
doomed, from 5 April on, to pay the price for both Lafayette and
Dumouriez. As we have seen, Dumouriez also dug Philippe-Egalité's
grave.

The fortunes of the Army of the Rhine were unenviable. So much of it was within Mainz that Custine was unable to prevent the Prussian forces from circling the place after crossing the Rhine slightly downstream at Bingen. Bingen's surrender in March, with considerable loss of equipment, invited comparison with Neerwinden. Now Custine fell back on Worms, from which, on 30 March, he sent a characteristic letter to the President of the Convention, blaming the setback at Bingen on the clumsy tactics of his subordinate Neuwinger.[87] When he abandoned Worms, it was good riddance: a contemporary engraving with the German title. "The pig-headed Jacobins are themselves forced to uproot the Tree of Liberty" is explicit.[88] By 4 April the Army of the Rhine was back in Landau: Mainz, some ninety kilometers distant, remained its only conquest.

Custine's constant practice in adversity was to accuse others for his failures and to offer his resignation: in the imbroglio with Luckner, in the troubles of February, and now again—an act to be repeated in May and in early July. From Landau, probably already aware of Dumouriez's strange maneuverings but not of his flight, he reverted to this strategy, no doubt anticipating vindication. Two swift replies came from Lebrun, the second of them acknowledging "the cowardly desertion of the traitor Dumouriez." The Council excused Custine's reverses; it "witnessed with grief" and refused his resignation, affirming "the nation's confidence" and applauding his "patriotism and military talents."[89] Custine needed little more ammunition. Yet a day or two later he had the disconcerting experience of seeing his high-minded aide-de-camp Lieutenant-Colonel Coquebert brandish a pistol in front of him while accusing him of treasonable communications with the enemy. Custine disarmed the officer, informing the President of the Convention that the incident had been "the result of an exalted imagination."[90]

His ego never flagged in victory or defeat until his days were numbered. He also wrote to the Convention: "Never fear, my fellow citizens, that any ambitious plan enters my thoughts: my soul rebels as much against the idea of exercising absolute power as that of enduring it." Yet the letter is a dialogue between innocence and Caesarism; for it approves "one dictatorship . . . inspired by high character and firm soul, guided only by virtue . . . a great person [who] should have no enemies but the ambitious . . . and the loathsome agitators."[91] There can be little doubt whose great soul the general had in mind. He then rattled off a dispatch to the newly formed Committee of Public Safety, announcing the arrival of his son with a new plan, "the only one that can save the republic," and demanding more artillery, more cavalry, and direct command over the Army of the Moselle "without delay."[92]

This is precisely when Marat was stepping up his denunciations: "A hundred to one that Custine will bring back to our borders only some tiny debris of his large army, already shorn of its cavalry. . . . I say there is no doubt that he is a traitor, a convinced counter-revolutionary. . . ."[93] On 1 April Robespierre had indicted the ci-devants at the Jacobin Club; its sessions of 8, 12, 15, and 17 April were spent in part in denunciations of Custine. Custine fought back in his accustomed style: "I regret that my character and steadfastness will always make me a multitude of enemies . . . all the enemies of order will conspire to destroy me. . . . I summon [you] today to the examination of my political principles and those of my whole life. . . ."[94]

Thus far Custine had successfully fenced with ministers and fended off the attacks of "agitators." But a decisive new weight was now added to the scale: Jean-Baptiste-Noël Bouchotte. Born on Christmas Day 1754, in the same city of Metz from which Custine had sprung, Bouchotte was a child of much humbler circumstances, the son of a military paymaster. A thorough patriot, in the tradition of Dubois-Crancé and Servan, he had risen to the rank of lieutenant-colonel. Proposed twice for Minister of War by the radical elements of the Convention, in October 1792 and February 1793, he finally obtained this post on 5 April 1793 in replacement of Beurnonville. In exposing his military program to the Convention on 10 April, Bouchotte declared: "The people will wage war, and will wage it well: my duty is to use all my means to insure this success."[95] France was verging toward a people's war. Political hatreds and the ambiguity between patriotism and professionalism still affected the army's reliability. Yet, as the Jacobin Dubois-Crancé had asserted in his report of February 1793: "Take a glance at our battalions [of volunteers] and you will see that all those who had some sense of the military art were chosen officers. . . ."[96] This raw material of the Grande Armée was the promise of the future; in the immediate present, following Dumouriez's departure and Custine's retreat, prospects looked sorry. As in August-September 1792, the *poussée populaire* was demanding a high price for failure and duplicity. On 10 March 1793, bending to this pressure, the Convention had established the Tribunal Criminel Extraordinaire, which was to become the chief instrument of the official Terror. "Soyons terribles," exhorted Danton, "pour éviter au peuple de l'être."[97] That was the atmosphere in which the Convention called upon Bouchotte to reanimate the war effort.

Bouchotte was not a bungler. Like Lazard Carnot, he, too, was intent on "organizing victory." But could one rely on the ci-devants to collaborate in this pure republican enterprise? Bouchotte's entire vision and experience predisposed him to think not. Already Marat and others were demanding that they be sacked and punished, pell-mell. But the upheaval in the officer corps could not happen at once: it had to be prepared by organized reporting of delicts, piecemeal measures, and a favorable political evolution. For even in April 1793 neither a majority of the Convention nor most of the officers and troops would have countenanced the dismissal of generals like Custine. Yet possibly by design, surely by fate, Custine would become the lightning rod for this bolt of democracy that Bouchotte and his Jacobin and sans-culotte friends were about to hurl.

A first measure was to use the power of the War Office to radicalize its personnel. Bouchotte seized the opportunity to restore the principles of Pache. He increased the number of his employees to 1880 (there had been 143 in 1787). They came from diverse, usually inappropriate, occupations, and were chosen for their "patriotism." Many were Cordeliers. Their professional performance was colored by their political fanaticism; army commanders and representatives of the Convention on mission alike bitterly attacked the functioning of their services in the coming months. Moreover, Bouchotte reappointed François-Nicolas Vincent, who had been dismissed by Beurnonville, and raised him to the position of secretary-general. Vincent, born in 1767 in Paris, the son of a prison concierge, was an ardent and violent clubist. He had played a leading part in the assault on the Tuileries on 10 August 1792. His installation made the Cordeliers the masters of the war effort. Vincent tyrannized the army and even threatened the Convention as it pleased him. He would finally be guillotined with the Hébertists on 24 March 1794 (4 Germinal, an II). While active under Bouchotte, Vincent sat at the center of an operation of spies and agents who regularly reported libelous and damaging information against targeted military commanders; he composed the dossiers that would be used for the cashiering and trials of the generals.[98]

Custine, whose brain was occupied with glamorous vistas of power, little suspected the destiny for which events in Paris were preparing him. Though stung by Marat's charges, he could not believe that his position was in jeopardy. Given France's perilous condition of defense, would he not be more indispensable to the nation than ever before? His appointment by the Executive Council, on 6 April 1793, to command the Army of the Moselle as well as that of the Rhine seemed to confirm this estimate. On 22 April he wrote lengthily to the President of the Convention, describing himself as "the constant enemy of disorder, of anarchy, and of all the *scélérats* who promote it." And he concluded: "Let the accusers know that there would be no happier moment for me than when I would be forced to prove to my fellow citizens all I have done to prevent our setbacks."[99] However, after complimenting Custine's services, the Committee of Public Safety cautioned him to rein in his wounded vanity: ". . . a newborn republic surrounded by enemies is naturally prone to anxiety and the liveliest agitation. . . . General, you are mistaken in fretting over accusations, in anticipating them, in involving the Assembly in them. We have but one object to fulfill, the fight against our enemies."[100] The cringing tone of Lebrun is no longer perceptible.

Marat stung many sensibilities with his arbitrary, though sometimes keen, thrashings. In one of its flagging victories, the Gironde attempted to stifle him by obtaining his accusation before the Convention. It was a Pyrrhic victory as well as an ominous precedent to send a Representative of the People before the Revolutionary Tribunal.[101] Predictably, and to the rejoicing of the Paris crowds, the Tribunal unanimously exonerated Marat on 24 April, and he was carried back to the Convention on the shoulders of the people. Heretofore somewhat of a pariah even among the regulars of the Montagne, Marat was suddenly invested with a halo of heroism. Already sick, perhaps unto death, he now took ever bolder leaps with his pen. Collaborating with Vincent's agents and seconded by the radical scribblers of the republic, he would conquer Custine with calumny, even from the grave.

8. Revolutionary Vengeance
in the North

After Dumouriez's desertion his tattered army was assigned to General Dampierre, a mediocre commander, suspect to the patriots besides.[1] However, Dampierre earned himself patriotic credentials by getting killed in a losing battle. As Gay de Vernon comments mordantly: "this glorious passing certainly saved him from the scaffold, where two of his successors [Custine and Houchard] would appear in their turn."[2] Bouchotte and several members of the Committee of Public Safety proposed that Dampierre should be replaced by General Kilmaine, a divisional commander who was an Irish mercenary without political ties. The appointment seemed confirmed on the evening of 9 May, but opinions were sufficiently divided for the Executive to canvass the local representatives on mission, Cochon, Debellegarde, Dubois-Dubais, and Briez. They did not feel that Kilmaine, whose advancement had been extremely rapid, had the talent to command an army. "Moreover," they wrote, "the Army of the North asks for Custine, and the wish of a republican army should be seriously weighed."[3]

Thus on 13 May the National Convention, advised by the Committee of Public Safety, directed the Executive Council to name Custine commander-in-chief of the Army of the North and the Ardennes.[4] From the commissioners of the Ardennes came a tone of suspicion. On the one hand, "Custine will restore discipline and make his military talent useful to no one but the Republic." On the other, "we shall avoid the danger of leaving a man at the head of the same army all too long, as [we have] done up to now with Lafayette, Dumouriez, and all our generals."[5] When the news of the nomination reached headquarters at Wissembourg on 15 May, the representatives of the people of the Army of the Rhine voiced support: "Judging by your letter that Custine is indispensable to you with the Army of the North . . . we have insisted that he take the command. . . . We are most sorry to see this general leave; we have great confidence in his military talent; we consider him the best general that France presently possesses."[6] It may be argued that the political dissensions of the Convention were reflected in the reports of its representatives on mission. Yet it appears, despite Marat's campaign of April, that Custine enjoyed the confidence of his army.

He received the order with mixed feelings. His position seemed secure and he had his unfinished business at Mainz. It would be no easy task to repair Dumouriez's damage. On the other hand, the Army of the North might prove a glittering challenge for his ambitions. Unfortunately, he resolved to have the best of both worlds: his parting shot was a massive and ill-prepared attack from Alsace on 17 May in which his forces, though superior in numbers, were mauled by the enemy. Liberally blaming everybody but himself for the defeat, he especially impugned his subordinate General Ferrière, who made a spirited defense of his conduct.[7] Custine left Alsace on 23 May, arriving on 27 May in Cambrai pursued by accusations.[8] Bouchette requested that the allegations, arriving from the front and also germinating in Paris, be examined by the Committee of Public Safety, which seems to have taken no action for a month.[9] Custine blamed his tardy departure for the North on "the torture of a colic which for days and nights allowed me no sleep."[10]

Custine's troubles were much magnified by indiscreet communications with the Duke of Brunswick, which had been ferreted out by the diehard Jacobin commissioners Soubrany, Ruamps, and Maribon-Montaut. For, in the course of his authorized secret diplomacy, in a letter of 5 May he had praised Brunswick for "his wisdom, his philosophy, and his love for the peoples he governs" and called him "the supporter of the oppressed and the pacifier of the world." He had even had kind words for the King of Prussia.[11] This was scarcely the language expected of a republican general who had earlier pronounced "guerre aux palais, paix aux chaumières." Custine defended his gaffe with belligerent self-justification. He cited his experience and knowledge of courts. His "[republican] principles . . . long and deeply reflected on did not produce the exaggeration of despising all kings just because they had the misfortune to be born on the throne."[12] That version of "mature republicanism" pursued him to his trial.[13]

Custine found the Army of the North in frightful disorder. Writing to Houchard on 30 May, he could only express "horror for the conduct of the atrocious Dumouriez."[14] Line battalions were reduced to three hundred soldiers; volunteer battalions to four hundred. Basic weapons were lacking.[15] He immediately investigated the loyalism of the officers and troops, and launched a "scrupulous examination" of their finances, equipment, and logistics.[16] On 4 June he lamented his situation to the Committee of Public Safety. His army was threadbare: if he attempted to attack with it, this would bring disaster; if he remained inactive, he would be accused of treason. He proposed to make a tour of inspection, then travel to Paris to expose a detailed military plan. If his views were not accepted, he would resign.[17] In point of fact, Custine had already

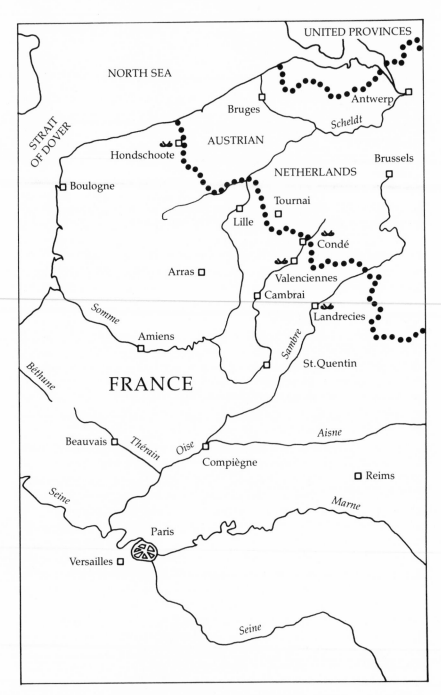

Front of the Armies of the North and the Ardennes, 1793.

conceived a plan in Alsace: it was quickly withdrawn when he saw the consequences of Dampierre's defeat.[18] He imposed his famous iron discipline: marauders, deserters, malingerers, and their accomplices would be summarily shot.[19] If that did not appeal to the government, they could relieve him.[20] He warned General O'Moran, one of his divisional commanders: "The debauchery and pillage inflicted by your troops should be repressed by the most terrible exemplary measures."[21]

Custine was in a murky situation: "je vais à tâtons," he wrote to General Tourville.[22] To the authorities he declared: "Everything here is so incoherent and unstitched that I cannot describe it and you cannot imagine it."[23] To Bouchotte he counseled "patience and the reorganization of the army."[24] But in a separate dispatch of the same day his rancor got the better of him: he chastised the minister for "ignorance and ineptitude" and threatened that "the time is no more when generals look upon a minister, especially an imbecile, like a god."[25] These reckless and insubordinate insults multiplied. A week later, Custine would be complaining to the Committee of Public Safety that "a minister in the pay of Koblenz [that is, the émigrés] could not be a better servant of the coalition of the kings."[26] In the meantime, he kept up an imperious barrage of requests for troops, weapons, clothing, and ammunition, and squabbled over the right to appoint and place his own officers: he especially wanted generals Leveneur and Stengel (the latter having just been acquitted by the Revolutionary Tribunal in connection with the defeat at Neerwinden).[27] Bouchotte kept a daybook of correspondence and activities; virtually every paragraph begins: "Custine demande. . . ."[28] Yet Custine's was now the critical front.

Custine did excel especially in drill and discipline. Immediately on arrival the new commander passed his army in review. "When he appeared," according to the Conventionals on mission, "the intoxication was general; he harangued the troops in the name of the Republic and said . . . memorable things to them."[29] Despite his Draconian measures, the soldiers responded positively; he began to test them in minor skirmishes with the Austrians. Gay de Vernon writes that no one else could have restored the situation so well.[30] Dubois-Dubais, a representative, concurred: "he has imposed the rule of order and the discipline that were lacking."[31] Even on 12 August, with Custine about to stand trial, his subordinate General Chérin felt moved to write from his prison in Amiens: ". . . the troops were drilled constantly; defeatism was blotted from the soldier's soul; his confidence in his leader and his will to fight were harbingers of success."[32] According to Custine, "the job is so difficult that I fear it goes beyond my strength."[33] Yet he succeeded.

When Fouquier-Tinville charged in his act of accusation at Custine's trial that the indiscipline and disorganization of the army were "a vain pretext," he flew in the face of all reasonable evidence.[34] June 1793 was, in fact, Custine's finest hour.

No matter. He had inherited a train of accusation that was creeping toward him like a slow-burning fuse. Not only was there Mainz to account for; in his new sector of operations, the fortresses of Condé and Valenciennes had been encircled in the week before his arrival. They were not well fortified or provisioned, were infested with enemy agents and spies, and were challenged by greatly superior forces; their almost predestined fall would expose the French to a coalition drive to the Channel, cutting off Flanders. Arriving in Cambrai in late May, Custine quickly decided that he would need massive reinforcements from the Rhine and Moselle armies to save the fortresses and blunt the threat. Mainz, he believed, could survive until August. As we shall see, his plan was eventually rejected. He unjustly acquired the blame for the fate of the northern frontier outposts.

In June 1793 the fragile French Republic faced not only a conventional military crisis and the inauguration of an English naval blockade, but internal anarchy and civil war. On 2 June, in the wake of a plebeian *journée* orchestrated by the Paris Commune, the Convention was purged by the arrest of twenty-seven Girondin deputies and two ministers, Lebrun and Clavière. Much of provincial France had thrown off central control. The sans-culottes saw the enemy everywhere, taking every delay and reverse to be undebatable acts of treason. Twenty-two days after the purge, the political theorists of the Montagne (notably Hérault de Séchelles and Saint-Just) presented the republican constitution of 1793, democratic and libertarian in its provisions. The nation and the army received their fundamental law with relief and enthusiasm, partly because it was now thought that a new assembly could be elected.[35] But this constitution would never take effect. Ironically, it is at the head of Saint-Just's draft of the document that he placed his famous aphorism: "On ne peut pas régner innocemment."[36]

Amid these commotions Custine strove to shore up the defense of the North. It is imputed that he was friendly with the fallen faction of the Gironde.[37] Hébert of course charged him with all these sins: "royalisme . . . rolandisme . . . brissotisme . . . buzotisme . . . fédéralisme."[38] If Custine certainly curried favor and influence with the government that the coup of 2 June swept away, it does not seem objectively true that he "paid with his head for his connections with the Girondins."[39] He rebuffed overtures from these fugitives in early July. His unpardonable sin was, rather, to rebuke the most powerful Montagnards in the wake of the Paris disturbances: "from the writings of Marat and the opinions of Robespierre, I looked upon the former as an agitator and the latter as an exaggerator."[40] And of course there was the constant stream of insult hurled against Bouchotte's "stupidity."[41] "General Moustache" did not have to practice complicity; his effrontery sufficed.

Custine's enemies prepared to trap him in the North. Three young agents of the War Ministry, Celliez, Varin, and Defresne, were planted in Cambrai and Lille for surveillance and propaganda. Their voluminous and repetitive dispatches against the aristocratic generals, as well as similar accusations posted from the Rhine by Garnerin and Gâteau, swelled the dossiers and were available to the radical journalists. On 5 June Celliez and Varin notified Bouchotte: "the soldiers . . . are in the best of shape [sic]; we cannot say as much for their commanders, but . . . the whole army knows which are the bad chiefs."[42] Marat was tied in with the attack. On 11 June, in a ferocious libel titled "Custine, tome second de Dumourier [sic]," he quoted Gâteau, the agent of Wissembourg, as writing: "in a short time Custine will be dictator of France in order to deliver her [to the enemy]; for he has already sold out."[43] What we witness is a well-plotted effort, originating in the War Ministry, to yoke Custine to all previous treasons and make him the symbol of a hated military aristocracy, seeking to abase it through the destruction of its most visible member. Custine's insubordination and ambition could only speed his downfall. The problem was how to snare him without causing panic in his army, where he still held the confidence of most of his officers and troops.

Bouchotte had both personal and political reasons for launching this operation. But Bouchotte was not having an easy time of it, for military inadequacies rebounded on him as well. In mid-June temporary pressures against Bouchotte's administration became so severe that the Convention authorized his replacement by Beauharnais, then commander-in-chief of the Army of the Rhine. That former noble had the tact not to put his head in the noose, and by 21 June Bouchotte was back on the job. Parisian politics now evolved slowly toward a consummated Jacobin dictatorship.

A sweeping campaign against all the ci-devants began. Hébert thundered: "It is not only Custine that we must discharge and banish; it is all the nobles in our armies, in the law courts, everywhere. The people must demand it!"[44] By July he was joined by a chorus of savage voices. The archival vision of the sans-culotte mentality is awesome. General Herlaut, a modern pro-Jacobin historian, writes that Celliez, Varin, and Garnerin "distinguished themselves by their revolutionary ardor, their zeal, and their intelligence."[45] This is true, except that their intelligence was that of the most narrow bigotry and poverty of invention, as judged by their missives to Bouchotte, Vincent, and others. Yet their cacophony was effective: during the Revolution some fifty-four army generals (almost all ci-devants) passed beneath the blade of the law.[46]

A few citations will suggest this volume and flavor. Custine is "entirely devoted to the cause of aristocracy and more treasonable even than Dumouriez;"[47] incessantly his "treason" is compared with that of Dumouriez and Lafayette; he has a "usurped reputation," is given to "excesses of debauchery," is a "*scélérat*," "meditates the ruin of the fatherland," and so forth.[48] Most of his generals are equally iniquitous. Of La Palière, "one sees nothing in his conduct but that of a *scélérat intriguant* [*sic*]"; Tourville "professes an implacable hatred for the patriots"; "Sabrevois is guilty of counter-revolutionary maneuvers"; Leveneur, "hated by his soldiers and despairing of leading them astray," has been appointed by Custine, "who knows his talents and character"; Dardennes is "a man who offends all good republicans"; Chérin is "an *intrigant* with no other merit than aristocracy"; Sparr "loves the Constitution of Condorcet"; Desbrulys (Custine's chief-of-staff) is "known for his aristocracy."[49] Constantly, lists of unreliable and counterrevolutionary officers are compiled; a composite of them includes: La Marlière, Leveneur, La Palière, Chérin, Champmorin, Vernon, Dardennes, Levasseur, Sta, Dangest, Sabrevois, Dufresnoy, Leblanc, Despouchez, Martin, Kermavan, Gobert, Jarri, Brancas, Dedouville, Stéphan, Van Mirthe, Bozancourt, Tourville, O'Moran, La Marche, Richardot, Amiot, Desbrulys, Saint-Martin, Margaron, Saint-Germain, Dru, Antoine, Halot, Sparr.[50] After Custine's cashiering in late July new lists and tales of intrigue continued to be dispatched: "to cut the evil at its root . . . the principal agents of all these counterrevolutionary plots should be sacked on the spot."[51]

The epithets *intrigant, scélérat, aristocrate*, and *traître* plied the shuttle from Cambrai to Paris. On 11 June Marat threatened to expose Custine's treasonable acts seriatim.[52] Hébert pilloried "the most idiotic and demented advocate of royalty."[53] But it was the more polite Jean-Charles Laveaux, editor of the new *Journal de la Montagne*, who swung the cudgels with greatest force. In a crescendo extending from 5 June to Custine's execution in late August, Laveaux devoted columns in no less than thirty-five of his numbers to attacks on the chief of the Army of the North, sometimes in the form of correspondence mailed to him, sometimes as signed editorials. His main theme: that Custine was a "scandal for the patriots."[54] He quoted Gâteau at the Jacobins on 5 July as accusing the general of "a number of horrible acts, the least of which deserves death."[55] Bouchotte had these papers sent to the armies to rivet the ardor and patriotism of the troops, especially to keep the Army of the North from becoming "custinisée." The first packet of *Père Duchesne* and the *Journal de la Montagne* arrived on 11 June; Celliez and Varin received it and distributed the copies, reporting "the joy of the soldiers." They repeated this message on 17 June; receiving another shipment three days later, they pleaded for further copies.[56] The reaction of the soldiers was probably mixed. But the Minister of Foreign Affairs felt compelled to write to Bouchotte: "I seriously wonder if such a tactic does not lead to the disorganization of that army. How will he be obeyed . . . if one covers his person with contempt at the very time when he is trying to restore the discipline that is so desired and so wanting? . . ."[57]

In Custine's absence his staff, probably at the instigation of Desbrulys, had Celliez and his secretary Compère thrown into jail, from where, on 2 July, Celliez addressed his colleague Varin with an obvious halo of glory: "I am surely guilty for I am in prison. . . . For me this adventure is one more title of patriotism."[58] To Bouchotte he wrote: "As you see, the patriots here groan beneath the weight of tyranny."[59] According to Herlaut, this event was regarded by the sans-culottes of Paris as "a declaration of war by Custine against the Revolution."[60] Marat demanded Custine's dismissal on 5 July; Hébert demanded his arrest, and threw in Biron for good measure.[61] Celliez, released on 6 July, went back to his business. On 13 July Marat's pen was stopped by Charlotte Corday. Hébert immediately accused Custine of "satisfaction . . . in seeing Marat immolated, massacred. . . ."[62] Marat's murder would now become part of Custine's guilt. Jacques Roux, Marat's self-appointed successor, clamored: "His head should fall beneath the blade of the law." A week later, with Custine now sequestered in Paris, Roux expostulated: "O shame! O madness of the eighteenth century! Who could believe that the French, who have shaken off the yoke of prejudice, would have entrusted the command of the armies to nobles?"[63] No one asked Roux if the press should be entrusted to ci-devant priests.

While the campaign of libels was swirling, an important jurisdictional matter fanned the flames. This contretemps was already set up when Custine arrived in the North. On 8 March 1793 the Executive Council had given command of the fortified city of Lille to General Favart, a bourgeois engineer officer. By inadvertence or design, Dampierre, before his death on 11 April, had named General Antoine-Nicolas Collier, ci-devant Comte de La Marlière, to the same post. Controversy broke out between the two generals.[64] The radical commissioners of the War Office insisted on the authority of Favart, a "pure patriot," as against the treacherous aristocrat. Custine wrote to Bouchotte ill-temperedly on 6 June, explaining his preference for La Marlière and lecturing the minister on his ignorance.[65] Favart complained a day later. On 10 June a Captain Calandini denounced La Marlière for conversations with enemy emissaries and for improper security precautions. Custine reiterated his backing of La Marlière on 11 June.[66] Bouchotte complained on 14 June to the Committee of Public Safety that Custine owed him "a more complete obedience";[67] with the support of the Executive Council he demanded submission two days later from the refractory general.[68] But here, it will be recalled, Bouchotte suffered a four-day eclipse of authority. On 17 June the Council hammered out a compromise: Favart would keep Lille, but La Marlière would have an independent field command, with the right to withdraw all but four thousand troops from the garrison.[69]

An aggressive political general Lavalette, who was in the habit of addressing his letters "Cher Sans-culotte,"[70] denounced La Malière on 20 June, and reported a conversation in Custine's circle where the replacement of Bouchotte by Beauharnais had been endorsed (it was of course unlikely; Custine probably wanted the War Ministry for himself).[71] By 25 June the fateful issue of the cannons had been raised. Custine had ordered Favart, under protest, to transfer sixty-six of his pieces from Lille for the defense of the Camp de la Madeleine; actually only forty-one were taken.[72] This was considered part of a plot to deliver Lille to the enemy, for Custine was already under fire for stripping Strasbourg of artillery and throwing it into Mainz. Lavalette repeated his accusations to Vincent on 25 June, 27 June, and 2 July.[73] La Marlière protested his "civic purity" to the Republican Society of Lille on 27 June.[74] Whatever his purity, there are no documents to show any conspiracy with Custine or with the enemy.[75] But there are repeated accusations of this by the Jacobins, echoed by the formal charge in Vincent's indefatigable trial testimony: "the atrocious project of handing over to the despots of the coalition one of the keys to the Republic."[76]

Custine continued to resist the War Office: "If Generals Favart and Lavalette cannot get along with General La Marlière, they must be sent to serve in another division."[77] The fall of Condé on 10 July aroused the worst fears of the Jacobins of Lille.[78] The generals' quarrels went on till the last week of the month. Lavalette found "no difference" between the conduct of Lafayette and of La Marlière.[79] Custine had now been ordered to Paris. On 20 July, Bouchotte confirmed Favart's command and ordered La Marlière to "account in writing for your military and political conduct in Lille."[80] Two days later La Marlière was stripped of his functions.[81] But the Conventionals attached to the Army of the North, favorable to Custine, published a proclamation the next day suspending Lavalette, arresting his secretary Defresne, and concluding that La Marlière and Lavalette would have an adversary proceeding (*débattre contradictoirement*) before the Committee of Public Safety.[82] It was not quite that. The renewed ("great") Committee of Public Safety, while embarrassed that Lavalette was a noble himself, had no difficulty in preferring his patriotism to that of La Marlière.[83] La Marlière met his death on 26 November 1793, two months after Custine. Lavalette followed them to the scaffold —on 10 Thermidor, an II.

We know of Custine's intermittent ineptitude and monstrous vanity. But we have no evidence of his treasonable intentions. Might he not have been driven to that pass? The question must remain moot. Custine's brain teemed with vast strategic plans. He chafed to move troops across the whole map of eastern France. Dumouriez no longer blocked his supremacy, but with Dumouriez gone, Custine was suspected of being "the next Caesar" by the true-blue Jacobins. On 2 June, Custine had announced to Bouchotte that he awaited the arrival of General Leveneur, "alone capable of commanding in my absence," so that he could make an inspection of the front.[84] When Leveneur did not arrive immediately, Custine submitted a plan. His armies would be massively reinforced from the Rhine and the Moselle. Effective superiority in the north would permit liberation of the besieged fortresses and attacks on Austrian supply areas. Then the forces would be speedily shifted south to relieve Mainz. The Committee of Public Safety ratified this plan on 9 June, and Custine acknowledged its acceptance "with extreme satisfaction" on 13 June.[85] However, Bouchotte protested in the Executive Council: among the unacceptable risks of the plan was undoubtedly that of placing so much military force in the hands of a suspect commander. Bouchotte gained an ally in the person of Beauharnais, his putative successor. Beauharnais, an ex-noble like Custine, was no hero of the *plebs*, but he had behaved with far more discretion. Moreover, behind polite formulas, he hated Custine, who had apparently denounced him as an *intrigant* to the Committees and the Executive.[86] After criticizing Custine's plan from a military angle, Beauharnais informed the Committee of Public Safety that he thought it unwise to "grant a single man the command or a sort of dictatorial influence over four armies [i.e. North, Ardennes, Moselle, Rhine], bestowing on him the responsibility for the defense of the frontier from Dunkirk to Lyons."[87] The political agents of the Army of the Rhine agreed. When the Jacobin commissioner Ruamps saw an order to Beauharnais to comply with Custine's memoir, he "almost choked with indignation."[88] But Beauharnais's intervention reinforced Bouchotte: on 19 June the Committee of Public Safety reversed its decision, tabling the Custine plan.

In his fury and regret Custine bombarded the Committee with letters defending his "plan which will leave little to be desired," and criticizing Beauharnais.[89] He repeatedly asked for Bouchotte's dismissal.[90] On 26 June he managed to have Leveneur named temporary commander while he set out on his inspection tour, not returning to his headquarters until 8 July. Would Custine's proposed operation have succeeded? Interestingly enough, the archives contain several letters from Carnot criticizing the plan.[91] Yet, after Custine's dismissal, the transfer of twelve thousand eastern troops allowed his successor Houchard to check the coalition at the battle of Hondschoote on 6–8 September, an engagement for which that brave but scarcely brilliant[92] commander was guillotined: though a commoner, he was considered a traitor for failing to exploit his success. It is at least clear that the denial of Custine's request doomed Valenciennes and contributed to his own extinction.

After the purge of 2 June certain "moderates" had fled to the provinces, notably Normandy and the Bordelais, hoping to raise forces for a strike against Paris. As their commander in Calvados, they had secured Custine's old friend Félix Wimpffen. Wimpffen wrote to Custine on 6 July, offering to be placed beneath his orders: "May it please heaven, brave and able general, that [this] cruel anarchy may finally be laid low by your rare talents."[93] Custine replied curtly: "I shall never abandon the majority."[94] To other petitioners from Caen he wrote: "I lament that Félix Wimpffen should soil his laurels by accepting an illegal command, but I cannot and must not imitate him."[95] To Bordeaux he suggested "peaceful means of persuasion" instead of "bayonets."[96] Simultaneously, he forwarded the rebellious correspondence to the President of the Convention with a denunciation.[97] Was he betraying his "friends" of the Gironde?

The episode is curious. Thirteen days intrude between Wimpffen's plea and Custine's posting of the packet to the Convention. By then he had been recalled to Paris under a cloud. He may have given the Girondin appeal ripe reflection, but we cannot know for certain. He had surely had a whiff of danger from all directions. On 23 June previous, he had been fuming to come to Paris to defend his plan.[98] But when on 5 July the Committee of Public Safety authorized the trip "after having taken all possible precautions that the army. . . will not suffer from [your] absence,"[99] he questioned the order, stating that he would remain at his post, and evoking vistas of death and resignation.[100]

It is not plausible that Custine's replies to the Girondins were confected in the hope of saving himself or that he was indulging in an act of betrayal. He had nothing to gain by the way in which he acted. He did not condemn the rebel correspondents self-righteously; rather he appealed to their spirit of national unity, asking them not why they wished to overthrow the National Convention but why they had not attacked the *monstres* and *scélérats* while still at their posts. And he did not fawn on the government: though deploring the "federalists," he went on to vicious recriminations against Bouchotte.[101] This was scarcely the best diplomacy to use on the eve of his confrontation with the renewed Committee of Public Safety, elected on 10 July. Custine, as a unitary French nationalist, probably had more in common with the Jacobins who proclaimed the "république une et indivisible" than he could have known. He thought them anarchists and agents of disorganization, scurrilous promoters of discord in the army and elsewhere. And of course that is very much they way they looked. For similar reasons he evidently could not abide the other sort of disintegration that the Girondins were encouraging. But this time he could not bluster his way through. He was caught in the same sack with the first Committee of Public Safety, which had been attacked by Marat on 1 July for connivance with Custine;[102] in a document by Vincent, calling the Committee of Public Safety "coupable" for not moving against Custine's "treason";[103] and by Hébert, who declared: "The more treacherous a general is, the more protectors he finds in the Committees."[104] Under extreme pressure on 10 July, the Convention installed (minus Robespierre, who replaced Gasparin on 27 July), the powerful figures of France's impending Revolutionary government.

These men had no patience with Custine. On 12 July Bouchotte urged the transmittal of Vincent's bulging dossier of accusations to the Convention, and the Committee and the Minister ordered Custine "to come immediately to Paris to confer about the situation and movements of the armies of the Rhine, the Moselle, and the North."[105] Temporary command was to go to General Kilmaine. Two days later Custine acquiesced.[106] It is not clear what he expected from the trip. His correspondence with his son in Paris was being intercepted. The latter wrote guardedly on 13 July: ". . . the presentation of your motives should be clearly, methodically, strongly, but prudently composed."[107] But once before the Committee, Custine could not contain his rage against Bouchotte and Vincent; the minister shot back that Custine had "a disturbed, jealous, and unbalanced mind" and coveted "all the authority he could get."[108]

The hostility of the new government determined Custine to take his cause before the public. When he appeared in the Butte-des-Moulins and Filles-St.-Thomas neighborhoods, where moderate and royalist sentiment had not been stifled, he was received with cheers, and on 20 July in the gardens of the Palais-Royal there were shouts of *Vive Custine!*[109] The government, which was now granting the demands of the Jacobin Club at about a day's distance, was persuaded to act. At the Jacobins the following day, Hébert, shrilly seconded by Vincent, called for Custine's head.[110] On 22 July in the Convention, Basire, claiming that Custine was distributing money to fan agitation, asked for a decree of arrest. The general was sequestered in the Luxembourg, though not yet formally charged. At the same time, the Executive Committee stripped him of his command, replacing him temporarily with General Dietmann, and voted the arrest of La Marlière. Valenciennes capitulated the next day. From prison Custine defended his "irreproachable soul" to the Committee of Public Safety and claimed he would have "no trouble in crushing these accusations to powder."[111]

Custine could still be dangerous if released. He enjoyed wide support in his command, and his rhetorical powers were not negligible. Amid the denunciations that Vincent was compiling, messages and manifestos in the general's favor were arriving. For example, on 25 July, the authorities of Arras (home of Robespierre) had written: "Instead of being placed under arrest, Custine ought to have been cited as deserving well of the fatherland for having created and organized an army in so little time."[112] Custine had obviously left no plot in his wake, only dismay. But Celliez and Defresne stepped up their frenzy of reporting, with repeated accusations against numerous officers still in place. Celliez wrote to Hébert: "Custine is not the only one to be chased from the army; there are still nobles, and we must not relax while any of them are left"; and to Bouchotte: "Seek every way . . . to strike the guilty; it is high time, or else we shall succumb to the powerful efforts of intrigue."[113] On 24 July Celliez and Varin denounced a plot by Leveneur, Dangest, Sabrevois, Bozancourt, Van Mirthe, and Despouchez to use arms against the Convention.[114] Dismissal and arrest would be the fate of thirty generals and colonels of the Army of the North in the month following Custine's incarceration; sixteen other cases remained pending.[115]

In removing Custine from his command, imprisoning him, and trying him for treason, the government had embarked on a double gamble: that his army would remain loyal to official orders and that its disorientation would not lead to a collapse of the front. Though a part of the army "experienced consternation" at Custine's treatment, there were no plans for any coordinated insurgency.[116] Several units demanded their general's release.[117] But despite a lack of confidence in Kilmaine and Dietmann, there was little disorder or desertion. Custine had reanimated the army too well for the front to collapse, and coalition strategy at this juncture was far from inspired. The north probably held because Custine had *not* been plotting with the enemy.

The last nail hammered into Custine's coffin was the surrender of Mainz on 28 July. Imprisoned successively in the Abbaye (of September Massacre fame) and then in the Conciergerie, he was not officially placed under arrest until 30 July. His ordeal of incarceration and trial was to last almost a month, a snail's pace compared to later Revolutionary justice. His papers were seized and seals were placed on his Paris apartment. On 31 July he requested access to his correspondence, adding with heroic resignation: "If they are thirsty for my blood, let it flow."[118]

In the first half of August witnesses were summoned, many from a distance, and Custine was interrogated about his papers. Finally things were in order for the trial. Coffinhal presided; Fouquier-Tinville was the public prosecutor. Custine was arraigned under Article Four, second section, first title of the penal code, which, in précis, stated that any "maneuver or communication" with enemies promoting their success against French territory or subverting the loyalty of French citizens, military or civilian, would be punishable by death.[119] Three questions of guilt were put to the jury. First, and of entirely general scope, had such crimes occurred during the present war? Second, had they caused Frankfurt, Mainz, Condé, and Valenciennes to fall to the enemy? Third, had Custine been guilty in such designs?[120] The charges were to this extent insidious: the first article of accusation could have applied to Dumouriez or any other individual; the second erroneously implied that Frankfurt and Mainz were French territories. Only the third article invoked Custine by name. But legal nicety was not the primum mobile of the operation run by Coffinhal and Fouquier-Tinville.

Fouquier-Tinville's act of accusation is a manuscript of thirteen and a half tightly written pages, charging Custine with conspiring with the enemy since the outbreak of the war, disobedience to his superiors, irregular conduct in the Kellermann affair, conspiracy to deliver Frankfurt and Mainz to the enemy, brutality of discipline, squandering his artillery where it could be captured, culpability for the dismal rout on the Lauter on 17 May 1793, treasonable interference with operations in the North, conspiracy with other noble generals, conspiracy with the Gironde, conspiracy with Dumouriez, treasonable guilt in the fall of Condé and Valenciennes, and plotting for the fall of Lille.[121] To these headings of accusation Vincent would soon add a host of others during the five hours that his testimony and the reading of his portfolio of documents consumed.[122]

In the latter half of August the comparative amenities of the court proceedings contrasted sharply with the repeated cries for vengeance from the press and the clubs. There is no reason to think that a show trial of major proportions was planned: the government's purpose was to eliminate the generals, not to scare them. But this Jacobin government was quite new, and its wheels of justice were not entirely well oiled. Two features in particular distinguished the trial from subsequent proceedings. It was public and, needless to say, well-attended and closely followed. Also, Custine was granted a liberty of self-expression that would never thereafter be repeated. Thus, although the jury was composed of hard-core Jacobins and the judicial machinery was totally at the disposal of the prosecution, the government feared the repercussions of an able and dramatic defense by Custine, a figure applauded just a short while ago.

The clubs were tense and agitated. Sometimes the orators of the evening were the witnesses of the morrow: their recriminations had furnished part of Vincent's brimming portfolio. As witness followed witness with sometimes lengthy and technical testimony, the "patriot" forces grew more and more upset. Robespierre, who had already accused Custine of "a thousand faults each punishable by a thousand deaths,"[123] now grumbled: "A tribunal established to propel the Revolution forward must not force itself into reverse by its criminally slow pace; it must be as active as crime itself."[124] On 20 August Laveaux feared a plot to save Custine.[125] François de Custine, at peril of his own life, was propagandizing for his father. There was even some apprehension that the jury was swaying. The entire session of the Jacobins on 25 August was filled with alarm at how the trial was dragging.[126] The pressure to finish with Custine was intense.

Forty-five prosecution witnesses followed the opening accusation: of these, several (including Lequinio, Léonard Bourdon, Cambon, Merlin de Thionville, and Levasseur) verged toward ignorance of the facts or neutrality; others, old enemies of Custine (notably Vincent, Laveaux, Charles of Hesse, Montaut, Celliez, Gâteau, and Garnerin), assailed him with multiple charges and insinuations. It must not be imagined that they doubted Custine's guilt: they had contributed the rope for the noose. Their particular charges and disagreeable vignettes were consolidated by

Vincent in his completed portrait of "Custine tout entier." Besides these, there were ten favorable witnesses, not the most prominent; for Custine's request to summon brother officers from the war zones had been curtly refused by Bouchotte and the Committee of Public Safety.

Custine's memory, calm, and presence were outstanding during the trial: he did not deny mistakes, but he parried his accusers well on virtually all occasions and was frequently able to demonstrate the absurdity of certain charges. For whatever it matters, the prosecution's case was not proved. A letter supposedly influential in the capitulation of Mainz was shown to be a forgery. No tangible proof was offered that Custine had acted against the nation when he took the cannons out of Strasbourg or Lille. The correspondence with Brunswick, though ill-advised, was not treacherous. Custine's "brutality" had received the sanction of the Representatives of the People. Seditious passwords (like "Condorcet"), issued to the Army of the North, had been the work of Leveneur while Custine was absent on inspection.[127] No scrap of paper showed him plotting with the Gironde, let alone the émigrés. He had committed mistakes of judgment, certainly not the pettiest, but hardly treason. As Custine responded to one witness, "If you could wage war as easily as was just said, there is no doubt that you would never lose a battle, you would win them all."[128]

Such a defense was of course irrelevant. Custine was guilty of three other cardinal sins: overbearing conduct gushing from an aristocratic ancestry; contempt for Bouchotte, Vincent, the sans-culottes, and the "agitators"; stalking too much in the shadow of Dumouriez, whom he actually despised. These congenital failings were more than enough to cost him his head: he was guilty by temperament, heredity, and analogy. Fouquier-Tinville made this clear when, in his opening accusation, he spoke of "Custine, alike in all ways to the perfidious and treacherous Dumouriez. . . ."[129] Coffinhal did likewise in his closing remarks to the jury, when he painted a composite portrait of the conduct of Lafayette, Dumouriez, and the accused.[130] In killing Custine the Republic would redress its previous mistakes and hesitations; it would kill a way of life. As Laveaux put it unambiguously: "The great, the only, the most necessary of all measures is going to be taken: there will be no more *nobles* in any positions in the Republic. . . . This is the cry of reason and good sense."[131]

Thus the trial came to its foreordained end. Custine was given the chance to summarize his defense, which he did in an hour and a half, just prior to Coffinhal's recrimination.[132] The jury retired to deliberate; a simple majority was required for conviction. At 9:00 P.M. on 27 August they returned their verdict of guilty on all three counts. There was a certain surprise, however, given the fact that the jurors were polled individually under the watchful eyes of the state. One juror disputed the first charge of treason; two the second; and three the third.[133] Two of these hardy jurors, Duplain and Roussillon, were immediately expelled from the Jacobin Club; the latter is alleged to have told Coffinhal, "There isn't enough there to whip a cat for."[134]

Custine's public defender disappeared from his side. The general said to the judge in pathetic tones: "I have no defenders; they have evaporated. My conscience makes no reproach. I die calm and innocent."[135] In a note he begged his son to salvage his reputation. Then he spent the watches of the night in meditation and prayer, alone or with his confessor, the Abbé Lothringer, who would soon minister to Philippe d'Orléans.[136] Lothringer was later apprehended and interrogated: it was charged that he had whispered with the victim in German.[137]

At about ten in the morning of 28 August Custine arrived at the place of execution, carrying a crucifix and a book of devotions. Sanson has described his last ride. "When the convoy drove out of the vault and appeared in the street, there arose, as always, a great clamor. General Custine became much paler than before; several times he repeated: 'Wasn't it they who applauded my victories?' As the shouts grew louder, he said over and over, 'that is the price of my services,' and the name of Dumouriez came to his lips without our being able to catch the surrounding sentence."[138] At the scaffold, Custine tried not to regard the instrument of death, and his eyes brimmed with tears. Then, after a last prayer, with a mixture of resignation and bewilderment, he submitted to the executioner, "not," as Sanson comments, "with the resolution that we [often] found . . . in simple citizens."[139]

Custine was never a simple citizen, but the product of a complex ancestral profession. Much as he tried to play the republican and wage revolutionary war, the mores of the regime were not his. Soon his son's life would be ended by the terrible blade; his grandson, a tiny baby, would live on through the Revolution and the Empire to become recognized as a gifted eccentric, and would write the remarkable *Russie en 1839*, the achievement that keeps the Custine name alive today. A week later, Revolutionary *journées* would encourage the Convention "to place Terror on the agenda,"[140] and the first "law of suspects" would be voted on 17 September in preparation for the bloodbath that Custine's trial, which we may describe as *of*, but not *in*, the Terror, had done so much to hasten.

Other generals would follow Custine to the scaffold—La Marlière,

Biron, Luckner, Beauharnais, even the poor commoner Houchard. A new breed would rule the army. But the relentless Jacobin fixation against the danger of military power would not be stilled; nor would the name of Custine cease to serve the patriots as a caution.[141] Even if France's generals would no longer be stigmatized as aristocrats born, they would continue to be feared as aristocrats made. As Robespierre, with his gift for crystalline expression, put it: "You do not know that your armies are permeated with treason. . . . Aristocracy is more dangerous than ever, because it is more perfidious than ever. Now it is in your midst, and, disguised beneath the mask of patriotism, it is striking blows that you do not expect."[142]

PART IV.
Jean-Sylvain Bailly
1736–1793

9. A Savant of the Old Regime

Jean-Sylvain Bailly was a bourgeois aristocrat; that is to say, he belonged to an "aristocracy of merit" which, by 1750, was invading the values of the three traditional orders, rendering them progressively fractured and incoherent.[1] He was born a commoner, committed to a certain station and style of life both by his middling, though ample, means and by his temperament. He lived a bourgeois life of ambition, frugality, and sobriety, except for a mild display of pomp that he affected during his tenure as mayor of Paris (17 July 1789–16 November 1791). Though he carried the weight of his ancestry far less truculently than a prince of the blood or a military noble, he was not a misfit creature of the Old Regime, for he obtained eminence within its rules and boundaries. He was not a convive of Versailles, Chantilly, or the Palais-Royal, nor did he draw his saber in America; but he was as typical and vital a part of the system that the Bourbons sustained as any cardinal, any noble of the sword or the robe.

Bailly was not a bourgeois of the legal profession or of commerce; his values were not especially theirs, except to the degree that all these commoners had an interest in wresting equal rights and equal respect from the privileged estates. He gained the reputation of an *homme de lettres* (if not quite a *philosophe*): unquestionably this caste mentality marked him more deeply than his bourgeois origins. For he participated freely, if prudently, in a favored milieu where advanced nobles and clergy mingled corporately with bourgeois savants in the glare of the *lumières*. What Bénichou has called the "sacre de l'écrivain" was now beginning.[2] As a writer and academician Bailly became part of a set of interlocking corporations that enhanced and reflected the crown's glory, while at the same time gradually undermining the sanctified precepts of its closed society and metaphysical supremacy. The great majority of the savants accepted, and depended on, what I have called the usufructory view of authority; they halted before the chasm of political upheaval. Busying themselves with practical reforms and the diffusion of scientific knowledge, they consigned their most subversive impulses to allusive utopian excursions or attacks on the perimeter of deferential superstition. Bailly was at most a fellow-traveler in these enterprises, content to seek, and when possible, obtain, the approval of his greater elders like Voltaire, d'Alembert, and Buffon. He was a courtier of the Academy and its elective monarchs.

One was not, of course, born to inhabit such a palace. One gained lodging in it by talent, patronage, and finesse. Unlike the many who failed and bore perpetual rancor in their hearts—the Marats, the Brissots, and the Carras of Revolutionary fame—Bailly was blessed not only with talented persistency, but with a head start. The son of Jacques and Cécile Bailly, *née* Guichon, he was born on 15 September 1736 in the very precincts of the Palais du Louvre, where his father, by a kind of quasi-hereditary appointment going back a century and a half, was curator of the royal paintings, a type of sinecure common in the Old Regime.[3] This comfortable existence of small renown permitted young Jean-Sylvain an atmosphere of security and culture in which to ponder a career. Not needing to venture himself in the world or take to the highways of France to seek his fortune, he blossomed steadily, like a hothouse plant. He could try on one talent after another until he found the vocation that fitted him.

His father introduced him to drawing and painting; his scientific bent was as yet stifled beneath hereditary apprenticeship. Young Bailly had a fling at literature, too, producing dramatic works of little merit and some unmemorable, fragile lyrics.[4] Finally he turned with ardor to the study of astronomy under the tutelage of the Abbé de La Caille, making rapid progress in astral observation and acquiring the knowledge and training that would lead him on to original discoveries as well as to the mission of popularizing a science which, in the eighteenth century, was still deeply involved with occult and superstitious beliefs.[5] Of his admired mentor, Bailly would later write: "The compensation of the wise man is to say as he is dying: I have only acted well on this earth, and no one, after my death, can bear any grudge against me."[6] Little could he have suspected that his own end would come in a rage of politics and a ravaging of reputation. As Bailly progressed to fame, his character took on a certain aloofness, which it was not difficult to connect with hours and weeks spent alone with the telescope, focusing on the radiant displacements of cold planets set at an inhuman distance. Indeed, his childhood had been marked by solitude and self-sufficiency.[7]

This future aristocrat of the intellect grew into a strikingly tall and skinny man, with "a pinched face, small, heavily lidded eyes, a regular but conspicuously long nose, and a dark complexion . . . severe . . . almost glacial . . . though with a few traces of merriment."[8] He disclosed neither a calculating nor a choleric personality.[9] Yet his taciturn presence commanded. Contemporary portraits render him something like a Swiftian Houyhnhnm, equine, grave, and serene.

Bailly's generous, mildly libertine father smoothed his path to independence; in May 1754, fourteen years before his death, he transmitted his office as *garde des tableaux* and its emoluments to his son. This undemanding post, guaranteeing an income of at least 1500 livres a year, together with the solicitude of La Caille, provided the indispensable resources for astronomical research.[10] This occupied the young man completely: he had nothing of the *mondain* about him and was destined not to marry until the ripe age of fifty-one. In 1760, well trained to conduct his own work, he set up a small observatory with telescope on the upper story of the Louvre's south gallery.[11] From here he began a series of meticulous observations of the satellites of Jupiter, first identified by Galileo in 1610, establishing their diameters and systems of rotation—a handsome feat of eighteenth-century science. His findings were recorded in three memoirs, which occupied Bailly from 1762 to 1771.[12] The exploit won him a coveted place in the Académie des Sciences in 1763. Henceforward, this solitary erudite would be in the company of the best minds of France.

He still wished to gain reputation as a writer. He was advised, for lack of anything better, to participate in the modish exercise of writing windy eulogies of the fabled dead and submitting them to competition. By the mid-eighteenth century, the eulogy had become a highly acceptable path to literary acclaim: in part a revenge of the philosophes, with their yearning for posterity, against the church, whose preoccupation with the preparation for death and the uncertainties of the beyond struck at worldly pursuits.[13] There were specialists in *éloges*: Thomas, for example, who had gained prizes in 1759 (Marshal de Saxe), in 1760 (d'Aguesseau), in 1763 (Sully), and in 1765 (Descartes). Bailly's eulogies, considered "remarkably mediocre" by his enemy Condorcet,[14] dealt with such subjects as Charles V, Corneille, Molière, Leibniz, and the Abbé de La Caille. Mostly brittle, mechanically skilled compositions, they captured no first prizes for their author, except in Berlin (Leibniz). Yet we find in them passages useful to our understanding of the author.

In his eulogy of Charles V. Bailly wrote: "he was king because he was a father: powerful and respected monarchs, you are fathers because you are kings!"[15] Although this awkward chiasmus exploits obsequious rhetoric, an enrooted respect for royalty remained a first principle of Bailly's politics. He would later write in his *Mémoires*: "I always personally loved the King, but with the measure of devotion suitable to the circumstances and to reason."[16] Love was tempered by gratitude: the Baillys, father to son, had been royal pensioners for well over a century; doubly so in the case of Jean-Sylvain, who depended for facilities and stipends on the royally sponsored academies to which he had been elected. But there was just a hint of protest, too—on behalf of the meritocracy. In the eulogy on Corneille, Bailly makes this point unoriginally, but with force: "Corneille never enjoyed the honors he so well deserved. They would have been his in Athens, in a republic where men born equal create a distinction of their own; he could not obtain them in a monarchy where [dignities] of place are everything, where men are nothing, and where genius alone has no [claim to rank]."[17] How many bourgeois intellectuals idealized the democracy of the ancients, not wishing to have it, except as a means of condemning present injustices? A few pages further along Bailly adjusts his mock-Athenianism: "Reason can only rule the multitude under the name of opinion, whose authority is shared between the kings and the great writers. Thus legislation and philosophy should unite for the happiness of the world."[18] This reasonable marriage of monarchy and learning is clinched in a later work: "In a monarchy . . . the tastes of the prince become those of the people, royal subsidies attract the man of genius, and the impulse given to the nation paves the way for his successors."[19] On the whole, the Republic of Letters found comfort in the Political Monarchy. As we shall see presently, this view collided abruptly with the Jacobin estimate of science, literature, and philosophy.

Bailly touched upon another important problem in the *Eulogies*: the way in which the historical consciousness was related to the spread and progress of learning in a monarchical society. "Among all peoples," he wrote in the Corneille eulogy, "centuries of shadows came before the light, and those centuries show only greed, war, and the talent for destruction . . . but finally the forms of government were fixed, and civil peace abided in the shade of the laws."[20] This sentence not only recalls Voltaire at his most complacent, but it suggests a growing concern with the genetic exploration of man: his combination of perceptions, his acquisition of technique and rational procedures, his submission to rational morality, in brief, his "education."[21] The eighteenth century inhabited an unstable middle ground between elegant but reductionist systems of reason and the investigation of human diversity in space and time. Was reason's flexibility so great as to encompass that flux with its norms? As Cassirer writes: "The philosophy of the eighteenth century from the outset treats the problems of nature and history as an indivisible unity. It tries to attack both types of problems with the same intellectual tools; it endeavors to ask the same questions and to apply the same universal method of 'reason' to nature and to history."[22] Bailly was among the first to undertake the difficult task of constructing a rational history of science. As we shall see, it committed him to an exaltation of the savant's role.

It is not accidental that Bailly wrote on Leibniz, that bifurcated genius who, paramount among the system-builders of his time, has also been awarded a role in the creation of "historicism."[23] Defining philosophy as "the employment of reason extended to everything surrounding us and returned to our own compass,"[24] Bailly in his Leibniz eulogy attached special importance to the historical study of jurisprudence: "Laws are founded on man's knowledge in depth of the human species; but how many differences can we not find within that species? How many are the nuances that philosophy discovers in traversing the earth from one pole to the other and in retracing the great river of time to the very origin of the world?"[25] To go back to the origin of the world: was this not "reason" applied simultaneously to nature and history? Although the philosophes played incessantly on the normative equation of origins with images of a natural justice yet to be obtained, Bailly was a committed scientist; he could not have written, like Rousseau: "Let us then begin by setting aside all the facts; for they are of no relevance to the question."[26] Both Bailly and Rousseau shared an interest in sidestepping the biblical rigors of anthropological explanation, but their projects were not the same. Paradoxically, Rousseau's poetry may have struck closer to the truth than Bailly's scientific fantasies.

Bailly's science is not to be understood in the fashion of the nineteenth century. His tendency, like that of his longtime patron Buffon, is dualistic. In him the materialist's creed of matter in motion cedes to an almost lyrical notion of wonder at the starry heavens, which were his special province. Compared to the materialists, Bailly's moral preoccupations were even a bit Panglossian. But he shared the special talent of the Enlightenment, especially in his *History of Astronomy*, of bringing new discoveries within the intellectual horizons of the educated man, believing that knowledge and human improvement were partners. *Coeli enarrant gloriam Dei*? Not exactly: Bailly was a deist without personal religion. But the stars directed him toward the source of man's wisdom in space and time. He announced his project in the Leibniz eulogy: "The origin of peoples is the worthiest object for the curiosity of a philosopher."[27] A singular conundrum that fascinated a culture where "the leading idea . . . [was] not the idea of progress but that of nature. . . ."[28]

Bailly savored rustic promenades where he could commune with his own thoughts. From the Louvre they often led him to Chaillot, then almost a country village, and to the authentic verdure of the Bois de

Boulogne. A few months after the death of his father, in 1768, he rented a cottage in Chaillot whose modesty would have satisfied Rousseau. Later he purchased his own dwelling at 21, rue de Chaillot. Here most of the writing of his monumental *History of Modern Astronomy* and *History of Ancient and Indian Astronomy* was undertaken; here also he no doubt worked out the speculative theory of a primordial, wise race of astronomers that had transmitted knowledge to early civilizations, but had left no trace of itself. His biographer Arago, also an astronomer, has described his method of composition: "Each morning Bailly set out early from his modest house in Chaillot; he walked in the Bois de Boulogne, where, in the course of lengthy strolls, his potent intelligence planned and joined conceptions that would charm the future, adorning them with all the fineries of language."[29] The withdrawal to nature was a means of clearing the head so as better to return to the world of intellectual controversy in Paris.

Bailly's manners were simple; his ambition was transparent. Temporarily patronized by d'Alembert, who encouraged him to put himself forward as successor to Grandjean de Fouchy, the ailing and less than competent permanent secretary of the Academy of Science, Bailly was later played false by that illustrious sage, who threw his support to Condorcet. A eulogist of Bailly accuses d'Alembert of being "unjust and wicked. . . . The words liberty and equality were continually on his lips, but he wanted only liberty for himself and no one as his equal."[30] Though there was little that was lovable in Condorcet, d'Alembert surely backed the best man. However, the result of this contretemps was a history of animosity between d'Alembert and Condorcet on the one hand and Bailly and his sponsor Buffon on the other. When Condorcet presented his eulogy of Buffon to the Academy of Science in 1788, he put in a few nasty digs.[31] D'Alembert and Condorcet were able to bar the portals of the Académie Française to Bailly until 1784, when he was finally seated among the "forty immortals."[32] Even during the Revolution, Condorcet and Brissot attempted, unsuccessfully, to drive a wedge between Bailly and Lafayette when the two were closely associated in the Paris municipal government.[33] As for Buffon, he and Bailly quarreled when Bailly refused to pledge his vote to the Abbé Maury for a *fauteuil* in the Académie Française.[34] Academic infighting was Bailly's chief preparation for later civic responsibility, an important incubator of his reactions.

Bailly was eventually heralded as the "member of the Three Academies"—Sciences, Inscriptions et Belles-Lettres, and the Académie Française—sharing this distinction with Fontenelle (and, it seems, Malesherbes).[35] It is not precisely true that the walls of the first two sanctums simply fell at the blast of his trumpet.[36] His election to the scientific academy was obtained against two opponents by one vote and by virtue of a blank ballot; his admission to Belles-Lettres was not by ballot at all, but by a category of appointment exercised by Louis XVI.[37] While scarcely diminishing Bailly's luster, these slight corrections illustrate the undercurrent of faction in the Republic of Letters and temper a myth that Bailly would leave in his wake. Still, with the great philosophes dead and others, like Buffon and Raynal, teetering on the brink, Bailly was acclaimed a torchbearer of the *lumières*.

He always bore that torch prudently. Accused after his publication of *Lettres sur l'Atlantide de Platon* (written to a decrepit and bored Voltaire) of attacking the Mosaic cosmogony, he retracted his position for fear of persecution.[38] While sympathetic to the aims of the *Encyclopedia*, he politely declined to contribute.[39] Political liberty was not his mania, and the idea of political violence shocked him. As Lafayette recounts: "At the moment when Bailly was elected deputy he had taken no part in the French Revolution [i.e. the "pre-Revolution"], and the single political remark cited from him before this time was one disapproving of revolutions (I cannot recall it)."[40] The passage that escaped Lafayette's memory, written in 1778, reads: "Let us never wish for revolution; let us pity our ancestors for those they have experienced. In both physical and moral nature, good descends on us from heaven only slowly, little by little—I almost said, drop by drop. But everything that is sudden and instantaneous, all that is revolution, is a source of woes."[41] Bailly's later political career is thus an irony: for he passed fifty-two years without divulging a seditious political thought. Daniel Roche expresses Bailly's position well in an important article in which he guardedly isolates the social and mental factors that distinguish the academicians from the collaborators of the *Encyclopedia*: "The basic difference from the *Encyclopedia* resides in the fact that the academies are not only marked by a respect for the traditional social structures, but also thereby importantly affected in their [internal organization] . . . more dependent on the urban environment and in line with the socioeconomic structure of the Old Regime."[42]

Bailly is Roche's academician, par excellence. What, then, was an academy, especially a great academy, where Bailly mingled with other "immortals"? According to the *Encyclopedia*, an academy was intended to obtain the "perfection" of an art and was composed of "persons of distinguished capacity, who exchange knowledge and reveal their discoveries for mutual benefit."[43] According to Roger Hahn, the premier academy, Sciences, had "by the middle of the eighteenth century . . . become the major symbol for the advancement of learning of the enlightened world."[44] This was a world of elite consumers formed by the social patterns of the Old Regime, progressives of the head rather than the heart. The institutions that served them were indebted to the monarchy for their charters, privileges, and pensions. They were royal in two senses: by foundation and, ultimately, control; and by mission, being frequently entrusted with royal errands and projects. With the exception of the Academy of Science, royal preference interfered with their choice of members and influenced the judgment of talent in their professions.[45]

The academies were certainly not ignorant of their amphibian nature: "Fontenelle knew all too well that his institution was fashioned [not only to serve truth and advance learning, but] to satisfy another more parochial force as well. He was sufficiently realistic to proclaim that the Academy had two acknowledged masters, science and the crown."[46] The Académie Française had begun under the impulse of the Cardinal Richelieu in 1636. Its flattering device was a l'immortalité—hence the phrase "forty immortals"—no doubt gratifying to the intellectual's amour-propre. The Académie des Sciences owed its origin in 1663 to that other great royal minister Colbert: its applications of science held out promise for improvements in navigation, warfare, and architecture and an opportunity "to fulfill the dream of centralizing all the cultural activities of the realm around the monarchy."[47]

It is to be stressed, therefore, that the image of the academy was neoclassic and antifeudal. Predictably its views of prestige and authority would clash with the aristocratic mode. The academy was more strictly monarchical (usufructory): royal bounty made possible the progress of intellectual inquiry. Yet at the same time, academies encouraged the pretensions of a new and mixed aristocracy: their members could be at the same time an elite and corporate element concerned with the welfare and instruction of humanity, responsive to but superior to society. The aims of the academicians and the aims of the state were, to be sure, closer in Colbert's time than in Maupeou's; but, on the whole, the alliance was natural and helpful to both parties. Tensions with ecclesiastical norms grew; but, after all, orthodoxy had lived in a state of armed truce with libertinism and skepticism in the Grand Siècle. Despite its proportion of progressives (many of whom, like d'Alembert and Condorcet, were its leaders), the academy contained tinder within its precincts that could be ignited only by an external explosion.

Bailly's equation of princely patronage and scientific advancement did not stamp him as a reactionary. Earlier, Fontenelle had written: "Societies —and only societies protected by princes—can succeed in amassing those materials [necessary for knowledge]. Neither the *lumières*, nor the care, nor the life, nor the facilities of any individual can suffice. There are too many experiments, too many different kinds of experiments."[48] This judgment did not flag on the eve of the Revolution; consider Lavoisier: "These bodies, having an active strength, not only will preserve through the ages the original impulse given them by a great minister [Colbert], but their active strength will destroy the resistance which ignorance, superstition, and barbarism might raise against them."[49] Condorcet's opinion was no different: "The sovereigns alone possess the means of making [the ordering of knowledge] successful independent of time and chance. They alone can prescribe and see to the systematic execution of these long and laborious works whose glory can have no material reward. Who will organize these great undertakings . . . if it is not a prince who knows how to judge his projects, not according to the life of a man, but according to that of nations?"[50] Of course there are fundamental tensions in Condorcet's thought between scientific elitism and political liberalism.[51] But we must acknowledge the usufructory royal premise from which men like Condorcet, Lavoisier, and Bailly started, and the environment of the academy from which they were weaned to politics. Academic patronage was not only a *fleuron* of Frederick II, Catherine II, and Joseph II, but of the plodding and pious Louis XVI. Royal commissions of *cognoscenti*—to study epidemics, hospital conditions, city lighting, agriculture, architectural standards, hygiene, and other matters—blossomed toward the end of the Old Regime. As Hahn writes: "On the eve of the Revolution, the Academy had truly become an adjunct of royal authority. As a consultant and arbiter in the realm of technology, it was the final court of appeals."[52]

Academicians did not, in the 1780s, believe that they lived in the best of all possible worlds, for they were neither blind nor uncaring. Moreover, they respected the primacy of merit over ascribed status. But the mixed government of the academies well reflected the political confusions of the waning Old Regime: monarchical sanction and mission; aristocratic psychology toward the *crédules* and *ignorants*; and democratic communication of knowledge. The doctrine of natural equality and the ideology of natural talent—the notion that made judges and constables out of ordinary untrained citizens—ran against the grain. Yet, as the Revolution gathered shape and momentum, the academies themselves were riven by political as well as personal disputes. Learned corporations tend to harbor insidious divisions while presenting an elitist solidarity to the outer world. For example, in November 1789 the Duc de la Rochefoucauld (later to be stigmatized as a reactionary) led a battle to reform the organization of the Academy of Science along lines of the political regime coming into being. The "bitter factionalism" of the revolutionary era was reproduced within its walls.[53] Finally, and most importantly, the talents of the French had, by the late eighteenth century, outgrown the privileged academic sanctums. There were ultimately two alternatives: to reform them or to abolish them. Condorcet, who favored reform, well knew that the tests of truth—and perhaps taste as well—could never be an affair of mere majorities or raucous assemblies. Yet his belief that knowledge in the human and moral "sciences" could be brought into much greater harmony with the methods of validation used in the physical sciences suggested at least a rapprochement of public power with scientific guidance.[54] The Jacobins, some *savants prétendus* and others contemptuous of practically all intellectual elitism, could not countenance such a halfway house. For, the Revolutionaries either passionately believed, or had come to scorn, the notion that the sciences will, in the words of Groethuysen, "teach man what is just and good . . . instruct him in what is beautiful . . . provide him with historical examples from which he can derive profit . . . shake his prejudices and reveal new possibilities of happiness. . . ."[55] If they scorned science, their solution was, in Saint-Just's phrase, "institutions."

Bailly did not, like Lavoisier and numbers of others, attempt to fulfill the role of savant during the Revolution; politics occupied him entirely. But, precisely because of this deep plunge into politics, his representative quality as a pre-Revolutionary academician takes on added significance. We have already glimpsed some of the biases of his status and self-image. They contributed to his claim of objectivity in the midst of events where no participant could avoid taking sides. In his *Mémoires* Bailly cites his "spirit of moderation (*mesure*) and judgment (*calcul*) about what one wanted to get, or could hope to get, about all one could wish for or all one could lose, a spirit that has always guided me, and that I would willingly call wisdom. . . ."[56] Further on he asserts that he has "never been connected to any faction (*parti*) nor been a party to any intrigue."[57] He persisted with the same claim in 1793 while under arrest, with his life hanging in the balance. But such a contention is absurd. His instincts were those of a savant and an academician (unperturbed by the care of a wife and children), prudent and mildly progressive, humane but elitist, royalist by habit and conviction, dedicated to slow and lawful change, Voltairean in faith, and somewhat at sea in the obstreperous confusions of politics. He remained half-glued in the Old Regime.

Among Bailly's numerous writings, the *History of Astronomy* is his finest literary achievement and also a reliable clue to the core of his political thought. It is a vast and meticulous account of both scientific progress and its heroic explorers. Bailly worked and reworked this magnum opus to reach out to a wider audience. In his second edition (from which I cite), he carefully distinguished between the narrative history of astronomical discovery and the scientific technicalities of the discipline (textually isolated for the learned reader in a sequence of "éclaircissements"). This was an original approach to the history of science.

Bailly's Preliminary Discourse is fundamental to the political understanding of an academician: it mixes the pride of the savant with the responsibilities of scientific diffusion. At the outset, the substance of history and the work of the great scientists are joined: "While great men propel the sciences, increasing the number of true propositions by new discoveries, history broadcasts these truths; history makes knowledge descend from above, like waters gathered on mountain peaks that rush down to the plains and are distributed by canals. . . ."[58] But elitism is modified by two other factors: the first is the mission to spread scientific knowledge to the less enlightened; the second is a confidence that the many can be inspired by science, even if they remain unable to grasp its proper method. History may even lead people to science; the ontogenic-phylogenic parallel is introduced to stress the point; "One does not have to be learned to read the history of science; but it can help one to become learned. . . . Once the human mind was young, and it was poor before it became rich. . . . Idea was raised upon idea; interacting at the same time, one led to the other. We do not have to go back over all that, beginning with the earliest notions; the path is traced; anyone can make the trip, because it has already been made. The individual should be able to catch up with several hours of reading what it took the human race countless centuries to understand."[59] Bailly is arguing here that knowledge, linear and progressive in character, is a transmissible accumulation of the experience of others. But since men no longer have to make the experiments for themselves, science itself becomes a sort of revelation or catechism. Given sufficient faith in its ordering, one might even leap to the technical *éclaircissements*. Finally, there is the dialectic of the "genius" and the "race": the human race learns at a snail's pace what great men transmit to each other by leaps of intellect.

Bailly's confidence in the nonscientific intelligence is not of course a premonition of intellectual democracy. He conveys, rather, the conception of a hierarchical structure, allowing for a flow of information within the educated portion of the population adequate to insure enlightenment and stability: "In an enlightened nation the educated classes form a level wide enough at its base, and narrow at its summit. As we ascend, people know more (*la lumière des individus augmente*) and their number is fewer: perhaps a unique man is in a class by himself and at the pinnacle of intelligent beings."[60] But there is an imperative: the ignorant should rise; the savants should descend to meet and guide them. The paths cross in a bourgeoisie of the intelligence, where the historian is the mediator of intellectual status: "Obviously this [education] should be different for each of the different classes; thus it is of necessity that they all hearken to the historian, who is placed at the level of the middle class."[61] Scientific history is not unvarnished truth: it is a way of making truth practicable to the ordinary mind. The naked order of truth is apparently foreclosed to our intellect (d'Alembert had also said this in his *Preliminary Discourse to the Encyclopedia*).[62] Beneath it is scientific method, "the way of seeing . . . most favorable to our feeble conception." Finally, there is history, which, veiling the laws of nature with an account of their discovery, exhibits nature as most men are accustomed to treating it: "first of all vast and complicated, later becoming more and more simplified by the collective work of men and centuries," vindicating reason in diversity.[63] The perspectives of history and science converge in the process of enlightenment.

Bailly, like many of his confrères, resisted—not too successfully—carrying these conclusions into politics. "Political history," he writes, "has too often forgotten the human race in being concerned with a small number of men; kings were its sole preoccupation, and we read only the account of their terrible passions and their ever costly glory." But the history of science depends on the principle denied to politics; for while "political history exhibits [or should exhibit] the works of men assembled in nations, speaking in the interests of all, encompassing the customs improved or corrupted by the multitude," in science "the multitude plays no role; the multitude does not understand [the sciences] or looks on them with indifference: those who cultivate them are a class apart (*une classe isolée*)." Moreover, "Individuals reweave the thread of work and research. Thus these individuals alone—whose mission is to guide and raise the human mind—are the authors of progress."[64] It follows then that "science is only the product . . . of genius; and its history is the history of men and what they have thought (*leurs pensées*)."[65] Unfortunately the masses show a capacity to dominate (*faire la loi*) the "small number of superior minds."[66]

Altogether, the account is rather incoherent. Bailly, the devoted and entrenched academician, seems to deny the corporate capacity of science to interact with society, especially in view of the historical vulgarization he supplies for the uplifting of ordinary minds. And his appeal to "genius" is precisely the argument used as early as 1782 by Brissot to anathematize the stuffiness of the academies and to urge on science a kind of Rousseauian democracy and humility.[67] Bailly's "rewoven thread" scarcely accounts for the corporate supremacy of what has been called "the community of normal science." Bailly was evidently carried away by the episodic drama of the astronomers' lonely search for truth.

And what of the political innuendoes? Were politics and science really so separable in theory and practice? For Bailly's position we must look ahead to his *Mémoires*, which cover the first year of the Revolution. In a passage to which we shall return for other purposes, Bailly lamented the comparative paucity of savants in the primary assembly of the Third Estate of Paris in 1789, because "the *gens de lettres* [i.e., men like himself] are . . . among the most enlightened men, if not always about specific objects, at least about general matters: they have exercised their minds the most and they know best how they ought to be used."[68] This led to the corporate conviction: "I have always thought, and I still think, that a bit more of the philosophical spirit would not have been a bad thing (*n'aurait pas nui*) for the Constituent Assembly."[69] Bailly's notion of "genius" must thus be tempered by his commitment to the milieu of the academic aristocracy; the discontinuity between the concerns of politics and science, used rhetorically in the *History of Astronomy* to insist the more firmly on the role of scientific elites in human progress, must be modified by the conviction that savants possess superior political judgment. All this is of great importance in understanding Bailly's political evolution.

The *History of Astronomy* was also the first revelation of Bailly's most constant anthropological fixation: his first hint of the theory of an antediluvian, Hyperborean people, now vanished without trace, that had gained wisdom from astronomy:[70] "This science . . . seems to have been the accomplishment of a people from that part of the world placed at the latitude of forty-nine or fifty degrees."[71] Bailly's fancy engaged him in an intellectual dialogue with Voltaire. Voltaire had lent his *imprimatur* to the ancient Brahmins as the founders of knowledge; it seemed to him an eminently reasonable way of demolishing the claims of Scripture. Bailly sent a specially inscribed copy of his work to Voltaire at Ferney with the requisite note of flattery. Though the aging sage recognized Bailly's history as "a masterpiece of science and genius," he could muster no enthusiasm for the Hyperboreans.[72] His wit had certainly not left him in his waning years: "Nothing ever came to us from European and Asiatic Scythia except tigers to eat our lambs."[73] "For more than twenty-four years I have lived in a climate covered with snow and frost just like theirs. . . . I have reached the conclusion that one could hardly be expected to observe the stars assiduously beneath such a mournful sky."[74] Bailly tracked the dying Voltaire like a bloodhound: ". . . *I persist in desiring that you believe in my ancient lost people.* I have no less esteem for the Brahmins, whom you have taken under your protection. They would be very proud, knowing they had you for an apologist."[75] Bailly knew the practical rewards of "a detailed discussion" with Voltaire.[76] He overwhelmed him, philosophe to philosophe, with a mostly one-way correspondence of over three hundred pages in which, amid a catalog of miscellaneous erudition, he attempted to show identities and similarities in the isolated cultures of India, China, and Babylonia, and to argue that they must owe this feature to the Hyperboreans, "author of all the philosophical ideas that enlightened the world."[77]

Not content to let the matter rest, Bailly issued a companion volume in 1779 of new letters to Voltaire, all of them written in early 1778 just before the death of the octogenarian. Here he maintained that the Hyperboreans were actually the subject of the Platonic myth of Atlantis. The question of myth or fable was certainly not a new one. Fontenelle had expressly accused myth of being the production of "poor savages who . . . could explain the effects of nature only by the crudest and most palpable things they knew."[78] Fontenelle was not impressed with "original wise peoples." But as Bailly's ardor for the Hyperborean astronomers increased, he pushed their geographical origin farther and farther north, well beyond the fiftieth degree. His views were worked out still more elaborately in a posthumously published work, the *Essai sur les fables*, whose purpose was "to unravel the mythological chaos that has come down to us from antiquity . . . and . . . to arrive at the original founding people (*peuple instituteur des autres*), thus tracing the highway of truth [as it spread] over the globe."[79]

I have dwelt on this episode because it bears on Bailly's intellectual temper and his relationship to the Enlightenment, matters important to his position in the Revolution. A modern scholar, E. B. Smith, has accused Bailly of participating in a "naive optimism which brought about the French Revolution . . . a curious mixture of rationalism and illuminism."[80] This is not the place to meditate on the intellectual currents that met in the Revolution, but some clarification about Bailly is necessary. Essentially, Smith makes two charges against Bailly: that his "wild speculations" were indebted to the illuminist Court de Gébelin and that he was a Freemason.[81] With regard to the second point it is only necessary to recall that Masonry was not a preserve of intellectual freaks. Besides, the Lodge of the Nine Sisters, which Bailly is alleged to have joined in 1784, was no ordinary chapter: it included Benjamin Franklin and an assortment of *gens de lettres*. But finally, whatever the likelihood, there is no documentary evidence that Bailly was ever a Mason at all.[82]

Although Bailly's Hyperboreans may have stretched credulity, their contemporary reception was probably due less to the outlandishness of the hypothesis than to the eternal pastime of intellectual sniping. Even if influences came from Court de Gébelin, contemporaries gave more respect to his *Le monde primitif* than Smith allows. But behind all this we see an old combat continuing. D'Alembert, Bailly's enemy, indeed called him a "frère illuminé," and this carries some weight because d'Alembert himself resolutely rejected Freemasonry.[83] But d'Alembert's caustic epithet was intended mainly to reach Voltaire, who was himself inducted into the Grand Orient in the last year of his life. "Bailly's dream," d'Alembert wrote, "about the ancient people, which has taught us everything except their name and existence, seems to me one of the most hollow that man has ever dreamed."[84] It must now be recalled that Bailly had profusely praised Buffon, his patron, toward the end of his *Lettres sur l'origine des sciences*. Although the two men had quarreled over Maury by the time that Buffon's *Histoire naturelle des Epoques de la Nature* appeared in 1788, Buffon could still declare against the "Brahmin theory" and write: "It was in the northern regions of Asia that the stalk of human knowledge pushed forth . . . from the fortieth to the forty-fifth degree of latitude. . . . This earliest people was very contented (*très heureux*) because it had become very wise (*savant*) . . . already [having practiced] three thousand years of astronomical studies."[85] If this was "illuminism," then a ranking philosophe, who had done his major work at mid-century, was also an illuminist. Obviously we have to do with a party quarrel.

Bailly's other work belies the charge of illuminism. In 1784 he chaired a committee for the Academy of Science and the Royal Society of Medicine, whose members included Benjamin Franklin, Lavoisier, and Dr. Guillotin, to look into the phenomenon of "animal magnetism," a general theory of illness and cure propagated by Franz Anton Mesmer, "doctor of medicine of the Academy of Vienna," who had moved to Paris in 1778.[86] Mesmerism was not an underground cult; it had been subscribed to by numbers of distinguished people, including Bailly's later collaborator Lafayette. Court de Gébelin died beside a Mesmerist tub in 1784, the very year when his alleged disciple was attacking the therapy with the tools of science.[87] In investigating Mesmerism, Bailly's committee first witnessed the apparatus of cure: a great oaken tub, placed in the middle of a large circular room, pierced with a number of holes from which movable rods of iron protruded. Arranged in circles around the tub, each patient could grasp his own rod, which he applied to the portion of his body stricken with illness. In addition, the patients were joined together by a rope passed around their bodies, and they had physical contact by linking their thumbs with the index fingers of their neighbors. In the meantime, a pianoforte played various melodies, punctuated occasionally by the sound of singing.[88]

The savants, some of whom had chronic aches and pains, then submitted themselves to the treatment and observed the reactions of other patients as well. "None of them felt or at least experienced anything that could be attributed to the action of magnetism."[89] When they repeated this experience three days in a row, their opinions were unchanged.[90] They determined that the only positive effects of "animal magnetism" were due to credulousness; "armed with philosophical doubt," the experimenter could discover no benefit whatever.[91] "The experiments . . . rigorous and decisive," said the report, "authorize us to conclude that the imagination is the true cause of the effects attributed to magnetism."[92] Mesmerism was at best a kind of hypnosis. Moreover, "any public treatment where the methods of magnetism are employed can only, in the long run, have abusive effects."[93] Mesmer quickly fled the country. Bailly's report was a careful piece of preventive science.

Bailly's next practical mission for the Academy of Science was an inquiry into hospital conditions, undertaken in 1785. He was editor of the first report, filed in November 1786, which proposed the construction of four or five new hospitals on the outskirts of Paris in indigent neighborhoods. However, the real moving spirit behind this investigation was Jacques-René Tenon, not Bailly.[94] Unfortunately, the project was canceled in the ensuing political crisis: Loménie de Brienne pocketed the appropriation for the immediate needs of the state.[95] Bailly went on to produce a salient report on slaughterhouses (1788).[96] These activities, as well as his literary laurels, called him to the attention of the Paris electors a year later.

Obviously, despite his fixation on the Hyperboreans, Bailly was not an irrationalist or illuminist. Nor is there any evidence to stamp him as an incipient revolutionary. In the stars he identified an indwelling purpose; yet he used the methods of free experimental inquiry. Bailly believed in reason as defined by his greater intellectual ancestors: "When, in a century of *lumières*, one calls reason to his assistance, reason should end up as his master."[97] This was not just a theoretical reason exclusive to academic pursuits, but also a practical reason destined to overcome "outmoded privileges and absurd prejudices."[98] As we shall see, the notion of privilege and prejudice stopped far short of the ultimate demands of revolution: those limits bred in Bailly a stubbornness and an innocence, mixed with a vanity of achievement, that would cost him his life.

10. Difficulties of a Statesman

In 1789, writes Delisle de Sales, "France . . . had an inkling that the man of letters with great talents, who never stooped to intrigue, could be a statesman, and she placed a portion of her omnipotence in Bailly's hitherto clean hands."[1] The truth is more complicated. France was not a coherent actor: Bailly was funneled into politics. In Bailly's words, hearing of the summoning of the first Assemblée des Notables in December 1786: "I was struck. I foresaw a great event, a change in the situation, and even in the form of government. I did not foresee the revolution that would ensue, and I don't think that any man could have foreseen it. . . ."[2] One day, it seems, Rivarol (the wit, later an ultraroyalist journalist) said to him in jest that his talents would soon be required, for only the astronomer's art with digits could cope with the financial ills of the realm.[3] Yet a veil of scrim seems to hang between the momentous shocks of the Revolution and Bailly's appreciation of his part. There is perpetually an air of amazement in his memoirs: "I had no way of foreseeing the great scenes and revolutions to be played in that theatre [the Hôtel de Ville], nor the role in which I was to be cast in that very place."[4] Only his political experience in the world of science and literature had prepared him for his destiny.

The Revolution came to disturb his tranquillity and fame. He had been quietly married in 1787 to a cheerful and supportive widow, Jeanne Gaye, née Le Seigneur, two years younger than himself. Their brief life together was companionable and affectionate: Madame Bailly called her husband "Coco," a name cruelly picked up by journalistic detractors. At Chaillot she was a cordial hostess with her hot chocolate, but she did not find politics glamorous or go out in the social world, except to one or two official receptions while Bailly was mayor of Paris.

After 24 January 1788, when the Ministry published the letter of convocation and electoral regulations for the Estates-General, political excitement ran high in the city. In Bailly's words: "There was talk about who the deputies from Paris would be; lists were passed around; and it was said in public (*dans le monde*), and especially in the Club des Arts where I was a member, that I would be a deputy. However, I wasn't on those lists. Those who were had pretensions, and I had none."[5] The "lists" were probably like the documents published by Chassin, where one reads among the most conspicuous names: La Rochefoucauld, Lally-Tollendal, Condorcet, Duport, Hérault de Séchelles, Sieyès, Dr. Guillotin, Target, Brissot, Chénier, Bernardin de Saint-Pierre, Pastoret, and Chamfort, persons "known for their enlightenment as well as their zeal for the public welfare."[6] However, the Abbé Maury assured Bailly: "You will be a deputy. . . . I have just rented an apartment in Versailles, and you will be welcome every day at my table."[7]

The Parisians, last to meet in primary assemblies, compose *cahiers*, and elect deputies, had to do everything in a great rush and could not even join their colleagues for the opening session in Versailles on 5 May. This may have been a tactical move to keep the center of the political revolt off balance.[8] Finally, though, the assemblies were convoked for 21 April. Royal Paris was divided into sixty "districts"; these formed the electoral units of the Third Estate. The "commons" was still a very exclusive electoral body: winnowed by the exclusion of women and of the more indigent who paid less than six livres of taxes, it mustered only 11,706 voters in the primary assemblies (out of a total Parisian population of more than half a million). They in turn chose 407 "electors" to edit the general *cahiers* of the Tiers and choose the twenty deputies to Versailles from Paris *intra-muros*.[9]

Though living mostly in Chaillot, Bailly voted in the district of Feuillants, the area around the Louvre and Tuileries. Arriving early in the morning at the voting place, the scientist was informed by a young passer-by that he would be named an elector.[10] Once involved in the deliberations of the neighborhood assembly, Bailly felt suddenly transported: "I was breathing fresh air; it was phenomenal to be something in the political order, just by one's quality as citizen, or rather bourgeois, of Paris; for at that time we were still bourgeois and not citizens. . . . Yet this assembly, a tiny, tiny part of the nation, felt both the strength and the rights of the whole."[11] Bailly was here recording the experience of fraternity and arrogation of sovereignty by the smallest portions of the political whole, things that would later vex him so often. "During the meeting," he writes, "we received several delegations from the nobility and the commons. This collaboration . . . already announced the higher unity of the realm and the mixture of orders."[12] It was disappointing that the clergy had sent no well-wishers.

After a lavish exchange of compliments and pledges of concord, the Feuillants turned finally to their *cahiers* and elections. Unfortunately there is no extant *procès-verbal* of these proceedings, nor is there a local *cahier*.[13] The secretary for the occasion was Marmontel. Of the seven *électeurs* allotted to the district of Feuillants, Bailly was the first chosen by his peers.[14] Whether it was his intellectual reputation or his quality of participation, or both that impressed his colleagues we cannot know for certain. According to Delisle de Sales, "Bailly . . . was no orator; he was not up to soothing the billows of a stormy assembly with sweeping eloquence."[15] Probably the Feuillants, a moderate constituency, sought a spokesman of common sense and polite tenacity. And no doubt Bailly's *lumières* helped him to win his place. Later, in the Assemblée des Electeurs, the scenario would be somewhat different.

That meeting held its plenary session on 23 April in the great hall of the Archbishopric of Paris. Inasmuch as royal officials presided, the first independent act of the political body was to remove them and to elect its own officers.[16] Against Bailly's wishes the estates dispersed. The leading figure of the Tiers was the academician and lawyer Target: he was chosen to preside. Bailly, who "hardly knew eight or ten persons," nonetheless received forty votes for president, and was subsequently named secretary.[17] He kept the minutes, a source he drew on copiously when he composed his own memoirs in 1792. He pleaded lack of skill in his job: at one point a error in his bookkeeping allowed the Abbé Sieyès to be chosen the twentieth and last deputy of the Tiers of Paris, when the Assembly had already voted to exclude nominees from the other orders.[18] Bailly was pleased with his mistake, for "no one had named him to the Estates-General. The Third Estate had to avenge him and repay its debt. . . ."[19]

Before electing its deputies, the Tiers had the responsibility of drafting its general *cahiers de doléances*. For this purpose six committees were appointed: constitution; finance; agriculture and commerce; religion, clergy, morals, education, hospitals; legislation; and city government. From his secretarial chair Bailly beamed on their labors: "It is in such moments, when the seed of liberty is sprouting, that it is beautiful to see how a people tackles its legislation."[20] Under the direction of Target, the constitutional committee not only attempted to draft a rudimentary national constitution, but conceived of prefacing it with a Declaration of the Rights of Man. It almost entirely anticipated the work of the National Assembly. The Declaration of Rights stated in part: "In every political society all men are equal in rights. . . . All power has its source in the nation and can be exercised only for its happiness. . . . The general will makes the law; public power assures its execution."[21] Paris was not abashed to declare the nation's sovereignty, even within the confines of its small assembly, prefiguring the later course of the Revolution. The future mayor applauded his colleagues' wisdom, though he questioned their audacity in calling themselves sovereign.[22]

The *cahiers* occupied the electors through 10 May (five days late for Versailles). Then they were ready to turn to elections. Bailly was pleased to hear that he might be declared ineligible because he received income from government stipends: "I was quite content in my peacefulness and mediocrity. With no great gift of speaking and excessively shy, I thought I could add little to the Estates-General. . . ."[23] Lavoisier, a guest at Chaillot, dissented from this opinion.[24] Despite some exclusionary motions, the Assembly did not exempt Bailly from the honor of serving. Indeed, just before the balloting started on 12 May, a friendly noble paid this compliment: "If it were possible, M. Bailly would be a deputy of all the three orders, just as he is of the three academies."[25] Bailly evolved from reluctance to modest enthusiasm within ten pages of his memoirs. By a plurality of 173 votes out of 377 cast he was elected first deputy of the Tiers on the first ballot. The voting for the twenty seats continued for another week.

Bailly's pathway to still higher eminence is not mysterious, if we accept that his modesty concealed a certain resolute comportment. Once first deputy of Paris, he was naturally made *doyen* and later presiding officer of the Tiers Etat—for Paris was the real capital of France and the foyer of the Revolution. Then the Tiers created the National Assembly and imposed it. Since Bailly performed both bravely and astutely in those trying days of 17–27 June, it was natural that he, as a commoner, should be first president of the legislature. Finally, on 15 July, when a mass of Parisians gathered at the Hôtel de Ville acclaimed Bailly as their mayor, they were designating a *real* Parisian who was both on the spot and very much in view. It is, however, the election of 12 May that was decisive for Bailly's career. We need to review it more carefully.

Of the 407 electors of the Paris Tiers there were 8 military officers, 7 *gens de lettres*, 8 professors, 12 academicians (Bailly is counted here), 13 artists or architects, 23 practitioners of medicine or pharmacology, 32 royal or municipal officers, 170 jurists (lawyers, notaries, and other *gens de justice*), and 137 properly so-called bourgeois (merchants, bankers, manufacturers, artisans, as well as a few *rentiers*).[26] Only about forty had backgrounds in any way similar to Bailly's; with but a few exceptions (Marmontel, Target), they lacked his luster. In his memoirs Bailly has included a long digression on professional categories:

> Literary men are . . . the most enlightened. . . . The *gens de lettres* weren't [in the Assembly] in sufficient numbers to assert themselves; there were two dominant classes: the merchants and the lawyers, who were most in a position to appreciate [the *gens de lettres*]. The literary people lost; they should have stood together [with the lawyers]; both were the freest groups under the

> Old Regime: public authority was never able to silence a courageous lawyer, and it feared the free, proud intelligence of the outstanding writers: exile and *lettres de cachet* were often their reward. Why, then, did so few [*gens de lettres*] have leading places in the Revolution? I won't hide the fact that several of them were ultracautious; that in the midst of the great conflict of powers several took a wait-and-see attitude without rushing to acknowledge the new and legitimate authority. These were the tactics of weak men; but for others this hesitation had a more honorable reason. The *philosophe* loves liberty, he understands the dignity of man, but he asks especially for peace around him; he wishes for enlightenment to spread and for humanity to recover its rights, but gradually and without effort: he is afraid of shock and violent revolution.[27]

This is an extremely revelatory passage. Bailly has distributed himself into several *personae*: the aristocrat of the commons; the patriotic intellectual who has stepped forward to serve the nation; and the philosophe who hesitates for "a more honorable reason" and shuns violence, like Bailly in 1778. This mixture of participation and disinterestedness may have impressed Bailly's colleagues in the Assembly.

They may also have been won over by his conduct as a man of reason and compromise. Convoked in haste and confusion, the Paris assemblies were at first so intoxicated with political freedom that "each district believed in its sovereignty. Citizens who hardly knew each other made friendships; public-spiritedness took shape."[28] But by the time that the Assemblée des Electeurs had been formed, fraternity was beginning to dissolve and required discipline. Paris *intra-muros* had to lean heavily on a kind of "representation of interests": "the *esprit de corps* [of the professions] had a lot of influence, and things were worked out only by a kind of verbal horsetrading, where it was agreed that votes would be cast for those whom the different corporations had designated. Thus deputies were named from all the professions practiced by the different members of the electoral assembly."[29] If this is so, it is not difficult to see why Bailly might have been acceptable to most of the competing elements. There was pressure from the liberal nobility on his behalf; and when the Abbé de Montesquiou, speaking for the clergy, praised him as "the friend of the poor and the scribe of the hospitals" (for his report of 1786), his breadth of support was clear.

But there was a simpler and more immediate cause. No doubt the weight of his legal reputation, combined with his eloquence and presence, would have caused Target to be chosen first deputy. However,

Target had already been picked as deputy by the assembly of Paris *extra-muros*. One could be elected by multiple constituencies; but it is likely that in its haste to get to Versailles, the commons of Paris *intra-muros* found it unnecessary to pay Target any further compliments. Thus Bailly led the Paris Tiers to the Estates-General. It was not a delegation of overwhelming talent, aside from Sieyès, "adopted" from Chartres. The Parisian nobles, who included Clermont-Tonnerre, La Rochefoucauld, Lally-Tollendal, Duport, and Lepeletier de Saint-Fargeau, were far more prominent. Yet, as events too familiar to be repeated here showed, the Tiers was the center of revolutionary action.

When Bailly became leader of the Tiers, this was again accompanied by mixed feelings. He recommended his legal colleague Camus (later also a Conventional), but he felt that some Parisian should receive the honor: in consequence, he was elected: "I stammered, wishing to demur. . . . I [felt] I would lose [my literary reputation] in a moment. Taking care not to go on at great length, I insisted that the honor caused me deep distress." But he quickly muffled his malaise: he accepted "because I felt that the choice had been made chiefly to honor the Paris delegation, and that it had fallen on me because I was first deputy. . . . I let myself be escorted to the presidential chair."[30] When the National Assembly was constituted on 8 June, Bailly's presidency was renewed.

Bailly presided with tact and decorum. What he lacked in dramatics, he compensated for in proportionate behavior. He dealt with the other estates; he dealt with the personnel of the monarchy; he moderated the rashness of his colleagues: he was a diplomat. This student of myth knew how to extract both gravity and power from the black costume of the bourgeois that was legally the uniform of the Tiers when it assembled. He staunchly insisted, and obtained, that the manners of the commons should reflect the dignity of the nation and not be base or groveling in the presence of the king.[31] On 20 June, when the Tiers Etat endured its famous royal lockout from the Salle des Menus Plaisirs and retired to the Jeu de Paume, pledging "never to disband but to meet in any place that circumstances may require, until the constitution of the kingdom shall be laid and established on secure foundations,"[32] he stepped in front of his estate to swear the oath first without hesitation.[33] It is Mirabeau's forceful challenge to the "bayonets," in the face of Dreux-Brézé's order to disperse on 23 June, that we remember. But there were no bayonets in sight. Bailly's response seems more politic and totally explicit: "The nation when assembled cannot be given orders."[34]

Bailly helped to achieve the transformation of the legislature with a minimum of faction and friction; he could even speak of "moments of grandeur [when] the Assembly was truly Roman."[35] But beneath the exultancy was a core of caution. Bailly respected the monarchy profoundly. He rejoiced to hear that Louis XVI had said of his election as *doyen* of the Tiers: "J'en suis bien aise, c'est un honnête homme."[36] He objected to the divisive hatred injected into the nation's political climate when his colleagues of the Tiers referred to the nobility and the clergy as "privileged classes."[37] Even amid the enthusiasm of the oath of the Jeu de Paume, Bailly was impressed that the crowds had shouted *Vive le roi!* Despite the "despotism" of the Ministry, Bailly felt that the Assembly was "joined in heart and mind with the King, having no designs against his legitimate authority."[38] Willing to accompany his cohorts through the breach of Revolution, he became quickly preoccupied with limiting the penetration and controlling the occupation. No doubt his personal influence was circumscribed. Lafayette would later write of Bailly: "He played no part in the great insurrection of the French people except that of having worthily presided over the Assembly in an interesting period. He did not play a part in the subsequent debates of the Assembly nor did he speak on any question, or serve on any committee. . . ."[39] But the tenor of the observation is misleading. After 15 July, Bailly had his hands full with a municipal administration; the "member of the Three Academies" could not easily wear two hats like the more vigorous Lafayette. Yet he was a personage in view from the start. Barère's memoirs are instructive on this point: Bailly and Mirabeau were the "two men [who] attracted my attention most particularly." "M. Bailly," Barère writes, "was terse (*peu communicatif*), though full of gentleness and good nature. . . . [As opposed to others] he was austere in his principles, forthright in his conduct, and energetic in his spirit."[40] Barère was an ambitious young place-seeker; he must have sensed, rightly or wrongly, that Bailly was worth cultivating.

On 12 July, the king clumsily staged a reactionary coup, combining military movements with the dismissal of Necker. Paris rose to resist this affront with the well-known consequences. Already, on 11 July, the formation of a *garde bourgeoise*, a military force to defend against royal troops, was being debated. Bailly professed ignorance or innocence: "not belonging to any faction, nor in touch with any intrigue."[41] Yet, on the following day, the accustomed prophecy arrived at Chaillot: "Don't you know the rumor that's going around? They say you will be Prévôt des Marchands."[42] In the quaint nomenclature of that time, this meant Lord Mayor, the largely ceremonial role of the leader of the bourgeoisie of Paris. But the Tiers was in the process of becoming the nation, and on 14 July there could be no turning back.

According to Bailly's own account, 15 July was the day on which his peace of mind ended: "Though I have had shining days and moments of satisfaction, I have not been happy since."[43] This day opened at Versailles with a delegation of deputies to the royal presence. The king announced to the delegates: "I am inseparable from the nation; I place my trust in you."[44] The monarch then received the applause of the people, while the band of his Swiss Guards touchingly played the melody "Où peut-on être mieux qu'au sein de sa famille?" In Paris, in the wake of the Bastille episode, the 407 designated electors and other patriotic elements were preparing a transfer of power. The victorious procession from Versailles arrived at the Hôtel de Ville amid tumults of cheering. When the crowd quieted, there was the inevitable and interminable eloquence, in praise of Paris, in praise of the nation, in praise of the king, "father of his subjects." Lally-Tollendal seduced his auditors and received a crown of laurel; the archbishop proclaimed a Te Deum; Liancourt announced the king's authorization of a bourgeois militia. As the meeting gave signs of breaking up, Lafayette was made commander of the Paris National Guard by acclamation. Then, as the *procès-verbal* continues: "At the same instant every voice rose to proclaim M. Bailly Prévôt des Marchands. A single voice was heard to say: not Prévôt des Marchands, but mayor of Paris. And by general acclamation all those present repeated: yes, mayor of Paris."[45] It is reported that Bailly was greatly shaken, and wept. His own account virtually reproduces the experience of 12 May: "I stammered . . . I naively thought I could be Prévôt des Marchands, with the title of mayor of Paris. . . . I was enticed by the honor, without appreciating the burden. Had I known, I would have tried to refuse."[46] Bailly also thought that he would have created a bad impression by refusing. But the acclaim soon charmed him. Orphans applauded him as he passed the Enfants-Trouvés: "their pure voices seemed to add a heavenly element to the blessings of the multitude. . . . I would have liked to hug them; I made myself a promise to improve their lot."[47] The next day, when the conquering hero arrived in Versailles, Madame Bailly was "mortally anxious" and "not very satisfied" by his new honor.[48]

Bailly did not regard his *viva voce* designation as mayor legitimate until it had been duly ratified by the sixty districts of Paris. This appeal to the districts presaged forthcoming jurisdictional battles between the neighborhoods and the municipality during his tenure and far into the Revolution. But for the moment there was no friction displayed in the summons by the provisional legislature of Paris (the 407 electors) to the districts.[49] Lafayette's nomination as chief of the National Guard was handled in a similar fashion. The enthusiasm of the districts fortified

Bailly's confidence. Praise flowed in by letter and by delegation. For example, Prévost de Saint-Lucien of the district of Sainte-Elizabeth bestowed the following encomium on 22 July: "All [the citizens] know, as well as cultured Europe (*l'Europe littéraire*), that a lively and fruitful imagination, deep and elegant learning, a pure and flowery style, a natural eloquence in your writings, as well as in your speeches, long ago gained you entry to the leading academies of France. . . . But what [most] excites their respect and kindles their love is that real, noble, masculine courage you have displayed in the most critical circumstances." Bailly's academic reputation was now seconded by a solid respect for his civic bravery. Plaudits came from other municipalities that had experienced lesser Bastilles; "you have," one letter from Pont-à-Mousson declared, "just carried through, in a seemingly effortless way, a revolution that will hardly be believed by our grand-nephews."[50] Undoubtedly this flattery convinced Bailly that he was suited to be something more than a mere Prévôt des Marchands.

On 17 July Louis XVI prudently journeyed to Paris to acknowledge the new municipal administration and to receive its homage. Bailly, accompanied by three hundred deputies, met the monarch at Chaillot, where he presented the keys to the city and "spoke with the fullness of the heart." "Sire," he proclaimed, "I bring to Your Majesty the keys of the good city of Paris; they are the same ones that were presented to Henri IV: he had reconquered his people, but now it is the people who have reconquered their king."[51] Though Bailly could speak bluntly, as a bourgeois to a king, kingship was for him an abiding principle of good order. The "Henriolatry" of his speech (a philosophe theme) gives an accurate clue to Bailly's political preference: a condominium of the hereditary representative of the nation and the talents of the nation, excluding the drones, the reactionaries, and the ignorant. In his speech of 6 June Bailly had said: "Sire, your faithful commons will never forget what they owe to their king. They will never forget the natural alliance of throne and people against the diverse aristocracies. . . ."[52] This was formulaically sincere, but also disingenuous. For Bailly was an accredited member of one of those aristocracies. Still, at this time, he felt that his views accurately reflected the universal welfare, hence his constant claim to neutrality and objectivity. He took immense pride in the National Assembly, seeing it as a sort of superacademy speaking for the nation. The condescension of Versailles angered him. Writing of the reaction to the oath of the Jeu de Paume, he grumbled: "You simply do not address men who are the chosen and elite of the nation, enlightened by the great advances of human knowledge . . . with language suitable only for an ignorant multitude."[53] The Ministry was shockingly unaware of the quality of the men with whom it was doing business.

Another indicator of Bailly's politics is his interpretation of the "rights" of the nation. Like so many others, Bailly had his own project for a declaration of rights; its tenor is well expressed as follows: "Surely it is a very lovely philosophical idea to base the constitution on the declaration of the rights of man; but these metaphysical ideas lead the multitude astray more than they enlighten it. It is a way of isolating man and making him forget that he is surrounded by his fellow beings. If you teach him his rights before his duties, you are setting the stage for abuses of liberty and for individual despotism."[54] He criticized the final Declaration on the same grounds.[55] Unadulterated popular sovereignty also worried him. Although "at the moment when a nation recovers its rights, it has complete exercise of them . . . what about prudence? We need to know the forces pro and con. One has the right to want everything; but in wanting everything, might one not lose everything? . . ."[56] Amid his ardors, Bailly began to sound the note of pessimism. "The assembly," he recalled, referring to the violence of July 1789, "rightly looked on disorder as an obstacle to its work."[57] Early political societies, like the Club Breton, disturbed the national solidarity.[58] Bailly attributed the "grande peur" in part to the fear of good citizens, but also to "brigands . . . set in motion by those who wished to precipitate the revolution."[59]

Not only did Bailly open a Pandora's box of administrative anarchy when he consented to become chief municipal officer of a semi-ungovernable city, but he was in constant suspicion of a plot to drive the Revolution leftward and out of control. He was convinced that from 14 July on "there was an invisible motor . . . not satisfied by the destruction of despotism and the gain of liberty. . . . It must have had many agents, and, in order to have devised and followed through [its] abominable plan, there must have been a deep mind at work and plenty of money."[60] Bailly never directly identified the "mind." Was it the Duc d'Orléans? Bailly records only one meeting with the Duc on 27 June for some routine affairs; he had then "no suspicion of the maneuvers . . . that would be attributed to him."[61] Or was it Mirabeau, who tried very hard to push Bailly out of his job and have it for himself?[62] Could he have had some other plot in mind? Here are Bailly's words relative to late August 1789: ". . . enough had been done against the arbitrary monarchy. But many people, then in hiding, had no wish to stop there." Factions existed: against the constitution; against the monarchy; and against the person of Louis XVI. "All acted from different points of view but with combined effect."[63] The most permanently dangerous of these factions, and the most inclusive, seems to have been the *republican*.

In Bailly's view, the republican plot was incarnate in Brissot's plan for the organization of the municipality, presented to the Assembly of Paris on 12 August and published in the *Patriote français* (no. 16) two days later. Brissot envisaged extensive municipal and provincial self-government, local powers distinct from those of the National Assembly, but united by common rules of administration, "the *federal* tie uniting all the parts of a vast country." This suggested the eighteenth-century truism that large republics had to be federations. Bailly fulminated: "why . . . the word *federal*? I ask if the result of this plan would not be a large democratic (*populaire*) state, divided into thirty or more republics, themselves divided into 44,000 small republics [i.e., the communes], and all united by a federal connection?"[64] Bailly was a moderate centralizer who preferred a more descending scheme of city government; he saw the city as a microcosm of the regime. "I believe I can conclude," he wrote, "that the republican faction already existed and had for a long time, because its plans were already formed. . . ."[65] Brissot would eventually be caught by crossfire from the centralizers of the Left. In 1792 he wrote, perhaps disingenuously, that republicanism "is a phantom created by the moderates to set their faction against the patriots. . . . The *enragés* . . . would ask for another king if they could dethrone the constitutional king."[66]

More than republicanism was involved. Though Bailly's entry to the Hôtel de Ville had been widely applauded, he began to cultivate enemies once his thankless work began. For some of his detractors he was an academic snob; for others, a creature of Lafayette, or a hidden ultra, or simply an incompetent. Brissot, who hated academies, saw little connection between Bailly's intellectual prominence and the public agenda. He castigated him as "a mannekin whom others move at their pleasure" and summarized: "Bailly, the man of the Old Regime, could not be the man of the Revolution. Never had there been such a well-certified political booby in such high office."[67] Camille Desmoulins had already roasted Bailly for his civic ostentation, "his carriage . . . mounted guards . . . lackeys in livery . . . opulence of furniture . . . prodigality of dining."[68] Bailly defended his pomp, as distinguished from his personal habits: "the leading official of the greatest city in the world should . . . make a show of brilliance around him . . . as symbol (*dépositaire*) of its dignity."[69] In other words, the mayor was a mini-monarch of the constitutional order, a bourgeois and elective king of his domain, something of a doge.

Bailly had enormous administrative problems in a time of mounting political disorder, and often had his hands tied by the new shape of municipal government. He had entered a transitional situation lacking precedents. For several months his jurisdictions tended to coexist and collide with the royal ministry and, thereafter, with the National Assembly. Also, his powers and functions as mayor were initially quite undetermined and provisional; the authority to give Paris an official political status rested with the Constituent, which dallied with the issue until 27 June 1790.[70] It was almost impossible, except case by case, to specify the division between legislative and executive initiatives in the municipality. Several bodies of competence were in play. The first, and least nettlesome, was the departmental council under the presidency of the Duc de la Rochefoucauld. Then there was Bailly's municipal administration—the executive—which came to birth in a period when sovereign legislative supremacy was a keystone of political doctrine. It was Bailly's function of *presiding*, rather than of *acting* independently, that gave his office a certain consistency: "Bailly's influence did not stem from any independent authority which he was able to exercise as mayor, but from the prestige that was his as head of the Commune *and* from his position as presiding officer of the assemblies and departments in the municipal government."[71] These included a general council, a municipal council, and a municipal bureau (i.e., executive committee of the previous). Bailly could veto their decrees, but the veto could be reviewed and overridden.[72]

At the outset there was no semblance of a regular municipal body in Paris except the 407 electors who, three months earlier, had made the academician their chief deputy. Tradition dictated that this assembly dissolve itself, having fulfilled its duty of *cahiers* and elections. But there was nothing to replace it. However, on 30 July the communal assembly, no doubt encouraged by Mirabeau, ordered these electors to disband.[73] It was this "Commune Provisoire," chosen separately from the districts, that clashed constantly with Bailly over both forms and substantive issues, notably when it accepted Brissot's plan for municipal organization and forwarded it to the National Assembly, with slight modifications. Paris had also sixty "districts" or primary assemblies (later reduced to forty-eight "sections" by the National Assembly's reorganization decree of 27 June 1790). These were presumably the sovereign source of the legislature and committees of the Commune, being closest to the people. Failing to make his views regarding office, administration, and powers prevail with the Commune, Bailly appealed on 30 August 1789 to the districts for support, suggesting that they, too, should compose a reorganization plan and create an executive council over which he would preside. This was decentralization for the sake of centralization: Brissot and the Communal Assembly were indignant; but Condorcet and the advanced journal *Révolutions de Paris* were favorable.[74]

Bailly's tactic was dictated by prudence, not any passion for direct democracy. The bitter fight over jurisdiction lasted from August 1789 till a year later, when Bailly was fortified by a popular election in which he received 12,550 out of 14,010 votes cast.[75] But although the Assembly's membership of three hundred was renewed in September 1789, Bailly faced almost the same opponents as he had a month earlier. The municipal rupture was exacerbated by the role of the districts and of the National Assembly.[76] In effect, three theories were in competition: Bailly's notion of a presiding and countervailing executive at the top of a centralized pyramid; the Commune's view, which, attacking the monarchical character of the previous scheme, favored conciliar and representative, but not direct, government; and, finally, the doctrine of the districts, emphasizing their sovereign right to assemble and to intervene by petition or direct action in the affairs of the central administration. These ideas faced off during the entire ascendant course of the Revolution, with significant changes of spokesmen and motives: a secret of the Jacobin mastery of the Year II would be to combine them all in a single political juggernaut.

When Bailly found cooperation with the Communal Assembly unattainable, he clarified his views to the districts: "The powers of the city of Paris, under the authority of the King and the National Assembly, are just like those of the kingdom. . . . The legislative power resides in you, Messieurs; you have the right to make the local laws. . . . The executive power resides in the municipal administration . . . which should be in constant activity and never halted or hindered in its course [and therefore] the least divided and the most concentrated. . . ." The latter asked the district leaders to give "advice" to the mayor's "collaborators." It ended on a familiar cadence: "I have no ambition to command; I felt much more at ease . . . when all I had to do was obey. . . . [but] we must vest in a chief a superiority of influence that preserves our unity."[77] This neatly summarizes the monarchical view of city government.

Finally, it should be mentioned that, friends as they were, the close presence of Lafayette made Bailly vaguely uncomfortable. "I did not command him," Bailly writes; "I did not know that this was my right; but my confidence in him could not have been better placed."[78] Enthusiasm for Lafayette was constant because of "his talents, his name . . . his likable personal qualities," whereas often "the civilian chief was forgotten . . . no enthusiasm for him . . . [only] truth and justice *sans accompagnements*."[79] In praising Bailly's "loyalty, integrity, humanity," Lafayette does not hesitate to vaunt his own superior popularity and scope of action.[80] Commenting on Lafayette's inclusion in a meeting to discuss the organization of the Paris administration on 25 July 1789, Bailly observes caustically that he should not have been there, "for he is its instrument and should be ruled by it."[81] Still, on all important issues they stood together. On his part, Lafayette writes that their common enemies "made unbelievable efforts to set them apart, but in vain."[82] When Lafayette retired as commander of the Paris National Guard on 8 October 1791, Bailly spoke as follows: "I dare to hope that from time to time you will remember your former colleague, who was always united with you and who, since we shared the defense of Paris together, now asks you to share the feelings you will preserve for the city."[83]

As we have seen, Bailly waged jurisdictional war with other municipal powers; he sensed a republican conspiracy enveloping Paris and the nation; and he soon faced sharp criticisms, especially concerning his competence. Shortly before he left office in late 1791, a pamphlet echoed this charge: "Probably M. Bailly is the man most often at sea (*étranger*) in the administration. He has that in common with scholars who don't understand anything or who don't want to understand anything about politics."[84] "Get a good rest and reap your harvest," the critic advised. Bailly was presumed venal *and* incompetent. However, by the time this brochure was composed, he was being taxed not so much with incapacity as with sanguinary treason. In point of fact, he depleted his small savings while in office. And even the unsympathetic Aulard concludes that "no serious charge was lodged against his administration."[85]

Long before, the radical leaven of the Revolution had begun its work in the districts. At first Mirabeau had fished in these waters;[86] but later Bailly was increasingly harassed by a more plebeian leadership. When, in early 1791, a delegation from the section of Gravilliers attacked him at the Jacobins, he chided them about rumors set loose by "the enemies of the Revolution . . . frightened by the public power you have formed. . . ."[87] This was not his only altercation with the sections.[88] Bailly deeply resented these attacks, for he felt that he had battled for the most critical needs of his city. His early correspondence with Necker is "nothing but a long series of painful observations regarding the supply of Paris in grain, in wood, in charcoal, and concerning the poverty of the municipal treasury."[89] Necker grew weary of all these demands.[90] But Bailly exerted himself resolutely to see that Paris was fed and financed under his administration. Despite mistakes, it was a shining achievement.

From late summer of 1789, Bailly was deeply worried about political agitation, especially in the Palais-Royal, which "deserved our most serious attention because we were not in the dark (*nous n'ignorions pas*) about a formidable faction, working for [. . .], in the name of [. . .]."[91] But the lines between political boldness and lawlessness were blurred. Bailly and Lafayette had an incessant exchange of correspondence, occasionally testy, about the effectiveness and decorum of the National Guard.[92] Above all, one is struck by the rhythm of law and order, the play of the seasons. On 6 February 1790, Bailly wrote to Lafayette: "I think, Monsieur le Marquis, that the days are getting longer and it seems that we have nothing more to fear by way of agitation or insurrection on the part of the enemies of liberty."[93] Thus revenue could be saved by cutting back on street lighting. But, on 21 October, "the long nights, Monsieur, mean that we are entering a period where we must take all precautions for public safety."[94] Patrols and protection adjusted to the alternance of dark and light, with crime and revolution mingled in the shadows.

Bailly was not spared by the royalist Right. An exhortation running to 176 pages taxed him with his famous statement: *Ne souhaitons jamais de révolution.* It urged him to "*become yourself again and be the ardent apostle of your own doctrine, just as you have been its deserter.*"[95] An earlier pamphlet had lashed him for his part in transporting the king to Paris. "Throw yourselves at the feet of your king, French people; you still have time," the author advised. But even in 1791 Bailly was not disposed to do this; he was respectfully reproaching the monarch for his mistakes and evil counselors. On 18 April he forwarded an admonitory document to the Ministry, signed by, among others, La Rochefoucauld, Sieyès, and Talleyrand.[96] And in a letter of his own, dated 21 April, he implored: "Sire, we pray you, send from your presence those men who, veiling their frustrated vanity beneath hypocritical fears, trouble your frank and loyal soul and incur the honest distrust of a people jealous of the heart and the confidence of its king."[97] These and other documents substantially refute the charge of the revolutionaries that Bailly was involved in the plotting of the flight to Varennes. In 1791 he could well doubt that Paris had reconquered its king.

However, it was the radical press and, increasingly, the sections and clubs that thrashed Bailly, as well as Lafayette, for a catalog of offenses, from early 1790 on. We have already noted Desmoulins's disapproval. On 25 May 1790, Marat expostulated: "When a man of letters, a savant, a member of the three leading academies of France, a deputy of the National Assembly, is capable of betraying his trust and plundering the state, in whom . . . ought we to place our confidence?"[98] Of course the "ami du peuple" despised academicians with a jealous rancor. A journalist of the *Orateur du Peuple*, writing just after the renewal of the Commune, had come down on the same point: "[At the installation] M. Bailly's speech was drawn entirely from the old dictionary of the academy, except for three or four mistakes in French. He went wild over the *goodness of the king*; and he dared, under the reign of liberty, to say—this phrase probably picked up from the old bowing and scraping (*dans quelque coin de l'ancienne police*)—*we obey the men we love*! But mark my words, M. Bailly, since 14 July the French no longer obey men, they obey the law!"[99] Marat hurled anathemas constantly in the *Ami du Peuple* after the year 1791 had turned.[100] Two examples will suffice: "Make no mistake that Bailly and Mottié [Lafayette], those base servants of the monarch, those consummate hypocrites (*tartufes*), authentic models of villainy vomited from hell to achieve your ruin, are at the head of the conspirators."[101] "The Ami du Peuple will know no peace until Bailly and Mottié have been brought face to face in public with their spies, and until these monsters, who are both spies and robbers, have paid for their murders on the wheel."[102] On 26 May 1791, Marat asked for the heads of Bailly, Lafayette, and their municipal subordinates in case the royal family should succeed in escaping from the Tuileries.[103]

Such incitements to violence and murder against the Paris authorities came within less than a year of Bailly's convincing victory at the polls, with France at peace, and more than two years before the flowering of the Terror. The radicalization of Paris bred on hunger, impatience, rumor, deception, and an inchoate spirit of revenge. But it was also heavily fueled by a self-appointed intelligentsia that the Old Regime had humiliated or driven into dark corners. Deficient in what would later be called *moeurs républicaines*, the "member of the Three Academies" was already suffering his path to the scaffold to be traced.

11. The People's Massacre

At this pivotal point in our account, the sequence of argument needs to be restated. Bailly, as a "member of the Three Academies" and royal pensioner, was no less an aristocrat of the Old Regime than many members of the privileged estates who made their bow to politics during the earlier, more liberal phases of the Revolution; the status of the intellectuals, in relationship to the *grands*, had changed conspicuously since 1750. Unlike most of the *gens de lettres*, he had stepped forward. But his political instincts and inclinations were moderated by his prior elite experience. His style of politics was indebted to his natural reverence for the monarchical institution and to the lessons of statesmanship gleaned in an academic environment. While believing in enlightenment, he was far from worshiping the people. He was both a political product of the usufructory model and a politician well bound to consensualist convictions and rhetoric. His administration of Paris reflected his political understanding. Both it and the distinct markings of his previous career made him suspect to the radicals of the lumpen-intelligentsia and, by 1791, a foe to be crushed. Marat and others were asking for his head well before July 1791. It is plausible, on the grounds just mentioned, that they would finally have had it even if the Champ de Mars episode had never taken place, although it is obviously impossible to prove this. Although one might imagine that Bailly's academic aloofness and detachment, his willingness to trust scientific proof and experiment, would have served him well in a political confrontation, and that the failure of that training betrayed him, my contention here is that the opposite is more likely to have been the case. For science—including the science of administration—was as much to be defended against the passions of unthinking mobs as against the conceivable errors of the investigator. Priestley's scientific equipment was destroyed by a mob in England. Bailly could not countenance a similar fate for his administrative apparatus: rightly or wrongly, he acted like a scientist defending his instruments. He also acted like an academician defending his prerogatives and amour-propre: the two cases melt into each other, and yet are distinct. The Jacobin onslaught on the academy at large will be described in the next chapter.

When Bailly was brought to trial in November 1793, he was convicted on two counts: (1) connivance with Lafayette and others in the escape of the royal family from the Tuileries; and (2) responsibility for the fusillade that cost the lives of about fifty Parisians on 17 July 1791. The first charge appears to be mere fabrication. But since the second one is very serious, we are obliged to examine that incident in considerable detail. We shall not of course hold that Jacobin-style logic was faulty in convicting Bailly for the massacre or that it was not the immediate and sufficient reason for his execution. We shall instead show that, although there were extenuating circumstances in the deplorable event, it was entirely consistent with the portrait we have drawn and the political fatalities of Bailly's position. The Bailly of the Champ de Mars remains inexplicable if we are not familiar with the Bailly of the Louvre, of the academies, and of the *Histoire de l'Astronomie*. Our method compels us to dwell more than cursorily on certain episodes (in the case of d'Orléans, the *journées d'octobre*; in the case of Custine, the June–July events in the Army of the North; later, in the case of Malesherbes, the coup of Maupeou). The Champ de Mars is a moment requiring careful scrutiny.

Bailly was mayor of Paris when, on 20–21 June 1791, despite the precautions of his constitutionalist jailers, the king and his immediate family fled the palace, were apprehended at Varennes, and returned to the capital under guard. As chief municipal officer he was intimately concerned with the decisions that had to be made when the monarch was found missing. There is no evidence that he helped the monarch to flee; indeed it was calamitous to him, and to Lafayette, that this should happen. It is also very likely that the "member of the Three Academies" had no part in Feuillant designs for a moderate monarchy in the period of the king's suspension. "After the return from Varennes," he writes, "up to the presentation of the constitution [13 September 1791], I never appeared at the Tuileries. I made that my rule (*loi*), and I swear that during the whole time I saw neither Louis nor his widow. . . . At the moment when he was suspended from office all [our] relations were equally suspended; I had no right or reason to visit him."[1] Bailly received only unfavorable mention in the famous papers of the "armoire de fer," opened just before the king's trial in December 1792, and he seems not to have been party to the reconciliation of Lafayette with the Lameth brothers and their faction in June 1791.[2] Such entanglements would still remain tributary to Bailly's major public crime, the "massacre of the Champ de Mars," to be described below.

Already, in early June, the leftist press—the *Révolutions de Paris*, the *Ami du Peuple*, the *Journal Universel*, the *Orateur du Peuple*, and even Brissot's *Patriote Français*—was arousing the people to insurrection.[3] François Robert's *Mercure National* and, in a more speculative vein, Nicolas de Bonneville's *Bouche de Fer* had been urging the republic for several weeks.[4] The political positions of a new stage of the Revolution were coalescing rapidly under the pressure of events and over the issue of the restitution of the king. What has been called the embryo of a "Tory party,"[5] led by Duport and Barnave (Mirabeau having died in April), had been forming since May. Its principles were: (1) a bicephalous constitutional monarchy with a strong legislature, libertarian but elitist in character; (2) a closure of further revolutionary action; and (3) the political monopoly of the possessing classes. The king's flight gravely jeopardized this project. Yet the constitutionalists had no realistic alternative but to recapture Louis, pardon him, reform him, and promote him to titular head of their party.

Opposing these moderates, a new democratic Left, uncoordinated but spirited, was taking shape. Its bulwark was the *plebs*, but the plebs could not have moved without vanguard direction.[6] Their most audacious rhetoric came from the radical press and the Cordeliers, less frequently from the Jacobins. There were a handful of cooler, more meticulous spokesmen in the Assembly itself: Robespierre, Grégoire, Prieur, Buzot, Reubell, Pétion. The king's evasion gave these forces redoubled energy and fury; but they did not have, or share, a coherent plan for the new regime. Their justified suspicions that they—or the populations they addressed—were being excluded from the body politic promoted in them a reverse wave of self-righteousness: the monarchical constitution was null without even being promulgated; *they* were the sovereigns. A hypothesized regency for the Duc d'Orléans was regarded by some as a kind of halfway house between traditionalism and democratic novelty: we have already noted the failure of Laclos's plot. Mobilized in the advanced clubs and newspapers, the democrats formed a kind of antistate: this opposition could easily be perceived as anarchic. That such an anarchy could be mastered by a Montagnard executive under the aegis of Terror would have surprised most astute observers in 1791. Indeed, it was not evident until July 1793 that this could be the case.

In July 1791 these radicals—i.e., the left Jacobins, journalists like Marat, Bonneville, and Fréron, and militants of the Cordeliers and some of the sections of Paris (who would be thrown into temporary disarray by the Champ de Mars violence and its aftermath)—had several major points of contact: (1) they wished a change of dynasty or, more likely, form of government; (2) they wanted Louis XVI deposed and judged; (3) many also wished for the dissolution of the National Assembly; (4) they wished equal political rights for virtually all adult male citizens; and (5) they believed that effective national sovereignty resided foremost in the primary assemblies, closest to and most representative of the people at large.[7] The incendiary democrats had no axiomatic theory of violence to achieve their ends. Yet some of their leaders had already preached violence. Marat had written: "Today you have stupidly let your implacable enemies gather strength, and maybe it will be necessary to strike down five or six thousand; but even if it were twenty thousand, there is not a moment to lose."[8] And Fournier l'Héritier ("l'Américain") had a plan for the Cordeliers Club: ". . . to base a respectable and sacred form of government on republicanism . . . to beat down the idol of royalty and deal in the same way with its dirty hangers-on . . . sounding the general alarm, capturing Bailly and Lafayette, jailing them so as to try them, and making them pay with their heads for the guarantee they swore to us about the perjured veto."[9]

Bailly was essentially the instrument of the constitutionalists and later, inadvertently, their scapegoat. But the astronomer–mayor, probably a more fervent royalist than they, was not a nincompoop; he did not exactly fall into the trap of the Champ de Mars with his eyes shut. Bailly was sick and absent from his job for several weeks in early 1791.[10] His glory had become a burden. Nothing suggests that he aspired to any power behind the throne; rather, he longed for a peaceful retirement to his house in Chaillot. Yet he was reflexively inclined to quell disorder if the national interest as determined by the Assembly so dictated.[11] The radical press was now attacking him constantly. After the flight to Varennes, Fréron had thundered: "Lafayette lives? And Bailly still breathes? O Parisians, you are without spirit and energy. . . ."[12] Given a sufficient excuse and the approval of the lawmakers, Bailly could forsake his natural prudence and march behind the drum to a confrontation. He was not willing to be an *homme de lettres* who "hesitated." Yet his academic background poorly prepared him for negotiations that might have avoided battle with the plebs.

Fear of the consequences of democratic agitation pressured the Assembly toward a restoration of the monarchy. The national holiday of 14 July was approaching, with its two models: the violence of the Bastille (1789) and the fraternity of the Festival of the Federation (1790). Given the circumstances, a reenactment of fraternity was out of the question: Lafayette's white horse would have to be left in the stable. Thus, on 13 July, the Assembly received a report blaming the king's departure on the machinations of Marshal de Bouillé, now safely in emigration. Competitive petitions demanding that the status of the monarchy be decided by the primary assemblies of the nation or by the regular process of abdication were circulating.[13] France became a monarchy again. This was considerably more than a holding action, for it abrogated the legality of the antimonarchist petitions. Under law it was impermissible to petition against a decree of the Assembly (the right of petition was, moreover, reserved to individuals, not clubs). Yet, as can be imagined, this hasty tactic, declaring the king inviolable, only served to overheat the *demos* and to set it against the Assembly. On 15 July about four thousand demonstrators gathered on the Champ de Mars, vexed and angry, threatening to march against the deputies. Various plans of action circulated among the clubs. Cooler heads, among them Robespierre, estimating the balance of forces, advised caution for the present. The leaders of the constitutional majority faced the contingency of violence. As the American ambassador, Gouverneur Morris, wrote the same evening: "A good smart action would, I think, be useful rather than pernicious."[14] At this point, the moderates quit the Jacobins, reducing the club to its hard-core radical membership. However, the democratic leaders and the several thousand followers they commanded were determined to make a show of negation the following day on the Champ de Mars, assembling, presumably after a parade through Paris, to sign a petition authored by Robert of the Cordeliers, demanding not simply the judgment of Louis XVI by the primary assemblies but the institution of a republic.[15]

Before proceeding to the fatal events of 17 July it will be useful to summarize:

1. The Assembly committed a deceit (or, if one prefers, an act of raison d'état) on the nation in exculpating Louis XVI for his act of flight. It did this in the conscious attempt to preserve a constitutional monarchy and to stifle further revolutionary action.

2. The hasty decision of the Assembly was stimulated by the fear of an extension of the Revolution by the sections and clubs, roused by the neo-Roman rhetoric of the press: "When the Romans, the first free people, saw that the country was in danger and that the interests of all were at stake, they gathered in a popular assembly (*comme peuple*); the senators [i.e., the Constituent Assembly] made it the order of business in their meetings (*venaient prendre dans leurs assemblées*) to take up matters that [the people] assigned them (*dictaient*); never did the Senate reach its own conclusion (*prononçait seul*) about such important interests."[16] There are about three hundred signatures on this petition; Hébert's is prominent. A plebs without educated leadership could not have struck such a tone.

3. The form of the petition of the Champ de Mars, which obtained approximately six thousand signatures on 17 July, was illegal, for it not only contravened a decision of the National Assembly declaring Louis XVI inviolable, but it also called for the judgment and deposing of the

king. However, the gathering of the petitioners received an ambiguous sanction from the government.[17] They obviously believed that their action had been declared legal.

4. The National Assembly called the tune: it was now the executive as well as the legislative branch. Greatly disturbed by the popular demonstrations in mass, it had replied with police measures and stringent warnings to the municipality of Paris. Bailly and his colleagues responded to government directives that pressured the city to act in the national interest as defined by the legislature. Whatever our judgment of Bailly's political sagacity, this obligation can introduce extenuating circumstances for his action. It is a critical point on which we are obliged to look at the evidence, even if it was of no consolation to Bailly when the Revolutionary Tribunal processed his death warrant.

The facts of the Champ de Mars are well established, except for two important items: the exact conditions under which the National Guard opened fire on the crowd, and the number of deaths and injuries caused by the discharge of their bullets. There can be general agreement on the following points.

First, the Cordeliers, who were the impresarios of the rally to sign the antimonarchist petition, though intending no violence, still hoped that their gesture would have wider repercussions in the city and in other parts of France. They attacked the Assembly directly by urging it to disband, for their petition spoke of "convoking a new constituent body to proceed in a truly national manner with the judging of the guilty party [the king] and, especially, with the replacement and organization of a new executive power."[18]

Second, the leaders of the constitutional party, while not fearing an immediate armed insurrection, had taken steps to isolate the gathering from such trouble spots as the Bastille and the Place de la Grève. After all, Lafayette and others had been threatened with death.

Third, it is plausible that, in the words of Louis Blanc, "even while rejecting a coldly calculated plot . . . the leaders of the constitutional party wanted a *coup d'Etat* and lost no opportunity to strike."[19] Their whole tone of discourse before and after the incident reveals neither surprise nor shock, only temerity and self-congratulation, followed by repressive measures.

Fourth, although, as we shall see, the point has been subject to dispute, the National Assembly was sending strong signals to the municipality and the department of Paris that it wished all subversion and disorder squelched and the ringleaders prosecuted.

Fifth, the Paris National Guard, which would become the instrument of the repression, was hostile to the plebs. Although the radical press made concerted efforts to deflect the allegiance of the Guard[20] and although Chaumette would later claim that "more than two thousand national guardsmen of all the battalions of Paris and its outskirts . . . signed [the petition],"[21] the forces of order sent from the Hôtel de Ville to the site of the carnage treated the demonstrators as enemies.

Sixth, the perceptions of the Hôtel de Ville regarding the evolution of the situation on the Champ de Mars were garbled, despite the dispatch of eyewitness emissaries and the receipt of their reports.

Seventh, much was made by the authorities, in castigating the disorders, of the presence of foreign (i.e., ultraroyalist) agitators and foreign money. This was a theme launched by the Assembly in its precipitous actions of 16 July.[22] But already on 14 July we have the draft of a letter to the National Assembly, presumably by Bailly, recommending a total census of the inhabitants of Paris and stating: ". . . a large number of foreigners have rushed to Paris . . . with different opinions, interests, and motives. . . . If legal surveillance does not allow us to pierce [their designs], it at least authorizes and obliges us to know the numbers and occupations of the nondomiciled persons presently living in Paris."[23] The minutes of the municipality for 17 July refer explicitly to the fear of foreign agitation—"foreigners paid to sow disorder, preach rebellion, proposing to encourage large rallies in the criminal hope of misleading the people"—as an argument to break up public gatherings.[24] But we cannot conclude that in July 1791 the French state was threatened by foreign agitators. The recurrence of this theme leaves little doubt that the moderates were trying to head off the plebs by sowing a little xenophobia.

Finally, Bailly, who believed viscerally in the existence of a republican plot,[25] could be swayed, even counted on, to suspend his scruples if persuaded that the regime itself was in danger, even though the evidence might not be incontrovertible. We sense in the climates of opinion of mid-July 1791 not only a great quarrel over the meaning and benefits of liberty, but also a spectacle of two sides rushing toward a confrontation, the one seemingly haughty and pragmatic, the other steeped in accumulated rancor and self-styled virtue. Fraternity was over and, with it, the ability to speak a common language, to mean the same things with the same words. The politics of elite consultation was coming unraveled; the politics of class struggle was yet to be articulated: a state of war, impoverished by a lack of theoretical guidance, exalted by emotional self-certainty, was coming into being.

By all accounts, 17 July 1791 was, like 6 October 1789, prolonged beyond the normal limits of a day. By nine o'clock in the morning petitioners were arriving at the Champ de Mars to record their protest at the "altar of the fatherland." Within an hour or so, two men—believed counterrevolutionaries; impudent voyeurs, according to Rudé and Reinhard[26]—were killed and their heads placed on pikes. This news, received without clarification by the Paris Municipal Council, which had been in session for some time, caused that body to delegate three of its members, Le Roulx, Regnault, and Hardy, to go instantly to Gros-Caillou, accompanied by a battalion of the National Guard, to ascertain the facts and "to employ all means within the limits of prudence to disperse the gathering, and even, in the case that murders have really taken place, to announce martial law and display armed force."[27]

Bailly used the opening part of the municipal session of 17 July to brief his administration on the subject of gatherings and seditious activities during the previous days. He reviewed the assignment of patrols and commended the loyalty and zeal of the National Guard. In view of the precautions taken by the city government and measures which it was in a position to take, he felt that "public tranquillity would not be bothered."[28] The Council then passed a resolution to broadcast to the citizens of Paris by all available means a prohibition against gatherings in public places. It was at this point, at 11 A.M., that the two murders at the Champ de Mars were announced.

Bailly and his colleagues had been counseled to preach severity by the National Assembly. Its temporary presiding officer Treilhard (later a Conventional of a different stripe) had addressed the following letter to the mayor of Paris on the same day:

> Word has gotten round, Monsieur, that the enemies of public welfare, whose audacity grows each day, have been ceaselessly stirring up new disorders and that at the Champ de Mars their perfidious orders have led to criminal excesses. The National Assembly has charged me with warning you so that you can immediately initiate the most secure and rigorous measures to halt these disorders and to identify the plotters (*auteurs*). I have no reason to doubt that you will hasten to conform with the wishes (*intentions*) of the Assembly and give it a precise rendering of all you have found out as well as your actions for the restoration of order and public tranquillity.[29]

Regarding this letter, to all appearance strongly worded, Aulard inquires rhetorically: "Was that conceivably a formal order to proclaim martial law without further inquiry?"[30] Yet it surely placed a grave burden of decision on the Paris municipality. This text alone will not suffice. In another archive we come upon the unsigned draft of what seems to be the same letter, dated a day earlier, 16 July 1791, in slightly higher-pitched language:

> The National Assembly has been astonished to learn that one of
> its decrees [declaring Louis XVI inviolable] has provided the
> occasion for a few provocateurs (*quelques séditieux*) to seek to fool the
> people and disturb the public peace: movements we shall always
> consider insufferable (*toujours répréhensibles*) become criminal when
> they rise in resistance to the law. Unswervingly attached to the
> support of the Constitution, resolved to implement (*faire respecter*)
> the laws which can alone assure property, safety, liberty, and
> the happiness of the people, the National Assembly, wanting no
> reticence in the face of such disorders (*ne veut pas que l'on ferme les
> yeux sur de tels désordres*), commands you to employ all means
> granted you by the Constitution to repress them, to identify and
> punish their instigators, and to protect the peace of the citizens from
> all assault.[31]

A separate but companion draft reads: "The Constitution has placed in your hands the pursuit of crimes that disturb the public peace. . . . Record these crimes. Hunt down the instigators, so that the laws may punish those who have dared to take them lightly (*méconnaître*), and recall to their duties those who might have been tempted to follow their example."[32]

These drafts of Treilhard are indicative of the mood of the Assembly's contacts with the city. It is reflected in the tenor of the minutes of the extraordinary session of the Paris Council held on 16 July, where Bailly reported a "fermentation" that had "the criminal hope of causing disorder, so as to attack and overthrow the Constitution."[33] Nowhere in the Treilhard documents is the proclamation of martial law specifically recommended. However, the euphemism "all means granted to you by the Constitution to repress them" would seem to cover the case. Bailly was not reluctant about a show of force, but he and his Council acted within a boundary of superior orders. This is the defense that Bailly put forward in anticipation of his trial: "The municipality could not forget that if the law expressly made it responsible for maintaining public order, it had been even more specifically charged by both the speech given the night before by the President of the National Assembly and by his letter of the morning after to take rigorous measures."[34] Thus, still according to Bailly, "if there are guilty parties, they can therefore only be the representatives of the nation."[35]

Toward one o'clock in the afternoon, the three commissioners dispatched by the Paris authorities encountered Lafayette at the Champ de Mars. There were only a few hundred people milling around. They were signing the petition and listening to the oratory of Peyre, the chief of the Cordeliers, and La Rivière, the delegate of the Jacobins. The approach of the guardsmen worried them. There was some fraternization between the people and the Guard; but some stone-throwing was causing anxious moments. Rumors were spreading, exaggerating the situation for those who were not on the spot.[36]

The Paris commissioners tried to wind down the gathering. Given the orderly comportment of the crowd, its leaders besought the delegates of the city to report this fact to the Hôtel de Ville. Le Roulx, Regnault, and Hardy agreed, but they advised the leaders of the agitation that the crowd must disperse upon signing the petition. Peyre, of the Cordeliers, accepted this compromise, insisting that a delegation of the petitioners accompany the officials back to the Place de la Grève. This request was in turn granted, as well as a fatal concession to allow the dissidents more time to collect signatures. Fatal—for by midafternoon the number of demonstrators had increased about tenfold, to five or six thousand. It seemed that the republicans were having the better of the negotiations with the city authorities. The commissioners were impressed by the fact that calm was being maintained. This discipline of calm encouraged the crowd to swell. Lafayette had withdrawn his troops to the Place des Invalides.

The Champ de Mars—then rebaptised the Champ de la Fédération— was a spacious but dangerous assembly area for a dissenting crowd. Essentially a barren field intended for the maneuvers of the Military School, it was set back from the Seine, bordered by stone-filled ditches, dominated by a commanding slope, and encircled by an iron fence with only five access points. Despite its vastness within, affording freedom of movement to large numbers of people, it was a trap from which no large crowd could escape in a rush. Provocateurs could handily use the terrace above the Altar of the Fatherland to agitate and alarm anyone in their vicinity.

At the Hôtel de Ville, some four miles distant, on the Right Bank, according to the minutes of the Municipal Council, "messengers arrived constantly; their news became more and more disturbing (*inquiétantes*); from minute to minute public peace was being undermined. . . . Already

. . . four persons had been [officially] taken to the Hôtel de Ville, arrested for having thrown stones at the National Guard. One of the rebels . . . had a loaded pistol on him . . . and admitted . . . that he had thrown a heavy stone at an officer of the guard on horseback.''[37] The delegation of the dissidents accompanied the agents of the municipality back to the Hôtel de Ville, even while the crowd was seething and swelling on the Champ de Mars. They arrived about 6 P.M., only to find that the Council, acting on its own uncertain information, had declared "that martial law is to be immediately declared, that the drums should beat the *générale*, that a warning cannon shot should be fired, and that the red flag should be displayed."[38] A replica of this red flag would be ceremoniously burned, over two years later, at the foot of Bailly's scaffold.

The commissioners were "astonished" to see what stringent measures were being prepared.[39] Despite their inability to clear the Champ de Mars, they had concerted their efforts with Lafayette and had left the place in a state of relative calm. They had spent hours in prudent diplomacy and had come back to report this, only to find that the Municipal Council, persuaded by rumor, was preparing an exaggerated riposte. The *procès-verbal* of Le Roulx, Regnault, and Hardy tells us:

> there was a large gathering of men and women on and around the Altar of the Fatherland. We went to the Champ de la Fédération . . . with the general [Lafayette] . . . [where] we received a delegation of citizens. They were members of the Cordeliers Club, but assembled peacefully and unarmed to sign a petition to the National Assembly: we went among them to be assured that this was the case. They promised us that those who signed it would leave immediately. The Guard stayed for security purposes; everything was lawful and fortunately we were not obliged to use any severe measures. Some individuals who insulted the Guard were arrested. The members of the Club are to send a deputation with us to the Municipal Council *as soon as everything is quiet* [my italics]; then we will come back, Messieurs, and make a more detailed report.[40]

Evidently though, the commissioners had not rigorously pressed the issue of disbanding after the petition was signed; nor had the radical leaders sought to impose this promise. Everything was not quiet. By the time Le Roulx, Regnault, and Hardy had returned to the Hôtel de Ville, they were scarcely better informed about the situation than the authorities. Yet theirs was the best advice that Bailly had.

According to other testimony found in the same dossier, a different light is cast on the subject. Leaders of the Cordeliers were stirring the people to reprisal as early as midday. An orator, who had elicited cries of "nous ne voulons plus de Louis XVI," caused his listeners to swear an oath to "perish rather than suffer the least assault on its liberty": "After this, the same person, identifying himself as the president of a club revealed to me by several persons standing close to me as the Cordeliers said: 'Citizens, I must denounce to you a crime against the *sovereignty of the people*, committed by the Comité des Recherches of Monsieur Bailly. . . .' "[41] For the radicals we may presume that there were two motives: achieve the embarrassment, and eventually the capitulation, of moderate authority; do this by means short of violent confrontation and likely defeat. For the authorities also, two motives: contain the insurrection at this point so as to implement the constitutional monarchy; provoke conflict if necessary. However, the three commissioners—and probably Lafayette also, up to a point—regarded their main task as pragmatic compromise and the avoidance of bloodshed.

The crowds on the Champ de Mars had not departed; the Paris authorities were driven to rash action by rumors; and the three commissioners, having been unable to disperse the crowd, failed to impose prudence on the authorities. Through stubborn efforts they managed to get a futile hearing.[42] There is no evidence that Bailly swayed his colleagues to declaring martial law, though he certainly favored it.[43] Probably, without apprehension of dishonor, he was working hand-in-glove with the policies of the National Assembly, becoming, in words used about him in another context, "the interpreter of the dominant faction."[44] He did not shirk the responsibility as chief municipal officer any more than he had hesitated on the occasion of the oath of the Jeu de Paume. The minutes do not record any serious opposition. Bailly marched in the van of the civilians. La Rivière, the Jacobin who had come with the commissioners, threw up his hands: "So that is how a city government is roused against its citizens!"[45] Events were out of control.

At 6:30 P.M. Bailly and the other magistrates set out for the Champ de Mars, preceded by a detachment of infantry with three cannons, at whose head the red flag of martial law was displayed. The procession took over an hour to reach its destination, pausing in Gros-Caillou to collect Lafayette. The late summer afternoon was somber, overcharged with sticky heat, and threatening rain. Chaumette, whose article in *Révolutions de Paris* provides the most detailed and damning account of the episode, speaks of the complacency of the crowd, its disbelief in a show of force.[46] Had the people not assembled peacefully and been granted time to sign their petition?

The martial law obliged the authorities to publish three summonses to the crowd to disperse before resorting to any act of force. But, as we read in the *Révolutions de Paris*, "on suddenly hearing the drumbeat . . . the people recalled that they were acting within the law, and thus they remained. . . ."[47] Once again, we must imagine these several thousand citizens spread out in groups over part of a large field of military maneuver, most of them no doubt clustered on or around the Altar of the Fatherland, where, at separate points, the petition was receiving signatures. The Altar was itself dominated by a steep slope on which numerous demonstrators were gathered. Scarcely had the advance files of the National Guard come into view,

> when a discharge [of fire] was heard: *don't move, they are firing point blank, they are obliged to come here and announce the* [martial] *law.* The troops advanced; they fired a second time; there was no new reaction from those surrounding the Altar. But when a third round of fire had taken quite a toll (*ayant fait tomber beaucoup de monde*), people fled; only about a hundred persons remained on the Altar. Alas! they paid dearly for their courage and their blind respect for the law. Men, women, even a child were massacred, massacred on the Altar of the Fatherland![48]

Lafayette had given orders to his Guard to behave with calm. It seems that the regulars withheld their fire, but that the more unseasoned troops, tense to the breaking point, were unhinged by stones flung by members of the crowd, especially from the dominating slope, and opened fire without waiting for a command. The crowd did not receive three summonses to disperse and the Guard's patience did not survive the crowd's hoots and missiles. The official minutes record that "hardly had the municipal magistrates entered the passage leading to the Champ de la Fédération when a large . . . number of persons stationed above the slope to their right and left . . . began to chant in different cadences: down with the red flag, down with the bayonets! At this point, the Mayor stopped and commanded [the troops] to halt."[49] The account insists that the first volley was fired in the air and that only subsequently, under physical provocation, did the Guard take aim against the people. But there is no sure way of establishing these events.

Panic ensued. The minutes note tersely: "Since the municipal administration was unable to carry out Article Six of the martial law, the National Guard resorted to the powers of Article Seven: it used force because violence of the most criminal sort had made the summonses impossible. . . ."[50] Bailly estimated the deaths at about eleven or twelve, with an equal number wounded.[51] At the opposite end of the spectrum,

Marat wrote of four hundred dead, mostly corpses dumped into the Seine.[52] Chaumette indignantly settled on the figure of about fifty;[53] this is the number that modern historians have accepted as probable. The authorities conceded, therefore, that they had not been able to announce the state of martial law effectively. Nor is there any reason to see why the crowd was prepared in the slightest to expect an imminent show of force. Fournier l'Américain had not been able to convince anyone of the danger.[54] If Bailly and his municipal colleagues did not cause the massacre, it is certain that they made the collision inevitable. They had not connived for the victims to enter a death trap, but they had helped make it one.

The massacre was routinely justified by the ruling powers, whose stake was in public order and in teaching democracy a lesson. When Bailly, from the prejudices of his position, reported the events of the Champ de Mars to the National Assembly, he received the following exoneration: "The National Assembly has learned with sadness that enemies of the happiness and liberty of the French, usurping the guise and the language of patriotism, had led a few men astray, making them seditious and rebellious to the law. And so you were forced to exchange measures of rigor for measures of persuasion, which, up to then, you had used so successfully. The National Assembly approves your conduct and all the measures you have taken. . . ."[55] The document is signed by the presiding officer, Charles de Lameth.

The ascendant Feuillants now undertook what can be described as a *petite terreur bourgeoise* through indictments and prosecution.[56] Yet Chaumette, Bonneville, Marat, and Fréron were able to thunder accusing words as the temporary curtain of silence fell. Marat subscribed to the theory that the rock-throwing had been the work of the agents of Lafayette, primed to instigate the massacre; he also implicated "l'atroce Bailly" in these maneuvers.[57] Chaumette left us the detailed and passionate account of the event, already cited. And Fréron kept up his attack: "Messieurs Bailly and Lafayette are deeply guilty, compromised, and revealed as villains. We conclude that this unforgettable event was plotted and prearranged; that the National Assembly lent its helping hand to the conspiracy: thus the counterrevolution has proved effective."[58] "There is no doubt," he wrote, "Lafayette and Bailly want to restore the Old Regime."[59] And, "the scoundrels: they intend to swallow up the regime."[60]

The martial law, which had remained in effect after the Champ de Mars, was finally lifted on 5 August 1791: "Citizens, the municipality removes [the red flag], which it had displayed only with pain; it unfurls with joy the white flag, the sign of peace. Not that calm is totally assured

—there are still enemies of the public welfare in our midst . . . but a harsh law has provoked terror in them. . . ."[61] Ultimately, this relaxation was followed by the general amnesty proclaimed by the king in September when (with reservations) he accepted the Constitution. Desmoulins haughtily "resigned" his responsibilities of journalism to the hated Lafayette;[62] Fréron was supremely sarcastic: "The King pardons us, Lafayette pardons us, the Queen pardons us . . . Bailly pardons us, the National Assembly pardons us. What a collection of pardons and pardoners!"[63]

Arago, Bailly's sympathetic biographer but not his apologist in this affair, argues that his fellow astronomer was led or went astray in promoting the incident. Bailly himself later conceded that in promulgating martial law "the Council was mistaken."[64] It is clear, given the previous account, that martial law was an imprudent reaction to the undigested information at the disposal of the Municipal Council. Yet Bailly was certainly steered toward this course by his superior authority, the National Assembly. Was he guilty then of what has been called the "banality of evil"? Surely not: although a functionary, he was not an automaton. As for many conservatives in the eighteenth century, preserving order for him also meant preserving life. He had struggled to keep the Parisians from starving; he was not waiting for the moment when he could fell them with shot. Yet he had his values of order and legal responsibility; his deep fear of anarchy colored his response.

In some ways the Champ de Mars was a *champ des sourds*. "If we must weep over the loss of good citizens victimized by their zeal," Bailly wrote, "we can only accuse the destiny which, on this frightful day, caused the magistrates to go unheard and the public force of order to go unheeded."[65] This is more than an excuse; it is an insensitivity committed by a sensitive but limited man. It is also the voice of a prideful man of the Old Regime. Yet when Chaumette challenges: "reply [to us], Monsieur Bailly. You forbade any assembly in public places; had you the right to do so?" he, too, less consciously, is playing false.[66] For the leaders of the petition wanted to overturn the regime and were calling for insurrection and even assassination. Consequently, Aulard's charge against Bailly seems excessive, for the mayor was certainly following the orders of the government of France. Despite all this, the smugness of the authorities was deplorable.

Bailly had raked in the fire of both extremes. Testing his forces against the radicals did not make him the darling of the royalists. As the summer wore on, he began to yearn for retirement, although his term was still for another year. On 21 October, Desmoulins attacked him savagely at the Jacobins: "The ideas which our teachers drummed into our heads with the rod about the meaning of words, this academician, this *philosophe* asserted with the red flag. . . ."[67] On 12 November 1791, Bailly summoned the Municipal Council, gave a report of his administration, solemnly inviting anyone with grievances against him to report them honestly, convinced that he ought to respond to legitimate objections. Then he swore in his successor Pétion and left the meeting.[68] Pétion's inauguration speech paid Bailly no compliments, and the "member of the Three Academies" did not depart with acclamations ringing in his ears. He would return to live in Chaillot, in a desired obscurity, until June 1792, when his political and literary enemies of the Gironde hounded him and Madame Bailly out of their beloved house for indebtedness.

12. The Terror of the Savants

In the Revolutionary perspective, the Champ de Mars massacre was a sufficient cause for Bailly's liquidation. Had Fréron not declaimed: "What a monstrous knave, that Bailly! He says that every writer preaching murder will be brought to justice. Well, you be the first to go and get yourself hung, for your hands are stained with the blood of our fellow citizens."[1] Still, our context transcends the Champ de Mars: Bailly was a symbol of what true Jacobins distrusted and despised: an academic who had basked in the reflected light of monarchy. Larger questions of science, learning, and revolution are involved in our inquiry. Would Bailly have survived—for he showed no disposition to seek exile[2] —even if there had been no Champ de Mars? Would his discretion have saved him, or would he eventually have had to pay the price for Lafayette? Would he have suffered the fate of others more advanced than himself, like Condorcet? He would have needed luck, for the Jacobins deeply resented his corporate connections and his social principles. In their view, according to Charles C. Gillispie, "science was undemocratic in principle, not a liberating force of enlightenment, but a stubborn bastion of aristocracy, a tyranny of intellectual pretensions stifling civic virtue and true productivity."[3]

Before confronting that issue, we must follow out the career of Bailly. The former mayor of Paris was pursued by two sets of furies. Not only was he marked for reprisal by the radical journalists and clubs, but he was despised by Brissot and his faction. Brissot not only thought little of Bailly as a mayor, but was, like his former friend Marat, a failed academician. As early as 1782, in a treatise *De la vérité*, he had attacked the *raison d'être* of the academies. In the vein of Rousseau he had praised the solitary seeker of truth and castigated the learned societies as beehives of amour-propre. He advocated a democracy of learning: "The empire of science can know neither despots, nor aristocrats, nor electors. It mirrors a perfect Republic in which utility is the only title worthy of recognition. To admit a despot, aristocrats, or electors who by edicts set a seal upon the product of geniuses is to violate the nature of things and the liberty of the human mind."[4] Well before the Revolution, Brissot's doctrine challenged the mental structures of Bailly's world of elite opportunity. Later, politics, Condorcet's hostility, and questions of Parisian government would drive them further apart.

In the waning days of the monarchy the Gironde forced Bailly into difficult straits: the loss of his house and much of his library. The Baillys left Chaillot in the summer of 1792 and took refuge in Nantes, where they lived as unobtrusively as possible. As a registered citizen, Bailly swore allegiance to the republican constitution of 1793. He also took the precaution of writing personally to the President of the National Convention to defend his career and profess his loyalty.[5] In Nantes, he was close to the fringes of the Vendean counterrevolution, with which he had no contact or sympathy, although he was later interrogated on the subject.[6] He should perhaps have stayed in Brittany, but he obliged the urgings of his friend the astronomer Lalande to join him in Melun, east of Paris. After settling into his new domicile on 5 July with Madame Bailly and announcing his arrival to the authorities, he was detained by the local Comité de Surveillance three days later. "I ask you, fellow citizens," he wrote, "to give me back my liberty. My character, my principles, and my behavior are well established. Since the beginning of the Revolution I have not deviated for a moment; my life and happiness depend on its success. As a public figure, I was never entangled with any faction or party to any intrigue; I always walked in the straight path of duty."[7] Bailly had certainly sought seclusion and obscurity. But the Jacobin authority was determined, as far as its ingenuity could stretch, to establish the outlines of a single comprehensive plot against the nation: one in which the royal family and the court, Lafayette and Bailly, the Feuillants, the Brissotins, Dumouriez, and the Orleanists, backed by foreign agents and subsidies, were allied to strangle the Revolution in its cradle. Bailly's detention by the Committee of Melun and his subsequent delivery for arrest to the Paris authorities[8] were initially carried out in connection with the trial of Marie-Antoinette, summarily conducted in mid-October (the queen was executed on 16 October; 25 Vendémiaire, an II). Bailly's testimony was to be used to reinforce the evidence of treasonable plotting prior to the flight to Varennes; then it was to be turned against him as one of the two capital charges.

At the trial of the queen, despite the testimony (perhaps forced) by the royal children that they had recognized Bailly at the Tuileries, Marie-Antoinette staunchly denied his participation.[9] The search of his papers and personal effects, which had just arrived in Melun in cartons, revealed nothing compromising;[10] neither had earlier evidence brought forward at the king's trial. Why then the insistence, contrary to fact, that he had helped to plot the escape to Lorraine, when this was precisely the outcome that the constitutional monarchists had feared and tried to prevent? The answer is that the Jacobins abhorred complexity and fine distinctions. If they could limn the clarity of a single conspiracy, it would suit their virtue-and-vice image of politics and be less confusing to their plebeian supporters. Even to claim that Bailly connived with the moderates, but not the court, would have smudged this clarity. And so, at the queen's trial, the prosecutor asked Bailly bluntly: "Didn't you receive orders from Antoinette to carry out the massacre of our [best] patriots?" To which Bailly answered: "No, I went to the Champ de Mars only after a motion by the General Council of the Commune."[11] The hypothesis that Bailly, together with other moderates, had been accessory to the secret plotting of the flight and that, in turn, a similar cabal had prepared the Champ de Mars with the ultraroyalists is pure fantasy. However, it made both the queen and Bailly seem more contemptible to the nation and helped justify the rigors of Revolutionary government in preparation for the execution of the Girondins.

Bailly's denial of contact with the ultras, his profession of political innocence, his claim of only official relations with Lafayette, his affirmation of the Revolution and of his role as an unambitious citizen, and his denial of personal responsibility for the Champ de Mars episode[12] could not efface the "mistake" of martial law,[13] but did amount to a good legal defense. However, moderation was on trial; Lafayette was on trial; and so were the Old Regime and the dynasts. In addition to the charge of conspiring with the court, the trial dossier contained abundant material concerning the repression of the republicans and democrats in the month following the Champ de Mars. As Hanriot (later the Robespierrist commander of the National Guard) testified: "these men absolutely pushed the people aside and showed no compassion for their appeals (*se sont peu inquiétés des cris de la populace*)."[14] Class war also crept into the accusations: a contemporary writer attacked "those men who, having up to then formed a class unto themselves called the *haute bourgeoisie*, worked only for their own gain."[15] "*Veiller . . . réprimer . . . arrêter*" were their motives, *arrêter* meaning also "slaughter, assassinate, massacre."[16]

The trial was swift, its verdict unanimous and foreordained. Twenty-one witnesses appeared for the prosecution, seven for the defense. The major piece for the defense was Bailly's own hastily composed *J.-S. Bailly à ses concitoyens*, which, in about thirty-five concise pages, sketched his life and public acts for the benefit of the curious, declaring his loyalty and innocence, and pleading that the authorities should not "engulf in their anathema the friends of the people and first apostles of liberty."[17] On 14 Brumaire, an II (4 November 1793) the jury of the Criminal Tribunal handed down its verdict of guilty, asserting that "Bailly, together with Lafayette, used all means in his power to aid the escape of Capet, his wife, and the tyrant's family," and that "basely in the hire of the tyrant . . . to arrive at his goal, which was to arm the citizens against one another . . . to cause the massacre of the patriots who dared to speak the truth about the tyrant, he lent himself to the most odious maneuvers."[18] The document goes on to mention "his thirst for the blood of the people."[19] Bailly received his sentence with Stoic composure.

Not content with the execution of their victim, whose notoriety had been fully restored by his arrest and trial, the government decided to indulge in some further cruelty and theatrics. Bailly's beheading would not take place in the Place de la Révolution; rather he would be transported to the Champ de Mars, the scene of the crime: a replica of the red flag of martial law would be attached to the cart of the executioner, then ripped and burned at the foot of the scaffold.[20] The script turned out to be frightful.

The day of 12 November dawned drizzly and bone-chilling. The one-way ride from prison to the Champ de Mars must have seemed endless. Along its route "the carriage was greeted by deafening howls . . . a full battalion of cannibals was on hand. . . . [Especially] the women stood out by their boldness and exasperation."[21] Bailly was the object of a veritable "popular fury"; twice the crowd attempted to break through the guards and seize him.[22] The Abbé Morellet, a fellow academician then cringing in fear of his own security, recalled how "the unfortunate Bailly . . . was greeted with *bravos* and acclamations . . . to the total joy of the whole audience, and especially the women."[23] On his arrival, the scaffold was surrounded by some three to four thousand persons. Men threatened him; drunken hags (*mégères*) spat in his face.[24] The cold rain drenched the earth of the execution ground: mud and filth were flung at the accused along with vulgar epithets. The execution was delayed for more than an hour while Bailly waited at the scaffold: it took some time to burn the red flag. Finally, a sadistic onlooker shouted at the victim: "Bailly, you are trembling." "Because I am cold," the wretched man answered.[25] Previously he had said: "Posterity will judge us all."[26] According to our accounts, he sought no religious consolation. He died bravely when the blade fell. Sanson heard him murmur at the end, "Ah! now I am coming into port. . . ," as if it was not a moment too soon.[27] The hostile *Révolutions de Paris* described the drama with a much different emphasis:

> Bailly died on the scaffold after watching the red flag burned in front of him, that awful instrument . . . so [dangerous] in the hands of an official in the pay of a despot and a vindictive woman. Bailly called on posterity to judge him, when he would have done better to

remain silent. The execution took place on the Champ de la Fédération; nothing like making the punishment fit the crime. Along the
way, Bailly had ample time to hear that sensitive voice of the people
which is our real living posterity: *Give me back my father! Give me
back my wife! Give me back my children!. . . .*[28]

I have not been concerned to defend Bailly, or any other figures treated
here, but to document the implacable foundations of opposition between
them and the Jacobins, between the mentalities and political behavior of
those who, by social position, stood with a foot in both the old and new
orders and those who wanted to purge them from the commonwealth.
Without question, Bailly was killed mainly for his transgression of July
1791, having, unlike most savants, made himself politically prominent in
1789. H. B. Hill cites Bailly as the scientist par excellence whose professional instincts betrayed him in the Republic of Virtue after he had made
a promising start.[29] This is too strong. Yet, in the words of Thibaudeau,
an eyewitness, "there were among the revolutionary leaders those who
regarded enlightenment as an enemy of liberty and science as an aristocracy. . . . If their reign had lasted longer, or if they had dared, they would
have burned down the libraries, cut the throats of the scholars, and
plunged the world back into shadow. . . ."[30] Though it is excessive to
claim that there was actually a "Jacobin philosophy of science" that
"proposed to substitute for the image of nature with which science
confronts humanity a different one, one sympathetic to the ordinary
man,"[31] there were at least corporations of learned men, formed by royal
patronage, who were faced with the transformation of comfortable and
productive habits into a chilly regime of Jacobin virtue. Thus we return
to the theme with which the study of Bailly opened.

Earlier there was passing reference to a disappointed and frustrated
lumpen-intelligentsia. Here, it is appropriate to take up their quarrel with
the role-models of the Enlightenment and their ambiguous connection
with a republican and populist doctrine of antiintellectualism. As Darnton writes: "The Revolution turned the cultured world upside down. . . .
In destroying the old institutions, the new elite meted out a cruel revolutionary justice."[32] This pressure had been building up for at least a
decade before the political revolution. We have already noted Brissot's
tract of 1782, challenging the "Republic of Letters" with a democracy of
letters based on the operation of natural genius. The image of Benjamin
Franklin sometimes served as a mediate symbol between utility and
humility. But the lumpen-intelligentsia were torn between fighting their
purist battle for the natural intellect, as against the community of science,

and their aspiration to displace the reigning mandarins, a wish to destroy the system or to capture it with modifications. This conflict of aims of course resembled the Revolution itself. Moreover, vulnerabilities in scientific controversy rendered science and consequently all learning, in peril of "political forces of sufficient importance."[33]

Marat illustrates these tensions extremely well. While Brissot took up the literary cudgels in the 1780s, Marat bounced from job to job and from hope to humiliation: his ego was fragile and his hopes were preposterous. For such men, a science in flux was a function of their addled lives: they did not axiomatically opt for materialism or spiritualism, for phlogiston or oxygen, for patronage or anarchic poverty. They wanted recognition and a science that would be, above all, theirs. Here is part of an astonishing letter by Marat:

> The morality [of the mandarins], made for corrupted hearts, seduces the young people, and so their proselytes are very numerous. Every day they multiply; what a fearful society is forming, spread out over the whole face of the globe! . . .
>
> Already they have conceived the horrible plan of destroying all religious orders, and abolishing religion itself. . . . If some day their plans become more ambitious and they carry them into political matters (*affaires*), how can they be prevented from shaking up governments and overthrowing states?[34]

Marat later acquired his own intense desire to overthrow states. We must not take his establishment ideology too seriously: he was baring his teeth at the agencies that had spurned him. Later, when he felt that he had the gathered force of the people behind him, his chastisement of the mandarins would be perfectly consistent with a different political frame of reference.

In August 1790, Marat wrote: "For the good of science and literature, it is important that there should be no more academies in France."[35] But only in 1791 did he launch his consummate attack on mandarinism. In a work that accumulates all his frustration, he railed at the academies and lashed at the most hated savants. Apostrophizing Desmoulins, he declared: "Dear Camille, if you take the trouble to examine that mass of wrong and absurd opinions that disfigure even the exact sciences—those regularly published reveries about natural history, chemistry, and physics; that crowd of systems that destroy one another—you will be surprised by the confidence of these gentlemen in the enlightenment of the century and the ceaseless compliments they pay to the progress of reason and the reign of truth."[36] In his day Marat had received faint recognition and magistral rebuff. But had he not at least delivered an *Eloge de Montesquieu* to the Academy of Bordeaux? Perhaps this is why, while attacking the great academies as sinister forces, he tended to dismiss the provincial ones as frivolous: "Surely you mustn't confuse the provincial academies with those of the capital. The former are societies made by the vanity of big fish in a little pond (*petits importants qui cherchaient à jouer un rôle*) and by the boredom of puny amateurs seeking to kill time. But the latter are progeny of the arrogance of our royal ministers."[37] Marat's was not an isolated voice: "on the eve of the Revolution there was a well-articulated anti-academic position that had developed beyond the normal complaints of rebuffed seekers of academic praise . . . [voiced by people] jarred by the essentially autocratic and elitist nature of the academic system."[38] Bailly was one such; Marat did not attack him specifically in *Charlatans modernes*, for he had at least taken a fling at revolution. But he did rebuke the "member of the Three Academies" sharply in the spring of 1790 for "betraying and robbing the state."[39]

The most powerful assault on the academies was by Nicolas Chamfort, a noted dramatist, essayist, and aphorist. If Chamfort was slightly crazy, there was usually something quite sane, touching or biting, in the best passages of his wit. We owe him the epigram that "the poor are the Negroes of Europe."[40] He was a member of the Académie Française, an institution that he abominated. He welcomed the French Revolution in its full radicalism until it interfered with his literary independence in 1794. Then, visited by the police, he attempted suicide twice, once with a firearm, the second time with a razor, announcing that he "wanted to open his veins in honor of Seneca." He died shortly afterward, neither by suicide nor beneath the blade of the law.[41]

In 1789 he delivered a blistering indictment of the "forty immortals," intended to be read by Mirabeau, then the reigning tribune, to the National Assembly.[42] It begins with the functions of his academy: "the most important job is its dictionary. Everyone knows it is mediocre, incomplete, unsatisfactory."[43] A second duty was the reception speech for new members: "a man praised in his own presence by another man whom he has just praised himself, before a public entertained by them both. . . ."[44] The cardinal sins are false pride, false modesty, false eloquence, and especially false solidarity: "the struggle of petty interests, the combat of hateful passions, the circus-ring of paltry rivalries, the game of all those assorted, contradictory vanities of sword and mitre. . . ."[45] In the old days, when there were no citizens, there had to be "partial societies" and "colleagues."[46] But the events of 1789 have changed this. Some abuses have been abolished, but there still remains the spirit of hierarchy: "It would be vain to organize for [the purposes of] liberty bodies designed for servitude; for they will always seek to . . . extend their outrageous hopes for despotism."[47] Thus, such institutions should be closed forever, for they are stubbornly antirevolutionary.[48] "Spare the Academy a natural death," Chamfort urges. "Let it at least have the honor of expiring in memorable circumstances, buried together with even more powerful corporations."[49]

Chamfort was not alone in scalding the Académie Française. An anonymous pamphlet of the time suggests that it be maintained for the sole purpose of honoring the memory of Cardinal Richelieu, its founder, "the friend of liberty and, of all ministers, the most humane. . . ."[50] A recent historian refers to the savants' "reflex of distrust, contempt and fear" and the debasement of the Académie after 1790.[51] Now the assault reached out to science itself (excluding the science of war), previously revered as the central flame of the *lumières*. As "a royal institution, unwilling to break with the monarchy early in the Revolution . . . an aristocracy in a democratic world,"[52] the academy saw its existence threatened, just as Chamfort had urged, together with other "partial" societies and corporations uncongenial to the new politics. On 7 July 1792 Marat grumbled: "it is not true that the entire nation has risen against the despot, for he remains surrounded by his henchmen, the nobility, the clergy, the lawyers, the bankers, the capitalists, the scholars, the literary people, and their hangers-on."[53] As can be imagined, academic attendance dropped off sharply after August 1792. Even the eminent Académie des Sciences, whose utility was conceded by more moderate Jacobins, was menaced. Its main defender was Lakanal, a regicide and Jacobin. On 17 May 1793 he had the courage to praise it as "the leading learned society of Europe," to which Danton's ally Thuriot replied that it was nothing but "a privileged institution . . . the aristocracy of talents and knowledge."[54] Antoine Lavoisier was the mastermind behind Lakanal's efforts.

It is appropriate here to recount Lavoisier's sad adventure in conjunction with the destiny of Bailly's role. Whereas Bailly plunged totally into politics in 1789, leaving no further traces as an academician except the gibes of his adversaries, Lavoisier straddled the two worlds. The fate of this leading genius of French science instructs us in the hazards of the corporate world of the academy. He had entered that world in May 1768, just five years after Bailly. Like Bailly, Lavoisier took on a large burden of the collegial work of the Academy of Science, participating in many of its missions and reports, including the one on Mesmerism. He did distinguished work not only as the principal founder of modern chemistry, but as a geologist, cartographer, economist, agriculturalist, social reformer, and educational theorist.

Two months before his election to the Academy of Science Lavoisier had taken the fatal step of buying into the Tax Farm. We are told that he "entered the Farm to invest . . . so that he could devote himself more fully to the pursuit of science, which, he felt, would require a great deal of money."[55] His experiments were spaciously conceived and equipment was costly: now, far more than men like Bailly, he had an important source of independent income. Lavoisier was also an *anobli*, owing to his father's purchase of an office. At Fréchines in the Orléanais he developed a pronounced interest in social and agricultural questions, with views closely allied to Turgot's. He wrote an interesting statistical memoir on the "territorial richness of France."[56] He also made his debut in politics with election to the Third Estate of the Orléanais provincial assembly, reanimated by Necker in 1787: it was frequent in these bodies for petty nobles or clergy to be chosen to represent the commons. His paper "On the Summoning of the Estates-General" defended the doubling of the Tiers and voting by head;[57] as he put it, in good 1789 language, "the time of enlightenment has come; today we must speak the language of reason and demand the imprescriptable rights of humanity."[58]

Appointed to compose the *cahier* for the nobility of Blois, Lavoisier pointed out that "the purpose of every social institution is to bring the most happiness to those who live beneath its laws" and that "happiness should not be reserved to the few."[59] He defended property and security, the rights of the nation, the reform of criminal justice, and the hostility of his class to the great nobles.[60] He was elected a *suppléant* to the Estates-General, and his *cahier* was published the same year as a pamphlet. More closely involved in the pre-Revolution than Bailly and probably a bit more liberal, Lavoisier had a political mentality that was much the same —leaning somewhat more toward the usufructory than the consensualist view of authority. As he put it later in a curious letter to the king: "I am neither Jacobin nor Feuillant. I belong to no society or club. Accustomed to weighing everything in my conscience and my reason, I would never consent to allow any faction to dictate my opinions."[61] Apparently this neutrality meant that Lavoisier was not a militant; he belonged to the Club of 1789 and socialized frequently with both deputies and intellectuals in his wife's popular salon. Yet, constantly busy with experiments and administrative duties as Commissioner for Gunpowder at the Arsenal, Lavoisier was not in the thick of politics. Bailly, who bore cruel responsibilities, might have been a little envious of Lavoisier's cool profession of faith: "The man of science in the silence of his laboratory and study can also serve his country: by his work he is enabled to hope that he may diminish the sum of evils that afflict the human race . . . and were he to contribute . . . only to the prolongation by some years, even by some days, of the average life of man, he could aspire also to the glorious title of benefactor of humanity."[62] Thus Lavoisier, who neither exactly shunned politics nor took any appreciable distance from the dominant views of the Constituent Assembly, propagated the beautiful myth of disinterest that also attracted Bailly.

In early 1790 Lavoisier remained enthusiastic enough to write to Franklin: "we look upon [our revolution] as over, and well and irrevocably completed; but there is still an aristocratic party, making some useless resistance and very weak. The democratic party is in the majority and is supported moreover by the educated, the philosophical, and the enlightened members of the nation."[63] However, he worried about the arming of the people; obviously democracy had strict outer limits. And by 5 July 1790 Lavoisier conceded to the Scottish scientist Black that "the state of public affairs in France during the last twelve months has temporarily retarded the progress of science and distracted scientists from the work that is most precious to them . . ."[64] This was a pale harbinger of the four years to follow.

Perhaps because of his eminence, perhaps because of controversies in chemistry, perhaps because of his *anoblissement*, Lavoisier was a special target of hatred for Marat. He gathers the themes of the scientist's offenses to patriotism together in one or two pithy sentences: "I denounce to you the Coryphaeus—the leader of the chorus of charlatans—Sieur Lavoisier, son of a land-grabber, apprentice chemist, pupil of the Genevan stock-jobber [i.e. Necker], Farmer-General, Commissioner for Gunpowder and Saltpeter, Governor of the Discount Bank, secretary to the King, member of the Academy of Science. . . . Would to heaven that he had been strung to the lamppost on 6 August."[65] Marat returned to the fray in *Charlatans modernes*: "he has no ideas of his own . . . he changes his views as he changes his shoes."[66]

Lavoisier was now compelled to fight not only for his reputation but for his profession and the organized character of its work. Another eminent, but radical, chemist Fourcroy rose at the 25 April 1792 meeting of the Academy of Science to recommend that, following the judicious example of the Royal Society of Medicine, the corporation expunge from its membership roll all who had emigrated or were known to oppose the Revolution. Obviously this was the invitation to a blanket purge. By a motion carried on 29 April, the Academy, considering that its purview was science and not politics, voted to place the burden for dismissals on the Minister of Interior (then Roland).[67] Fourcroy, later a member of the Convention, pressed his case in the months to come. It was not exactly the nightmarish allegation, familiar since, that there was a "reactionary science" and a "progressive science." It was rather that the cohesion of science in a time of stress was undermined by politically unreliable elements. This claim threatened not only to interrupt important work, but to open the scientific field to a Jacobin strategy of denunciation.

The young Lakanal, guided by Lavoisier, sustained his tense battle for the autonomy and dignity of the scientists, obtaining a new decree for appointments from the Convention on 17 May, and on 25 May some appropriations for salaries. But, as he put it: "What rebuffs I met with! It was probably believed that [the scientists] were all opposed to the new state of things, and unfortunately there was some truth in this supposition. A course had to be steered through all these dangers."[68] Were the academies gangrenous survivals of the Old Regime? Were they pollutants of the new political community? Did they harbor and encourage counter-revolution? Was French science itself elitist and reactionary, undesirable in the Republic of Virtue? In defense of Fourcroy it has been noted that he objected strenuously to "the plan to destroy the sciences and arts in order to gain domination on a heap of rubble of human knowledge."[69] Obviously the cultural revolution was not as thorough as the political Terror. Still, the going was hard in 1793, and the academies were indeed closed and placed in limbo until they received their Napoleonic reorientation.

On 8 August 1793 the Abbé Grégoire delivered his report on the status of the academies to the National Convention. His strategy, influenced by Lavoisier and others, was to satisfy the general clamor against these elitist enclaves, but specifically to save the Academy of Science from dissolution and to make some allowance for reconstructing the other institutions. Grégoire's careful speech mingled some of the impudence of Chamfort with the prudence of Lakanal. "We should," he said, "be dishonored if our men of science were reduced to carrying to foreign shores their talents and our shame."[70] David, genial as an artist but poisonous as a politician, ruined these efforts. In an attack on the Academy of Painting and Sculpture, whose stodgy mandarins he despised, he added euphorically: "To speak of one academy is to speak of all. . . . In the name of justice, for the love of art, and above all for our love of youth, let us destroy these baneful academies, let us annihilate them, for they cannot exist under a free government."[71] This eloquence swayed the

Convention. Grégoire's careful proposition was gutted, so that only its first article carried: "All academies and literary societies, authorized or granted by the nation, are suppressed." Despite hopes for remedy, the decree stood. "It was not enough," as Hahn writes, "to find a substitute for the society's specific functions. When the Academy was destroyed, the scientists lost their identity as scientists and were offered only the unfamiliar alternatives of becoming functionaries, popular lecturers, or unanchored free spirits."[72]

Bailly was arrested, as we have recorded, about a month before these events, and he died three months later for a different reason. It was also on a different pretext that Lavoisier, who had been pursued since February 1793 by an inquiry of the Convention into the abuses of the tax-farmers, was silenced by a variety of enemies. Fourcroy and others had his name struck from the founders of the Lycée as a counterrevolutionary.[73] He was arrested by the authorities on 24 November 1793 (4 Frimaire, an II). With twenty-six others he was charged with counter-revolutionary conspiracy, and without respect for his capacities, he was summarily executed on 8 May 1794 (19 Floréal, an II) as a deviant citizen.

Although it is undeniable that the thrust of Jacobinism was hostile to advanced science, which plowed a furrow between elites and people at large, we need to establish some distancing between scientists and academicians. In the eighteenth century there was not a very great distinction between the two groups: scientists such as d'Alembert and Buffon were chartered *gens de lettres*; literary figures like Voltaire popularized science; men like Bailly were their own popularizers. Nevertheless, the elitism of science (acquisitions of knowledge beyond the ordinary man's understanding) and of academicism (the amour-propre of corporations of intellectuals buffered from the people) were of a somewhat different order. The hostility toward Bailly proceeded mainly from the second sort of suspicion. Still, both elements, abetted by his rashness at the Champ de Mars, contributed to his downfall and helped stimulate the Jacobin leveling of intellectual corporations.

Did the Republic, as Coffinhal is quoted as jesting, have no need for chemists; or, for that matter, astronomers? Did the Reign of Virtue destroy them as aristocrats? Neither Bailly nor Lavoisier died *because* he was explicitly a remnant of royally stimulated Enlightenment patronage. Yet the mentality of the reforming intellectual and the natural elitism of the scholar, frequently stigmatized by the radical press, accompanied them to the scaffold. One historian writes of "the curiosity that it was Chamfort who perished, not Morellet; Bailly, not Marmontel; André Chénier, not Raynal; Lavoisier, not Darcet; Condorcet, and not

Suard."[74] The irony intended is that the survivors frequented the *cercle holbachien*, considered impious and radical in the Old Regime, while the victims (guillotined, except for Chamfort and Condorcet) held more conventional views. But philosophical radicalism and political activism were not exactly congruous. In any case, many savants had reason to fear the Terror.[75] This was especially true if they, the laggards, had managed to survive many of the activists of 1789. Morellet relates that, when attempting to secure his *certificat de civisme*, he was rebuffed by Dorat-Cubières's blunt statement: "all academicians are enemies of the republic." When he argued the cases of Chamfort and Target, the reply was: ". . . and Lafayette, and Custine, and Bailly, and so many others, weren't they revolutionaries, too? What you have to be is a revolutionary of *10 août* and *31 mai* . . . neither your academicians, nor yourself, have done anything [for the nation]."[76] That was the atmosphere, if not the immediate cause, of Bailly's victimization, and the root-source of his politics. Mercier, a precious witness and perceptive raconteur of moods and events, wrote that "the probity and good nature of too scientific a man, too philosophical and too sensitive, perhaps, to occupy the highest places amidst the storms of a revolution were the first causes of so many atrocious crimes, the least noticed of which has been his own ruin."[77] This appears to have been the case. Virtue treated reason in 1793 as reason had treated royalty in 1789.

PART V.
Chrétien-Guillaume de Lamoignon de Malesherbes 1721–1794

13. A Philosophe, But Not Like the Others

Lamoignon de Malesherbes,[1] born on 6 December 1721[2] and executed under the Terror on 3 Floréal, an II (12 April 1794), was both the Tiresias and the La Fontaine of his political milieu. He warned and prophesied in vain, while bringing an almost peasant shrewdness to intricate matters of public judgment. Steeped in erudition[3] and meticulous in his research,[4] he despised the posture of pedantry and affected that of a country gentleman. "The greatest truths," he thought, "are ordinarily the simplest ones."[5] Malesherbes was a principled man who could fearlessly hurl simple truths at the all-powerful from his bastion, the Cour des Aides, without forfeiting his tact and private good-naturedness. The scion of one of the most esteemed families of the legal nobility, he showed a healthy contempt for caste and pomp, but when he believed the privileges of his order could be useful to the nation, he defended them fiercely. Respectful of tradition, he could be contemptuous of its abuses and bold in demanding its modification.[6]

He did not share certain illusions of his fellow intellectuals about the shining benefits of a "philosophical century," for he perceived that some of its energies were vindictive or destructive. His many enthusiasms—gardening and forestry, manufacturing, architecture, legal studies, the classics, the history of his country, travel, charity, vaudeville—were rarely abstract. Tolerant almost to a fault, he dealt tactfully with all the fanaticisms of his age, deploring them but seldom rising to their bait except when they became uncommonly vicious. He found the bitter disputes of Jansenism and Molinism unappetizing, but "écrasez l'infâme" was not his rallying cry.[7] Often himself hailed as a philosophe, he found the partisan spirit of the *gens de lettres* distressing, because "a sectarian leader (*chef de parti*) loses his philosophical independence, being often obliged to sacrifice his own feelings to the interests of his party and to support the quarrels of those he blames and even scorns privately."[8]

Repeatedly, Malesherbes castigated the despotic impulses of the monarchy and its privileged agents, yet he revered royalty all his life.[9] He believed in the virtues of aristocracy and ancient lineage—"our respectable and venerable nobility"[10]—yet reviled the pretensions of "les grands."[11] His sympathy with the "people" was genuine when he voiced their miseries in his remonstrances (he was cherished as a patriarch in the region surrounding his estate near Pithiviers), yet he did not believe them to be politically capable.[12] He yearned for the contemplative life, but spent years of labor preparing political memoranda, bolstered by historical erudition, and serving the nation in the office of censorship (La Librairie), in the magistracy, and in two ministries. He was the friend and protector of both Jean-Jacques Rousseau, the republican,[13] and Louis XVI, the last king of the Old Regime. Like Rousseau and other moral philosophers such as Hume, he believed that feeling was a more potent force than reason in men's actions.[14] A Stoic in his beliefs and bearing, he is nevertheless reported on many occasions to have shed tears.

With the exception of obtaining civil toleration for the Protestants of France in 1787, most of his work was a lost cause or a failure, neither inept nor uninstructive, but unable to crack the barriers of existing policy and prejudice. It is reported that at the time of his departure from his first ministry in 1776, Malesherbes lamented that he and Turgot had drawn the bulk of their knowledge from books, and were therefore poor competitors in the political game.[15] Yet, at about the same time, he wrote to the Comte de Sarsfield, contrasting his career with Turgot's: "M. Turgot was preparing himself constantly for a great role. . . . But I became a public man only in spite of myself. While I was in office, I busied myself only with small details, because that was the nature of my duties; they left me no time to think of other things, and I never judged the moment opportune for great projects, or wasn't sufficiently informed to undertake them. . . ."[16] This whimsical self-deprecation is a constant of Malesherbes's character. Perhaps Malesherbes found little, or too little, in an Age of Reason to rouse him to real heroism. The following observation on Rousseau is of interest: "If he had lived in a century when philosophers were persecuted, he would have been a kind of hero unknown to modern history because he would have combined the superiority of genius with the courage and devotion of a martyr."[17] Rousseau, then, had to play at his *personal* martyrdom; Malesherbes, of course, refused to do any such thing.

Malesherbes could thunder over the abuses of political justice in France (he was most direct and bold when he spoke for an institution); he could weep at the trail of ruin created by the despotic predilections of Louis XV or the naive misjudgments of Louis XVI, all the while finding bittersweet amusement in his own impotence and the defects of wisdom itself in an all-too-human world.[18] He knew that "a well-meaning man at Court is a foreign plant that a thousand insects set out to devour."[19] All the darker shades of Montesquieu's pessimism are cast in bold relief—for the decay is another generation advanced and the spectator has become the participant—but the satire is relieved and softened by a human piety reaching always toward, and sometimes losing itself in, a morass of experience. Malesherbes saw his time remarkably clearly and justly, but he did not know how to use the scalpel. He acted upon his society by example, insuring the gratitude of his contemporaries and posterity; never, either as a writer or a statesman, did he deliver any single stroke of genius that would shock or shame his century. As a leading noble, the son of a chancellor of France, and as a responsive member of the political class, Malesherbes stepped forward to repair certain contemporary evils and to guide the monarchy toward a better understanding of its role. But he did this with deliberate prudence (he taxed Turgot for his rashness),[20] and with the same fussiness of detail that caused so many of his writings, drafted and redrafted in crabbed handwriting, to remain in cartons in his library.

To this day, Malesherbes is regarded chiefly as the royal censor who was a "friend of the *philosophes*," the author of severe remonstrances against Louis XV, and the "admirable vieillard" who defended Louis XVI in 1792–93 at peril of his own life. Since he was neither a *ministre agissant*—like Turgot, Necker, or Calonne—nor the author of any French classics—like Montesquieu—he has become the symptom of flash points in French history and a symbol of pathos and paradox. That view scarcely does him justice. Yet it is the flaw of Malesherbes's public behavior and self-image, as much as the failure of subsequent connoisseurs of the period, that accounts for this destiny. The innumerable threads of Malesherbes's complicated intellectual tapestry of "simple truths" were never drawn together by the weaver himself: the synthesis is left to archeologists of another time, another mental and moral climate.

On 3 Floréal, an II, while leaving prison on the way to the scaffold, Malesherbes, whose eyes were failing badly, stumbled against a paving stone. "A bad omen," he observed. "A Roman would not go on with the ceremony."[21] Malesherbes had quite overcome the fear of death, but his quip may have conveyed a regret that his life had not been able to spare France from the Republic of Virtue. "Honor begins with refusing honors" was one of Malesherbes's maxims;[22] but this practice simply left honor to the dishonorable in a monarchy shy even of Montesquieu's sometimes sardonic specifications. Malesherbes was doomed both by his affability and depth of vision to be a facilitator and a catalyst rather than a leader, a subject of touching biographies rather than a "prophet armed." Indeed, he detested wearing his sword for court ceremonials and often got it caught between his legs.[23] In the dying moments of the Old Regime it was perplexing for this good man to know how to be a citizen.

If his citizenship had not been in the blood, the head alone might not have sufficed.

Malesherbes was descended from an important noble family whose roots can be traced back to the thirteenth century, when robe and sword were indistinct. From the sixteenth century on, the Bâville branch of the Lamoignons was distinguished in the law; its most famous member was Guillaume de Lamoignon (1617–67), Marquis de Bâville and Premier Président of the Parlement of Paris. Lamoignon's mind was of liberal cast; he contested the autocratic Colbert and had many friends among the literary figures of the Grand Siècle, conspicuously Boileau.[24] His grandson, Malesherbes's father, who bore his name, would become Chancellor of France in December 1750, succeeding the admirable d'Aguesseau. He was "a man of merit, but tough," according to Barbier, no lover of the parlements. Guillaume de Lamoignon was well known for his professional integrity, his legal erudition, and his Jesuit leanings.[25] Martainville writes that Malesherbes "had in his father an enlightened master, a tender friend, a model of every virtue."[26] However, this tenderness was restricted by an austere sense of duty and religious devotion. "The true and only knowledge useful to man is that of his duties because he is born to fulfill them," wrote Lamoignon de Blancmesnil.[27] And further, "it is religion which has disabused men of the pernicious maxims . . . that had deprived them of the knowledge of most of their duties."[28] Although Malesherbes would receive from his father a lofty sense of the magistrate's calling and of the nature of justice, he would inherit neither his Catholic piety nor his severe self-righteousness.

Malesherbes was born from Blancmesnil's second marriage to Anne-Elisabeth Roujault, whose family had been in the administration, the legal profession, and the Tax Farm: she produced in quick succession six children, of whom Malesherbes was the fifth, and she died in childbirth in 1734, when Chrétien-Guillaume was only twelve. Through Blancmesnil's first wife, Marie-Louise d'Aligre, Malesherbes was closely connected with another influential family of the legal nobility. The parlementary interbreeding did not stop here; even before his daughter's marriage to Louis Lepeletier de Rosanbo, Malesherbes was connected with that notable family, and, through his sister's marriage, with the Sénozans. Indeed, the Maupeou family—later the deadly enemies of Lamoignon, father and son—were cousins of lesser standing.[29] The principal aristocrats of the robe were both a corporation and a series of tribes in the Old Regime. The carnage of Terror would carry away, besides Malesherbes, five of his close family (his sister, Madame de Sénozan; his son-in-law and elder daughter, the Chevalier and Madame de Rosanbo; his granddaughter Aline-Thérèse de Chateaubriand and her husband), but it did not prevent his illustrious bloodline from forging nuptial links with two of the greatest names of the coming century, Chateaubriand and Tocqueville.[30] Thus the ancestry and the legacy of Malesherbes are involved with a wide span of literature and statecraft. The Lamoignon females transmitted the vigor of the earlier male lineage to later times.

In 1737, when Malesherbes was only sixteen but had already been for ten years a pupil at the Jesuit *collège* of Louis-le-Grand, his father, Lamoignon de Blancmesnil, addressed him a long and scarcely complimentary letter on his adolescent conduct.[31] In this "lettre exhortatoire" the stern parent accuses his son of failing to cultivate his "natural talents" and of "abandoning himself to laxity and disorderliness." "I know the fickleness (*légèreté*) of your character; for a long time I have sought ways to correct it . . . but I have always been pained to see how hopeless this was. . . . The more I am acquainted with your character, the more it causes me fright and alarm."[32] Apparently, the youth had been indocile to his teachers, impatient with the advice of his elders, ungrateful to his superiors (including presumably the aggrieved author of the letter), disposed to keep "libertine" company, and frivolous in matters of religion.[33] One remarkable passage merits attention: "You have within you a spirit of independence, carried sometimes to the extreme of ferocity, which makes you despise the advice given you. You bear that advice impatiently if it comes from someone who, by his age and character, deserves your deference; you try to avoid it; you are overanxious to know who has the right to give you advice, and when it comes from persons whom you don't think you ought to obey, you refuse to listen to them, you grow vexed and respond with insult and anger. . . ."[34] The mature Malesherbes conquered his quick temper; his sensitivity to rank resolved itself into a less impulsive judgment of rightness and fitness. But can we not discern here the critical spirit that rejects any automatic docility toward unexamined and arbitrary power?

"You are about to enter upon a trying (*pénible*) career," Malesherbes is warned.[35] Lamoignon approvingly cites his own diligence in preparation for the magistracy, "the fatigue (*peine*) I felt when, after having worked from daybreak to dinner—sometimes a very late dinner—I went back to my office, where, to refresh myself from the exhaustion of the morning, I found fifteen or twenty cases to judge or examine for the morrow. . . ."[36] Later the sixteen-year-old would push his own body to fatigue and weaken his sight with reading. How much his father's strictures influenced him it is impossible to say. However, the letter found by Pierre

Grosclaude bears the author's original signature and is therefore the copy received by his son and preserved. Blancmesnil's sententious remarks are intended, he writes, in the spirit of friendship, not of anger: he confesses in himself an excess of "vivacité." Nonetheless, the desire for religious conversion surfaces: "May God change your heart; it will be a great sign of his omnipotent grace."[37] "Only a complete change of life and of feelings can satisfy me."[38] For Lamoignon de Blancmesnil, the magistrate, service to God and service to the law were inseparable parts of his professional errand. It is because of his high sense of civic calling that he avoided the pitfalls of a narrow sectarianism. To dispense justice on earth was just as much a part of his creed as it would be of his son's endeavors. "The greatest good of life," he writes, "is to be useful to your fellow citizens; after ambition has brought you to the highest rank, your only wish can be to contribute to the felicity of others." Malesherbes is advised to "adopt as models those who enjoy public esteem."[39]

In his legal, literary, and ministerial career Malesherbes tempered the traditionalism and orthodoxy of the parent. Two of his attributed *pensées* make the point nicely: "The agedness of laws is sacred, just as that of man is venerable."[40] He, too, would defend the ancient laws and be revered as venerable. But, on the other hand: "A man well-born brags of something not belonging to him: the glory of his ancestors. Yet it is taken amiss when an unknown man of just desert speaks of his own possession, his talents."[41] The civic standards of Lamoignon would be Malesherbes's own. Though there would be dispute between the chancellor and his son over various issues (controversy surrounding the Jesuits, the management of censorship, the powers of the *cours souveraines*), the father endowed the son with responsibility and the son repaid the father with respect. If it was not a communion of love, it was a partnership of dignity.

Malesherbes's Jesuit education, apparently ending in that same year, was entirely in keeping with his father's penchant for a disciplined classical and religious regimen, although it was by no means common for the great families of the robe (infected with Gallicanism, if not Jansenism) to entrust their sons to the influence of the Society of Jesus. The son does not seem to have thrived in this environment. On leaving Louis-le-Grand,[42] he had the good fortune to receive legal training from the Abbé Pucelle, a vigorous and eloquent opponent of the bull Unigenitus and a stormy petrel in the religious politics of the early reign of Louis XV. Pucelle had a lasting influence on the intellectual and moral foundation of his pupil, counterbalancing the ethic of disciplined service with a spirit of liberty.[43]

In 1741 Malesherbes entered the magistracy as a substitute to the procureur-général; on 3 July 1744 he became Conseiller au Parlement de Paris. From the mid-1740s on, he pursued studies in chemistry and natural history, and acquired much of his knowledge and taste in literature.[44] A letter written to the Abbé Morellet in 1758, but apparently referring to this time, states: "For years my single passion was literature and I lived only with the *gens de lettres*."[45] Thus he was well prepared for the delicate task of directing the office of censorship (Librairie), which began in 1750.

On 4 February 1749 Malesherbes married Marie-Françoise Grimod de la Reynière, a wealthy young woman descended on both sides of her family from tax-farmers (the circumstance is not without irony, for the Cour des Aides, to whose presidency Malesherbes would succeed, was by its function the devoted enemy of the practices of the Tax Farm).[46] Two daughters were born from their union, in 1756 and 1758. Little is known of Madame de Malesherbes except one appalling fact: she committed suicide on 11 January 1771 in the forest of Malesherbes by means of a contrivance with a rifle and a ribbon by which the trigger could be activated.[47] There is a gracious exchange of letters between Rousseau and Malesherbes regarding the tragic event. On 17 January 1771, Rousseau wrote cryptically: "To the feelings that Madame de Malesherbes inspired in everyone who had the honor to know her, I add my special gratitude for her hospitality (*accueil obligeant*). But for me her memory remains even more cherished; for I saw that she could be deceived like many others, but that, like so few others (*presque seule*), she knew neither how to dissemble nor to deceive."[48] To which the widower replied: ". . . a deep melancholy was the principal symptom of the illness she had had for six months, and if you had seen her then, you would have noticed it and perhaps attributed to some other cause the cold reception she would have given you. . . . Release, me, Monsieur, from the pain of telling you more at this time."[49] The meager evidence permits no speculation on the cause of the suicide. Malesherbes would always have a close and affectionate relationship with his children and grandchildren, without hint of blame or rancor. It may be of some significance that Madame de Malesherbes's fatal act came at a moment of crisis in her husband's professional career: little more than a week later (19–20 January 1771), *lettres de cachet* were delivered against the Parlement of Paris, and within three months the Cour des Aides would be similarly dispersed.

Malesherbes found peace in the countryside. As he put it: "The spirit is sharpened in the city, but it grows tender in the fields."[50] As for the property of the chateau and the relations of the *châtelain* with his staff and the surrounding country population, there are numerous adulatory accounts. According to one biographer, Malesherbes devoted, on average, 12,000 livres a year to the upkeep and improvement of his land.[51] There he maintained, as a kind of welfare measure for his peasant neighbors, "immense and ongoing works projects."[52] Much of his interest was devoted to botany and arboriculture; he collected all kinds of seeds and plants during his travels and had exotic specimens sent to him from distant places. Conifers were his greatest passion.[53] According to Arthur Young, who visited Malesherbes on 13 September 1787, his spectacular plantings, which lined the road for four miles approaching the chateau, were the most exotic trees in France.[54] Beyond these visible signs of enlightened proprietorship, his charity to the neighborhood was legendary. He often overspent revenues on good works.[55] After his arrest on 20 December 1793, the officials of the municipality of Malesherbes had the boldness to post a notice certifying that he had been "always the most zealous defender of the rights of the people" and had "constantly deserved the esteem of this commune."[56]

Malesherbes counted among his acquaintances much of the political, literary, and scientific establishment of France as well as many correspondents in England, Switzerland, and, in later years, North America (including Franklin and Jefferson). He was a member of the three principal royal academies: Sciences (1750); Inscriptions et Belles-Lettres (1759); and the Académie Française (1775)—as well as the Royal Society of Agriculture.[57] His abiding and practically oriented interest in the French past—especially prominent in his work on the Protestants and in his constitutional and legal studies—was balanced by an avid curiosity for new developments, such as improved agricultural methods and the experiments in aerostatics that the Montgolfier brothers were conducting in Annonay.[58] In his investiture speech to the Académie Française, he struck a progressive posture amid somewhat overscaled rhetoric, calling for a dialogue between the *gens de lettres* and a "public tribunal."[59]

Both while a minister of Louis XVI (1775–76, 1787–88) and in retirement, one of Malesherbes's chief struggles was to obtain civil liberties for the Protestant minority of France. It is appropriate here to make some comment about his own religious convictions. Although officially a Catholic and the son of a devout magistrate, Malesherbes lost his orthodox faith at an early age and was never a practicing Christian thereafter. He abhorred fanaticism and superstition; on the other hand, he evidently believed, like Montesquieu, that religion was an indelible and salutary force in the stabilization of social morality. As censor he found "books contrary to religion" pernicious, a necessary exception to the liberty of the press: "even those who favor them by secret inclination would not dare to deny this principle."[60] "Religion" evidently meant, in the first place, the Catholic religion professed by a vast majority of the French (though Malesherbes's erudition did not extend to theology), as well as the more general sentiment of a God and a Creator. In the wider sense, it was a religion assimilable to morality itself: what may be broadly called neo-Stoic or deistic in eighteenth-century France. This much is implied not only in the tenor of Malesherbes's way of life, but also in his reported conversations with Louis XVI during the king's detention and in the way the magistrate met his own death. But his "Stoicism" was a very private creed; Malesherbes did not attempt to proselytize, and he left a largely Catholic descendance.

Conceivably, Malesherbes found some of the harmonies of the life and conduct he practiced in a latitudinarian version of Protestantism. He may have admired the Protestants not just because they were unjustly perse-cuted, but because their mores made some contact with his own. More-over, as he insisted, Protestantism could be *civic*. The following passage is of interest: "There is nothing in the principle of the Protestant religion that tends to lessen the submission of the subjects to their sovereign. . . . When one blames the Protestants for having taken up arms in the interest of religion, one forgets that the Catholics have done this every day exclusively in the interests of their ambition, or so as to satisfy their vengeance."[61] This is not to imply that Malesherbes was a secret Protes-tant, but rather that he saw them as a strength to the civil polity which France needed to create. He was not a man to embrace organized sects or bodies of doctrine. On the whole, his kinship with religious sentiment was philosophical, and is best identified in an unlikely source: his po-lemic against the natural history of Buffon, published four years after Malesherbes's death. Here, amid a generalized attack on Buffon's "meta-physics" and contempt for detail,[62] he writes: "It is not up to us to decide the extent of God's grandeur. . . . We can only know his intentions through his works; but we would be mistaken in wishing to judge his works by the intentions that we impute to him. . . ."[63] This is neither materialism nor a "cold" deism. A possible clue may be found in Males-herbes's warm praise of Leibniz in the same work. Leibniz was the "creator . . . of the most profound metaphysics . . . of all the philoso-phers, the one characterized by elevation of ideas and generality of views."[64] Was Malesherbes's own philosophical religion Leibnizian? It is a good guess.[65]

This man whose passion for nature interested him in its finest details was an enthusiastic traveler and meticulous observer of foreign customs.

Sometimes he journeyed alone, sometimes in the company of a servant, often away from the beaten track, with long stretches of tramping and hiking. A famous European, he frequently went under the incognito of Monsieur Guillaume. Numerous interesting letters and journals record Malesherbes's observations. Through Grosclaude's research, we know of Malesherbes's travels to the Auvergne (1751); to the Midi and parts of Spain (1767); to the Bordelais, the north of France, and Holland (1776); to Switzerland, Savoy, the Franche-Comté, and the Jura (1778); and to Brittany (1779).[66] No doubt there were other unrecorded adventures. A melancholy and, as it turned out, last dangerous trip that Malesherbes took was to Lausanne in 1791 to visit his younger daughter and her husband, the Baron de Montboissier, who had emigrated.[67]

In 1763, internal court politics, motivated by the controversy surrounding the expulsion of the Jesuits and the incessant remonstrances of their mortal enemies, the parlements, had caused Louis XV, guided by Madame de Pompadour, to demand Lamoignon's resignation from the Chancellorship of France. The octogenarian friend of the Jesuits refused to leave his (*inamovible*) office, and was exiled to Malesherbes. René-Charles Maupeou, father of the magistrate who will command our attention in the next chapter, was named vice chancellor. From this point on, Lamoignon de Blancmesnil was chief magistrate of France in name and privilege only; he resigned on 15 September 1768, four years prior to his death at the age of eighty-nine.[68] Many of his political predelictions at this time were not Malesherbes's own, for, as the latter put it, with him "the principles and administration [of Louis XIV] were always present."[69] However, the chancellor maintained a belief in the monarch's sovereignty, expressed as follows: while the king had the *power* to do anything, he did not have the *right* to do everything. When the king transgressed all resistances of the sovereign courts, he was using means evidently at his disposal, but also committing acts of tyranny. This was also Malesherbes's position. On a second count, there was also consensus between father and son. There had been certain refusals of the parlements to assemble to dispense justice, interferences with royal administration in the provinces, and illegal interventions in the case of the Jesuits. Though Malesherbes, unlike his father, had no love for Jesuits, he concurred in condemning the abuses. In sum, each believed in limiting both the pretensions and errancies of the monarch and the parlements, warding off despotism, on the one hand, and aristocratic particularism, on the other.[70] Thus Malesherbes gained an example of integrity and citizenship from his father. The openness, suppleness, and liberalism of his own policies—his *lumières*—would need to come from other sources. But

Malesherbes recognized his father's courage and virtues in the Latin epitaph he had engraved on his tomb: "vir justus/ morum rigiditate legis instar flecti nescia spectatus / constantia insignior / quam humanae conditionis vices corrumpere nec frangere valuerunt. . . ."[71]

If Lamoignon, in endowing Malesherbes with his stern values, did not make him a philosophe, he nevertheless provided his son with a facility that would test his tact, finesse, and enlightenment by entrusting the Librairie to his charge in 1750. By then Malesherbes was of course well steeped in the literature of his time and proud of the genius of his century; his "living with the men of letters" had made him a sympathetic connoisseur of the intellectual novelty cascading from French pens. His enthusiasm for literature and its producers was sincere. As he wrote to Morellet about his entry to the Librairie: "I desired nothing so much as to be able to render a service to those with whom I had passed my life."[72] "Genial thought," he remarked, "is the property of humanity."[73] In the same year that he became head censor he was also inducted into the Academy of Science.

However, Malesherbes regarded himself not as a philosophe agent within the walls of the establishment, but as a judge and protector of the rights of authority and public decency, on the one hand, and of the author's right to profess and the public's right to know, on the other. On balance, authority needed less protection than public expression, for, given its bent, it would stifle much useful knowledge by fanaticism or caprice.[74] Besides, Malesherbes regarded great literature with joyful appreciation. Of Rousseau he wrote, much later on: "I am convinced that the majority of judges who condemned him would be very annoyed if they could not read his works."[75] To put Malesherbes's work at the Librairie in perspective, it is useful to keep in mind that this role overlapped considerably with his tenure as Premier Président of the Cour des Aides. Between the years 1756 (when the battle of the courts against the royal power brewed up in earnest) and 1763 (when Malesherbes resigned as director of censorship), he was constantly involved in both tasks. (These same years, of course, spanned the Seven Years' War, an episode of great importance to the Cour des Aides, whose direct function was the registration and supervision of taxation.) The battles against despotism on the literary front and on the fiscal front were interwoven for Malesherbes in a single ongoing experience. In the one case the struggle was for the prerogatives of an institution (the *cours souveraines*) that for lack of anything better, spoke for a silenced public, whereas, in the other, the struggle was for the public's right to be instructed and to clarify its opinions. The linking notions are those of public happiness and public communication. As for literature, "what the public needs to know is the truth; it will always know it when there is permission to write, it will never know it otherwise."[76] As for taxation, Malesherbes remonstrates to Louis XV: "There are peoples so unfortunate that there is no regularly established communication between the sovereign and his subjects."[77] Or, put more bluntly, "such is the misfortune of royalty that the sovereign is often the only person in his kingdom who does not hear the universal cry of the nation."[78] As he wrote boldly to Morellet in 1758: ". . . my principle of liberty is not restricted to literature. . . . I am much inclined to extend it to the science of government, not even excluding criticisms of the operations of the ministry."[79]

The Librairie (which concerned not only censorship, but also supervision of printers and booksellers, regulation of imports by inspectors, and the granting of diverse privileges) was one of the more complex and delicate parts of the royal bureaucracy. Its direction called for firmness with some, amiable tact and deception with others: not just the writers, printers, and *colporteurs*, but also the police, a vigilant clergy, and an indefinite number of interested parties with influence at court. The history of censorship of books in France went back virtually to the invention of printing. An order of François I, in 1521, had subjected authors to the necessity of obtaining a preliminary royal authorization. At first, this responsibility had been vested in the theologians of the Sorbonne; then, in the middle of the seventeenth century, specific royal censors were appointed. By the time Malesherbes took office, the production and circulation of books had so increased that eighty-two censors were required.[80] When he left the Librairie in 1763, his liberal policies had not prevented this number from growing to 121. One scholar lists 117 in March 1762, distributed as follows: theology (14), jurisprudence (15), natural history, medicine, chemistry (18), surgery (3), mathematics (4), belles-lettres, history, etc. (60), geography, navigation, voyages (1), prints or engravings (1), architecture (1).[81] Over all publications, especially those that qualified as theology, philosophy, and belles-lettres, loomed the shadow cast by the zealots of Catholicism, sensitized not only by the assaults of the philosophes but by the Unigenitus conflict.[82] Malesherbes's "liberal" administration was characterized by "a care at all moments to commit no errors and not to let any be committed."[83]

Malesherbes was fond neither of censorship as a principle nor of the subsidiary abuses it entailed: arbitrary exclusion of perfectly anodyne works, special and privileged patents of authorization, pirated editions, depredation of the French book trade, fraud by authors and printers, endless intrigues and complaints by the *gens de lettres* against one another and against his office. Above all, he felt that it interfered disastrously with the nation's enlightenment. He subscribed to it only when it prevented: (1) attacks on religion; (2) attacks on good morality; (3) attacks on established government; and (4) defamatory writings.[84] However, Malesherbes was not as doctrinaire as his categories might make him sound, particularly with reference to religion and morals. He was rather inclined to view both of these formidable subjects under the heading of "good conduct," although in the administration of his office he scrupulously subjected (or attempted to subject) works like the *Encyclopedia* (vols. 1–7) and *De l'Esprit* to the prescribed theological censorship.[85] He really had little choice. In his *Mémoires sur la Librairie* he wrote: "The principles [of morality] are the same as those of Christianity. The law that avenges religion will avenge morality."[86] Malesherbes frequently expressed the view that the great utility of a work like the *Encyclopedia* far outweighed "several bad things" in it.[87] It was not only "an honor to French literature" but "a fairly important object of commerce." But we also find him writing to Madame Helvétius, who, after the suppression of *De l'Esprit*, was complaining of attacks on her husband by the devout party, that "my personal feeling should not influence my conduct of business and I cannot shut the mouth of authors who believe they must avenge religion and morals."[88] As he wrote elsewhere: "I recognize a great difference between works I don't care for and even disapprove of personally and those whose appearance I, as a public official, am obliged to prevent."[89] He allowed his preferences to stretch the flexibility of his office, but he never forgot the nature of his charge.

With regard to the two other headings—libels and attacks on political authority—Malesherbes was far more categorical. He disliked personal attacks that made no pretense of public enlightenment and attempted to curb them, although such polemics and libels were, and continued to be, the daily bread of the *gens de lettres* and their adversaries. He deplored the sectarian spirit wherever it abandoned the contest of ideas for the *ad hominem* destruction of reputations. He warned Rousseau that "the style of life you have taken up is too singular and you are too famous to avoid public scrutiny," but consoled him with the thought that all great writers make enemies.[90] When his friend the Abbé Morellet overstepped the limits of decency in his defamatory *Vie de Palissot*, Malesherbes raised no murmur when Sartine sent him to the Bastille in 1760.[91] He did not, above all, want the government to appear to take sides in writers' quarrels: "the main job of the government in these affairs is to punish all infractions without affording more protection to one literary faction than to another."[92] In effect, this principle was bent slightly in favor of the philosophes.

As for politics, Malesherbes recognized that "the freedom of the press concerning affairs of state is one of the most powerful supports of the liberty of a republic," but he knew that France was certainly not a republic. In France "the king is master; his ministers are powerful. The intention of the king is that their conduct, pro and con, should not be a matter of public debate."[93] This was a simple statement of fact. Aware of the fragility of the system, Malesherbes was constrained to write in his *Mémoires sur la Librairie* of 1759:

> At this time the most important object of the administration should be to suppress works whose authors dare to submit royal authority to examination. The censor's rule will be neither arbitrary nor ambiguous. He should stop all such material. The *philosophes* and savants will disingenuously claim that they are the firmest defenders of the sovereign power, and that these restrictions will deprive the public of a sublime theory. The rights of the throne are certain, founded more solidly than their vain speculations; and the discovery of an important axiom in morals or jurisprudence will never compensate for the evils that might result from . . . abusive controversy.[94]

Still, Malesherbes believed that although "divine power is the origin of all legitimate powers . . . the greatest happiness of the people is always its object and end."[95] He had two perspectives, two functions and advocacies: that of royal bureaucrat and that of judicial complainant. He tempered his censorship with an open spirit that encouraged the philosophes even if it did not always accommodate them.

In the famous case of the *Encyclopedia*, he averted a first crisis—brought to a climax in 1751 by the publication of the Abbé de Prades's article "Certitude" and the assaults of both the Parlement of Paris and the Sorbonne—by conniving to conceal personally the manuscripts of forthcoming volumes.[96] Through the efforts of d'Alembert, Madame de Pompadour, and Malesherbes's agile diplomacy with his father, the chancellor, the privilege of the great work was saved. A more vigilant theological censorship was then imposed; but it was simply ignored in many cases by Diderot and his printer Le Breton.[97] In the meantime Malesherbes had had to fight a subtle battle with Diderot over the article "Constitution Unigenitus"—a taboo subject in the reign of Louis XV—which was finally scrapped at the orders of Lamoignon de Blancmesnil.[98] Finally, in 1759, after condemnation of the *Encyclopedia* by the Parlement of Paris on 6 February, together with Helvétius's *De l'Esprit* and six other works, there was little for Malesherbes to do but concur in the chancellor's decision to revoke the publishing privilege.[99] This was duly enacted

by *arrêt du conseil* on 8 March, in language mainly composed by Malesherbes himself, with a few touches added by Lamoignon. The friend of
the *Encyclopedia* thus became its reluctant executioner, but only after
continued imprudences had forced his hand. In the event, he did all that
was possible to salvage the situation with the booksellers and subscribers
by securing permission for the distribution of the companion volumes of
engravings.[100] Malesherbes saved what he could of philosophical production. In so doing, he tried to increase the book trade in France and let
fresh breezes blow in his century.

But naturally some of his actions annoyed the philosophical party, as
well as their adversaries, the *dévots*. "If you knew M. de Malesherbes,"
d'Alembert grumbled to Voltaire, "if you knew about his lack of nerve
and consistency, you would be convinced that we can no longer count on
him for anything."[101] Voltaire, in Ferney, knew full well about Malesherbes; he had been plaguing him for special favors since early 1752 and
exhausting his patience.[102] In 1761 he wrote in anger to d'Alembert:
"M. de Malesherbes degrades literature, I agree; he is a *philosophe* and he
wrongs philosophy. . . ."[103] Yet Voltaire was sensitive to the loss when
Malesherbes retired from the Librairie in 1763.[104] Malesherbes had been
Rousseau's esteemed confidant;[105] as we might expect, it was Rousseau
who paid the highest compliment to his friend and protector. "In learning of your retirement," he wrote, "I felt sorry for the *gens de lettres*, but I
congratulate you. In ceasing to hold their leadership by your position,
you will always keep it with your talents. Busy with the charms of
literature, you are no longer forced to bear its calamities; you can philo-
sophize in peace, and your heart will support an easier burden."[106]

Philosophical peace was not exactly Malesherbes's destiny in the years
to follow, for the words of his legal remonstrances, launched against such
visible evils as oppressive taxation and stagnant justice, now rang out
with accelerating persistency. But, as we have seen, his affinity with the
philosophical prophets of his age was mediated by his role as magistrate
and administrator. He desired to be their "counselor" and not their
censor,[107] and he shared their friendship and a place in their intellectual
estate: unfailingly, he gained a reputation for advanced ideas. When Louis
XVI was forming his ministry in 1774, he would not at first hear of
Malesherbes. "Do not speak to me of him for any office," he told
Maurepas, "for he is an Encyclopedist and very dangerous."[108] Yet
Malesherbes had his bedrock of conservative faith, his ancestral habits,
which would eventually prove inhospitable to the new dispensation.

14. The Peaceful Profession
of Justice

By heredity Malesherbes succeeded to the Première Présidence of the Cour des Aides in 1750, at the age of twenty-nine, when his father gained the chancellorship. The Cour des Aides was one of the *cours souveraines* of France, which included the twelve parlements (Paris, Toulouse, Grenoble, Bordeaux, Dijon, Rouen, Aix, Rennes, Pau, Metz, Douai, and Besançon), two *conseils souverains* of lesser dignity (Colmar and Perpignan), and a variety of Chambres des Comptes and Cours des Aides in different locations.[1] These courts were of unequal size, importance, and jurisdiction. The Parlement of Paris was by far the most influential, having jurisdiction over about one-third of French territory; consequently, it cultivated interests and attitudes on a more national scale. In the *pays d'élection*, where local Estates had ceased to exist, the courts were the functional spokesmen against royal power as well as agents of royal power in society: besides Paris, Rouen (Normandy) was typically the most aggressive of them in the eighteenth century. Some provincial parlements incorporated the functions of Cours des Aides or Chambres des Comptes, or both. Elsewhere, these two other courts were often combined. The total "parlementary world," including these courts, scarcely exceeded two thousand individuals.[2]

Well into the seventeenth century, these legal bodies had served as a means by which enterprising commoners could accede to the nobility, though this was not the route traced by the Lamoignons, who were of old noble stock. The magistracy was hereditary, venal (purchasable), and irremovable. The requirements for the *anoblissement* of commoner magistrates varied among the jurisdictions. By the eighteenth century, the access of the *roturiers* to the parlements had become constricted, although the Cours des Aides and Chambres des Comptes were more open. Of entrants to the Parlement of Paris between 1715 and 1771 only about ten percent were commoners.[3] At Rennes, Aix, and Grenoble the proportions of nobles and *anoblis* were even higher, though in Colmar roturier participation rose to seventy percent.[4]

Traditionally, the sovereign courts had three major functions. First, they were responsible for hearing and settling litigation within their jurisdictions and for dispensing public justice. Second, they had the responsibility of registering new laws within their jurisdictions; the monarch could override their refusal only with a *lit de justice*. Finally, the courts could address remonstrances to the sovereign on behalf of some public complaint or accompanying the refusal to register a law.[5] Chambres des Comptes were restricted to litigation and legislation bearing on the use of public revenues and accounting for the estates of the crown; Cours des Aides concerned themselves with forms and procedures of taxation (*aides, tailles, gabelles*, etc.) raised by royal authority.[6]

In 1673 Louis XIV had severely restricted the powers of the courts, ordering them to proceed immediately to the registration of all laws "without any modification." But on 15 September 1715, the regent, Philippe d'Orléans, restored the right of preliminary remonstrance, thereby "reintegrating the *cours souveraines* into the discussion of public affairs."[7] The leaven of opposition began to work. As the century wore on, the remonstrances took ever bolder tones. After mid-century the word "arbitrary" would appear increasingly, sometimes accompanied by "fear" and "terror."[8] Moreover, the courts would sometimes have their complaints printed and disseminated to the public. Malesherbes is reported as saying: "Woe to the king who forces his people to argue over the principles of authority and obedience."[9] This is precisely the dispute that the reign of Louis XV procured.

Malesherbes was not steeped in the law like his father; his mind could not revel in its minutiae. But he was a magistrate who was able to give voice to the law for a more generalized political purpose. During his tenure the main issue of conflict between throne and parlement was fiscality and taxation, and it was the special vocation of his court to treat such matters. But this was merely the tip of the iceberg. Taxation was joined to the religious schism occasioned by the papal bull Unigenitus, issued on 8 September 1713 by Pope Clement XI, explicitly denouncing Jansenist Catholicism, and registered as a law of France on 15 February 1714 by the Parlement of Paris under the orders of Louis XIV. Not only did Unigenitus commit the large party of Jansenists to a relentless persecution, harrying them into the religious underground, but it interfered grievously with the autonomous traditions of the "Gallican" church in France: in denouncing Quesnel's ninety-first proposition, it legalized through the threat of excommunication the papacy's interference with the civil obedience of Frenchmen, up to and including the king.[10] This the Gallican parlementarians could not tolerate as a principle; were they not the guardians of the law? Nor did the cruelty toward the Jansenists, traditionally strong in the ranks of the *robe*, sit well with the magistrates. Jansenism and Gallicanism, which had previously existed on separate planes, commenced to fuse in a secular frame of reference.[11] A single example, from a remonstrance of 1756, will illustrate how closely political issues had come to dominate the long Unigenitus controversy: "Sire, the time has finally come when [the royal authority] should exercise its rights without discrimination (*indistinctement*) toward all citizens, because they are all indiscriminately its subjects. Never has it been more essential to use rigor in repressing those who aspire to erect an independent state within the State, pretending to spiritualize that which they would usurp."[12] Gradually, this battle called forth a Gallican opposition that would not only submit the prince to the "fundamental laws of the state,"[13] but would encourage vistas toward popular sovereignty: "Authority is more fundamentally attached to the society than to the chief who governs it. Those exercising it die and are replaced; the [social] body never dies."[14]

Finally, a mortal blow struck the Jesuits, pillar of papal supremacy and influential in royal councils. On 3 September 1759 the Society of Jesus was expelled from Portugal after an attempt, the year before, on the life of the king. Since the Jesuits had a well-known doctrine of regicide, French thoughts turned to Ravaillac, and the fears of Louis XV, who had escaped Damiens in 1757, were aroused. Encouraged by the Duc de Choiseul, the parlements struck again and again at this "foreign element," cementing far closer relations among the provincial courts in a ground swell of Gallicanism. Reluctantly, by edict of November 1764, the government consented to the dissolution of the Jesuits, for, as Cardinal de Bernis put it, "the destruction of a Society that it had always protected would [otherwise] have been achieved in spite of [royal] authority."[15]

Tax grievances added to the politico-religious controversies of the 1750s gave the parlementary caste a community of interest in an ideological context of freedom versus despotism. This presumption of parlementary unity struck at the manipulative capacities of royal power, for the royal doctrine held that the sovereign courts were merely separate and exclusive emanations of the king's jurisdiction and creatures of his will. The countertheory had been elaborately brought forward by the controversialist Le Paige, who maintained that all the courts constituted a single parlement, "having only been dismembered over a period of the last three or four centuries."[16] This led to a notion of "classes," enunciated by the Parlement of Paris in its remonstrances of 22 August 1756: "The metropolitan Court [i.e., itself] and all its colonies are the diverse classes of a single and unique Parlement . . . nourished by the same principles, bent upon the same object."[17] The presumptive "unity" of the parlements entailed the right of one of them to remonstrate over matters affecting the others, a claim of such grave affront to the monarchy that Louis XV felt bound to restate the principle of absolute sovereignty in his famous "séance de la flagellation" of 3 March 1766: ". . . what occurred in my Parlements of Pau and Rennes does not concern my other Parlements; I took action with those two Courts as my authority saw fit, and I owe no accounting to anyone."[18] The forces of opposition, thus defined, were steering toward the crisis of 1770.

Despite this parlementary coalescence, it must not be assumed that the magistracy of France achieved a single unity of design and purpose. Regardless of the traditional ideology of the courts, "royalty was the source of all justice; the king could intervene in any trial. Never having alienated his right to dispense justice, the king could use this right at his pleasure, either by thrusting aside his usual executors, or by remanding the issue to his Council, or by the appointment of special decision-making bodies."[19] Indeed there was a higher *cour souveraine*, the Grand Conseil, with jurisdiction over the entire realm, sensitive to the influence of the court, to which the king could refer cases as it pleased him.[20] The royal position still had advocates in the courts and could tempt ambitions. Maupeou and Terray, to be discussed ahead, were parlementarians. Indeed, in 1750 a young scion of the legal nobility—trained, however, in the Sorbonne—named Anne-Robert-Jacques de Turgot scratched off a fragment called "Plan d'un ouvrage contre le Parlement," in which he insisted that the monarchy must have "the last word."[21] Although as minister in 1774 Turgot supported the restoration of the parlements, it was without great enthusiasm: the expedients of Maupeou had simply proved worse and had been stigmatized by public opinion. He wrote to Dupont de Nemours that he did not "take a great interest in the broken pitchers."[22] Yet fissures in the unity of the *robe* did not thwart the capacity of the courts to obstruct legislation, rally public opinion to specific causes, and create unwanted aristocratic nuisances.

The Cour des Aides of Paris, created by the Estates-General under Jean le Bon in 1355, had been organized as a sovereign court by edict of 1411.[23] For a long time it had led a modest and precarious existence. Malesherbes's character and the issues of the times thrust it into a leading role. When Malesherbes took office, its personnel included, beneath him, a procureur-général, three avocats-généraux, nine présidents, and about fifty conseillers, distributed in three chambers.[24] It had, among other things, to confront the *vingtièmes*—surplus taxes on revenue, usually used to finance war. The vingtième, first imposed in 1749, was doubled by royal declaration of 7 July 1756, tripled in 1760 for a period of two years and renewed again in 1761. With the coming of peace in 1763, the third vingtième was suppressed, but the second was maintained for six years by edicts of 1767 and 1768.[25] Usually the Cour des Aides was called on to register the tax edicts only after they had been bludgeoned through the Parlement of Paris. However, Malesherbes's opposition was more than perfunctory. On 7 July 1756, in attacking the second vingtième, he specifically defended two categories of citizens: the merchants, who "by ponderous work, continual risk, and extensive connections (des combinaisons presque infinies) have found a way to create a taste for our arts in foreign nations and to enrich us with the product of their surplus (luxe);[26] and the peasants, "whose daily labor increases the value of the products of the earth and the sum of real wealth . . . men sunk in misery and work, whose threadbare existence alone would be a reason for granting relief."[27] Malesherbes's remonstrances were often distinguished by their concrete representation of the plight of the people (as he put it, "a people buried in taxes will finally refuse to pay them");[28] this portrayal was characteristically doubled by the legal argument: "The people have never so cruelly felt the weight of their wretchedness. . . . The order forbidding deliberation is the most crushing blow for the magistracy."[29]

Other taxes, especially the taille, caused the vigorous protest of the Cour des Aides. In 1768 Malesherbes and his colleagues held out a year longer than the Parlement of Paris in refusing to register a royal measure. The king responded in bad humor: "My Cour des Aides should not make it necessary for me to recall the laws granting its existence and the limits of its jurisdiction that forbid participation in the administration of my Estates."[30] Malesherbes's remonstrance had insinuated secrecy, cabal, and disorder: "On whose say-so is it possible to give credence to the assertion [that the people could bear this increase]? . . . Sire, it is in the night of silence that such a great operation was prepared; invisible hands traced for you the portrait of the condition of your peoples."[31] The author must have been a careful student of the passages on "oriental despotism" in Montesquieu's De l'esprit des lois; indeed that term occurs boldly in a private letter written after Malesherbes's exile, to Madame Douet in 1772.[32] A second point to note is the figurative pathos of Malesherbe's great remonstrances. As early as 1760 Auget de Montyon praised him for a "spellbinding (entraînante) eloquence, a brilliant imagination . . . a love for humanity carried to enthusiasm."[33] This eloquence merited him a fauteuil in the Académie Française in 1775. No doubt this was a quality also inspired by his intimacy with Rousseau, to whom he wrote on Christmas Day 1761: ". . . I love truth, I sympathize with all true passions. . . . I only have an aversion for injustice and falsehood."[34] Rousseau himself could have written the words.

Malesherbes had no illusions about the personal motives and political habits of parlementarians, an opinion he expressed to Turgot: "As for our magistrates of the Parlement, almost all have a common vice which, in my eyes, is the worst of all; it is the unconquerable habit of artifice (*finesse*) and falsity, which, joined to their facility for despotic speech, makes it impossible to do business with them."[35] Why, then, did he defend their prerogatives so forcefully? It was in part because only the courts could insure a semblance of invariant justice in France: "Vainly have the laws been made, for [now] one substitutes variable principles, what one likes to call administration . . . always subject to favoritism."[36] Thus remonstrances were "that unique residue of liberty [by which] the nation could make its voice heard to its King."[37] There was also professional pride: "In the peaceful profession of justice there are heroes as great as those of the armies, who even have the advantage of owing to nobody or nothing but themselves and their own virtue what the heroes of war share with millions of soldiers."[38] Malesherbes seems to have subscribed to the "unity of the magistracy" as well. This would be illustrated in practice when the Cour des Aides protested fiscally-related matters in Dijon and Rennes. And in a remonstrance of 1770 he referred the king to "your Courts, that former council of the kings, that unique interpreter of the sentiments of the Nation. . . ."[39]

Malesherbes's "constitution" was not specific, but it predicated a wholesome balance between the royal power and the subjects' rights and means of redress. "In a well-run (*policé*) country . . . all those holding sovereign power should have three checks on them: the laws, recourse to superior power, public opinion."[40] Remonstrances of 1768 speak of having "no other goal but the same as that of Your Majesty: preserving your state within the constitution it had under your predecessors, and opposing dangerous innovations."[41] This does not mean a reluctance for true reform; it is the loathing of an evolution in which "every order of birth, everybody, every rank, every dignity can no longer but fear the imperious force of absolute power. . . ."[42] Malesherbes never claimed that the sovereign courts were an ideal voice of the people. If deprived of this expression, "then . . . [the courts] would beg [the king] to be well advised to listen directly to his people through the voice of their deputies, in a convocation of the Estates-General of the Kingdom."[43] This was in 1763; in 1768 he repeated the advice.[44] He also recommended the creation of provincial assemblies in the *pays d'élection*, a measure later taken up by Necker.[45] And in 1771, after the Parlement of Paris had been fractured, he declared that "there exist in France, as in all monarchies, some inviolable rights belonging to the nation" and challenged: "Sire, ask the Nation itself."[46]

On 24 April 1767 a traveling merchant named Guillaume Monnerat

had been arrested in Paris on charges of trafficking in contraband to-
bacco. Thrown into prison by a *lettre de cachet* inspired by the Tax Farm,
he languished there until the end of 1768, when he provided evidence of
false arrest and demanded reparation. Refused by the Tax Farm, he peti-
tioned the Cour des Aides for redress. The Grand Conseil quashed the
case.[47] In Malesherbes's remonstrances, he attacked the Tax Farm as "an
apparatus of terror," and he condemned the hated *lettres de cachet*.[48] But
his most passionately wrought sentence was the following: "No citizen
in your kingdom is assured that he will not see his freedom sacrificed to
personal vengeance; for no one is great enough to be sheltered from the
hatred of a minister, nor small enough to escape that of a clerk of the Tax
Farm."[49] It was a grand indictment of despotism directed toward Chancellor Maupeou, who was not a man to forgive.

Although structural categories of controversy are endemic in such
language as Louis XV's "sans dépendance ni partage" or the parlements'
"classes, unité, indivisibilité," it is appropriate to turn here to personalities, if only because all politics was highly personalized in our period,
commented on and understood as such. From 1763 on, there had been a
running battle between the Duc d'Aiguillon, commander-in-chief of the
royal administration in Brittany, and the Parlement of Rennes, especially
its procureur-général René de La Chalotais, who had been extremely
vigorous in his campaign against the Jesuits.[50] *Lettres de cachet* were
issued against the Bretons on 28 May 1765.[51] On the night of 10 November, La Chalotais, his son, and two others were summarily imprisoned. The king sought to force a registration; the great majority of the
Parlement refused, and their offices were declared vacant. For three years
d'Aiguillon attempted unsuccessfully to create a rump parlement. In the
meantime, other parlements, conspicuously Paris and Rouen, had remonstrated in favor of the prisoners and the dismissed magistrates.
D'Aiguillon—an able but stubborn man, later a favorite of Du Barry—
resigned his office in August 1768; in the following July a part of the
former parlement was recalled. It seemed that compromise might be
achieved in 1769, for even the younger Maupeou, now chancellor, was
for the moment conciliatory. But La Chalotais was intransigent.

On 3 March 1770 the Parlement of Rennes opened a criminal proceeding against d'Aiguillon. Contrary to the king's advice, he demanded to be
judged, as was his right, by the Court of Peers at Versailles.[52] The trial
opened on 4 April 1770 under the presidency of Louis XV; as it proceeded, evidence was brought forth that not only tended to inculpate
d'Aiguillon for his acts of 1766 but to implicate the council and the
ministry. Perceiving the vulnerability of his highest officials, Louis XV

stopped the trial by *lit de justice* on 27 June and declared d'Aiguillon innocent. The Parlement of Paris retaliated on 2 July by excluding d'Aiguillon from the peerage; the king overrode this *arrêt* a day later. It was in his remonstrances of 10 July that Lamoignon, Malesherbes's cousin, spoke of "anxiety, terror, and desolation."[53] Then, on 20 August, two Breton magistrates, Lanoue and Goyon, were arbitrarily arrested upon leaving an audience with the king. A *lit de justice* of 3 September forbade the Parlement of Paris to devote any further scrutiny to the affair.[54] On 3 December Maupeou issued a terse edict forbidding the Parlement to use the terms "classes, unité, indivisibilité" to refer to the sovereign courts; for, as he put it, predecessor monarchs, in creating the courts, had done so "at different dates" and "independently of each other, establishing no sign of relations among them."[55] A *lit de justice* of 7 December enforced this edict.

Up to 1770 the Cour des Aides had not become entangled in the d'Aiguillon affair, which was outside its jurisdiction. However, with the arrest of the two conseillers of the Parlement of Rennes—soon after the Monnerat case—Malesherbes prepared sizzling remonstrances. This "unity" of action could be justified by the fact that the Breton Parlement sat also as a Cour des Aides. But in fact the issue was that of approaching conflict with the chancellor. Malesherbes's stinging message was that if such actions could be taken, no citizen was secure. "When one wants to use sovereign power to satisfy private passions," he wrote, "authority then threatens those who already groan beneath injustice, giving them the choice of committing acts that might be ascribed to disobedience or of suffering both outrage and oppression."[56] By this stance he further associated the fate of his secondary court, never before exiled, with that of the Parlement of Paris.

Choiseul's eclipse removed a last restraining force. The Duc de Choiseul, long in power as War Minister, had been relatively friendly with the *gens de robe*, sympathetic to political Gallicanism, and hostile to the Jesuits. However, he was hated by the *dévots* and the king's young mistress. His love of extravagance made him even more vulnerable, and some intemperate acts in foreign policy caused him to be disgraced and exiled to his property of Chanteloup by *lettre de cachet* on 24 December 1770.[57] D'Aiguillon, so recently under trial, quickly filled the vacuum of power, allied to Maupeou and the Abbé Terray, in what became known as the triumvirate.

René-Nicolas-Charles-Augustin de Maupeou had been on the fringes of power since 1763. In that year, the refusal of Lamoignon de Blancmesnil to retire had resulted in the appointment of his father René-

Charles de Maupeou to the unusual post of vice chancellor. At the same time, the son succeeded Molé as Président of the Parlement of Paris. When Lamoignon resigned in 1768, the king appointed Maupeou *père* chief magistrate on 15 September. By prior arrangement, engineered by Choiseul, he occupied the office for just one day and then relinquished it, together with the ministerial post of Garde des Sceaux, to his son. If Choiseul had foreseen future ingratitude, Malesherbes might have been made chancellor.[58] Maupeou rode the political currents as it suited his advancement. A contemporary draws the following portrait: "he was distinguished only by his cunning, by his indifference toward justice for its own sake, by his flexibility and by his intrigues on behalf of the powerful and all who could be useful to his views. [He was] a man without education, without wisdom, without knowledge, who showed no zeal or affection for the public good. . . ."[59] Against this imputation of narrowness and guile it must be said that Maupeou possessed one indispensable quality: that of knowing how to phrase with deliberate clarity the policy that his master of the moment—be it the Parlement of Paris or Louis XV—wanted.

Though the chancellorship itself was a commanding height, Maupeou also needed ministerial allies. On 16 January 1770, adeptly avoiding a trap set by Choiseul, he obtained from the king the appointment of the Abbé Terray as Controleur-Général (Minister of Finance). Terray had risen from obscurity and indigence partly through his natural skills, but especially by inheriting the fortune of an uncle and by cultivating useful patrons, not an unusual or disreputable tactic in the Old Regime. After buying himself an office as conseiller to the Parlement of Paris, he managed to gain appointment to its inner circle, the Grand' Chambre. Here he forged his alliance with Maupeou. Though his duplicity and immorality did not go unnoticed, Terray established a firm reputation as a fiscal watchdog. On behalf of the Parlement of Paris "he composed the famous iterative remonstrances of January 1769; he gathered the facts and demonstrated most energetically the horrible situation of France's finances."[60] While growing richer himself, he cynically struck at the prodigality of parlementarians and ministers alike. He and Maupeou shared a temporary popularity. Once in office, Terray reduced the annual cost of the state's indebtedness by 39 million livres through what might be termed an extortion from its creditors that impaired its future ability to raise money. In 1774 Turgot discovered heavy liabilities and extreme irregularities: not only had Terray borrowed lavishly, but he had sweetened the sinecures of Madame du Barry's favorites.[61]

As Minister of War and Foreign Affairs, the Duc d'Aiguillon brought high birth to the triumvirate. This favorite of Du Barry, saved from serious embarrassment when the king quashed his trial, matched Choiseul's previous luster and cemented the connection between king, royal mistress, and the two magistrate-ministers. Though by 1772 he had come to despise Maupeou, his animus against the Parlement of Paris had thrust him into the chancellor's camp at the critical moment.[62]

We have already noted the strengths and anomalies of both the parlementary and royal positions. If the law was mediate between sovereign authority and public rights, could it be said that this law emanated from the parlements? Evidently not; for they had no claim to lawmaking. By what right could they unmake or hinder the force of the law? The pretension of a hereditary and largely aristocratic corps of about two thousand individuals, "indivisible" or not, to speak for the nation was rather bizarre. The excuse for this pretension was "despotism." But the logic of the parlementary argument led, in spite of the desires of many of the magistrates, toward the unmentionable thesis of representative popular sovereignty. The royal argument was easier to state and to defend in theory. It reduced the sovereign courts to individual bodies of consultation, functional conveniences established by the king that he could dissolve or reshape if they became cumbersome and rebellious. Yet the royal appeal was blemished by its arbitrary and costly policies. In practice the crown knew from bitter experience that it needed courts of trained magistrates to dispense justice in France; though it had the power to fracture the courts, and occasionally did so, the crown found them difficult to replace.[63]

By late 1770, the self-styled metropolitan court, the Parlement of Paris, was no longer recalcitrant; it was unbudging. Maupeou and Terray, as vengeful as they were politic,[64] were determined to lay it low, expecting to create a rump substitute by co-options to the Grand' Chambre. They were also wrathful toward the Cour des Aides for its persistent badgering in the Monnerat case. Although the blow of exile did not fall on the parlementarians until 19 January 1771, the outcome was manifest in the *lit de justice* of 7 December 1770. Here it was noted that the Duc d'Aiguillon had taken his place among the peers and dignitaries for the first time since July. Maupeou made the royal doctrine crystal clear:

> When the legislator [i.e., the king] wants to declare his will, you are his organ and his goodness permits you to advise him; he invites you to enlighten him and commands you to show him the truth.
> Your mission is then over.
> The King, in his wisdom, weighs your observations; he poses

them against his own determining motives, and by this glance that takes in the scope of the monarchy he judges the benefits and disadvantages of the law.

At his command you owe him the most complete submission.[65]

As expected, the Parlement of Paris presented new remonstrances and suspended its functions. After the passage of the holidays it recalled to the king the existence of fundamental laws inviolable by royal edict, and refused obedience. But Maupeou's was a thesis in whose presence even the Parlement of Paris had to feel uncomfortable. The accurate reply was 1789.

The royal doctrine had complex resources for the punishment and reorganization of the sovereign courts. An interesting memoir composed about 1760 by Bourgeois de Boynes suggested an indirect and meticulous strategy that would have required three visitations of the parlement by the royal person, progressively stripping the recalcitrants of their functions, offices, and emoluments.[66] It would later be announced as royal policy when the parlements were recalled in 1774. But Louis XV and Maupeou chose a more precipitous form of action. Perceiving that the resistance of the Paris Parlement was total and even endemic in the heretofore docile Grand Conseil, Maupeou perpetrated his "terror." On the night of 19 January, all members of the Parlement received *lettres de cachet* containing a final summons to resume their duties. Then, on 21 January, 130 magistrates of the Parlement were exiled and their offices were confiscated by royal edict. On 23 January the Conseil d'Etat was bludgeoned into assuming the functions of the Parlement. Vigorous protests by the provincial courts poured in, and two princes of the blood (Condé and d'Orléans) seconded their complaints in an unpublished memoir.

Malesherbes had yet to play his outstanding role. Before examining this, it will be of interest to call attention to his persistent use of the word "terror" to describe the policies of Louis XV, for this is evidently one of the sources that influenced the career of the concept in 1793.[67] Malesherbes had adopted this term as early as 1756.[68] It meant for him: suspension of law; attacks by authority against the fundamental security of the person; arbitrary assaults on property, including offices; and the psychological state of being subject to these uses of power. There is a *pensée* of Malesherbes that reads: "let the prince who believes that he can reign over the ministers of justice by terror reflect on the fact that fear is the portion of base souls. . . ."[69] To anticipate somewhat: when his own court was falling, he apostrophized, "Sire, the terror that one wants to inspire in all the orders of the state has not shaken your Cour des Aides. . . ."[70]

The glory and terror of his court were now to follow. The remonstrances of 18 February contain some of Malesherbes's most exalted prose: "Our demand," he wrote, "is going to expose us to an implacable vengeance; but our silence would cause the whole nation to accuse us of treason or cowardice." He continued: "By what fatal accident, Sire, can one wish to force the most faithful subjects to recall to their master the laws imposed on him by Providence when he was given the crown? . . . You hold [the crown] only from God, Sire; but you are also beholden for your power to the willing submission of your subjects. . . ."[71] With a directness that even the Parlement of Paris had not dared use, Malesherbes unambiguously proposed the rights of the nation against those of the monarch. After asking for the Estates-General, he concluded: "The incorruptible testimony of [the nation's] representatives will at least inform you whether it is true, as your ministers ceaselessly proclaim, that the magistracy alone serves its interests in violating the laws, or if the cause that we defend today is that of the whole people *by whom and for whom* you reign!"[72]

Mortally offended by this language, the king refused to receive the Cour des Aides for a traditional presentation at the end of February.[73] Other consequences of the judicial upheaval need not concern this study.[74] The entire month of March was passed in fretful shadowboxing between the chancellor and the magistrates. On 22 March, Malesherbes took the bold step of ordering the annulment of all registrations made by Maupeou's transitional parlement and refusing to recognize its legal authority.[75] On 25 March the king ordered the registers of the Cour des Aides seized. A tense meeting between Malesherbes, accompanied by three senior colleagues, and Maupeou at Versailles on 27 March was followed by a brief, hostile audience with the king. Malesherbes was not able to preside over the last sitting of the Cour des Aides on 9 April; for on 6 April at Malesherbes, he had received a *lettre de cachet*, postdated the eighth, commanding him to remain on his estate.[76] Yet his spirit was present, and the other magistrates were well prepared. On 24 March he had written to the Duc de la Vrillière (whom he would replace in 1775 as Secretary of State for the Maison du Roi): "I have forseen what enemies I was going to incite against my court (*Compagnie*) and I have always been determined to take the position I take today, even if things should come to the last resort."[77]

In the same archive as the *lettre de cachet* there is a wealth of fascinating documentation, especially Maupeou's secret "plan for the supression of the Cour des Aides." It is a marvel of "terror," *ancien régime* style. Under four explicit headings, this operations plan precisely describes all steps that are to be taken, and by whom, from the posting of the Malesherbes *lettre de cachet* to the closure and exile of the court. No stone is left unturned.[78] There are also special memoirs of instruction to the Duc de Richelieu and all subordinate participants, as well as a document called "agenda," detailing all the orders for the sequence of the operation. To stress the punitive protocol of the coup, a note from Maupeou adds: "Once the suppression [of the Court] has been published, the dismissed officers have only the status of private persons (*simples particuliers*); thus the *lettres de cachet* should be delivered by musketeers and the addressees of the lettres should not receive the titles of Président or Conseiller."[79]

Clearly there was a will not only to disgrace the magistrates but to humiliate them. Nonetheless, when the Marshal de Richelieu and his bailiffs declared "we have extinguished and suppressed, we extinguish and suppress our Cour des Aides of Paris," the court reacted worthily. Avocat-Général Antoine-Louis Bellanger declared the act "illegal . . . a sham (*prétendu*) . . . without any consent on our part, against our conviction, against our will, and, we dare to say it, against the good of the state."[80] Richelieu had to threaten the magistrates to make them disperse. A *lit de justice* of 13 April transferred the functions of the Cour des Aides to the Grand Conseil, now refurbished as the organ of justice for Paris. Malesherbes dwelt in sorrow on his lands, suffering both from his disgrace and the death of his wife.

Was there a case for Maupeou? Many intellectuals could conceive only of reform from above—by a "legal despot" and an enlightened administration—and they reacted favorably. Voltaire regretted the banishment of the magistrates but he praised Louis XV for "bestowing on the nation the greatest good ever granted by any monarch."[81] The decree of Maupeou of 9 April 1771 suppressing the Cour des Aides stressed the same benefits that appealed to Voltaire:

> If the present situation of our finances does not allow for a decrease of taxes, we are at least eager to give a part of our people prompter and less costly resources against the abuses of tax collection. In our [new] Parlement of Paris and in the councils formed as a result of the edict of last February they will receive justice without charge, able defenders, and judges who, placed closer to them [i.e., territorially], will better sense all their griefs [*maux*] and hasten to make reparation. Finally, they will no longer be exposed to conflicts of jurisdiction that weary them with delays and exhaust them with useless procedures.[82]

The utility of such a reform is evident. But Maupeou's clumsy and arbitrary execution drove it onto the rocks, animating political jealousies and alienating public opinion and a large part of the trained magistracy. Maupeou was pilloried in hundreds of libels, collected as the so-called *Maupeouana*, and several times threatened with assassination.[83] After three years, even philosophes like Voltaire, d'Alembert, and Condorcet were ready for the return of the old parlements, just as they would later welcome Malesherbes's entry to the ministry.[84] Moreover, clever old Maurepas, whom Louis XVI called first to his side as counselor, detested Maupeou and had no desire to share in the unpopularity of any of his works.[85] The coup proved even easier to undo than it had been to enact.

Exiled to his estates, Malesherbes absorbed himself in research, but he also maintained a wide, semisecret network of correspondence with sympathizers, former colleagues, and other magistrates. He upheld the *esprit de corps* of his court and the magistracy as a whole in the expectation that their disgrace would not be final. He communicated through intermediaries with influential princes like d'Orléans and Conti or administrators who had amply reflected on Maupeou's failures, like Bourgeois de Boynes, then Minister of the Navy. And he exchanged opinions with Turgot.[86] Dramatically the picture changed with the sudden death of Louis XV and the ascendancy of Maurepas, a friend of the magistrates. Malesherbes now basked in the glory that his bravery and banishment had won him. Odes were written to his wisdom.[87] He was eagerly solicited by Turgot and others close to the young king for advice on how to restore the magistracy. These thoughts were communicated in a flurry of correspondence with Turgot and in four brief memoirs addressed to Louis XVI.[88] Malesherbes wanted a workable balance between justice and authority. He wished the honor of the deposed magistrates restored, but not vengefully. Sympathizing with legal reform, he refused to enter the ministry as Garde des Sceaux; for, he insisted, as former head of a sovereign court he would not be well placed to "persuade [his colleagues] to register voluntarily anything that would limit their power."[89] He jested that he would be sacrificing a life's reputation to a lost cause. He disingenuously pleaded incompetence, recommending Maurepas himself, Amelot, Portail, Miromesnil—and, preferably, Turgot—for the portfolio of justice (it was given to Miromesnil, Premier Président of the Parlement of Rouen, two weeks later).[90] He also had a plan for easing the old deadlock: the reestablishment of the former courts would be axiomatic, for their privileges had never ceased; the laws of Maupeou's parlements would be valid, for they had acted provisionally; a renewed Grand Conseil would sit in the place of any courts that refused obedience.[91]

Malesherbes addressed the king without impudence but without flattery. He pointed out that the love and confidence of the French people were dependent on the security of legal protection placed in the hands of a hereditary magistracy. He did not doubt that the scope of royal authority transcended the courts, but he held that despotic uses destroyed its effectiveness and rationale. Fixed laws were the precondition of the nation's happiness and stability, for "the property, life, and honor of the subjects are exposed to great danger when the laws are variable, the decisions arbitrary, and the judges uncertain."[92] Finally, he told the king, "of all [official] bodies, the magistracy is the one where principles of honesty and ancient virtues have been best preserved."[93] This didactic tone was adopted for a youth of nineteen; Turgot also tried to keep his memoirs to the monarch consecutive and simple.[94] The aim was to inaugurate the new reign in a spirit of conciliation and confidence.

Nonetheless, after 12 November 1774, Malesherbes was once again President of the Cour des Aides, speaking in the same tones of independence that had angered Louis XVI's grandsire. To be sure, the restoration of the exiled courts was a moment of joy and good feeling. The king's greeting to the returning heroes in his *lit de justice* was not entirely to their liking, for his edicts (composed by Miromesnil) emphasized submission and attempted, ultimately without success, to impose the Grand Conseil upon future delinquencies.[95] But, after remonstrances, the king retreated, and the Paris Parlement moved back into its comfortable living space. Malesherbes remained ebullient: "Justice is in the heart of the King; the nation has everything to hope for."[96] A week afterward, leading a delegation, Malesherbes told the monarch: "Yours, Sire, will be a reign of justice. . . . We had been asking for a legislator, Sire, and the first acts of your administration have caused us to recognize in Your Majesty the one destined for us by Providence."[97]

It was not a long honeymoon. The Cour des Aides produced its first remonstrances on 10 April 1775. And on 6 May Malesherbes gave vent to the longest protest he had ever written, ostensibly on the subject of fiscal griefs and the Tax Farm, but dwelling on the accumulated injustices of administrative despotism and arbitrary power that characterized the entire system. How could he have addressed a complaint of such scope and belligerence to a king scarcely seated and a ministry that he would shortly join? Of course Malesherbes did not then believe that he would accept a portfolio. But, beyond this, the "great remonstrances" are a kind of education of the prince. The king had to be made to see how deep in abuses the Old Regime was sunk, no matter who its master and its executants might be. The most interesting parts of the document were pleas for communication and decentralization: communication between monarch and nation, and defense of the interests of the voiceless multitude by provincial assemblies. The warning fell on barren ground.[98].

On 8 July 1775, Malesherbes, chosen for a new destiny, presided over his last session of the Cour des Aides. At his official resignation on 14 July he was told by his colleagues: "The King summons you to his side; you have made him hear the voice of truth, and that voice has inspired his decision."[99] Actually, the king had every suspicion of Malesherbes's reformative impulses, and Malesherbes every anxiety about his own political competence: their collaboration was secured only by the most assiduous persuasions of Turgot, Véri, and Maurepas and lasted but ten months.[100] Malesherbes was appointed Secretary of State for the Maison du Roi (a jurisdiction including not only the royal household, but also Paris, religion, and a host of police matters). The position ill-became his temper and talents, for it rubbed him up against all the place-seekers of the court and created embarrassing friction between his new duties and old loyalties. He felt both socially and professionally out of place in Versailles. But he was determined to support Turgot in his efforts to reform and to pursue matters important to himself—the toleration of the Protestants and the relaxation of the *lettres de cachet*.

Impolitic on this field of maneuver and self-deprecatory besides, Malesherbes hated the petty details of his office and the useless ceremonials of his surroundings. Despite his public popularity, knowledgeable contemporaries awarded him low marks as a minister. Malesherbes thought Turgot too rash, but he himself was too easily demoralized by depredations on his budget of thirty-three million livres a year. The Abbé de Véri quotes him as saying: " 'I could prepare the materials for reform, but anyone who expects much of that is making a big mistake; by nature (*caractère*) I am incapable of seeing it through; I am too anxious to believe that everyone who walks into my office is right.' "[101] But Malesherbes was not really disingenuous. He seconded Turgot loyally, even if they might disagree over timing and particular arrangements. He attempted to bring needed corrections to the government of Paris, to deal with poverty, begging, and vagabondage, to restrict the uses of the *lettres de cachet*, to encourage a reform of the prisons and penal legislation, and to obtain religious toleration, as well as to create economies in the royal household.[102] If his results were modest after ten months, this should occasion no surprise. Though Malesherbes exuded reluctance and Turgot a kind of enterprising zeal in power, and though neither was quite sure of the other in their last days in the ministry, both lost the confidence of the king when he grew wary of their reformative intentions and found them unacceptable to his wife.[103] The paths of Malesherbes and Louis XVI would not cross again until 1787, in darker moments when the realm was about to be uprooted. The former magistrate accepted his "disgrace" without bitterness and with a keen sense of relief, not failing to supply the monarch with some new memoirs. Despotism had receded, but chaos was growing.

15. The Political Thought of Lamoignon de Malesherbes

Malesherbes may be claimed as a serious political thinker despite his scattered and topical form of presentation, for he was a great touchstone of the monarchy's inability to reform itself. He is obviously, in the main, an exemplar of the "constitutionalist" tradition of French thought, but he is not merely a stodgy descendant of old formulas. Because of special developments in France—notably the heritage of sacral kingship and the thirst for a strong center of political order after the Wars of Religion—an unalloyed reverence for monarchy infected even the constitutionalist tradition and indeed helped shape it.[1] However, Malesherbes also shared, with the fugitive or disinherited Protestants whose cause became so closely his own, a skeptical view of royal power; thus he became an eloquent proponent of civil toleration within a progressively stagnant and unjust political order. The character of his doctrine, though never fickle, may be called Janus-faced. On the one hand, history and tradition meant much to him, and logical abstractions had little appeal. On the other, he saw benefits in novelty and had no wish to take the world backward in time, like many advocates of the *thèse nobiliaire*. He is presumed to have written: "There is a great advantage when what appears to conform to reason and justice is supported by the authority of past centuries."[2] But also, in a speech to the Cour des Aides of 1751, he proposed to fix the limits between respectable tradition and the prejudices that must be destroyed.[3] He could face the future because he felt an anchorage in the past: in this he was more consistent and complacent than Montesquieu, who is in many ways his kindred spirit. He had affinities not only with Montesquieu, but with Rousseau and Turgot. His distances from them are also worth recording.

Montesquieu and Malesherbes shared a horror of despotism and a willingness to suggest that France might not be exempt from its ravages. Although the tone and message of both writers are quite similar—and indeed it is certain that Malesherbes's conception derives from Montes-

The original version of this chapter appeared under the title, "The Political Thought of Lamoignon de Malesherbes" by George Armstrong Kelly, was published in *Political Theory*, vol. 7, no. 4 (Fall 1979), pp. 485–508, and is reprinted herewith by permission of the publisher, Sage Publications, Inc.

quieu's—it is well to keep in mind that Montesquieu was reflecting principally on the reign of the *roi soleil* (a past event), whereas Malesherbes was directly designating a present condition. Also, Montesquieu distinguished most carefully between a *monarchy* and a *despotism*, while Malesherbes appears to have believed that "despotic monarchy" was not a non sequitur.[4] As Montesquieu writes: "Monarchy is lost when a prince thinks he shows his power better in changing the order of things than in following it; when he takes away the natural functions of some officers and gives them arbitrarily to others, and when he is more enamored of his fantasies than of his regulated will."[5] This passage prettily describes Malesherbes's sense of the events of 1765–74. Yet Malesherbes, not being bound to Montesquieu's typology, was never so bold as to speak of the "loss" of monarchy. The difference, however, should not be overstressed; for Malesherbes's notion of despotism encompasses a mode of domination that is outside the rules, a situation where there is no longer any shared interest between the monarch and his subjects. As Premier Président of the Cour des Aides, Malesherbes saw as his main task that of protecting the country and the magistracy against "that apparatus of authority . . . always frightening to the people."[6] Otherwise, the result was "despotism, that form of government frightening to the people and contrary to the rights of humanity." And Malesherbes conceded that his court had had "the boldness to label as despotism a power exercised as a result of your [Majesty's] orders."[7] Malesherbes was among the first to speak in such tones, but by 1763 the Parlement of Paris was referring to "the humiliating condition of a subjugated people."[8] Later, in 1774, Malesherbes defined the matter in a memoir for Louis XVI: "Despotism ignores the forms that regulate the process of a paternal government and preserve it from the hazards of a sudden revolution; it ignores even more the general laws which secure the succession to the throne, the honor, life, liberty, and fortune of the subjects; it will not listen to remonstrances."[9]

We have noted that Malesherbes often employs the term "terror." As early as 1756, in reference to the arbitrary behavior of the commissions on contraband, he writes of "the terror that these irregular tribunals impose on the people."[10] In 1768, referring to the increase in the taille, he informs the king: "we can vouch to Your Majesty that the unique effect produced by the new operation has been to spread terror in the places where it was carried out."[11] Almost as frequently, though, Malesherbes chooses Montesquieu's haunting image of "silence," indicating both a void of moral communication and a condition in which people are neither privileged nor able to speak, in which there is no one to listen. Despotism is like Usbek's seraglio, where "a profound silence reigned throughout."[12] When the Cour des Aides remonstrated to the king on 9 July 1768, Malesherbes castigated the descent of "a night of silence."[13] Similarly: "The decadence of an empire begins at the moment when the oppressor is powerful enough to enforce his justice in silence."[14] The opposite of silence is productive dialogue between the sovereign and his people: this is one of the most prominent themes of Malesherbes's great remonstrances of 10 April 1775.[15] For, as he observes elsewhere, "such is the misfortune of royalty that the sovereign is often the only person in his kingdom who does not hear the universal cry of the nation."[16] When we add Malesherbes's theme of communication to Montesquieu's motto of silence, we perceive that he has displaced the emphasis of the latter on the transmissions of the *corps intermédiaires* in favor of a more extensive kind of public discourse.

If Malesherbes seems to advance somewhat beyond Montesquieu by urging that the king reach out more directly and locally to hear the pleas of the citizens, he is still at one with Montesquieu in regarding the legal apparatus of the Old Regime (including its heredity and purchase of offices) as the *dépôt des lois*, essential to the confidence and stability of the nation.[17] But, on the other hand, Montesquieu goes beyond Malesherbes in assigning a positive and active content to the concept of "liberty," in part because the ancient notion of civic or republican liberty resonated far more in the soul of the former Président à Mortier of Bordeaux. For Malesherbes, liberty most often occurs with a distributive meaning, and is less inclined to abstraction from its concrete manifestations, which are mostly "negative," rarely "participatory." There are few, if any, republican residues in Malesherbes: the consummate liberty for him is the free motion of justice guaranteed to particulars by the sovereign courts.[18]

As a leader of the *gens de lettres*, Montesquieu was Malesherbes's model of perfection. Gentlemanly and nonsectarian, he had not attempted to stir up quarrels: "No one overturned more altars than he did," Malesherbes wrote to d'Alembert, "but he never indulged in personal attacks, and when he felt obliged to reply to a few critics, he did this with so superior a moderation that he reduced them to silence."[19] However, the idolatry was tempered with a criticism of some of Montesquieu's methods and political positions. If Malesherbes could agree with Montesquieu that in a monarchy "the laws take the place of [republican] virtues,"[20] he seems not to have shared his emphasis on "honneur" and "grandeur."[21] Malesherbes had both a firmer belief in "royal authority," properly exercised, and the collaboration of the king and the nation than did Montesquieu. He even once accused Montesquieu of excessive partisanship for the nobility.[22]

With the nation on the verge of political upheaval in 1788, Malesherbes, having resigned from the ministry, addressed an important "Mémoire sur la situation présente des affaires" to Louis XVI. This document, later biographers have said, might profitably have been digested by the king, who apparently ignored it. In the course of the argument, Malesherbes counsels against summoning the Estates-General in the forms of 1614: "What the Nation demands is a new Constitution which has never existed in France."[23] Malesherbes, who did not share Montesquieu's Anglophilia, had also ceased to believe in the ultimate value of corps intermédiaires as buffering zones in a monarchy. "M. de Montesquieu might well regard the intermediary powers as a necessary brake for preventing the monarchy from degenerating into despotism in a country where no other brakes existed."[24] But if such bodies had traditionally checked despotism, had they not also had their share in oppressing the people? A France endowed with new representative institutions would no longer require such "brakes."

The intellectual relationship between Malesherbes and Rousseau is of a quite different order. Their political disagreements are too obvious to require explanation: if Malesherbes had any of the qualities of a democrat, they abided strictly on the plane of moral sentiment, and that sentiment was not conflated with politics, as the citizen of Geneva taught.[25] The distinction is well expressed in one sentence by Rousseau: "I cannot hide from you, Monsieur, that I have a violent aversion for the ranks of society (états) that dominate the others; I am wrong in saying that I cannot hide this from you, for I have no difficulty in confessing it to you, you of illustrious birth, son of the Chancellor of France, and Premier Président of a sovereign court."[26] Rousseau admired and trusted Malesherbes, but he despised those of his sort. And the reasons for his hatred were, at bottom, political, though mediated by a complex psychology, because they involved relationships of domination.[27]

Malesherbes, on the other hand, believed in the functional efficacy of the ranks of society and in fact felt to the end of his days that a "respect based on the right of birth has always been in the hearts of the French . . . who, despite the philosophy of the century, have maintained their old attachment for our respectable et antique noblesse."[28] Rousseau reveled in the fantasies of a republican universe; Malesherbes could scarcely have conceived it. And yet, notably for his time and station, Malesherbes had a concrete appreciation of the misery of the plebs and a desire to extend the respect of equality in the areas he thought possible. It is likely that his connections with Rousseau helped sensitize him to a moral practice for which his heredity had not conditioned him. One of these areas was the patronizing dependency of the profession of literature: "The patrimony of the *gens de lettres* consists only in what they receive for their works or in the charity of the powerful. But no situation is so obnoxious (*fâcheux*), or perhaps even so humiliating, as to be in need of the great or to depend on their whims."[29] This is a particular example of the way Rousseau felt about everything. We cannot leap from here to the conclusion that Malesherbes followed this thought very far into politics, for he had no axiomatic belief in the common man's capacities. But Malesherbes knew the difference between *être* and *paraître* (hence his studied negligence of his own appearance), and he recognized the costs of dependency relationships and the rejuvenating power of more basic feelings among men— especially friendship. When, after the ordeals of his trial and condemnation, Louis XVI inquired of Malesherbes how he could appropriately thank his other attorneys Tronchet and de Sèze, the old man had no hesitation in replying: "Embrace them!"[30] A glow of fraternity shines through the gesture.

As Malesherbes suggests in a letter to the Comte de Sarsfield, there are two sorts of inequality. There is "real inequality," anchored in function and custom, and there is "inequality of opinion." Only the latter is susceptible to "philosophical" reform.[31] The former is of three sorts: the superiority of administrators, the authority of judges, and unequal wealth. In the "feudal government" all these sources of inequality were placed in the nobility; gradual modifications of the constitution of the state have alleviated them.[32]

"Inequality of opinion" is of two kinds. First of all, there is the respect given by a person of lesser to one of greater rank, not only through fear or interest, but also through veneration. Then there is the homage rendered by a poor man to a rich man, independently of interest, because of his luxurious style of life. The first type of respect, Malesherbes claims, has not been diminished because of "the philosophy of our modern Quakers"; rather, this has happened because the nobles themselves have prized riches above birth and breeding.[33] "Effeminate manners" and extravagance have sapped the nobility; an austere and vigorous corrective of philosophy might do it some good. "The ruined nobleman is not as well treated [by the 'great'] as a rich commoner."[34] The "great" obviously benefit from both kinds of inequality. A resulting scandal is that the administration of justice shows them unjust deference: their crimes, especially in capital cases, go unpunished because they are fawned on. Here Malesherbes is especially severe toward his colleagues of the robe, who, being an "espèce de grands," are arbitrarily sensitive about dishonoring others of their kind.[35]

In the letter to Sarsfield Malesherbes made his modest contribution to the far-reaching luxury debate of the eighteenth century. Dating from the time of the Regency, political economists like Melon (cf. his *Essai politique sur la commerce* of 1734) and new-breed optimists like the younger Voltaire (cf. his *Le Mondain*), weary of the warnings of "golden age" moralism, had seen personal luxury and national wealth as partners. In 1742 David Hume clinched the connection between luxury and "civility" (*politesse*) that some of the worldly philosophes were aiming for: an "increase [in the sentiment] of humanity" would surely be forthcoming from those who "flock into cities; love to receive and communicate knowledge, to show their wit or their breeding, their taste in conversation or living, in clothes or furniture. . . ."[36] Fénelon's Bétique and Montesquieu's Troglodytes still had their punch, but they, of course, were fictions. Then Rousseau assailed his contemporaries' felicity in both his first and second discourses (1750, 1755), a civility that was mere appearance and a luxury that crushed and ruined the farmer and the citizen.[37] Turgot was only slightly less caustic: "Extravagant luxury . . . smothers taste. Men no longer seek for the pleasure which things afford to the senses and the mind; they no longer search their own hearts."[38] Duclos came down against *politesse* in his *Considérations sur les moeurs de ce siècle* (1751). Saint-Lambert delicately tried to adjudicate the controversy in his article "Luxe" for the *Encyclopedia*, urging his readers "to shed equally the prejudices of Sparta and those of Sybaris."[39]

For Malesherbes wealth is not a real, but a derivative power, fed by opinion.[40] In this part of the analysis, we receive some of the tones of Rousseau. "The greatest misfortune of a state is surely the poverty of the people; the second is perhaps the luxury of the well-off."[41] Luxury is defined not as the exhibition of wealth, but as the desire to spend more than one has. Among other things, this vice stultifies trade: the honest merchant knows that economic prudence is necessary to his designs. But poverty, frugality, and modesty are despised in French society; the desire to emulate the rich is constant, and it becomes humiliating not to make a show of extravagance. Thus, "we are made unhappy by the respect that opinion pays to wealth."[42] Philosophy can play a role in unmasking this pretense.

If men like Rousseau, d'Alembert, and others could convince the social world of that fundamental axiom, found "in everyone's mouth and in practically nobody's heart, that *poverty is not a vice*, then a great many people who are presently considered poor and unfortunate would find themselves as rich as Croesus."[43] A Rousseau will get nowhere simply by hating the nobility. But his influence is great when he says, "I despise wealth and I scorn the means by which I might acquire it."[44] The conclusion marks both the distance between Malesherbes and Rousseau and their affinity: "There will always be subordination to the various kinds of power because there will always be people who will submit to them willingly. But the man who can live from his estate (*patrimoine*) or who learns to live by his labor will be truly free and independent if he wishes. And that . . . is the greatest good that philosophy can obtain for men."[45]

Turgot was a more conventional kind of friend and a constant collaborator in matters of detail. Malesherbes knew him first in the 1750s,[46] and their affectionate relations continued until Turgot's death on 6 April 1781. They wrote constantly and saw each other often. The two comrades left ministerial office together in 1776. When Turgot died, his family asked Malesherbes to act as the executor of his political papers.[47] However, there was a gap between their ideals of politics.

First of all, there is an often noted difference of style and temperament. Turgot, too, was erudite, with a wide variety of literary interests, but he was more single-mindedly concentrated on administration and political economy and had long harbored the ambition to become a statesman. Philosophically, Turgot was an apt pupil of Locke and Condillac, a believer in the reason of things generated by the mind's immediate awareness of principles constructed out of a more or less abstract account of sense experience. This was not Malesherbes's tradition of thought.

Turgot is sometimes dismissed as a doctrinaire exponent of political cure in France. No doubt as an experienced administrator and a theorist of parts, he was not disposed to compromise with his opponents: he shot at the bread rioters in 1775. "Turgot demanded six years of despotism to establish liberty," Baudot is credited with observing.[48] But this aphorism is not strictly true; if it were, his understanding with Malesherbes would have been more difficult. Indeed, although Turgot flirted with some of the ideas of "legal despotism," he drew back in horror from the extreme conclusions of *économistes* like Mercier de la Rivière and Baudeau.[49] In 1774, defending the term "autorité publique" to Dupont, he heaped scorn on the economists' terms *tutélaire* and *protectrice*.[50] Turgot, whose personality admittedly was scarcely apt for the more circuitous charms of political persuasion, was, without betraying himself, an effective and enterprising minister during his brief term as Ministre de la Marine and Controleur-Général. But after a brief dalliance, Louis XVI was made to fear his leadership. Malesherbes attempted to slow Turgot's pace down, but he loyally supported his colleague in the matter of free trade in grain and the "six edicts," including the controversial suppression of the *corvées*.[51]

Above all, Malesherbes and Turgot disagreed in their estimate of the value of the sovereign courts. Turgot did not like the parlements and he paid them, at best, negative lip service, partly because Turgot, though of a *robe* family, was an economist and an administrator, and partly because he was a philosophe, "neither a courtier nor a parlementaire," as he put it.[52] Malesherbes felt corporate dread and girded for war as the show-down with Maupeou approached in 1770. The response of Turgot, then the *intendant* of Limousin, was quite the opposite. He even used the word "terror" in a contrary sense. He attacked the "independence" of the judges and the courts, and their claim of unity, writing of "the terror that the unity of the whole magistracy must inspire in anyone opposed to [its] pretensions . . . the certainty that any man charged with taking rigorous measures against [it] will lose fortune and reputation, be struck with the anathema of the laws to which [it] gives voice."[53] This more than routine diatribe sounds like an oracle of the *thèse royale*. Malesherbes wished to reform the delinquencies of the sovereign courts; Turgot found their very existence a roadblock to real political remedy.

In Turgot's famous article "Fondations," there is this passage: "Public utility is the supreme law, and it should not be counterbalanced by a superstitious respect for what is called the *intention of the founders*."[54] Although Malesherbes surely did not believe in any simplistic reverence for what was old, he did not think it either wise or possible to fashion the world anew, as Turgot's argument tends to suggest. In his perennial attempts to liberate the Protestants from civil bondage, Malesherbes avoided the pellucid arguments from "right" or "utility." Instead he tried to show that the historical intention of Louis XIV had been differ-ent from what the following century supposed and that, in any case, the results desired by the monarchy at a given moment had not been achieved.[55] Of course a part of this indirect method related to strategy, but it was not the strategy of "clear and distinct ideas" by which Turgot was wont to make his case.

Beyond the vital center of Malesherbes's doctrines, we enter an area of secondary principles that are largely programmatic in nature, although, in each case, remarkably consistent with the fundamentals. With Male-sherbes, rights and liberties are perceived as both human and traditional; they are not so much to be *asserted* as to be *recovered* by the elimination of abuses. Not only are most of Malesherbes's reforms derivative from his hereditary sense of participation as a magistrate in an ongoing project designated as "the nation" (meaning the French monarchy), but they are also responses of a public man dealing with particular items (the vingtièmes, the Tax Farm, the administration of the Maison du Roi, the book trade, the marriage of Protestants, etc.).

A first area is *finance*. Under this heading we treat three separate but related issues: taxation, commerce, and state expenditures. The first of these is the most basic category, for it proceeds directly from Malesherbes's concern for justice in its distributive and proprietary sense. Malesherbes, like many others, associated justice with property and regarded taxation as the alienation of property to the state. "Property," he said, "is the right of any people that is not enslaved: Taxes, although often necessary, are a derogation of that right."[56] Malesherbes was not accustomed to using the strict language of the natural rights tradition, but he assigned a central role to property in his conception of human security and independence. Despotism was in part the denial of judicial recourse and the prohibition of remonstrances; it was also in part the arbitrary confiscation of property by unjust taxation, a derogation of the rights of society's members. This was especially true of the vingtièmes, the surplus taxes added to finance wars and rarely withdrawn with the coming of peace.

The taille—most ancient of direct taxes—from which the nobility, the clergy, and certain other privileged officials were exempt, involved not only the derogation of property rights, but also offended the equal dispensation of justice and communication of grievances. Moreover, the taille was levied differently according to the status of the provinces and the kind of resources taxed, distinctions that would take us too far out of our way to describe.[57] During the reign of Louis XV a variety of attempts (some inspired by the reformist writings of the Abbé de Saint-Pierre) were made to rationalize or shift the bases for the collection of the taille; but each of these measures involved the system in further injustices. It was regarding the taille that Malesherbes, on 9 July 1768, advocated a system whereby local deputies chosen by the property owners of the province would supplant the intendant in deciding on the distribution of the tax burden.[58] The same issue led directly to his proposal, seven years later, for the establishment of provincial assemblies in the *pays d'élection*. The procedures and rapacity of the tax farmers (who collected indirect taxes) were another constant object of Malesherbes's attack on arbitrary administration.[59]

As for commerce, Malesherbes agreed with a long line of both mercantilists and économistes that the promotion of trade and production increased the prosperity of the nation, and that both were jeopardized by the tax policies and morale of the regime. In his letter to Sarsfield, he assailed the imitation of the profligate luxury of "les grands." Once the exemption from the taille was abolished and an equitable tax structure created, Malesherbes believed, "no [practice of] trade or any mechanical art or in general any profession permitted in the kingdom [should] in the future bring about the derogation of the nobles."[60] In recommending that the nobility practice trade, his motives were resolutely antifeudal though not necessarily antiaristocratic.

The costs of the court and ministry, and especially the royal household, were capricious, unproductive, and extravagant beyond measure. This was the bottomless well into which the fiscal property of the nation was dumped without recovery, causing huge debts and payments to state creditors. In 1775, when Malesherbes entered the government, nobody knew exactly how deep the sore festered. At almost the same time, Louis XVI was crowned at Rheims in a celebration of almost unbelievable pomp.[61] Malesherbes and Turgot could do little to check this damage; it had entered the mores of the ruling class. According to Malesherbes's calculations, the cost of the Maison du Roi had risen to 61,249,000 francs.[62] He thus began to initial requests for pensions with an unresponsive *cela ne se peut pas*. And he addressed a memoir to the king on 13 April 1776 in which he called attention to the crisis of spending, recommending that the Maison du Roi be run on principles more natural to an ordinary household and suggesting that the king himself take the first step in achieving economies.[63] His plea for frugality fell on deaf ears. He would repeat this same message of urgency eleven years later.[64]

A second area is *justice*. In Malesherbes's remonstrances there is the constant refrain that the ideal justice of a monarchy is a circulatory system, with the sovereign courts mediate between a sovereign lawgiver and an articulate citizenry. In general, the parlementarians were quite content with a "closed politics" in which their largely hereditary bodies assumed the right to aggregate the will of the people for purposes of royal instruction, whereas Malesherbes took a more liberal view of the situation. The dogmatic authoritarianism of Louis XV and his ministers and royal officials often called forth a recalcitrance of the judicial process, a tactic of which Malesherbes disapproved. Moreover, many of the *gens de justice* were autocratic in their own right, regarding their courts and offices as petty aristocratic republics in the midst of the monarchy. As such, they dispensed a privileged justice, scathingly castigated in Malesherbes's letter to Sarsfield. Malesherbes was never timid in placing the blame: "If there are a few abuses that the courts commit against the sovereign power, mustn't they also be reproached for some against the justice due the citizens?"[65] It was the perfect triangle—king, courts, people—that Malesherbes was seeking to establish. He also wanted a regular, active, impartial justice guaranteed by fundamental laws and animated by civic responsibility.

It was Malesherbes who encouraged the Abbé Morellet to translate Beccaria's influential *On Crimes and Punishments* into French in 1766.[66] Malesherbes himself was not willing to endorse the abolition of capital punishment, but he regarded it as an especially grave measure. He wished the execution of any corporal penalty suspended until the highest court, the Grand Conseil, had had an opportunity to review the case in the full light of the evidence.[67] While in the government, Malesherbes also paid close attention to prison conditions: he personally visited the Bastille, Bicêtre, and Vincennes, and he was able to liberate some prisoners. As he reported to the king: "At the Bastille and Vincennes I found more than half of those committed there for more than fifteen years insane or fallen into such frenzy that it was no longer possible to give them their freedom."[68] His research into police and prison reform ranged far afield, to other parts of France and to foreign countries.

Not least was that burning issue of the Old Regime, the *lettres de cachet*. Although Malesherbes's thoughts on the subject were not known to a wide public until 1789, long after similar works by Mirabeau, Linguet, and others had appeared, his concern for this abuse was already prominent in the remonstrances connected with the Monnerat case of 1770, where he had exclaimed: "God did not place the crown on the head of kings for any other reason than to assure men their lives, the liberty of their person, and the tranquil possession of their goods."[69] As minister, he was not of course in a position to abolish a practice that he considered odious, but he made every effort to control and curtail it.[70] Malesherbes employed the historical method in his memoir against the *lettres de cachet*: he attempted to show how their use had arisen in a time when kings dispensed seigneurial justice personally. Now, when there had long existed regular channels of justice, this practice was a mere residue of feudal barbarism. He expressed the wish that the king would "put the finishing touch on the happy changes introduced by custom into our administration, renouncing illegal banishments and imprisonments, just as his predecessors long ago gave up dispensing criminal justice personally."[71]

Shunning both the abstraction of the legal philosophers and the institutional one-sidedness of the propaganda of the *robe*, Malesherbes saw justice not just as an ideal, not just as an office or performance, but as a method subject to criticism, a system subject to correction, and a practice subject to humane reform.

We turn next to *civil liberties*. Categories overlap: when Malesherbes was flailing the taille or the *lettres de cachet*, he was promoting the image of freer men, subject to the law and not to whim, in prudent possession of the rights cherished by the eighteenth century. But his most lasting work was in the field of toleration and the extension of citizen rights to the Protestant minority. The project cost him twelve years of patient effort, from the time of his first ministry to the midst of his second. By then, of course, the king had had to call the Swiss Protestant banker Jacques Necker to his councils.[72] Malesherbes's ministerial portfolio of 1775 included jurisdiction over "la religion prétendue reformée"; he went after this charge with accustomed diligence. Ever since the revocation of the Edict of Nantes in 1685, the Protestants, mainly located in the South, had endured fluctuations of persecution, pursued both by the intransigent majority of the higher Catholic clergy and by a shortsighted policy of raison d'état which judged them harmful to civil peace and capable of constituting a "nation within the nation." Louis XIV had been convinced that severity would cause the Protestants to convert to the religion of the state. It was a monumental error.

The denial of civil status to the Protestants had left them in a position that was not only exceedingly cruel, but confusing besides. Not only was the protection of the state denied to their forms of worship and not only were they forbidden any access to the meager participation in public life that the French of this time enjoyed, but their marriages were considered null (defined as concubinage) and their children were legally bastards. Under Louis XIV they had at least been allowed a pro forma Catholic marriage, but under Louis XV even this wan benefit was refused on the ground that it was a profanation of the sacrament. Two possible paths of reform were open: either to return to the earlier solution or to grant a legitimacy to marriages performed in the absence of a priest. Malesherbes attributed advocacy of the latter view to both Louis XIV and later to Joly de Fleury, but argued that these views had been overcome by the power of the church and the narrow-mindedness of the Royal Council. Malesherbes believed this solution preferable.[73] However, it carried other consequences in its wake, for it presumed a civil, as well as a religious, status for the subjects of the king by introducing a contractual form of marriage as an alternative to the sacramental one. In short, it pointed toward a purely secular citizenship, perhaps even toward the subsequent civil constitution of the clergy of 1790.[74]

It would require all of Malesherbes's scholastic shrewdness to overcome the pious scruples of Louis XVI. Although the preparation of his plea was arduous, his intricate historical method served him well in the long run, penetrating the king's ancestral intelligence in recesses where Voltairean thunderbolts could not have reached. Yet in 1775 the time was not yet ripe. Leaving office with his policy unfulfilled, Malesherbes devoted much of the next decade to efforts on behalf of the Protestants.

He wrote the first draft of his great "Mémoires sur le mariage des protestants" in 1779, although they were not published until 1787.[75] Throughout the years 1784–87 he was in ever closer touch with the Protestant chiefs. With the publication of his treatises, intended "neither for the *philosophes* nor for those who hold the political principle that the government should look upon all religions with indifference,"[76] the cards were on the table. It was one of the few instances that Malesherbes's writings were printed in his lifetime. A freethinker, he could not resist making the following dig at the Catholic clergy in a "secret note": "They do not dream that they themselves have contributed to [religious indifference] by the seductions and motives of temporal advantage (*intérêt*) that they have so long employed to tempt the heretics to sacrifice their religion."[77] On 17 November 1787, despite the misgivings of the king, the Edict of Toleration was signed. The two memoirs of Malesherbes, hurried to press, had been read in the Royal Council and had been the decisive factor. Many other preponderate events were taking place; the Old Regime was collapsing under pressures impervious to the reasoned judgment of a minister or the moderation of a magistrate. But a career crowned with frustration had finally known one sweet success.

Malesherbes was deeply concerned with the spread of knowledge, but he was not a stereotyped enlightener. His own thought gravitates toward the particularity of the concrete without, for that matter, abandoning its consistency. Its overlaps of category are circumstantial, but rarely haphazard, a characteristic that stands out in Malesherbes's attitude toward the freedom of the press. While still head of censorship in 1759, he composed five memoirs touching on all the problems and jurisdictions of the Librairie, in which he had strongly insisted that there could be no public enlightenment without the freedom to publish and to know. But he had also argued, as we have seen, for restrictions on works injurious to morals, religion, the established government, and reputations.[78] He discriminated carefully between liberty and license. In 1788, with the Estates-General about to assemble, Malesherbes composed his *Mémoire sur la liberté de la presse*.[79] It repeats many of the arguments of the earlier *Mémoires sur la Librairie*, but goes beyond them in view of the momentous happenings, for, as he puts it, "we have arrived at the happy moment when the king himself demands enlightenment from all his subjects."[80] Now the balance of the argument lies in favor of noncensorship: "Everything is expected of the Assembly that is about to gather. So as not to disappoint the hopes of the nation, its true wishes mus˙ be carried by its representatives to the foot of the throne. Accordingly, this scattered nation must receive an enlightenment that will reach it in its very dwellings. This is not to be hoped for without the freedom to publish."[81] After reviewing the errors and ill effects to which censorship is subject, Malesherbes concludes: "The freedom demanded today for authors writing about the interests of the nation is incompatible with any kind of censoring."[82] Yet Malesherbes is ultimately willing to surrender all power of the authorities over printed matter. His idea is to make censorship voluntary for the author (in which case nothing he prints can be legally faulted). If the author chooses to publish without this precaution, he can be pursued for sedition, blasphemy, or defamation as the case warrants.[83]

Malesherbes expressed himself on two other issues relative to enlightenment. The first question concerned a proposal for national education, a matter much mooted following the expulsion of the Jesuits in 1764. In 1780, at the request of his cousin Lamoignon, then President of the Parlement of Paris, Malesherbes wrote a memoir extensively canvassing his views on education, with particular application to a proposed reorganization of the University of Paris. The magic idea of national education, launched by La Chalotais's *Essai d'éducation nationale* of 1763, was in the air. Amid his many interesting comments, Malesherbes attacked this notion on three essential grounds. In the first place, the university was rarely innovative in the propagation of new knowledge. In Malesherbes's own days as a student no one had breathed a word of the discoveries of Newton or Leibniz. The proposed bureaucracy would insure that "all the new truths [would] be available to the entire public long before appearing in the schools."[84] Second, the notion of a national education, more appropriate to Sparta than to France, would have the effect of reducing learning to a kind of odious common denominator, ignoring the social need for various sorts of specialization.[85] And third, such a system was an illicit infringement on the right to choose an education freely, according to the wishes of the parents of the student, according to the demands of one's station in the social order, and according to the traditions of the local community.[86] Malesherbes's ideal, seemingly foreign to the French temper, endorses a fruitful pluralism: "Let there be many different institutions (*maisons d'éducation*), and in each of them let the instructors teach the way they think best. Then education will improve."[87] This injunction is accompanied by an equally striking plea for decentralization. The people of the provinces know what is best for themselves: "leave the administration to the municipal bodies, enjoining the [royal] commanders, *intendants*, and bishops to assist them with all their power."[88]

He also wrote a memoir on the reorganization of the academies, which dates from 1789–90, a period when these institutions were, as we know, under heavy attack by certain factions of the Revolution. In the context of that time, the piece is a bit backward-looking, for the work and distinctiveness of the three premier academies (of which Malesherbes was a member) are, on the whole, defended uncritically. However, Malesherbes does argue that academies should in no way sacrifice their independence to any benefactor, be it the monarch or the National Assembly. He does not appear to have conceived that the life of these institutions might be in danger.[89] He had lost contact with some of the passions of the holocaust to come.

In June of the tumultuous year 1788 Malesherbes sought to be relieved of his governmental charge, "for this situation is not suited at all to those who distinguish themselves fighting the ministers for the rights of the people."[90] During July Malesherbes passed several days in Paris, "confined to total solitude,"[91] putting his thoughts on paper. The result was his "Mémoire sur la situation présente des affaires," addressed to the king, an early and prophetic summarization of the political wisdom of the Enlightenment by a man who was neither a philosophe nor a believer in "legal despotism," but a reverent royalist who wished to shift the monarchy to more secure foundations.

Malesherbes's memoir assumed a vast social and intellectual change in the nation, a decline of aristocracy and the irreversible progress of the commons. As was his custom, the paper passes from specifics—the bankruptcy of the treasury—to deeper formulations of political doctrine. Unless the nation is made copartner with the king, not for the duration of the emergency but for all future time, it will be impossible to obtain the necessary resources. For decades controversialists had engaged in obscure arguments about the nature of the "French constitution." Now Malesherbes will have the boldness to insist that this shadow must become substance:

> The time is past when one can seek to mislead the Nation. . . .
> Let us speak clearly. What the Nation is asking for is a new Constitution that has never existed in France. Not only is this what the Nation is asking, but this is the way the King has set his steps in all that he has

done for the last year and a half. . . . It is inevitable ever since the King consented to make public the state of his affairs and to consult the Nation on ways of recovery. The Nation, which sees itself ruined because this Constitution did not exist during earlier reigns, has the right to ask for it and the King is obliged to grant it.[92]

We see Malesherbes demanding not a constitution that would be defined in terms of the juridical "estates," but rather in terms of an integral nation exclusive of privilege and function: "The Nation is composed of all the subjects of the King and all individuals who have their residence (*établissement*) and possessions (*fortune*) in France and whose persons and goods are governed by the laws of France."[93] From here it is but a short step to the demolition of a royal ideology which, with a variety of inflections, had served the French monarchy since the time of Charlemagne.

None of Malesherbes's version of ascending government was exactly novel in France or in antecedent political thought. But up to July 1788 no royal minister or counselor (d'Argenson and Turgot had kept their more radical views speculative or private) had dared to state the implications of modern constitutionalism so boldly to the monarch. Malesherbes did not blink. *Corps intermédiaires* are swept aside: neither clergy nor magistracy is endowed with any special rights that the nation itself has not granted. Indeed, the king himself is not exempt: "The sovereign is the perpetual representative of the nation. . . . The power of the King is none other than that which the Nation has conferred on him."[94] The premises of Malesherbes's regime are both clairvoyant and anachronistic in terms of the new order. The powers of the king will undoubtedly be reduced; but as an irreplaceable hereditary representative he will gain in the affection of his subjects. The powers of the parlements will be reduced, too, for the nation's deputies will supersede them, but they will still have the indispensable role of administering justice. Finally, the provincial assemblies will have a more vigorous part to play, especially in deciding on direct tax assessments. The national representatives will regulate the disputes of the provinces; and the monarch, chiefly responsible for the "bonheur de la nation" and guarantor of its unity, will adjudicate in the last instance between conflicting powers of government.

Uniquely bold for a minister, Malesherbes's plan was bypassed or breached by much of the work of the Constituent Assembly. That body diminished the power of the monarch and exalted the power of the legislature far beyond Malesherbes's wishes; it abolished the ancient divisions of the kingdom (he had never conceived this); it put an end to his cherished sovereign courts and instituted a wholly different system of justice; it prescribed an equality of citizenship that he had only hinted at; and it founded its construction on metaphysical principles for which he had little taste. Yet Malesherbes clearly foresaw that the assembled Estates-General would become a permanent legislature and the source of continuing reforms: "When the Nation demands the Estates-General, it is not exactly asking for what it really wants; as for the educated persons who demand it, they are certainly asking for the restoration of the former Estates-General only because they see this as a way of later getting National Assemblies of a different sort, never before seen in France."[95] Moreover, "other assemblies will improve on the work of 1789, and provided that the two orders which are only a tiny portion of the nation are denied the right of monopolizing the national suffrage, time and reason's progress will take care of the rest."[96]

Time ran out, and reason's progress confronted unfamiliar elemental forces. Malesherbes had preached an Enlightenment somewhat more Gothic than that of the radical philosophes. Sainte-Beuve's evaluation places too much emphasis on Malesherbes's prudence, but it is essentially correct: "this was a man of the old days . . . a *philosophe*, yet not like the others . . . wanting only to maintain and regenerate."[97] Experience had taught that the straight road was not usually the shortest way home. The contemplative magistrate could not avoid being drawn into the whirl-pool of revolution, whose vortex he obeyed through a sense of duty that superseded all inclinations. A part of his efforts and a part of his climate of opinion had helped to prepare that dramatic sequence; a part of his spirit had been forewarned of its disillusion; a part of his desire had been to cushion its shock. Ultimately Malesherbes's political thought was grounded in his magistrate's love of order and sense of justice. Yet his views went far beyond the horizons of the parlementary caste with which his new enemies identified him.

16. Vanished Supremacies

The peacefulness of his estate and the occasional company of the *gens de lettres* would have been the desired fulfillment of Malesherbes's old age. Yet he reluctantly took his place in the Royal Council in the spring of 1787, urged by his cousin Lamoignon and largely motivated by the wish to secure the edict of civil and religious toleration for the Protestants. He would depart on 25 August 1788. In the meantime, the storm clouds of revolution gathered with astonishing speed, the city of Paris endured constant agitation, and the *révolte nobiliaire* spent itself in the far greater tempest of political change that would produce the National Assembly.

After his vain effort to enlighten the monarch, Malesherbes took leave from the affairs of state. The great opening moments of the Revolution found him a spectator, rusticating on his lands. To be sure, he kept in contact with events through his wide circle of friendships—Rabaut Saint-Etienne, Lafayette, Boissy d'Anglas, the Duc de la Rochefoucauld, and others. And he was not one to underestimate the epochal quality of the times: he knew that the French crisis was unique in his country's history.[1] For a brief time, he was hopeful that this unparalleled surge of political energy would root out abuses and restore stability.[2] Soon he became greatly worried. He could not have been reassured by the *journées* of October 1789, when the crowds included in their chants: "A bas les Parlements!"[3] He had a certain disdain for the pretensions of the deputies: early sources record him telling his intimates: "Ils nous perdront, ces petits messieurs. . . ."[4]

From long years of experience Malesherbes was a connoisseur of the deficiencies of the sovereign courts, but he regarded them as a fundamental part of the realm. Moreover, his son-in-law Louis de Rosanbo was Président of the Chambre des Vacations of the Parlement of Paris. However, the abolition of the parlements was much on the mind of the advanced leadership of the Tiers, many of whom had pleaded as lawyers before these courts. In the vision of the progressives of the *robe* (some of them nobles, like Hérault de Séchelles, Lepeletier de Saint-Fargeau, and Adrien Duport), the sovereign courts were a part of that *féodalité* condemned by the national revolution. The courts were offensive to their doctrines of natural right: the unpopular registration of the edict summoning the Estates-General "in the forms of 1614" by the Parlement of Paris on 25 September 1788 had claimed antecedent and particular rights as its justification.⁵ And the bourgeois lawyers were envious of the nobles of the robe who had lorded it over them for so long.

The first attack was mounted by the liberal noble Alexandre de Lameth on 3 October 1789: he moved a decree for the *mise en vacances* of the parlements. Lameth was strongly seconded by Target, who asserted that the literal powers of the sovereign courts had expired with the creation of the National Assembly. It was logical to phase out the parlements at a time when the ancient provinces and territorial jurisdictions of France were also being abolished. Lameth's decree passed: the parlements were sent on holiday, with minimal judicial activities continuing to be exercised by their caretaker sections, the Chambres des Vacations.⁶ Hereupon, the Président of the Paris Chambre des Vacations, Lepeletier de Rosanbo, privately circulated a letter, dated 5 November 1789, expressing his body's "profound consternation."⁷ The parlementarians now perceived that their fate was intimately linked with that of the monarch. This was the beginning of the so-called *complot des parlementaires*, important in the sequence of events leading to Malesherbes's eventual arrest.

Under the Old Regime the parlements were accustomed to remonstrate against abuses of their privilege and function. This was now no longer within their power: the king could not act, and the National Assembly would not receive their protests. Moreover, they had lost the support of public opinion. There were recriminations and episodes in the parlementary citadels, notably Toulouse, but to no avail. Conservative and highly status-conscious by nature, many of the parlementarians commenced to drift toward counterrevolution. Especially in Toulouse and Bordeaux their fraternal networks served as conduits for antipatriot opinion and brochures.⁸

On 24 March 1790 Thouret, a Norman lawyer and leading antagonist of the Parlement of Rouen, read a report of the Committee on the Constitution, in which he cited the "corrosive effects" of these ancient, particularistic bodies and called for their suppression. It was in this atmosphere of impending doom that Malesherbes, on 26 July 1790, wrote to his friend Barthélemy-Gabriel Rolland d'Erceville, former President of the Chambre des Enquêtes of the Parlement of Paris:

> Alas, Monsieur, for the past two years I have been working on lots of things familiar to me that I could foresee occupying the debates of the National Assembly. I took the precaution of keeping them private when I saw how things were going. . . .
>
> In times of violent passion words of reason are best kept under wraps. To disclose them would even do injury to reason, for the

enthusiasts would stir up the people against the very truths which, in other times, would be received with general approval.[9]

This letter would later become a damning piece of evidence against Malesherbes. He was not a man to subscribe to Burkean diatribe, but he had begun to fear the future.[10]

By motion of Desmeunier, on 6 September 1790, the National Assembly decreed that 30 September would be set as the date for the dissolution of the provincial parlements and 15 October for that of the Parlement of Paris. They would be replaced nationwide by an entirely novel system of elective magistrates. Hébert exulted in the *Père Duchesne*: "Ils foutent enfin le camp, ces sacrés coquins de juges! . . . Les voilà rasés . . . on n'est plus dupe de leurs singeries!"[11] The Chambre des Vacations of the Parlement of Paris held its final, mournful session on 14 October; then government bailiffs sealed its doors and escorted its members away from their high calling and into obscurity.[12] Almost immediately, elections for the new judiciary were held; certain liberal members of the old aristocracy, including Lepeletier de Saint-Fargeau, Dionis du Séjour, and Hérault de Séchelles, had no trouble with popular suffrage.[13] Louis de Rosanbo was also elected, but swiftly he resigned and retired to Malesherbes, for he was the repository of the dangerous secret protests.[14]

The most damning of these papers was a letter drafted by Rosanbo and signed by all members of his Chambre, half of whom would later pay for it with their lives under the Terror:

Estimating that, in the midst of the ruins of the monarchy, it is vital for the stability of the throne, the glory of the nation, and the happiness of the citizens of all orders and classes that there should survive a monument preserving the principles by which it has been governed for so many centuries; and that in present circumstances this obligation is especially incumbent on the magistrates of the Chambre des Vacations, since, as a part of the superior court of the kingdom, they alone can compensate for the silence of the princes and peers and magistrates from whom they are separated—the undersigned, renewing their protests of 5 November against the first assaults upon the laws and the Constitution of the state, have decreed that they never intended to give any approval to the different statutes that they have recorded; that this recording was done only on condition of eventual acceptance by the entire court; that, since this condition could not be obtained, all recording thereby becomes null and void; that they cannot acknowledge as the

general wish of the nation the result of the deliberations of an
assembly which should have been composed of the three orders of
the Estates-General, but which is actually denatured and constituted
solely by its own authority as a National Assembly; that finally they
protest, and will not cease to protest, against all that has been done
by the deputies to the Estates-General, who, in this so-called
Assembly, against the express intent (*teneur*) of their mandates, have
not only exceeded their power, which consisted principally in
paying the state's indebtedness, in providing for the necessary
expenditures by an equal assessment, and finally in inaugurating a
judicious reform in the different parts of the administration, but
have even abused it by violating every kind of property, by de-
spoiling the clergy and bringing about a contempt for religion, by
destroying the nobility, which had always been a stalwart support,
by the depredation of royal majesty, attacking its authority and
reducing it to an empty phantom, and last by the confusion of
powers which is destructive of the true principles of monarchy.[15]

The document states unequivocally that the National Assembly has been
illegitimately constituted, thereby denying the constituent power of that
body; it defends "feudal" property as inalienable according to the fundamental laws of the kingdom; it further insists on the necessary validation
of all national legislation by act of registration with the sovereign courts;
and it raises, albeit passively, the standard of restoration. In this one huge
turgid sentence the conservative doctrine of parlementary constitutionalism (close to Burke in all respects) indicts the work of revolutionary
change just begun. Moreover, the words are composed by Malesherbes's
son-in-law and cherished friend. It is small wonder that the Jacobins,
unearthing this text at Rosanbo's house in December 1793, were convinced that they had stumbled into a mine of royalist treason. Malesherbes was not an ultra. Yet his halting path to the scaffold began not
in December 1792, but in October 1790, mapped by a parlementary
intransigence for which he had little sympathy.

What Malesherbes deplored was the vitiation of the monarchy. On this
subject he wrote to his friend Boissy d'Anglas, on 22 November 1790.
The immediate issue was the executive power of the monarch: should he
promulgate decrees without ministerial countersignature; should he be
commander-in-chief of the armies? A motion of Alexandre de Beauharnais proposed to strip him of these prerogatives. But did the nation wish
to have only the simulacrum of a monarch? Malesherbes thought not; he
was convinced that the vast majority of the French were attached to

royalty and wanted a king who could *rule*. As for himself, "I believe that we must have a king in France. If things reached the pass where each citizen was asked for his opinion, I would support this with my vote, for I am too old and too little trained in arms to support it otherwise. But I feel I would be obliged to offer my body to the noose and my house to vandalism, rather than hide my way of thinking or act evasively about this principle, which is the most cherished feeling of my heart, and which I consider to be the fundamental law of my country."[16] These words ring with as much conviction as Malesherbes had ever put into any remonstrances. His fidelity to the king was solidly planted in his conception of the nation, and he did not consign his thoughts to secrecy on this occasion, for he authorized his correspondent to share them with Rabaut Saint-Etienne. Even the flight to Varennes could not shake the old man's politics.

In the spring of 1791, with heavy heart, Malesherbes undertook his final trip abroad. This was no carefree expedition of "Monsieur Guillaume," but a visit of duty to his younger daughter Françoise-Pauline de Montboissier and her husband, who had emigrated to Lausanne. If there was reactionary sentiment in the Rosanbo family, it was not to be compared with the hatred of the Revolution felt by the Montboissiers. Malesherbes could not approve his daughter's politics, but he adored all his children and grandchildren. The pathetic letters of Madame de Montboissier, written from Switzerland to the family at Malesherbes, cautious but disaffected, would later be added to the Terror's dossier of accusation. During the visit, Malesherbes renewed a number of friendships cultivated at the time of his previous trip of 1778.

The dramas of 1792 were about to afflict the nation. In their midst, Malesherbes would periodically forsake his quiet country life and return to Paris to be near the threatened king, thus honoring his declaration to Boissy d'Anglas. According to Bertrand de Molleville, the aging magistrate attended the *lever du roi* each Sunday, even though he despised the ceremonial costume worn on those occasions. He exchanged no words with Louis XVI, satisfying himself with the assurance that the monarch perceived his presence.[17] Then he returned to his beloved estate with its modest comfort and stately forest.

The days 20 June and 10 August thundered past. The king was deposed and made a prisoner of state. The Legislative Assembly dissolved; the National Convention gathered. Dizzily, France became a republic. Her borders were breached by the Prussians; she regathered strength and thrust the invaders back. Finally, after some political circuitousness, Jean Mailhe, a deputy of the Haute-Garonne, speaking for the Committee on

Legislation, presented to the Convention on 7 November 1792 the report that would serve as the basis for the trial of Louis XVI. He argued that the ex-king was justiciable (contrary to the Constitution of 1791) and that the Convention itself, as repository of the sovereignty of the people, should serve as the court of judgment.[18] The Convention decided that it would at the same time fulfill the roles of prosecutor, grand jury, jury, and judge. All questions, including those of guilt and punishment, would be settled by a simple majority of those present and voting. Thus, when on 11 December 1792 the royal prisoner first appeared before the Convention for interrogation, it was without benefit of counsel. Barère presided and directed the questioning.[19] The hostility of the occasion was ill-disguised, but at the end of the session the Convention almost unanimously granted the defendant the right to obtain legal assistance for his defense.[20]

The king's first choice for a defender was Target, who haughtily refused, citing his state of health and his republican principles. Tronchet, another former Constituent, then accepted, though without great warmth, as a "duty to humanity." But on the very day of Louis's interrogation Malesherbes, now seventy-two years old, touchingly offered his services: "Twice I was called to the [Royal] Council of the man who was my master at a time when everyone was avid for that job; I owe him the same service, when it is now a function that many people find dangerous."[21] Numerous others (including émigrés like Lally-Tollendal) stepped forward. But Malesherbes and Tronchet were accepted by the king. On 16 December, Malesherbes wrote to the President of the Convention, asking to add a third attorney, "since it is physically impossible for two men, one of them over sixty and the other over seventy, to prepare a defense against an accusation under more than forty headings in such a short time."[22] Thus Romain de Sèze, a young Bordeaux lawyer with acknowledged powers of oratory, became a part of the team. The three men worked effectively and frictionlessly against the brutal deadline set by the Convention; Louis's defense plea was to be heard on 26 December. In the meantime, the Assembly was partially occupied by the diversionary measure initiated by Buzot and other moderates against the Duc d'Orléans (Egalité) and the remaining Bourbons.

Malesherbes and his colleagues had difficulty in obtaining and assembling the pieces of evidence they felt necessary for the defense. A letter of 19 December requests one of these documents; another, dated 27 December (after the *plaidoirie* of the defense), asks for another packet, forwarded from London by Bertrand de Molleville, the former Minister of the Navy.[23] Amid the severity of winter, the defenders worked from dawn until late into the night, not so much to save Louis XVI from inculpation (which was hopeless), but to save him from death (which was believed possible). Only the defendant himself was convinced that the end of his days had come; his thoughts were already directed toward the problem of obtaining a nonjuring priest to hear his final confession. He later implored Malesherbes to make this contact for him, conceding that it was "a strange errand for a *philosophe*."[24] At one point Malesherbes asked his sovereign what country he would choose for exile if the Convention decreed deportation. "Switzerland," Louis replied; "history shows it is mildest for fugitive kings."[25] "But, Sire," the magistrate persisted, "what if the French people, restored to their senses, called you back; would you come, Your Majesty?" "Without relish, but for duty's sake," was the reply.[26]

Every day, no matter how crushing his legal chores, Malesherbes visited his distinguished client in the Temple for several hours, often from noon until six o'clock in the evening.[27] Since any ostentation was then perilous, he would travel in a simple fiacre. It is said that each time that he, or the other lawyers, arrived to consult with the king, they were stripped down and ignominiously searched and compelled to change clothes for fear that they concealed some weapon with which the prisoner might take his life.[28] However, a more reliable account has it that the law forbade such treatment of the defenders and that Malesherbes willingly emptied his pockets in the presence of the municipal jailer. At a time when "heroic suicide"—inspired by the example of Socrates, Cato, and Seneca—was about to achieve a certain vogue, there was little likelihood that the Most Christian King would choose the pagan example. For, said Malesherbes, "if the King were a *philosophe*, if he were of the religion of the old Romans, where a kind of honor was attached to suicide, the King might kill himself; but he is of the Catholic religion, which forbids this. The King is as pious and convinced as a man can be, and the fear of displeasing God would always stay his hand."[29]

On 26 December 1729 de Sèze delivered his remarkable statement of defense to the Convention and Louis XVI himself added some final touching words. All three attorneys had a hand in preparing the defense plea, although the final draft appears to have been the exclusive work of the spokesman. De Sèze's words were heard in respectful silence. The attorney did not, it seems, attempt to stampede his auditors with high-flown pathos. According to one royalist spectator: "the King himself had made [de Sèze] strike out eloquent passages that might have shaken the Assembly, not wishing, as he put it, to owe *his salvation to pity* (*attendrissement*), *but to the justice of his judges*."[30] De Sèze argued on several fronts:

citing the Constitution of 1791, he denounced the illegality of the trial (a point previously made by the deputy Morisson in a speech of 13 November); he questioned the forms of the trial ("I look around for judges, and all I see are accusers"); he remarked on the anomaly of treating Louis neither as a king nor as a citizen; he invoked the doctrine of ministerial responsibility; and he concluded with a catalog of the virtues of the accused.[31] Then the ex-monarch spoke briefly, declaring that his conscience was clear and that he was innocent of shedding the blood of his people.[32] There was no hint of the idea of paternalistic kingship in the defense: that aura, which came so unnaturally to Louis XVI, had been dissipated before the mortal blow to his own person was struck. While the king's defense was unfolding before the Convention, it is recounted that the defendant exchanged some snatches of quiet conversation with Malesherbes, in which the old magistrate, as was his habit, used the forms of address "Sire" and "Your Majesty." Overhearing this, one of the deputies, Treilhard, whose views had prudently changed since his days as a rather conservative *robin* and member of the Constituent, said angrily to Malesherbes: "What makes you so bold as to use words that the Convention has forbidden?" "Contempt for you," was the answer, "and contempt for life."[33]

Malesherbes and other royalists were counting heavily on the cohorts of Brissot, Vergniaud, and Madame Roland to save the king's life, for it was believed that they could sway the majority of the Assembly. But these men, never as cohesive a faction as has sometimes been claimed, were divided by litigious disputes, tactical concerns, and emotional cross-pressures.[34] They were not—as the ascendant Montagne would simplistically charge—royalists at heart; above all they wished the trial proceedings to be a show of enlightened justice, not a vengeful carnival. As against their hesitations, the unity of the Montagne became a rallying point for the politic and the undecided. And so, in a feverish political atmosphere, the Convention, in its *séance permanente* of 16–17 January 1793, decreed the death of Louis XVI by a margin of five or twenty votes, depending on how the count is interpreted.[35] The king's defenders took it as a good augury that, on the question of the penalty, the *appel nominal*, which was made by departments, would begin with the letter "G"; for they expected the beginnings of a landslide when the tabulation of the Gironde began. But all they received was death in their own hearts: "There was redoubled interest in the hall when, after eighteen or twenty votes divided between death and banishment that had come from the representatives of the Haute-Garonne and the Gard, Vergniaud, the first of the Girondins, climbed the steps to the rostrum. The word *death* dumbfounded everyone. . . ."[36] Unconditional death for the ex-monarch was voted by 366 Conventionals. Henceforward, they would be known as the "regicides," banished from France under pain of execution by the restored monarchy of 1814. For the time being they were either exultant or uncomfortable accomplices in the creation of a Jacobin republic with all its advancing rigors of purity and revenge. Correspondingly, Malesherbes would swiftly become a hero of the very ultras who had scorned him and despised his ideas for forty years.

There was one last chance for the defenders: an ensuing vote on reprieve (*sursis*), which made little sense after the ominous finality of the death sentence. The three attorneys obtained permission to address the Convention one last time. Without result, Tronchet and de Sèze denounced the verdict as illegal, insisting—as had the Breton deputy Lanjuinais, early on in the debates—that the penal code required a two-thirds vote (if so, however, it would have been on the question of guilt or innocence). A request for the appeal to the primary assemblies of the nation similarly received short shrift.[37] When it was Malesherbes's turn to speak, he attempted to support his colleagues, but tears overcame him.[38]

It befell Malesherbes to inform his royal client of the verdict and, under the king's instruction, to caution a group of young royalists that no attempt was to be made to rescue him by force. The king had repeatedly urged Malesherbes to withdraw from the case and not expose himself to its obvious perils. At the end of his will, composed the night before his execution, Louis XVI graciously thanked his attorneys for the troubles that they had endured.[39] In these last moments of their friendship it was Louis's task to solace Malesherbes. According to the reported words of the latter, "One last time I had the honor of speaking with the King. At the moment of taking leave, I could not hold back my tears. 'Tender old man,' the King said, shaking my hand, 'don't cry: we shall see each other in a better life. I am sad to leave a friend like you. Adieu! Do control yourself on your way out; you must. Remember that they will be watching you. . . . Adieu! Adieu!' "[40]

Quite overcome with grief, this instant hero of the royalists suffered through the last hours of the king's vigil. It is said that on 21 January, after the execution, a spontaneous demonstration of acclaim took place in front of Malesherbes's Paris dwelling on the rue des Martyrs and a crown of laurel was left behind.[41] His safety had been prejudiced by his gesture. According to the early historian Lacretelle, Malesherbes told his intimates: "Robespierre's glance follows me everywhere. . . . I can still hear the sound of his voice telling me that he was willing to excuse my tears. That man must really hate me, for he would like to pass for being virtuous, but surely his virtue is not mine."[42] This seems apocryphal. Though Robespierre was a prime mover at the trial of the king, his star had not yet risen so high as to blaze down vindictively on all Malesherbes's waking moments. Still, Malesherbes suffered no illusions of invulnerability. With his "mépris pour la vie" he determined not to emigrate; perhaps, as he wrote to the Comte de Provence abroad, circumstances would require him to stand forth once more as the defender of the queen and the king's sister, then in prison. "I might eternally reproach myself," he wrote, "if I did not remain at my post."[43] The old man left the consolation and comparative safety of Malesherbes in the early summer of 1793 to sniff the wind in Paris, where the Jacobins were consolidating their power. When, at the beginning of September, he offered his services for the defense of Marie-Antoinette, he was immediately rebuffed and forbidden to come to the capital.[44] Thus, the better part of 1793 was passed with his family at the chateau, where, attempting to submerge his chagrin in daily activity, "he lived . . . with nature, far from the passions that were stirring up the world. . . ."[45]

The young Comte de Tocqueville, who arrived at Malesherbes on 31 January 1793 as the fiancé of the magistrate's granddaughter, Louise de Rosanbo, leaves the following description:

> We led a very gentle life at the *château* of Malesherbes: everybody got together at mealtimes and kept company for a while. Then we parted, each to his own occupation. At nine in the evening, we would all gather in the salon. M. de Malesherbes would arrive; he singled out some member of the company and launched himself into stories. . . . At midnight he retired and went to lie down, fully clothed, on his bed, where he would sleep for a few hours. . . .
>
> Spring, summer, and autumn went by with the gentle and peaceful rhythm of the life of the *château*. But the horizon was growing darker and darker. The terror that the Convention wished to impose on all of France reached further each day; the prisons were filling. M. de Malesherbes had been warned to leave France. It was correctly feared that the rulers of that time, incapable of appreciating his devotion, would make him pay with his head. But this courageous old man would not think his mission over as long as a member of the royal family remained in chains; he foresaw that the Queen would be brought to trial, and he desired the honor of defending her. . . .[46]

Malesherbes might have died for being the man of December 1792— and, in part, this would be difficult to deny, given his later action in the case of Marie-Antoinette—but he died principally for less lucid and more complicated reasons. Though the despisers of royalty were surely glad to be revenged on him, they did not kill him simply because he had rushed to the side of the doomed king. Malesherbes died because he was a particularly indigestible part of the Old Regime, a part that the Revolutionary leaders had vowed to extinction. It was lost on these men that Malesherbes had been a discriminating reformer; they saw him as a notorious aristocrat, epitomizing the former *noblesse de robe*, hostile to their designs, in league with their enemies. If, in the words of Saint-Just, one could not reign innocently, it was equally true that certain persons could not be born innocently. There was more than a perfunctory excuse for intruding on the "gentle and peaceful rhythm" of the chateau of Malesherbes with gendarmes and *sectionnaires*. The threads of the story go back to the dispersion of the parlements in 1790 and the secret *arrêt* composed by Lepeletier de Rosanbo. Malesherbes would die less as a martyr to royal devotion than as an accessory to the *complot des parlementaires*, which, in the Jacobin imagination, reached out with its sinister strands to London, Koblenz, and all compass points of the counterrevolution.

For reasons still obscure, a denunciation of Louis de Rosanbo was made to the revolutionary committee of the Faubourg Montmartre. Rosanbo, who had lived in Malesherbes in 1793, had his Paris domicile within the section of Bondy. Its committee was therefore alerted; with alacritous enthusiasm these patriots, together with the Montmartrians, descended on Rosanbo's house in mid-December and fairly tore the place apart. They discovered, among other items, "a bust of Louis XIV given by him to a Le Pelletier who was Minister of State."[47] This was enough to cause them to order Rosanbo's arrest. Further investigations procured still more interesting evidence of treason: dubious correspondence and, well-hidden in a packet sealed with wax, the incriminating order of 14 October 1790 and a letter of the same date to the king, ending with extensive compliments to the royal family that the excited sleuths described as "tant de bassesses." They now decided on the arrest of the entire Rosanbo family and the search of the premises of Malesherbes.

Meanwhile, obsessed with the notion of plots and intrigue—some of which were real enough, for the idea of legitimacy was at stake in France as well as the reality of power, and France was at war—the Revolutionary Government determined to move against the former parlementarians who had not fled the country. While it might seem that a document written in 1790 was ancient history, it was as timely to the revolutionaries as any proof of the moment. For, as the report from which these details have been drawn, stated:

> Established by the well-expressed wishes of the people, the Constituent Assembly had pronounced the destruction of all the Parlements of the kingdom. That measure was necessary; a beneficent magistracy was to supplant these so-called fathers of the people who were really only executioners. The gratitude of the people greeted this great reform (*bienfait*). But how could one imagine that an ambitious corporation, the secret enemy of a new regime which was disclosing a happy destiny to the people, would not protest against the supreme will and would not, following its custom, conspire in the shadows? . . .[48]

The men of Bondy conveniently forgot that a goodly number of the Constituents were also their enemies and victims.

The revolutionary constables visited Malesherbes on 26 Frimaire, an II (16 December 1793), where they arrested Rosanbo and sequestered all the papers they could find. According to their account, "they found letters from *émigrés* and an exchange of letters with the children of Citizen Rosanbo [in London], motivating [us to add to the arrest warrants] the names of Malesherbes and the children of Rosanbo [i.e., the Chateaubriands and the Tocquevilles]."[49] We take up the story in the words of the Comte de Tocqueville:

> On the morning of the 19th, two new members of the Revolutionary Committee of the section of Bondy arrived with the mission of arresting M. de Malesherbes, Madame de Rosanbo, and all her children, and of transporting them to Paris. M. de Malesherbes had already gone out of doors; he was saying a last farewell to his gracious gardens, which he would never see again. He made haste to return, and he received the commissioners with a serenity inspired by the courage of his soul and the peace of his conscience. . . .
>
> On the morning of 20 December, we climbed into two carriages, with a commissioner and an official of the village of Malesherbes in each one. The officials had offered to make this wretched trip so that we would be spared the discomfort of a police escort. . . .
>
> At eleven in the evening, we dismounted from our carriages in the court of a building occupied by the Revolutionary Committee of the section of Bondy. . . . We were taken into a low hall where the members of the Revolutionary Committee were sitting, all of them in red bonnets, the distinctive sign of their bloodthirsty patriotism.[50]

Officially, the case of Rosanbo was distinct from that of the other members of the Malesherbes family. This was a matter of both form and convenience; the clarity of the "complot parlementaire" allowed for the incrimination of twenty-five other legal colleagues from Paris and Toulouse. Indeed, in the days to come the parlementary carnage was terrible, mounting into the hundreds.[51] Rosanbo and his codefendants were charged with "conspiracy against the sovereignty and security of the French people," "rebellion against the constituted authorities," "maintenance of intelligence and correspondence with the external enemies of the state," and "maneuvers of all sorts designed to stir up civil war."[52]

For some weeks the family was held in detention at Port-Libre (formerly the convent of Port-Royal); it was during this time that Malesherbes's many observations about the period of the king's trial were recorded by interested fellow prisoners. But on 29 Germinal (18 April 1794) Rosanbo and the parlementarians were transferred to the Conciergerie to appear before the Revolutionary Tribunal. At this point, Malesherbes, grasping for straws, addressed a memoir to Fouquier-Tinville, the Public Prosecutor, hoping to extenuate the effect of the document of 14 October 1790. It was the last "history lesson" he would deliver. In this memoir, dictated to his granddaughter Aline-Thérèse de Chateaubriand, he pointed out that

> in 1790, the time of the so-called protest, there existed neither
> republic nor liberty. I will say to you in all frankness that such was
> the purpose of a dominant faction of the Constituent Assembly,
> only too well known, that it amounted to nothing less—as Saint-
> Just recently declared in a report for the Committee of Public
> Safety[53]—than taking the crown from the former king and putting
> it on the head of d'Orléans. Under these conditions, the members of
> the Chambre des Vacations, somehow placed between the usurper
> and the former monarch, took the side of the latter and believed it
> their duty to protest in his favor. These protests took place con-
> stantly and were indeed popular under the Old Regime, which had
> still not been destroyed.[54]

Malesherbes went on to add that before liberty had come to the French, the rules made it impossible for Rosanbo's Chambre to authorize laws without the consent of the full Parlement. He then attempted a tortuous defense of Rosanbo's protection of the damning document, and concluded with praise of his son-in-law's civic and moral qualities. This lengthy missive was recopied and transmitted to Rosanbo before his trial.[55] It was a fatalistic complicity of survival in an upside-down world that men of reason and good will had not made. In the terror of the moment, it was an act of family devotion.[56] The allegation of the Orleanist plot could scarcely have been serious in October 1790; in any case, that was not what motivated the Parlement's impotent displeasure.[57] Malesherbes undoubtedly knew that he and his closest kin were doomed. Nevertheless, he would spend his energies fighting for them, just as he had fought for the king. Only when it came to his own case would he lack words.

The lines of Rosanbo's "plot" blur into the general charges against the family in the evidence of packets of extensive correspondence, letters generally composed with great circumspection but unfailingly smacking of the émigré mentality. As the Committee of Bondy writes in one of its reports: "The Committee observes that in its research of correspondence made [among the papers of] the citizen and the citizeness Rosambo [sic], letters were found relative to public affairs casting suspicion on the following persons. . . ."[58] Here Malesherbes is named in the first instance, and then the rest of his family. The report concludes with a profession of revolutionary ardor: "The Revolutionary Committee of the Section of Bondy has not wasted a moment and will not rest until it has finished the mission with which it was charged by the Committee of General Security."[59]

The letters referred to are found indifferently in the Rosanbo and Malesherbes trial dossiers (W 351/ W 731). For example, on 15 October 1792, Madame de Rosanbo hears from her sister: "I have learned with great pleasure that you will prolong your stay at Malesherbes. In these times one should avoid the capital, which is the center of tumult, and you could not be living in a more peaceful place than where you are."[60] From Tournoi, on 20 May 1792, Madame de Chateaubriand receives this letter: "I often suffer from your decision to remain in France despite all the horrors going on there and those that seem inevitable in the future."[61] "Each day brings us news contradicting what we heard the day before. We don't know what to believe, what to wish for, still less what to say, what to hope. . . . That is our sad occupation, and perhaps it will be ours for the rest of our days," Madame de Montboissier had written to her sister from Lausanne on 18 June 1791.[62] Carefully underlined in red or blue pencil for the attention of the Revolutionary Tribunal, these and dozens of similar utterances, contained in the letters that Malesherbes and his elder daughter had the imprudence to keep, were the stuff out of which the counterrevolutionary plot was fabricated. They were offensively "uncivic": that was what really mattered. Their danger to the French state was null. Malesherbes's letter of 1790 to President Rolland, which we have already examined, was thrown into the bargain.

Louis de Rosanbo perished on the scaffold on 2 Floréal, an II (21 April 1794). A few hours later, toward seven-thirty in the evening, Malesherbes, Madame de Rosanbo, and the young Chateaubriands, in their turn, were questioned before the Revolutionary Tribunal. The basis of the charges was their uncivic correspondence; the minutes of the questioning are laconic, typical of the accelerated Terror. Asked if he had not "conspired against the liberty of the French people and said that [he] would use every means to destroy the Republic," Malesherbes replied simply: "I never said that."[63] Madame de Rosanbo was similarly terse. However, Fouquier-Tinville's act of accusation painted the portrait of a plot emanating from the coffers of London and striking at the vitals of the republican enterprise: ". . . Lamoignon-Malesherbes has all the characteristics of a conspirator and a counter-revolutionary. The papers found in the possession of this ex-magistrate prove that he worked ceaselessly to bring back the Old Regime; that he was the center around whom were gathered the other conspirators that have just been struck by the blade of the law and that he directed all their measures."[64]

Revolutionary justice needed no further proof or evidence than this, especially against a man who is said to have written from prison: "I am ready for anything: they will not forgive me for having defended the unfortunate Louis XVI; still I say at the top of my voice that I am proud to have sacrificed my existence for him. . . . I would do it again if the situation demanded."[65] In the same parody of justice that swallowed up Malesherbes and his family, room was made for a mixed lot of victims, including the prominent Constituents Le Chapelier and Thouret and the parlementarian Duval d'Eprémesnil, who had so actively opposed the crown in 1788.

On the following day, 3 Floréal (22 April), they were led to their deaths. We have scant testimony of Malesherbes's last moments; those who recorded his acts were still in prison, and the Sanson memoirs are mute on the subject. We do know that the old man faced his end with perseverance, enduring the horror of seeing his child and grandchildren precede him to the guillotine. His surviving relative Clérel de Tocqueville (whose hair turned white in prison) attributed to Malesherbes a last-minute turn toward religion.[66] But this is quite out of character. Malesherbes's spirituality was totally private, never manifesting itself in any traditional or organized devotion. He was not, like his son-in-law Rosanbo, a Freemason;[67] neither does it appear that he sought the consolation of the religion of Louis XVI when his end came. Within weeks, the magistrate's sister, Madame de Sénozan, and two of his secretaries, Baufre and Pierson, followed him to their deaths, all accused of counter-revolutionary plots.[68]

Two points should be emphasized in conclusion. The first of these is the range and perspicacity of Malesherbes's diagnosis of the Old Regime and his trenchant efforts to reform it with the meager means available. Until Grosclaude's substantial archival discoveries, this wealth of ideas had been distinctly subordinated to emotional themes. Secondly, we should repeat an important irony. Malesherbes's vindictive death, although prefigured by his demonstrative royalism, was more directly a result of his hereditary network of parlementary connections. He died for his king; but he also died under the burden of a birthright. If it was not until April 1794 that the Jacobins got around to killing the Prémier Président of the Cour des Aides and if they did this at a time when the Terror seemed determined to make a clean sweep of all hostile forces, there was still political reason in the act. As one of the leading physicians of a moribund political order, Malesherbes, too, had to share in its fate. For he was contaminated by contact with the diseased members and had committed the cardinal error of believing the patient operable.

PART VI.
Aristocracy and the Republic of Virtue

17. Conclusion

Four cases of victimization by the Jacobin Terror, studied in considerable biographical detail, cannot permit us to extrapolate the complex rationale—regional, personal and vengeful, micropolitical, or even haphazard—that would account for the killing of some thirty-five or forty thousand persons, and the imprisonment of perhaps five times as many others, by the government of the Year II.[1] However, we have cleared away a lot of the debris that concealed the major structural outlines and implicit meaning of the Terror. Although biography has been used for this experiment, it has never been asserted that the Terror was an aggregated bundle of psychological reactions, either by the executioners or the victims. A richness of personal detail has been used to exemplify and symbolize Jacobin repression in France, by relating individuals to roles, roles to significant parts of the social spectrum, and the latter to ideological models of authority current at the time. There is a legitimate explanatory history that builds by such devices, not crudely and inductively, but representatively and symbolically, without committing the psychological fallacy.

As I pointed out much earlier, this work goes only part way to securing a definition of Jacobinism. Although enough of Jacobin doctrine has been canvassed in these pages for us to treat it as something less than impenetrable, we have not made the attempt here to analyze its particulars or to give the creative aspect of Jacobinism due credit. Having come this far, it would still be possible to construct a moral or prudential defense of Jacobinism—for we have not been arranging a parade of dead heroes. The title of this chapter is, therefore, in part a conclusion and in part an irony. Surely if there is one single bold thesis to the work, it is that Jacobinism, in a position to organize Terror just as it organized victory, attempted to uproot all those elements of the social body that it perceived as aristocracies, within the course of a revolution largely prepared and launched by aristocrats. Jacobinism's definition of aristocracy was drawn first from surviving residues of the mentalities of the Old Regime and persons in whom its corporate attitudes seemed embodied, secondly from the extension of vendettas, through this justification, to other parties. The many opportunistic elements of real-life Jacobinism do not refute its ground swell of moral outrage and its doctrinaire political vision. But here we face the irony. For we have said little or nothing about the "Republic of Virtue." There were republicans in France, such as Dupont de Nemours and Condorcet, who shared few, certainly not most, of the aspirations of the moving spirits of the Terror. As for virtue, it was widely acknowledged that Robespierre was incorruptible and that civic or patriotic virtue (often in the form of surveillance or denunciation) was what the Jacobins intended; but was a Malesherbes not also considered virtuous in the eighteenth century? One way of conceiving the Jacobin notion of regeneration is to compare it to a tide-cycle. The outgoing tide would purge and liquidate the corrupt aristocracies, the *corps* and *communautés* of yore;[2] the incoming tide would refresh the ramparts of a new order, a polity of citizens, created by means of what Saint-Just called "institutions": "Institutions are the guarantee of public liberty; they moralize the government and the civil status; they repress the jealousies that produce factions; they found the delicate distinction between truth and hypocrisy, and innocence and crime; they implant the kingdom of justice. Without institutions, the strength of a Republic rests either on the merit of fragile mortals or on precarious methods."[3] Needless to say, the precarious methods were uppermost: the main concentration of Jacobinism was on the outgoing tide. We may brutally speculate that their ideal polity fortified by "institutions" (creating, in Rousseau's words, "a miracle which could have happened only as the result of a sudden enthusiasm for morality and virtue spread throughout a whole people,"[4]) would have travestied civilized life, for the "whole people" had actually to be created by excision. But the point must remain moot, like the Constitution of 1793. What we do know is that the purge could not last; that Western nations resolutely resisted Jacobin solutions in the coming century; and that numerous new nations today—without exactly employing the French rhetoric of Jacobinism or having a literary culture to sustain it—are often tempted by, or submitted to, similar ideals.

Further speculation on the ideal Jacobin regime is, however, inappropriate at this point. We are instead bound to summarize what our findings have been in the sphere to which the biographies bear witness: the character of the Jacobin elimination of aristocracies from the body politic. The Terrorists regarded their work as purification. This, in turn, entailed multiple differences of meaning—and consequences—that the French Revolution had for those who had applauded its first motions but could not become a part of its radical intensity, and for those who willingly denounced and executed them. It also entailed a linguistic adaptation of the categories of virtue and vice, heroism and crime, *patriotisme* and *perfidie* which seem simplistic from today's vantage point following upon our interpretive assimilation of Romanticism, positivism, Marxism, Freudianism, and a quantification of attitudinal data far outstripping anything dreamed of by Condorcet in his project to capture the history of common humanity.

I shall attempt first, then, a summarization that mediates the role and "institutional attitude" with the personal life-trajectory of our four subjects, in the hope of showing their disparity and significance. The disparity is itself significant, for we have developed at least presumptive evidence that the Jacobins, or, better, the mentality that organized and sustained the Terror, did not distinguish nicely between the crimes or plots of segments of the former society and the transgressions of individuals—at least not on a scale of analysis useful for any broad historical purposes.

The institutional attitude that best characterizes d'Orléans is that of *prince frondeur*. *Fronde* waged by princes of the blood assumed a large residue of *féodalité*, a diminution of Bossuet's dictum that "the public power is in the person of the prince" and a presumption of family interference in the affairs of state. The outstanding model was, of course, the "Great Condé," a prime mover in one of the strains of the actual Fronde during the minority of Louis XIV.[5] The practice of fronde challenged absolutism by ancient, frequently familial, means: it did not aspire to usurpation, pure and simple, especially in our period, and adopted constitutionalism with muted enthusiasm. It was a reaction against the centralizing, bureaucratizing tendencies of the monarchy by means of a "countercourt" or a counterclientele through which offended princely jealousies could be expressed without radical subversion of the system. We have already seen some of the ways in which the d'Orléans family contributed to this tendency. Fronde entered the perspective of the major political encounters of Louis XV's reign, the strife over the application of Unigenitus and the opposition of the sovereign courts, notably the Parlement of Paris, coming to a climax in Maupeou's coup d'état of 1771. It was an unstable element of the coalescing crisis of the regime. Numerous princes—Clermont, Conti, d'Orléans—incurred the royal displeasure. Finally, the inauguration of the renovated Palais-Royal and the spread of Freemasonry under the nominal auspices of the later Philippe-Egalité concentrated the countercourt and the counterculture at the top.

Meanwhile, in the years 1649–1714, England had seen tumultuous and irregular dynastic displacements: a king executed; two protectors; a king restored; the revolt of a king's illegitimate son; a king banished; and, finally, a total change of dynasty. In later Hanoverian times, rudimentary habits of government and opposition had attached themselves to the regular mechanism of the royal succession. Although France, by contrast, prided itself on exemplary stability, none of these events went unnoticed by purveyors of fronde. It was conceivable that the royal will could be bridled and even that usurpation itself could be constitutionalized.

Everything that figured in the formation of a man who assumed the title of Duc d'Orléans in 1785 cast him perfectly in the role of *frondeur*. This is not to say that he was without competitors: Provence and the Prince de Condé, during the first siege of the monarchy and after emigration, gave evidence of this. But d'Orléans held trumps. He loved "liberty," and liberty was in the air. He had animus and vast wealth, and he alone, both by disposition and advice, had anticipated the evolution of fronde from a condition of closed to open politics. Yet in 1787, and even in 1789, his attitude was still largely that of a countercourtsman, a popularity-seeker, and a troublemaker. He was not the agent of the political millenium; he was disposed to act negatively and jealously in the bubbling disorder of the Old Regime. When despised, he was regarded by his critics not as the harbinger of deep political change, but as a new version of Guise or Cromwell (who had a universally bad reputation in the eighteenth century). If admired, he was seen by his adulators as a kind of restorer, a prince, who, if he had dynastic pretensions—as I believe he did for Louis-Philippe—lacked dynastic instincts.

But Philippe d'Orléans both fulfills and denies our institutional portrait. He did not go the way of the Comte de Provence (with whom he shared many positions in 1788). Instead, he cultivated his English taste for liberty, severed his tactical connections with the conservative *parlementaires*, defied family solidarity in the worst of crises, allowed his lieutenants to build him a rudimentary political apparatus suited to the new politics, fished in the murky waters of leftist pamphleteering, had his children raised as "virtuous citizens" by Madame de Genlis, gravitated toward Jacobinism, renounced his rights to succession, embraced the Republic, forged connections with the Montagne, and voted for the death of the king. These acts, whose authenticity we have no reason to doubt, carried him far outside the predictable orbit of reaction by a frustrated prince, even if we allow for the remarkable events surrounding him. Yet the whole comportment of the Red Prince shows that there was a part of his disposition that refused to let go of older images and echoes. These emerge most evocatively in his hopes for his posterity. The passage from Fronde to Revolution was not an easy glide for the Duc d'Orléans. He was a reservoir of contradictions, hamstrung by his desire for liberty, essentially a liberty of private morality (so unlike Jacobinism's civic or public liberty), kept afloat by his immense advantages of birth and wealth, errantly steered by his compass of political conviction. This is, to a considerable degree, how he experienced himself: he lacked both the great criminality of a Machiavelli and the stout impulses of a Roman republican citizen. We cannot escape his elephantine presence; yet it shrinks to puniness compared to the *persona* it might have served.

It is not difficult to grasp why others, who had experienced this same French history, tended to see d'Orléans in a magnified frondeur image, rushing to his countercourt or abominating him as a vicious and homicidal prince. Nothing that d'Orléans might say or do could convince others that he was a compulsive republican who had forever renounced his Capetian rights and his title of *premier prince*. Not only did his morals make him highly offensive to purists like Robespierre; there was a general feeling that as long as he lived, the crown of France was closer to a flesh-and-blood head. The Republic had no need of frondeurs, royal aristocrats masking as plebs-worshipers. It is all very easy to say that from the Jacobin point of view it was totally necessary to fortify the republic by eliminating all those who might claim the crown. But they did not kill Louis XVII. Nor did many sincere republican deputies to the Convention (like Condorcet) even wish Louis XVI killed. D'Orléans's supposed republican guile helped to make him unsavory; his radiance as a great prince, useful up to a point, also targeted him for purification. Not only was his unsavoriness an object-lesson; it could be used fictitiously to contaminate others. D'Orléans even lucidly detected that political associates shied away from him as if he carried a contagious disease.

The prevailing institutional attitude of the Comte de Custine was that of *liberal military aristocrat*. Each of these three words has the value of a variable. Aristocracy here means descent from the *noblesse d'épée*. The military role is also crucial, for the notion of war as the preeminent aristocratic function was widely accepted by virtually all French society before 1789. The French nobles were regarded as an especially martial race, avid for combat with the enemy or with each other: despite anti-duelling legislation, they drew the sword on occasions of the point of honor far more frequently than other Europeans.[6] And, as we have seen, they clashed venomously in other ways. Liberalism enters the picture when we examine the sociology of the officer corps. Liberal officers tended mainly (and predictably) to be found among the highest-born, "court nobles" or at least those with a visible station and fortune, not those who accepted the military career as the only alternative for having a livelihood (though there are exceptions, like Dumouriez). This fact correlates with their access to education and *lumières*, their exposure to Parisian society and to travel, often their participation in the American

Expeditionary Force, and, eventually, their broad involvement in the aspect of the *révolte nobiliaire* that stressed the recovery of a voice in government rather than a retrenched defense of their estate privileges and the meager means of "living nobly." However, such men were not socially self-effacing or opposed to the *règlement Ségur* of 1781. A generalized ethos regarding the nobles as the logical persons to wield the French sword was thus fortified a decade before the fall of the monarchy by a preferential edict. To be a military aristocrat, even liberal, was therefore not only to want a voice in the affairs of the realm, but to be the consummate aristocrat.

Paradoxically, the great French military model of the age of Louis XV had none of this precise caste formation, but was a Protestant mercenary, Maurice de Saxe. Despite his extravagance and dissolute behavior, Saxe was acknowledged to possess the attributes of great generalship. When the *Encyclopédie* attempted to set forth all the qualities esteemed in a military commander, it could do no better than cite in detail a commentary by Saxe.[7] A contemporary eulogy for him declared: "It seems as if Maurice existed only for great deeds. . . . As soon as he ceased to conquer, he disappeared from the surface of the earth."[8] Saxe's career emphasizes, among other things, that the military aristocracy of the Old Regime was somewhat of an *internationale*: hence, in a manner thoroughly offensive to the new "patriotism," the Feuillant ministers Narbonne and Delessart had no hesitation in seeking the services of the Duke of Brunswick as the French generalissimo in January 1792, and Custine fell into deep trouble for his later correspondence with Brunswick.

Although liberal military aristocrats played at revolt in 1788, the disorienting rebellion went only skin-deep. At heart, the officer's oath was to his king, the commander-in-chief; his life, regimen, and mentality were firmly rooted in the symbols of authority of the Old Regime; his career was a testimony to his hereditary status. Though many joined with enthusiasm in the work of the Constituent Assembly, they strove to remake the civil part of France, while leaving the military part relatively untouched: an anomaly. There were limits of fealty and self-interest not to be transgressed. Depending on the man, at some stage in the Revolution (oath-taking, the flight to Varennes, 20 June 1792, the execution of the king, etc.) he would abandon his command or be pushed aside, even though the prospect of glory in war continued to attract him and he would not have been welcomed among the émigrés. Predictably he would be inclined to emigrate, despite this. If he did not emigrate, he would at least resist the radicalization of politics, which seemed destructive of all sane military discipline. Lafayette, Lameth, Latour-Maubourg,

Montesquiou, Wimpffen, and many others deserted; of the major figures of the liberal nobility only Custine, Biron, and Beauharnais attempted to ride out the storm, and all were guillotined.

Custine was born to the *épée*. No doubt because of his childhood experience and his later veneration for Prussia, he took Saxe for his model. He had only some of Saxe's qualities. At his best moments he could conduct a political negotiation, drill raw troops, march an army, and infuse spirit with his martial rhetoric. But his flawed ego, his vindictiveness, and his incapacity to earn the friendship and trust of brother officers and politicians often nullified his talents. He was not quite like the others: he had fought in America and adopted Freemasonry, but he held his idealism on a fairly tight leash (except for oratorical display). He felt that he had been promoted too slowly. Beneath dense layers of hereditary pride he gained the habit of treating others as obstacles, fools, or enemies. He could not bear to confess an error and was thus profligate in his placement of blame on others. There was a basic conflict between Custine's highly illiberal personality and his political professions. He disapproved of the king's execution on largely prudential grounds, although his leap to republicanism was not made with conviction. However, his self-image as an illustrious military leader was far more important to him than the nature of the regime. He was essentially a monarchist because he was a believer in strong government, just as he was a believer in rigid military discipline: the Republic seemed to promote inferior demagogues and bureaucrats who would bring in anarchy. Yet Custine did not conspire with the enemy.

Firmly convinced of his indispensability to the nation in the highest posts of war and strategy, Custine did not follow the predictable path of a liberal military aristocrat in many respects. On the other hand, he was stridently and thoroughly aristocratic in his basic institutional reflexes: toward civilian "bourgeois" authority, in his conception of European strategy, in his treatment of command functions and relations with fellow officers, and in his conduct of war. This perilous tension deprived him of choosing the route of Lafayette, the constitutionalist, and Dumouriez, the clever place-seeker; but it exposed him to the suspicion that he, stereotyped as a military aristocrat and an especially offensive one besides, would shortly act as they had. Moreover, Custine's downfall was the critical factor in the Jacobinization of the army. His arrogance finally played into the hands of his destroyers when he had believed that it would intimidate them. They neither could nor wished to unravel his vexing conduct from the generalized aristocratic plot in which they had come to believe. Precariously Custine remained a "patriot," but with all signals crossed and in an untenable contretemps with the Jacobin republic. His trial did much to convince the government to organize the official Terror.

Bailly's institutional attitude was that of the *academician*. The academy, as we have seen, is not so easy to encapsulate, for its interior organization, relatively free, allowed for all sorts of prejudices and perspectives. The savants were individualists, nevertheless assimilable for the most part to the general *esprit* of their learned corporations. However, the academies were aristocracies of talent and intellect, only incidentally of birth.[9] By 1750 they were becoming vested aristocracies of their own kind. They were the indispensable core of French science and culture. The monarchy was proud of their establishment and sought their advice on matters of welfare, taste, and technique; would-be savants competed jealously for their prizes; and the academicians themselves appreciated their attachment to state patronage (which, among other things, lightened their dependence on private handouts from *les grands*).

Of course there was a fly in the ointment: the academies, too, were breeders of *sociabilité politique*. They were, to a certain degree, purveyors of subversive knowledge, heralds of modified disaffection from social, religious, and political orthodoxies. They leaned toward the usufructory view of political authority, which was not the official ideology. In one sense, the academies promoted the social implications of the *lumières* and helped to make them respectable (in a way that the *Encyclopedia* was not respectable); yet, in another, they cushioned the shock of radical criticism through the delegations of intellectual authority that they enjoyed. Most of the ferment took place outside their walls. Moreover, much of the literature of the period escaped the dilemma of censorship; fine arts and architecture were scarcely politicized; and science and medicine pursued their own courses, despite some troublesome moments with the church and its organs of opinion.

To be sure, many a reformer, many a free-thinker, even a few philosophes dwelt within the groves of *académe*. But the academician was not typically a subversive. The extreme forms of subversion were more likely to be found in underground literature (cf. Jean Meslier), in the production of scandalmongers like Morande, or in the recriminations by aspirants on whom the academies had shut their doors tight. The academician was just barely prepared for 1789. Though the Republic of Letters was internally a democracy, its instincts were highly aristocratic, and its major organs were sponsored by a king. The National Assembly dismantled "féodalité" with hardy dispatch, but even the Academy of Science had fierce arguments over the reform of its own rules, and the

other academies lagged further behind. Predictably, our typical academician would be wary of the Revolution. Not only would he have a bond
of allegiance to his royal patron, but he might take the stronger position
that monarchies were the best support for science and culture. On the
other hand, as an enlightened man, he would be inclined to applaud
much-needed political and social reforms, all the while believing his own
vested interest valuable to humanity. He would lose respect for courtiers
and ministers who exalted breeding over talent. But he would not grant
that talent was a public right, like representative government. He would
fear and hate the democrats who preached their notion of "virtue"
against genius and talent. He would dread any political disorder disrup-
tive of his work or the corporate regularity of his life.

The cleavage among savants was pronounced in the Revolution. A
few endorsed the new ways wholeheartedly. Some emigrated, many
protested (like old Raynal), some were killed, others lay low. As Bailly
notes, few of the eminent *gens de lettres* stepped forward at the outset. The
Abbé Morellet has given us the sad saga of the waning months of the
Académie Française. As we have seen, the community of learning was
scourged and shaken.

Bailly belonged to the bourgeois-aspirant part of this mixed-estate
aristocracy. He was more uncomfortable in it than if he had been born
noble or had simply been more aggressive like d'Alembert (who was
baseborn). Bailly required the nurture of intellectual patrons. Yet he had
two great advantages: he was a Parisian, and he came from an artistic
family supplied with a royal pension. Nonetheless, even after admission
to all three of the major academies, he still felt compelled to prove his
worth in the correspondence about the Hyperboreans and other subjects
that he forced on Voltaire. And his actions as mayor of Paris (the pomp of
the Hôtel de Ville, the ambiguous feeling toward Lafayette) display the
same insecurity. Strangely, for one who later became a political victim,
Bailly had always been careful in his literary career to steer clear of
dangerous subjects. Though he was one of the few of his kind that
stepped forward in 1789, he was far less radical than many in the Old
Regime.

Bailly had made himself an aristocrat according to the rules of the Old
Regime, an aristocrat of the *lumières*. He is prototypical of our portrait in
one way and not in another. He devoted a huge portion of his life to the
corporate activities of the academy. It is fair to say that he gained from
this a deep indoctrination in procedures and patterns of public behavior.
But, on the other hand—partly by choice, partly by chance—he dove
into politics in 1789, moving from smaller to greater eminence. He was

now known, painted and sculpted, as an *homme d'Etat*, which appealed to the self-esteem that lay beneath his modesty. He mildly chided colleagues who had not followed his example, while claiming to understand their reticence. And thereupon he forsook his "tranquillity" for the business of politics. Thus his personal career and his institutional career were not simultaneously consummated, which is why the last part of our Bailly narrative is written in an "as if" frame of reference.

The "member of the Three Academies" freely chose his fatal political career and yet regretted it. He was both sacrificing himself to the nation and gaining an honorable place in the new aristocracy. Despite his many moments of chagrin and surprise, it is clear that he carried the attributes of his academic aristocracy into politics: his laborious tenacity, his insistence on formal procedures and dignity, his wish for liberty without license, his instinct for corporate rules, his love of order, his claim of neutrality or objectivity, his inherent royalism. Indeed, he also believed that the man of the intellect had a special aptitude for the affairs of state. The Jacobins sensed, and detested, this temperament many months before he became responsible for the Champ de Mars. Although Bailly was executed by the Revolutionary government for being the chief municipal officer at a public massacre, his preformed instincts and mentality contributed much to his reaction on that occasion. Although the academy is a mediation in the case of Bailly's death, it is a significant one. It might easily have caused him yet another death. His politics had been shaped by the routines of a corporate aristocracy.

Despite his awesome range of activity we can place Malesherbes, without much dispute, within the institutional context of the *noblesse de robe*, for his activities as an *homme de lettres* and as a royal minister were conditioned by his primary allegiance. As we have seen, the eighteenth-century *parlementaires* (I use the word for shorthand) were the *vox populi* by default. The sovereign courts were frail reeds on which to stake outcomes that engaged the interest or vanity of a royal official, but they were the only constant vehicle for the protection of the law and, furthermore, the only institutionalized obstacle to new laws yet more oppressive. They were also the rallying point for the Gallican opposition to ecclesiastical interference in affairs of state. Their better men were steeped in the law and showed it great respect, but they were counterbalanced by placemen and prejudiced aristocrats. When they "spoke for the nation," they usually spoke with a certain accent. They were a labyrinth of families and connections, and there was more than a casual relationship between wealth and office, since justice had to be bought. Finally, many of the courts served local rather than national interests. When, in the decade prior to the coup of Maupeou, the sovereign courts declared their own ideology of *classes, unité, indivisibilité*, this was indispensable to the preservation of any constitutional balance in France but also indicative of a federative "republic" of aristocracies within the monarchy. Yet, if the parlementary strength had collapsed in 1771, France would have been governed "despotically" by court nobles and favorites, not by enlightened technicians. The restoration of the Parlement of Paris and the Cour des Aides by Louis XVI in 1774 caused great popular rejoicing.

The events of 1787–89 far exceeded the aristocratic conception of politics cultivated by the magistrates. From the point when the Parlement of Paris rejected the representational demands of the Tiers, it was predictable that the parlementaire would gravitate toward veneration of a no longer menacing royal power and toward hostility to a Revolutionary threat involving offices, social status, and the whole hereditary edifice, indeed toward counterrevolution. This is indeed substantially what happened when the parlements were dismissed, and later dissolved, by the Constituent Assembly.

Contextually, Malesherbes occupied somewhat the same position toward the parlementaires as did Lafayette with respect to the liberal military aristocracy. Both enjoyed the advantages of high birth and wealth: in each case, these were enablements, not nostalgic grazing pastures; in each case, the man was in the forefront of reform, and attention came to be focused on him as such. Neither was a *parvenu*. Yet his youth and the limits of his *lumières* made Lafayette a kind of "new man," while Malesherbes's critique of the morals and politics of his age went back virtually to where the disorder had first been planted: the Regency. Intellectually he was a bridge between Montesquieu and the men of 1789. Malesherbes was deeply, though discreetly, inspired by the *esprit philosophique* of Montesquieu, Voltaire, Rousseau, Helvétius, Turgot, and others. He fought many liberal combats (Protestants, press, *lettres de cachet*, for example) that carried him outside the premises of his hereditary mentality and associated him with the mixed estate of the Republic of Letters. Politically, he believed in a stable order promoted by a wise exercise of royal majesty at the top, local liberties and grievance procedures for citizens at the bottom, and the regular practice of humane justice as a mediate and animating force. His remonstrances for the Cour des Aides, often daringly couched beneath the obligatory *politesse*, are a consistently developing plea for this harmony. In terms of 1789 they seem piecemeal and timid: they resist the scourge of despotism, but they do little to substantiate a new political order. For all their passion, they are essentially precautionary, not a herald of paradigm change. This is in part because of Malesherbes's intrinsic loyalty to the institutions of his country, but also in part because of his sense of realism and his limitations as a participant-actor.

Malesherbes never ceased to regard the nobility as an indispensable buffer against royal power, although he felt that its pretensions had to be cut to size and that its estate prerogatives needed thorough revision. At the same time he profoundly revered the monarchy and wished for a far closer communion between king and people. In his *mémoire* of 1788 he in part anticipated Mirabeau's notion of popular monarchy.[10] That advice was ignored, and it was probably too late. Malesherbes never—even in debunking the need for *corps intermédiaires*—disputed Montesquieu's defense of a specialized administration of justice, reinforced by the heredity and independence of offices. His welcoming of the Estates-General and recognition of their desire to become a national legislature did not preclude his fretfulness at their tampering with the magistracy. The Revolution increasingly alarmed him. Aristocratic discipline and notions of service had set Malesherbes apart from the individualist and utilitarian tendencies of the bourgeois lawyers; the brutality of the Republic stunned him, while preparing him for the sacrifice of his life. In the end, he could express himself only through a persevering loyalty to the symbols whose bearers he had been unable to reform. Yet the political horizon of his ideas far outreached the normal boundaries of his offices and the mentality of his caste, even though the Jacobins chose to regard him as the epitome of reaction and treason.

There is no very solid linking trait among our four subjects except for their unhappy destinies. Malesherbes remained the devoted royalist *bon gré mal gré*; d'Orléans renounced his birthright for the republic; the two others, for reasons we have taken up, fall somewhere in between. Yet they are closely connected by two other factors. All four moved resolutely into the world of the new politics compared with most others who shared the same background and institutional attitudes. And all four fell under Jacobin suspicion to a large degree because they could not efface the stain of their pre-Revolutionary or aristocratic past, by habit, by conviction, or by accident. They were not only representative symbols of what the Jacobins abhorred—aside from their personal flawed strategies—but as symbols they inhabited a greater reservoir of symbolism generally referred to as the *complot aristocratique*. That symbolism had the double purpose of confirming the Jacobins in their splendid image of virtue and of alerting the agents of the nation to a concentrated force of turpitude that patriotic vigilance could conquer. I do not claim that these victims were the best and brightest of an older order trying to make accommodations with the new; but their relationship to the live forces in that older order subsumes a great many other cases and dependencies, and helps us to confirm a portrait of the Terror and its meaning. However, history is sloppy: no formula reduces its sound and fury to smart theories. If we claim an insight, we do not write Q.E.D. at the bottom.

Just as the comparative experiments of institutional role and person cast light on the more shadowy areas of the Jacobin Terror, we may also be instructed by the careers and destinies of d'Orléans, Custine, Bailly, and Malesherbes in tracing the breakdown of authority patterns in the French state as the crisis of the Revolution approached and washed over the Bourbon dynasty. D'Orléans was in a sense fixated in the logical realm of the absolute royalist model by reason of inheritance and succession. The claims of his ancestor, the regent, to exercise plenitude of power on behalf of the minor Louis XV was rooted in these assumptions, as communications with the Parlement of Paris make clear. But Philippe d'Orléans himself was in full rebellion against this doctrine. He exhibited some mild affinities with the pattern I have called Aristocratic I in some of his displays of fronde, but his early political alliances (up to 1788) identified him very closely with the premises of the *robe* (Aristocratic II). Thereafter, he evolved swiftly toward the strong rhetorical mirage of consensualism, which dominated his public displays on most occasions during the Revolutionary period. The consensualism endorsed by d'Orléans was, however, impure or superficial on two counts: (1) it was strongly identified, to the exclusion of much else, with his "goût dominant," private liberty, which he mistakenly assumed to be the ruling passion of the Jacobins and, indeed, the French people at large; (2) it bent back tortuously on, and conflicted with, "the education of the modern prince" that he had prescribed for his male children. D'Orléans was only indirectly affected by the usufructory ideology; at least it did not modify or temper his abrupt passage from monarchism to republicanism. Yet it seemed for a while to be the main justification for his pretension to the regency.

Custine appears, despite his oath as a royal officer, to have become decisively emancipated from any strong attachment to the absolute royalist dogma, at least by the time of his appearance in politics. What residues of it that may have remained were transformed into the wish for strong government, preferably centered in one individual. By hereditary instinct he had absorbed and continually demonstrated in his behavior tendencies of Aristocratic I; one cannot say that he favored the supremacy of the *ancienne noblesse* in any of his public declarations, but he subscribed to it compulsively in military, as opposed to civilian, affairs. In other words, he was an aristocrat of the principal aristocratic *métier*. Custine was neither by background nor by temperament committed to the premises of the Aristocratic II model: insofar as he was preoccupied by such matters as justice and constitutional balance in the state he had unhesitatingly reached a consensualist position, further reaffirmed in his flattery of the Tiers and his wish to abolish implicit estate distinctions in the Constituent Assembly through new elections. Intermittent but important strains of the usufructory ideology infected Custine's prewar positions: in part they substituted for the absolute royalist mystique; in part they appealed to his penchant for discipline and efficiency. As one scans Custine's somewhat confused political stances, one becomes aware of an incipient streak of Bonapartism, greatly tempered by the habits of the Old Regime.

Bailly registered some residual emotional attachment to the symbolism (minus the dogma) of the absolute royalist model, without of course any religious commitment to it. As a bourgeois intellectual, he could be described as neutral, and possibly somewhat hostile, to the aristocratic models of authority; at best he appreciated them prudentially. Bailly's major temperamental element was the usufructory view of monarchical authority, a tendency shared with most of his fellow intellectuals. Indeed, as mayor of Paris, bourgeois constitutional king of a small but important domain, he cast his administration in this image once it had been legitimized by consensualist processes. It was of course under the rubric of consensualism that Bailly won his spurs in politics; as its defender he had his most heroic episodes. Nevertheless, he perceived and feared the open-endedness of consensualism, especially the ease by which it could reject a monarchy that he revered. Bailly hoped to combine both the majesty and public efficacy of the royal executive with a disciplined expression of the national legislative will.

Malesherbes, far more coherently but with no less futility than the others, grasped the outlines of a constitutional order in which each of the doctrines of authority would have its role to play. His filial appreciation of absolute royalist doctrine was much sobered by his fear of despotism, but he could not conceive of a France that was not based on a strong, affectionate, and reverential feeling for the king, a king separable from his counselors of the moment. He similarly harbored an attachment for the subsidiary role of our "antique et respectable noblesse," but saw its functions greatly reduced from what Montesquieu had thought in the age of politics coming into being. As a noble of the robe himself (Aristocratic II), he believed that the parlements had to relinquish their claim to be the nation's voice, but he never ceased to think that the "peaceful profession of justice" should remain their prerogative in an independent judicial climate. Malesherbes conceded to Turgot and others many claims of the usufructory position, in economics, in administration, and in "reform from above," so long as this did not abrogate the processes of justice traditionally guaranteed by the sovereign courts. Finally, he had come by 1788 to favor and prophesy the formation of a national legislative will, a genuine "voice of the nation" dominated by the commons, which, however, whether as an initiating force or as a sounding board of grievance, could scarcely be described as "sovereign" in his mixed system.

This analysis not only helps to sharpen our perception of how, as transitional, confused, or mixed attitudes toward legitimacy and authority in the state, the political postures of these four men betray an anchorage in ancestral habits, but why they were offensive to the modeling of the Republic of Virtue, whose essential project was to moralize the French with brand-new institutions and to transform a single individual will into an indivisible collective will. We can also judge the disintegration of traditional French authority patterns by examining these cases.

There have been many ingenious explanations of Jacobinism and Terror in the last century and a half of French historiography. Most of them are partly true. All have their place: the struggle of ideas and institutional paradigms; early prefigurations of class conflict based on competing relations of production and the shape of a society in which juridical categories and their attached privileges mocked economic reality; crises of wages and prices; the perils of foreign and civil war; the mobilization of the *plebs* and its pressures upon the tribunes to purge the system; the effort of the tribunes to control and mollify the plebs; the collision of secularization and public fervor; the recovery of a fantastic "Roman" ideology; vendettas of would-be elites attempting to profit from disorder; and the insatiable thirst for an egalitarian justice that would sever the Gordian knot of privilege. The last item in this catalogue—and I pass no judgment on its own wisdom and justice—seems to me to have the advantage of taking Jacobinism seriously, and it is supported by the findings of this study.

To repeat: Jacobinism—its Republic ("revolutionary until the peace" —but *what* peace, since the civil war was regarded as coterminous with the foreign one?) and its Terror—are best explained as a sanguinary crusade against *aristocracies*, wherever these are to be located. This thesis does not reject the possibility that the Jacobins might construct their own aristocracies (e.g., of "republican" wisdom and virtue), for they would be regarded as "magistracies" (*à la* Rousseau) and not as aristocracies in the hated sense. Neither does it contradict the obvious fact that many Jacobins did not practice what they preached or emerged quite "demythified" in the Directoire, the Consulate, or the Empire. We are speaking here of a range of persons extending roughly from Danton and Barère to Marat, Hébert, and Billaud-Varenne. But it is really the doctrine of action and institutions that we are specifying, as well as the justificatory propaganda involved. If "the *sans-culottes* are only definable collectively in terms of what they were against—and they were against an awful lot of people, an awful lot of attitudes, and an awful lot of institutions,"[11] this is also true to a considerable degree of the Jacobin organizers of the "official Terror." Their aggregating concept of lethal reproof was "aristocracy."

I shall close with a few brief remarks that link this study with work that remains to be done. In *Père Duchesne*, no. 29, Hébert gives vent to his hatred of a whole variety of aristocracies. He identifies them principally by behavior pattern, by species of hypocrisy rather than corporate interests. Among his targets of attack are "those of good faith . . . because their personal interest is more important to them than the general interest. . . . They are the least blameworthy"; "others, who would like justice done but find the means for doing this too violent and [therefore] speak out against liberty . . . because the peaceful existence they lead . . . seems preferable to . . . the conquest of that liberty"; "others . . . aristocrats by vanity [who] are the most to be feared . . . who would overturn everything . . . for the sake of vengeful satisfaction"; "another kind of aristocrats . . . by profession . . . interested above all in money"; "another class of aristocrats cleverer than the others . . . who take no side, but study the situation so as to jump on the right side . . . a so-called *marquis*, a pious writer with impious tastes . . . who preaches, in turn, patriotism and aristocracy. . . ."[12] The net is cast very wide indeed: aristocracy here becomes a mania of stigmatization. The tone of Hébert's article shows us how his political contempt not only reproduced some of the criticisms of existing social ways made on certain occasions by our four victims, but could have been turned on any of them, as it was, at a moment's notice.

It is indeed true that by 1789 the notion of aristocracy had come, at least in some circles, to be extended to portions of society far wider than the privileged estates and royal officials.[13] Yet the spacious employment of the term—with its future implications of Jacobin indictment—obviously has its moorings in the visible institutional aristocracies of the Old Regime. French manners, as Voltaire so well knew, descended from the top. And as Malesherbes acutely observed, this inspired jealous emulation, artificiality, and luxury in the lesser ranks. Hypocrisy derived from the vanity of social superiority, encrusted in its neo-feudal and rococo forms: the patriot responded with a mixture of envy, scorn, and hate, or with visions of a utopia in which there was no time for "philosophy" to seep in but where purification was a first order of business.

It was not nearly enough to catch the monarch red-handed in a conspiracy against the virtuous parts of the nation and to cut off his head. The monarch himself was comparatively trivial: Saint-Just was well aware that this was but the first step. For, "the nobility used to make sport of the kings, who were only then as they are now the greatest dupes of their land. The aristocracy, abhorred for its crimes, weighed upon the earth; probity was ridiculous in its eyes; it invented passions and stupidities to stimulate its satisfaction; it trampled down the countryside; it insulted misery and made fun of heaven and earth."[14] Now aristocracy itself would be trampled, not only so that France might live but so that, rid of a millenial curse, she might live with "virtuous institutions."

The further assertion is then that the Jacobins attacked both the parts and the whole of aristocracy with their "force coactive." They pursued it to the depths of its institutional crannies, in some cases completing the work of the assemblies of 1789 and 1791 (e.g., the church, the parlements, the estates), in others initiating the real task of purification (the army, the academies, certain other parts of the bourgeoisie). As for their victims, the Jacobins had specific reasons for killing many of them, but these reasons were swallowed in a more global vision where the discrepant boundaries between personal public behavior and role-occupancy tended to melt away, where a species of retributive justice mingled with premonitory deterrence achieved the proportions of a continuing spectacle of ritual delegitimation.[15] Finally, all these initiatives, inspired by an unremitting war of patriotism and purgation, were conceptually dissolved into a single mission, a single *raison de République*, undertaken against a gigantic historical misfortune, a single plot against "humanity" and "nature," a single treason. The individual acts of accusation delivered by Fouquier-Tinville and his colleagues, the brusque specificity of the trials, the convergent lives and the parallel deaths of d'Orléans, Custine, Bailly, and Malesherbes were ultimately modes of a single substance.

In an afterthought to his brilliant interpretation of *The Nightmare*, a well-known pre-Romantic painting of Fuseli (Füssli), Jean Starobinski describes an imitative vignette of the Revolution called *Le cauchemar de l'aristocratie* by P.-J. Sauvage. Asleep in the midst of a tormented dream is an allegorical female figure. Crowns, scepters, a coat of arms, a Maltese cross are prominent at the foot of her bed. The emblems of her nightmare, so close that they almost touch her heaving breast, are a Phrygian bonnet and an equilateral triangle. It is not an incubus that is pursuing this incorrigible woman, but the austere symbols of equality and republicanism.[16] In 1793 they would be joined by the blade of the law.

Notes

Abbreviations to the Notes

AAT   Archives de l'Armée de Terre, Vincennes
AN   Archives Nationales
BN   Bibliothèque Nationale
OBI   D'Orléans Papers, Bibliothèque de l'Institut de France

Chapter 1

1. Merleau-Ponty, *Humanism*, p. 91.
2. I have written more detailed observations on this work in a paper "Authority, Ideology, and Terror in the French Revolution," prepared for delivery at the Northeastern Society for Eighteenth-Century Studies, October 1980.
3. Furet, *Penser*, pp. 18–20.
4. Furet, *Penser*, pp. 58–59. Subsequent quotations in this chapter will be cited in the text.
5. See White, *Metahistory*, esp. pp. 7–27.
6. The title of Furet's introductory essay is "La Révolution française est terminée."
7. See Furet, *Penser*, esp. pp. 218–21.
8. Ibid., pp. 82–85.
9. Cf. certain essays of Georges Lefebvre and some of the recent writings of Richard Cobb, which relate the "humble annals" of the poor or the eccentric.
10. Furet, *Penser*, pp. 68–69.
11. Skinner, "Meaning and Understanding," p. 27.
12. Bossuet, *La Politique tirée*, p. 185.
13. Le Paige's principal work was *Lettres historiques sur les fonctions essentielles du Parlement, sur le droit des Pairs et sur les lois fondamentales du royaume*, 2 vols. (Geneva, 1753–54).
14. The notion is given crystalline expression in d'Holbach's article "Représentans" for the *Encyclopedia*.
15. Van Kley, "Church, State," p. 635.
16. See esp. Taveneaux, *Jansénisme*, pp. 185–200; and Van Kley, *Jansenists and the Expulsion*.
17. See Derathé, *Jean-Jacques Rousseau*, pp. 84–92.
18. See Censer, *Prelude to Power*, passim.
19. Furet, *Penser*, pp. 66–67.
20. Goubert, *L'Ancien régime*, Vol. 1.
21. Aulard, "Patrie, patriotisme," p. 325.

22. Goubert and Denis, *1789: Les Français*, p. 40.

23. Ibid., p. 43.

24. Shennan, *Parlement of Paris*, p. 284.

25. Mounier, *Considérations*, p. 24.

26. Ibid., p. 26.

27. Lanjuinais, *Oeuvres*, 1:139.

28. See esp. Van Kley, *Jansenists and the Expulsion*, pp. 23–29.

29. For one view of the changing character of the nobility and its values, see Chaussinand-Nogaret, "Aux Origines," pp. 265–78.

30. See Mably's argument in his *Observations*, esp. vol. 1, chaps. 1–5.

31. Sieyès, *Tiers Etat*, p. 132.

32. See Seligman, *La Justice*, 1:357.

33. D'Alembert, "Eloge de Saint-Pierre," in *Eloges historiques de l'Académie Française, Oeuvres complètes*, 3:252.

34. Furet, *Penser*, pp. 49–50.

35. *Le Patriote français*, no. 47.

36. See the exchange between Cazalès and Volney, *Archives parlementaires* 11:622–23.

37. See Baker, "French Political Thought," 295–98.

38. Rousseau, *Social Contract*, in *Oeuvres complètes*, 3: II,vii.

39. Helvétius, *De l'homme*, sec. x, chaps. 9–10, in *Oeuvres complètes*, 4:370–79.

40. Cf. Marat: "it is in the very midst of this Convention that we find the *foyer* of the Counter-Revolution." To the Jacobins, session of 13 May 1793, in Aulard, ed., *Société des Jacobins* 5:197.

41. *Manifeste très pressant et très essentiel* . . . , in Découflé, Boulanger, and Pierrelle, *Etudes d'histoire*, p. 6.

42. *Le Patriote français*, 21 September 1792.

43. Aulard, ed., *Société des Jacobins*, 5:243.

44. For Lavater's character reading of Hérault, see Palmer, *Twelve Who Ruled*, p. 15.

45. G. P. Müller, *Aus Lavaters Brieftasche* (Munich, 1897), pp. 52–56, passim.

46. "Deffinition du modéré, du feuillant de laristocrate [*sic*] . . . ," anonymous address sent to the Convention, quoted in John Hardman, *French Revolution Documents*, 2:58.

47. Cordeliers Club, 22 June 1793, in ibid., p. 117.

48. *Père Duchesne*, no. 259, p. 6.

49. Robespierre, to the Jacobins, 21 Messidor, an II (9 July 1794), *Oeuvres complètes*, 10:523.

50. On various aspects, see Groethuysen, *The Bourgeois*; Plongeron, *Conscience religieuse*; and Vovelle, *Religion et Révolution*.

51. For a fascinating account, with remarkable photographs, of the destruction and recovery of the statuary of the principal portal of Notre-Dame, see Giscard d'Estaing, Fleury, and Brandenburg, *Les Rois retrouvés*.

52. Even when Cazalès, the spokesman for the ultras in the Constituent Assembly, provoked Barnave, of the Left, to a duel on 11 August 1790, its

honorable outcome promoted the friendship of the two men and the applause of the Assembly. See Chevallier, *Barnave*, pp. 155–60.

53. Madame de Genlis, *Mémoires*, 1:282, 290; 2:149–57, 167, 232–41, 335.

54. Bibliothèque Nationale (*BN*), fonds français 22,133, fol. 56.

55. Maugras and Croze-Lemercier, *Delphine de Sabran*, p. 137; see also pp. 71–72.

56. Tocqueville, *Democracy*, 2:102–3.

Chapter 2

1. See Scudder, *Prince of the Blood*, p. 89.

2. Louis-Philippe-Joseph d'Orléans, "Exposé de la conduite," p. 5.

3. Duc des Cars, *Mémoires*, 1:73.

4. Louis-Philippe, *Mémoires*, 1:25.

5. D'Orléans papers, Bibliothèque de l'Institut de France (*OBI*), Ms. 2048/16.

6. For a temperate and readable account of the Regent, see Shennan, *Philippe*.

7. Voltaire, *Précis du règne de Louis XV*, in *Oeuvres historiques*, p. 1313.

8. Voltaire, *Siècle de Louis XIV*, ibid., p. 945.

9. *Nouvelle Biographie*, 37–38:815–16.

10. Louis-Philippe, *Mémoires*, I:9.

11. Amadée Britsch, "Philippe-Egalité," p. 338. D'Orléans's paternity has been questioned; his mother is reported to have said: "When you fall among thorns, how do you know which one stuck you?" Laurentie, *Histoire*, 3:359.

12. "All together," wrote Target, "they are that [Court of Peers] which is not the nation, but which, for more than eight hundred years, especially the last six hundred, has substituted as much as possible for the lack of national assemblies." See *Lettres d'un homme à un autre homme*, in *Maupeouana*, 1:183–84.

13. "Apanage," in *Encyclopédie*, 1:521–22.

14. Hyslop, *Apanage*, p. 1.

15. Louis-François de Bourbon, prince de Conti (1717–1776) was a military man who became disillusioned with Louis XV's conduct of the realm and struck fronde-like alliances with the parlements in his later years; the king called him mockingly "mon cousin l'avocat." He was the chief of the princely opposition to Maupeou in 1771.

16. Quoted in Scudder, *Prince of the Blood*, p. 21.

17. Cf., for example, Gamache, *Récit*, pp. 7–12.

18. Letter, undated 1791, *OBI*, Ms. 2051.

19. Louis-Philippe, *Mémoires*, I:10.

20. Britsch, "Philippe-Egalité," p. 350.

21. Ibid., p. 358.

22. See Hyslop, *Apanage*, pp. 29–47.

23. See Castelot, *Prince rouge*, p. 29.

24. Walzer, ed., *Regicide and Revolution*, p. 11.

25. See Lacour-Gayet, *Marine militaire*, p. 119.

26. Manceron, *Hommes de la liberté*, 2:34.

27. Ibid., 2:35–40.

28. For d'Orléans's army commission, see *OBI*, Ms. 2048/174.

29. Bossuet was preceptor of the Dauphin, son of Louis XIV; Fénelon the preceptor of his grandson, the Duc de Bourgogne.

30. Much of the following is from Morand, "Philippe-Egalité," 304:290–93.

31. (Anon.), "Exposé des changemens à faire," p. 6.

32. (Anon.), "Observations sur la destruction de la promenade du Palais-Royal," pp. 1, 34–35.

33. (Anon.), "Réflexions sur la clause de la donation du Palais Cardinal, depuis Palais Royal," pp. 1–4.

34. Morand, "Philippe-Egalité," pp. 292–93.

35. Britsch, "Philippe-Egalité," p. 490.

36. See especially Archives Nationales (*AN*), AF^{IV} 1470.

37. When advised in 1793 to seek safety in America, Egalité flatly refused: the Americans had no opera.

38. (Anon.), "Etat de situation de M. Louis-Philippe-Joseph," p. 1.

39. Ibid., p. 3.

40. (Anon.), "Contrat d'union du duc d'Orléans."

41. Ibid., p. 4.

42. Ibid., pp. 11–14.

43. See note 22, above.

44. Chevallier, *Histoire de la Franc-Maçonnerie*, 1:160–61.

45. Martin, *Franc-Maçonnerie*, p. 29; cf. Chevallier, *Histoire de la Franc-Maçonnerie*, 1:322; and Ligou, "Franc-Maçonnerie," p. 108.

46. Chevallier, *Histoire de la Franc-Maçonnerie*, 1:173.

47. Ligou, "Franc-Maçonnerie," p. 105.

48. *AN*, R^4 283.

49. Chevallier, *Histoire de la Franc-Maçonnerie*, 1:197, 276.

50. [Montjoie], *Histoire de la conjuration*, 1:53–57.

51. Martin, *Franc-Maçonnerie*, p. 16.

52. Ibid., p. 29.

53. Ibid., p. 87.

54. Ibid., p. 125.

55. Ibid., p. 152.

56. See Chassin, *Elections et cahiers*, 2:331; and Le Bihan, *Francs-Maçons parisiens*.

57. *Journal de Paris*, no. 55, 24 February 1793; also *OBI*, Ms. 2048/127.

58. *OBI*, Ms. 2048/128.

59. [Montjoie], *Histoire de la conjuration*, 1:120–21.

60. Etienne and Martainville, *Vie politique*, p. 1.

61. Ducoin, *Etudes révolutionnaires*, p. 111.

62. See Britsch, "Philippe Egalité," p. 478; Scudder, *Prince of the Blood*; Castelot, *Prince rouge*; and Dard, *Acteur caché*, esp. pp. 134–35, 144–47.

63. "Jean-Georges-Charles Voidel à ses concitoyens," p. 5.

64. Talleyrand, *Memoires*, 1:152.

65. Bacourt, *Correspondance entre Mirabeau et la Marck*, 1:68.

66. Barnave, "Introduction à la Révolution française," in *Oeuvres*, 1:106.

67. See below, chap. 3.

68. Dumouriez is accused, but without proof, in Barère, *Mémoires*, 2:314. See also testimony of Clermont-Tonnerre, in *Procédure criminelle*, 2:80–81.

69. Dumouriez, *Mémoires*, 2:80.

70. Mounier, "Appel au tribunal," p. 264.

71. Malouet, *Mémoires*, 1:247.

72. Madame Roland, *Mémoires*, 1:56.

73. Barère, *Mémoires*, 2:73.

74. Ibid., 1:295.

75. Ibid.

76. Ibid., 2:293–94 and 294n.

77. Louis-Philippe, *Mémoires*, 2:238.

78. "Epitaphe de feu Mgr d'Orléans," in Malherbe, *Oeuvres poétiques*, p. 71.

Chapter 3

1. See note 15, previous chapter.

2. *OBI*, Ms. 2048/10.

3. D'Orléans, "Exposé de la conduite," pp. 4–5.

4. Ibid., p. 3.

5. Necker, *Administration des finances*.

6. See Olivier-Martin, *Droit français*, par. 292, pp. 377–78.

7. Chen Ta Ming, *L'organisation des Assemblées*, p. 50.

8. Brienne, *Journal*, p. 23.

9. The *arrêtés* of the *bureaux*, not published, are found in *BN*, nouv. acq. 23,617, folios 5–13 and 19–21.

10. Brienne, *Journal*, pp. 55–56.

11. The *procès-verbal* of the Third Bureau (d'Orléans) can be found in Ms. 841, Bibliothèque de l'Institut de France.

12. Ms. "Extrait des souvenirs de la Vicomtesse de Loménie," in Brienne, *Journal*, p. 122; cf. p. 56.

13. Egret, *Pré-révolution*, p. 154.

14. Cited in ibid., p. 177. See Brissot's scathing account of Ducrest's pretensions: Brissot, *Mémoires*, 2:65–66.

15. Hyslop, *Apanage*, pp. 198–99.

16. Ducrest, "Vrais principes," pp. 21, 24–25.

17. See Lefebvre, *Coming of French Revolution*, p. 27.

18. Talleyrand, *Mémoires*, 1:192–93.

19. Quoted in [Montjoie], *Histoire de la conjuration*, 1:95, 102.

20. Text cited in Olivier-Martin, *Droit français*, par. 508, p. 699.

21. See "Procès-verbal de l'Assemblée des Notables . . . 1788."

22. Ibid., p. 78.

23. Ibid., p. 214.

24. Ibid., p. 221.

25. Ibid., p. 230.

26. Ibid., p. 232.

27. D'Orléans, "Exposé de la conduite," p. 11n.

28. Dard, *Acteur caché*, p. 146.

29. Brissot, *Mémoires*, 2:69.

30. Duc de Castries, *Mirabeau*, p. 377.

31. See Dard, *Acteur caché*, pp. 139–44. According to Grace Dalrymple Elliott, Laclos was introduced to d'Orléans by the Vicomte de Noailles: Elliott, *Sous la terreur*, p. 20.

32. "Aujourd'hui prude, hier galante;/ Tour à tour folle et docteur:/ Genlis, douce gouvernante,/ Deviendra dur Gouverneur;/ Mais toujours femme charmante/ Saura remplir son destin:/ On peut bien être pédante/ Sans cesser d'être Catin." In anon., *La vie privée*, p. 74. My translation.

33. "Change donc, ma fille,/ Ta plume en aiguille;/ Brûle ton papier;/ Il faut te résoudre/ A filer, à coudre./ C'est là ton métier." Quoted in Brissot, *Mémoires*, 2:11. My translation.

34. Quoted in Castelot, *Prince rouge*, p. 152.

35. Brissot, *Mémoires*, 2:64.

36. Dard, *Acteur caché*, p. 162.

37. Hyslop, *Apanage*, p. 201.

38. See Castelot, *Prince rouge*, p. 264.

39. Dard, *Acteur caché*, p. 155.

40. See Bailly, *Mémoires*, 1:52.

41. Louis-Philippe, *Mémoires*, 1:103.

42. Ibid., 1:115.

43. Hyslop, *Apanage*, p. 248.

44. Dard, *Acteur caché*, p. 166.

45. See Bellanger et al., *Histoire générale de la presse française*, 1:431–34.

46. Lefebvre, *La grande peur*.

47. Of the hundreds of pamphlets of its time, *Qu'est-ce que le Tiers Etat?* has alone become a classic; it passed through three editions in 1789. The most readable edition, with an extensive introduction (pp. 7–117) is R. Zapperi's (Geneva, 1970).

48. D'Orléans, "Exposé de la conduite," p. 6.

49. Talleyrand, *Mémoires*, 1:209–10.

50. D'Orléans, "Exposé de la conduite," p. 6.

51. Dard, *Acteur caché*, p. 166. There is a voluminous work of 1789, attributed to the Duc d'Orléans, called *Traité philosophique, théologique et politique de la loi de divorce*. It is conceivable that Laclos wrote it.

52. Dard, *Acteur caché*, p. 168.

53. Britsch, "Philippe-Egalité," p. 493, suggests that they may have been the work of the Marquis de Limon, then a member of the Conseil de la Maison d'Orléans. This seems unlikely.

54. D'Orléans, *Instructions*, pp. 1–7, passim.

55. Martin, *Franc-Maçonnerie*, p. 156.

56. Ibid., p. 158.

57. Dard, *Acteur caché*, p. 168.

58. The Duc claims that his *Instructions* showed that he had understood what the French were thinking: "My ruling passion for liberty had tied my personal interest to the public interest." *OBI*, Ms. 2049.

59. Hyslop, *Apanage*, p. 249.

60. Ibid., p. 250.

61. Chassin, ed., *Elections et cahiers*, 3:276.

62. "Procès-verbal de l'Assemblée Nationale" (1789), 2:7–9.

63. For example, [Montjoie], *Histoire de la conjuration*, 2:10.

64. Quoted in Alissan de Chazet, *Vie politique*, p. 28.

Chapter 4

1. Louis-Philippe, *Mémoires*, 1:103.

2. See Dominique, *Paris enlève*, pp. 59–60.

3. Ibid., pp. 128–29.

4. It was especially Mounier's notion that king and Assembly should be inseparable (he liked to play the honest broker between them); but he would have preferred Soissons or Compiègne.

5. Louis-Philippe, *Mémoires*, 1:113–14.

6. Mounier, "Appel au tribunal," pp. 59–60.

7. See Lefebvre, *Coming of French Revolution*, p. 165.

8. All these charges were made or suggested in the testimony taken by the Châtelet: *Procédure criminelle, instruite au Châtelet de Paris*, (hereafter cited as *Procédure au Châtelet*). For a condensation, see the appendix to Dominique, *Paris enlève*.

9. D'Orléans, "Exposé de la conduite," p. 17.

10. Ibid., p. 22.

11. "Véritable intérrogatoire et véritables réponses," p. 2.

12. (Anon.), "Intrigues secrettes de Louis-Philippe-Joseph d'Orléans," p. 4.

13. (Anon.), "L'assassinat de la Famille Royale: plan présenté à Mgr. le duc d'Orléans," p. 8.

14. Rémusat, *Mémoires*, 2:346.

15. Bailly, *Mémoires*, 1:62, points out that Lafayette's proposal had the fault of "not being always clear and precise."

16. Lafayette, *Mémoires*, 2:313.

17. Ibid.

18. Mounier, "Appel au tribunal," pp. 11n–12n.

19. Lafayette, *Mémoires*, 2:313; also 2:355, mentioning Bailly.

20. Ibid., 2:272; and see Mortimer-Ternaux, *Histoire de la Terreur*, 1:435–37.

21. Lafayette, *Mémoires*, 2:334–35.

22. Ibid., 2:416.

23. *Procédure au Châtelet*, 2:38.

24. Lafayette, *Mémoires*, 2:336–37.

25. Ibid., 2:355.

26. Speech of 2 October 1790, quoted in ibid., 2:357.

27. Ibid., 2:415.

28. D'Orléans, "Exposé de la conduite," p. 19. See also "Brouillon pour discours à la tribune de l'Assemblée Nationale," *OBI*, Ms. 2048/120.

29. Dard, *Acteur caché*, p. 193.

30. Bacourt, *Correspondance entre Mirabeau et La Marck*, 1:127–28.

31. Duc de Castries, *Mirabeau*, pp. 376–77.

32. This is indicated in the document "Instruction du Roi à S.A.S. Mgr. le duc d'Orléans," in d'Orléans, *Correspondance*, pp. 40–42.

33. Ibid., p. 36.

34. *AN*, F[7] 4385[1].

35. Mirabeau, *Lettres de cachet et prisons d'état*, 1:25.

36. Bacourt, *Correspondance entre Mirabeau et La Marck*, 1:154–61.

37. Ibid., 1:111.

38. We may speculate that Mirabeau outweighed Bailly enough in popularity to have had his post of mayor on 17 July 1789, had he not been absent attending to the funeral of a father he hated (the Marquis de Mirabeau, the "ami des hommes"); when Mirabeau later in the year aspired from his eminence in the National Assembly to ministerial rank as well, Lanjuinais introduced a successful resolution imposing an absolute separation of powers.

39. See Welch, *Mirabeau*, p. 291.

40. Bacourt, *Correspondance entre Mirabeau et La Marck*, 2:15–16, 19–24.

41. Ibid., 2:20.

42. Ibid., 2:31.

43. Chateaubriand, *Mémoires d'Outre tombe*, 1:178.

44. Duc de Castries, *Mirabeau*, p. 338.

45. Marat's great diatribe against the savants is *Les charlatans modernes, ou lettres sur le charlatanisme académique* (Paris, 1791).

46. See *Journal de la République française*, no. 84, 25 December 1792, p. 8.

47. Gottschalk, *Marat*, p. 58.

48. Marat knew England well, having been there from 1765 to 1777.

49. Walter, *Marat*, pp. 185–86.

50. "Marat, l'ami du peuple, à Louis-Philippe-Joseph, Prince français," in Chèvremont, *Marat*, 2:107.

51. The Châtelet is described as "a royal jurisdiction . . . the *prévôté* and *vicomté*

of Paris . . . a *bailliage* and by far the most important in France." For further information, see Olivier-Martin, *Droit français*, par. 411, p. 556.

52. These and other details in Dominique, *Paris enlève*, pp. 263–68.

53. Ibid., p. 267.

54. *Procédure au Châtelet*, 2:38.

55. Lafayette, *Mémoires*, 3:139.

56. D'Orléans actually tried to perform as a diplomat; see his letters to Montmorin in *Correspondance*, pp. 56, 72, and ff.

57. Ibid., p. 104.

58. Ibid., p. 113f.

59. Lafayette, *Mémoires*, 2:483.

60. *OBI*, Ms. 2048/150.

61. D'Orléans, *Correspondance*, p. 156.

62. Ibid., p. 162.

63. Bacourt, *Correspondance entre Mirabeau et La Marck*, 2:69–77. This important document is worth reading in full.

64. Ibid., 1:186.

65. *Orateur du Peuple* 1, no. 42, p. 335.

66. Ibid. 1, no. 43, p. 340.

67. Ibid. 2, no. 2, p. 5.

68. *Ami de Peuple*, no. 243, 7 October 1790, p. 1.

69. Ibid., no. 242, 6 October 1790, p. 5.

70. *Révolutions de Paris* 5, no. 57 (7–14 August 1790), p. 216.

71. Ibid. 5, no. 65 (2–9 October 1790), p. 630; also pp. 638–44.

72. Hébert, "Philippe d'Orléans et le ci-devant Comte de Mirabeau," pp. 4, 8.

73. Duc de Castries, *Mirabeau*, p. 467. For a complete account of these debates, see "Journée du 6 octobre 1789."

74. Etienne and Martainville, *Vie politique*, pp. 79–81.

75. Chabroud, *Rapport de la Procédure du Châtelet sur l'affaire des 5 et 6 octobre 1789, fait les 30 septembre et 1er octobre 1790, à l'Assemblée Nationale, par M. Charles Chabroud*.

76. Ibid., pp. 101, 107, 116.

77. Ibid., pp. 2–3.

78. Ibid., p. 6.

79. Ibid.

80. Ibid., p. 41.

81. Ibid., pp. 43–44.

82. Cf. Michelet, *Histoire de la Révolution*, 1:316 and 349.

83. Elliott, *Sous la terreur*, pp. 25–26.

84. See Mounier, "Appel au tribunal," esp. pp. 57, 224–25.

85. Cf. "Journée du 6 octobre," pp. 11–13, 19, 117–19, 124–26, 134.

86. "Compte rendu par une partie des membres de l'Assemblée Nationale."

87. *AN*, C 45/423.

88. *Orateur du Peuple* 1, no. 43, p. 344.

89. "Grâce donc à notre assemblée,/ La vertu triomphe d'emblée;/ Pour être un grand homme, en effet,/ Il ne faut plus que son décret./ Rendons à notre personnage/ Constitutionnel hommage,/ En répétant à tout venant,/ Ma foi, c'est un grand innocent!" *Actes des Apôtres*, no. 179. My translation.

90. Louis-Philippe, *Mémoires*, 1:139.

91. Dard, *Acteur caché*, p. 289.

92. Louis-Philippe, *Mémoires*, 1:140–41.

93. Darin, *Bossuet*, p. 113.

Chapter 5

1. (Anon.), "Au régicide d'Orléans," p. 3.

2. (Anon.). "Le portefeuille de Louis-Philippe d'Orléans," p. 35.

3. (Anon.), "Le sieur d'Orléans tout entier," p. 2.

4. (Anon.), "Non, d'Orléans, tu ne régneras pas," p. 1.

5. See, on this, Reinhard, *Chute*, p. 132. Reinhard's is by far the best *événementiel* account of this period.

6. *Orateur du Peuple* 5, no. 36, p. 304.

7. *Ami du Peuple*, no. 501, 25 June 1791, pp. 5–6.

8. *OBI*, Ms. 2050.

9. Ibid., 9 April 1791.

10. Ibid., undated 1791.

11. Ibid., 23 May 1791.

12. Louis-Philippe, *Mémoires*, 1:142–43.

13. Ibid., 1:140.

14. (Anon.), "Réponse de M. Delaclos à M. le duc d'Orléans," p. 4.

15. (Anon.), "La faction d'Orléans mieux dévoilée," p. 4.

16. Madame de Genlis, *Mémoires*, 4:11.

17. Aulard, *Société des Jacobins*, 2:545–47.

18. Madame de Genlis, *Mémoires*, 4:88.

19. Ibid., 4:92.

20. Quoted by Tournois, *Histoire*, p. 288.

21. Louis-Philippe, *Mémoires*, 1:160n–61n. Indeed, Louis-Philippe did have the morals of a Spartan; he, the colonel of a regiment, wrote a remarkable letter to Madame de Genlis on 3 April 1792, avowing his virginity. *OBI*, Ms. 2048/221.

22. Barnave, "Introduction à la Révolution française," *Oeuvres*, 1:134.

23. See the discussion in Reinhard, *Chute*, pp. 130–31.

24. Cf. Robert's speech at the Jacobins, 30 November 1792: "I think that M. Brissot is a republican, but not a republican like the Jacobins. There are republics and republics. Venice and Geneva are republics, but that certainly isn't what we want." Aulard, *Jacobins*, 4:531.

25. Quoted by Dard, *Acteur caché*, p. 308.

26. Aulard, *Jacobins*, 3:17.

27. Brissot, *Mémoires*, 2:282.

28. Ibid. Brissot may not so easily have escaped the imputation of Orleanism because of his previous connection.

29. Aulard, *Jacobins*, 3:20.

30. Dard, *Acteur caché*, pp. 322–23. Also, Bailly to Lafayette, 16 July 1791, "Correspondance Bailly-Lafayette," *BN*, fonds français, 11,697.

31. Laclos later rejoined the army, survived the Terror and the reaction, and died in 1803.

32. See his correspondence with Duportail, *OBI*, Ms. 2048/174.

33. *OBI*, Ms. 2048/69.

34. *AN*, C 190/160[4].

35. *OBI*, Ms. 2048/82.

36. Ibid., 2048/88.

37. Ibid., 2048/101, 102.

38. Castelot, *Prince rouge*, p. 204.

39. *AN*, F[7] 4385[1], 26 July 1792.

40. Ibid., 4 August 1792.

41. Ibid., 18 August 1792.

42. Ibid., 26 August 1792.

43. Louis-Philippe, *Mémoires*, 2:241.

44. *OBI*, Ms. 2048/108, 9 September 1792.

45. Louis-Philippe, *Mémoires*, 2:184–90.

46. For example, Etienne and Martainville, *Vie politique*, p. 118.

47. Louis-Philippe, *Mémoires*, 2:214–15.

48. Etienne and Martainville, *Vie politique*, p. 119.

49. *OBI*, Ms. 2048/122, 123.

50. Louis-Philippe, *Mémoires*, 2:293.

51. Ibid., 2:294–300.

52. *Ancien Moniteur*, 4, no. 353, pp. 763–68.

53. Ibid.; and Barère, *Mémoires*, 2:293f.

54. Aulard, *Jacobins*, 4:589.

55. Ibid., 4:590–91.

57. Ibid., 4:592.

57. *Journal de la République française*, no. 84, 25 December 1792, p. 1.

58. Robespierre, *Lettres à ses commetans*, no. 11: "Sur la proposition faite de bannir tous les Capets," *Oeuvres*, 5:487.

59. Ibid., p. 509.

60. *Père Duchesne*, no. 220, p. 2.

61. *Mercure français*, 21 December 1792.

62. *AN*, BB[30] 163/dos. 1–2.

63. Louis-Philippe, *Mémoires*, 1:320.

64. Cf. Monin, "Philippe-Egalité," p. 448.

65. *OBI*, Ms. 2048/119, 16 January 1793. A letter of d'Orléans to his youngest son, the Comte de Beaujolais, dated 1 January 1793, makes no mention of the king's trial. Ibid., Ms. 2051.

66. Cf. the dozens of reports assembled in *AN*, AF[IV] 1470.

67. Ibid.

68. Aulard, *Jacobins*, 4:387, 401.

69. Dumouriez, *Mémoires*, 2:349.

70. Worrying about Chartres's vacillations toward moderation, the Jacobins had, however, dispatched Basire to the front to shore up his politics. See Louis-Philippe, *Mémoires*, 2:315.

71. Ibid., 2:349.

72. Dard, *Acteur caché*, p. 381.

73. Aulard, *Jacobins*, 5:113f.

74. *Ancien Moniteur*, 16, no. 97, p. 60.

75. *OBI*, Ms. 2048/115.

76. *Ancien Moniteur*, 16, no. 97, p. 60.

77. Louvet, *Vérité*, pp. 49, 51.

78. Aulard, *Jacobins*, 5:121.

79. *Le Publiciste de la République française*, no. 168, 14 April 1793.

80. *Ancien Moniteur* 16, no. 103, p. 112.

81. Aulard, *Jacobins*, 5:140–42.

82. *AN*, C 252/438.

83. *AN*, AF★ II2/217.

84. *AN*, C 252/443.

85. Marat complained: "D'Orléans has been sent to Marseilles so that his trial can be kept hidden from the vigilance of the Montagne and the patriots of Paris." *Le Publiciste de la République française*, no. 216, 14, June 1793.

86. Scott, *Terror and Repression*, p. 86.

87. Ibid.

88. *AN*, BB[30] 163/dos. 1–2.

89. Ibid., 11 April 1793.

90. Ibid., dispatches of 11, 14, 16 April 1793.

91. Ibid.

92. Ibid., Minister of Justice, undated.

93. *AN*, F[7] 4389.

94. *AN*, F[7] 4385[1].

95. See 'Véritable intérrogatoire et véritables réponses"; and "Lettre de Louis-Philippe-Joseph Egalité, ci-devant d'Orléans, envoyée hier à Paris."

96. *AN*, F[7] 4389.

97. *Le Publiciste de la République française*, no. 212, 10 June 1793.

98. Ibid., no. 216, 14 June 1793.

99. Louis-Philippe, *Mémoires*, 2:310n–311n.

100. See chap. 2, no. 63, above.

101. Sanson, *Mémoires*, 4:294.

102. Gamache, *Récit*; see chap. 2, n. 17, above.

103. Cf. *AN*, W 285, "dossier Lothringer."

104. Sanson, *Mémoires*, 4:300.

105. *Révolutions de Paris* 17, "Du ci-devant duc d'Orléans," pp. 189–90.

106. *AN*, C 280/166.

107. *AN*, C 281/774.

108. *AN*, C 285/827.

109. *AN*, C 285/832.

110. Minogue, *Liberal Mind*, p. 23.

Chapter 6

1. See Gay de Vernon, *Mémoire*, p. 47.

2. Carré, *Armée française*, p. 10.

3. Gay de Vernon, *Mémoire*, p. 75.

4. Thanks to the Curator of the Municipal Library of Nancy, I have, in photocopy, several accounts of the revenues of the Custine estates: in 1778, for example, there were revenues of approximately 17,958 livres, expenses of 14,478 livres, and withdrawals of 2780 livres; by 1787, the respective sums had grown to 78,149 livres, 43,285 livres, and 34,181 livres.

5. Archives de l'Armée de Terre, Vincennes (*AAT*), GD/1264, 1ère série.

6. Chuquet, *Expédition*, p. 34.

7. Madame de Genlis, *Mémoires*, 1:290; 2:149–52.

8. He wrote: "The only thing I fear is an inactivity that would prevent me from proving to the King my zeal and attachment to his service." *AAT*, GD/1264, 1ère série.

9. Ibid.

10. Verger, "Journal of the Most Important Events that occurred to the French Troops under the Command of M. le Comte de Rochambeau." In Rice and Brown, *American Campaigns*, 1:142.

11. Acomb, *Journal of Von Closen*, pp. 149–50.

12. *AAT*, GD/1264, 1ère série.

13. Rice and Brown, *American Campaigns*, 2:178.

14. Blanchard, *Guerre d'Amérique*, 1:64.

15. Quoted by Babeau, *Vie militaire*, 2:137.

16. Bluche, *Vie quotidienne*, p. 154.

17. Manceron, *Vent d'Amérique*, p. 243.

18. Tuetey, *Officiers*, p. 331.

19. Babeau, *Vie militaire*, 1:16.

20. Servan, *La seconde aux grands*, quoted in Carré, *Armée française*, p. 15.

21. Quoted by Babeau, *Vie militaire*, 2:83.

22. Tuetey, *Officiers*, pp. 161–75, passim.

23. Ibid., p. 129; Babeau, *Vie militaire*, 1:189; 2:88.

24. See Bien, "Réaction aristocratique," Jan.–Feb. 1974, pp. 23–48; Mar.–Apr. 1974, pp. 505–34.

25. Bien, "Army in the French Enlightenment," p. 75.

26. "La législation réduite à sa plus simple expression," anon. pamphlet cited in Découflé, "Aristocratie française," p. 45.

27. Hartmann, *Officiers de l'armée royale*, pp. 2–3; Babeau, *Vie militaire*, 2:138. The statistics are drawn from the Guibert Report of 1787.

28. Hartmann, *Officiers de l'armée royale*, p. 5.

29. Besenval, *Mémoires* (1786), cited in Bien, "Army in the French Enlightenment," p. 71.

30. Hartmann, *Officiers de l'armée royale*, p. 5.

31. Ibid., p. 97.

32. Ibid., p. 6; also Tuetey, *Officiers*, p. 33.

33. Babeau, *Vie militaire*, 2:140.

34. Bien, "Army in the French Enlightenment," p. 78.

35. Babeau, *Vie militaire*, 1:367.

36. Ibid., 1:166. See the magistral investigation and summary of all these forces in Corvisier, *Armée française*, especially the summary, 2:990, stressing humanized treatment, stricter garrison rules, and upper command *désarroi*.

37. Quoted in Babeau, 1:299.

38. Cited in ibid., 1:351. The Duc de Choiseul, War Minister of the time, held that the foreign soldier was equal to three men: the one who had been purchased, the one whom the enemy could no longer purchase, and the French peasant released to till his fields.

39. Ibid., 1:248.

40. See Kelly, "Duelling," passim.

41. Babeau, *Vie militaire*, 2:171.

42. Carré, *Armée française*, p. 10.

43. Chevallier, *Histoire de la Franc-Maçonnerie*, 1:197.

44. Ibid., p. 195.

45. Martin, *Franc-Maçonnerie*, pp. 35–36, 44.

46. Hartmann, *Officiers de l'armée royale*, p. 28f; and Carré, *Armée française*, p. 14. The condensed comment in Corvisier, *Armies and Societies*, pp. 166–70, is crisp and accurate.

47. Hartmann, *Officiers de l'armée royale*, p. 49.

48. Ibid., p. 68.

49. *Cahier* of Les Essarts-le-Vicomte (Bas-Sézanne), in Goubert and Denis, *1789*, pp. 74–75.

50. Madame de Genlis, *Mémoires*, 2:335.

51. Ibid., 2:167.

52. See Le Bihan, *Loges et chapitres*, p. 320.

53. Declaration signed by Miaczynski, *AN*, W 99.

54. *AN*, W 100.

55. Lort de Sérignan, *Duc de Lauzun*, p. 296.

56. Madame de Genlis, *Mémoires*, 2:153–54, 233.

57. *AAT*, GD/1264, 1ère série.

58. Gay de Vernon, *Mémoire*, p. 105.

59. (Anon.), *Vies et mémoires des Grands Capitaines*, Vol. 2, *Custine et Dumouriez*, p. 27. The memoirs are not by Custine, but are a royalist libel.

60. Maugras and Croze-Lemercier, *Delphine de Sabran*, p. 37.

61. Gay de Vernon, *Mémoire*, p. 48.

62. Chuquet, *Expédition*, p. 41.

63. On the French hatred of Prussian disciple, see the *cahier* of the Tiers Etat du Bailliage de Saint-Sauveur-le-Vicomte, in Goubert and Denis, *1789*, p. 213.

64. Gay de Vernon, *Mémoire*, p. 47.

65. Custine, "Apperçu rapide," p. 27. Cf. Marat, *Journal de la République française*, no. 84, 25 December 1792, p. 8: "More than three hundred predictions fulfilled prove that I know how to judge men and affairs."

66. Custine, "Discours prononcé en l'Hôtel de Ville de Nancy."

67. Custine, "Plan à consulter."

68. Ibid., pp. 7–11.

69. Ibid., p. 11.

70. Ibid., pp. 15–16.

71. Ibid., p. 15.

72. Custine, draft pamphlet "Adresse d'un Citoyen ami de la Constitution, à ses concitoyens" (1791), *AN*, W 101.

73. Custine, "Apperçu rapide," p. 12n.

74. Custine, "Plan à consulter," pp. 26–27.

75. Custine, *Déclaration des droits du citoyen français* (printed, copy found in the Bibliothèque Historique de la Ville de Paris).

76. Letter to *Gazette nationale*, 10 February 1791.

77. Custine, "Second compte rendu . . . de ses opinions de l'Assemblée Nationale, le 12 septembre 1789," in *Comptes rendus*, p. 405.

78. Each *compte rendu* was published separately, but the most convenient source is given in the bibliography under Custine, "Comptes rendus," *Archives parlementaires*.

79. Custine, "Premier compte rendu . . . ," p. 398.

80. Ibid.

81. Ibid., p. 401.

82. Custine, "Quatrième compte rendu . . . ," p. 428.

83. Ibid., p. 433.

84. Ibid., p. 424.

85. Custine, "Adresse d'un Citoyen ami de la Constituion," *AN*, W 101.

86. Custine, "Premier compte rendu . . . ," p. 412.

87. Custine, "Troisième compte rendu . . . ," p. 421.

88. Custine, "Cinquième compte rendu . . . ," p. 446.

89. See Chill, *Power, Property, and History*, pp. 6–8.

90. Custine, "Troisième compte rendu . . . ," p. 413.

91. Ibid., p. 419.

92. Custine, "Second compte rendu . . . ," pp. 406–7.

93. Custine, "Troisième compte rendu . . . ," p. 419.

94. Ibid., pp. 414–17.

95. Ibid.

96. Ibid., p. 415.

97. Custine, "Quatrième compte rendu . . . ," p. 425.

98. Ibid., p. 438.

99. Ibid., pp. 422–23.

100. Custine, "Cinquième compte rendu . . . ," p. 452.

101. See Bertaud, ed., *Valmy*, pp. 189ff.

102. A *demi-marc d'argent*, according to M. Reinhard's calculations (*Chute*, p. 179), was roughly equivalent to twenty-seven livres.

103. Custine, "Cinquième compte rendu . . . ," pp. 439–41.

104. Custine, "Quatrième compte rendu . . . ," p. 427.

105. Custine, "Opinion sur la loi sur les Emigrans," pp. 3–4.

106. Ibid., p. 2.

107. See Maugras and Croze-Lemercier, *Delphine de Sabran*, p. 80.

108. Custine, "Second compte rendu . . . ," p. 412.

109. *Révolutions de Paris*, 4–11 June 1791.

110. *AAT*, GD/1264, 1ère série.

111. Baudot, *Notes historiques*, p. 9.

112. Custine, "Adresse d'un Citoyen ami de la Constitution," *AN*, W 101.

113. Hartmann, *Officiers de l'armée royale*, p. 244.

114. Ibid., p. 276; also Reinhard, *Chute*, pp. 158–160; Carré, *Armée française*, pp. 22–23; and "Rapport des commissaires de l'Assemblée Nationales envoyés dans les départements du Rhin et des Vosges, fait par Custine, Chasset, Regnier de Nancy."

115. Hartmann, *Officiers de l'armée royale*, p. 288.

116. See Bertaud, *Valmy*, p. 189f.

117. Custine, "Apperçu rapide," p. 12n.

118. Hartmann, *Officiers de l'armée royale*, pp. 341–43.

119. Custine, "Apperçu rapide," p. 31n.

120. *AN*, W 101.

121. Custine, "Apperçu rapide," p. 22.

122. Ibid., pp. 34–35.

Chapter 7

1. The chief pacifists were Barnave, a constitutionalist, and Robespierre, a radical. All the contestants had their special reasons for preferring peace—or usually war. See Reinhard, *Chute*, p. 245.

2. Quoted by Fugier, *Histoire des relations internationales*, 4:19.

3. Quoted by Reinhard, *Chute*, p. 247.

4. Hartmann, *Officiers de l'armée royale*, p. 528.

5. Quoted by Chuquet, *Expédition*, p. 9.

6. Carré, *Armée française*, p. 24.

7. See Bertaud, *Valmy*, pp. 143–44.

8. There was much ill feeling between the two sorts of units, subject as they were to different regulations, pay scales, and emotional commitments.

9. Bertaud, *Valmy*, p. 155.

10. *Le Patriote français*, 5 January 1792.

11. See Sorel, "Mission de Custine à Brunswick," 1:163.

12. *AN*, F⁷ 4402.

13. Ibid. Letter of 22 January 1792 to Delessart.

14. Commissioned by Narbonne, *AN*, W 99.

15. For Custine's explanation, see Buchez and Roux, *Histoire parlementaire*, 29:269; also Gay de Vernon, *Mémoire*, p. 11.

16. Luckner to Custine, 28 April 1792, in *AN*, W 99.

17. Ibid.

18. Luckner to Custine, 23 May 1792, in ibid.

19. Circular order signed de Broglie, 20 May 1792, ibid.

20. Luckner to Custine, 23 July 1792, in ibid.

21. Quoted by Chuquet, *Expédition*, p. 44. This is true: the Lauzun Legion had been under the orders of Custine's Saintonge Regiment in Virginia. See Rice and Brown, *American Campaigns*, 1:134.

22. Chuquet, *Expédition*, p. 47.

23. Ibid.

24. Ibid., p. 27.

25. Ibid., p. 68.

26. *AAT*, GD/1264, 1ᵉʳᵉ série.

27. Gay de Vernon, *Mémoire*, p. 48.

28. Chuquet, *Expédition*, p. 47.

29. Ibid., p. 57; Gay de Vernon, *Mémoire*, p. 49.

30. Chuquet, *Expédition*, p. 69.

31. [Baraguey d'Hilliers], *Mémoires du général Custine*, 2:46–47.

32. Gay de Vernon, *Mémoires*, pp. 56–57.

33. Chuquet, *Expédition*, p. 37.

34. Ibid., p. 143.

35. Ibid., pp. 101, 109.

36. Ibid., p. 147. Chuquet claims that Dumouriez also supported Custine in this instance. This seems false. Cf. Louis-Philippe, *Mémoires*, 2:323–24.

37. Chuquet, *Expédition*, p. 148.

38. *AN*, W 99.

39. The letter of 31 October 1792 is quoted in *Mémoires du général Custine*, 2:28–30.

40. Ibid., 2:32.

41. *Vies et mémoires des Grands Capitaines*, 2:139.

42. Chuquet, *Expédition*, p. 37.

43. Custine to Pache, 14 November 1792, *AAT*, B² 29.

44. Quoted by Chuquet, *Expédition*, p. 154.

45. Custine to Minister of War, 26 April 1793, *AAT*, B² 29.

46. *Mémoires du général Custine*, 1:175.

47. Ibid., 1:167.

48. See especially the libel "Custine Tout Entier," a diatribe of sixteen pages, accusing Custine of treason, ineptitude, debauchery, and theft—probably inspired by Vincent.

49. Gay de Vernon, *Mémoire*, p. 75.

50. See *Journal de la Montagne*, letter to the President of the National Convention, no. 33, 30 June 1793.

51. *Mémoires du général Custine*, 2:170–99.

52. Chuquet, *Expédition*, p. 154.

53. Ibid., 158f.

54. Ibid., p. 169.

55. Custine to President, National Convention, 28 April 1793, *AN*, W 99.

56. Gay de Vernon, *Mémoire*, pp. 103–4.

57. Custine to Clavière, *AN*, W 99.

58. Gay de Vernon, *Mémoire*, p. 108.

59. Madame Roland, *Mémoires*, 1:3.

60. Custine to Pache, 22 January 1793, *AN*, W 99.

61. Cf. Dumouriez, *Mémoires*, 2:126–27; but also Louis-Philippe's rendition of his conversations with Dumouriez: *Mémoires*, 2:324–28, 375–76.

62. *AN*, W 99.

63. Dumouriez to Minister of War, 10 February 1793, *AAT*, B¹★ 107.

64. Custine to Minister of War, 7 February 1793, in ibid.

65. *Mémoires du général Custine*, 2:230.

66. War Minister to Dumouriez, 14 February 1793, *AAT*, B¹★ 107.

67. Beurnonville to Commissioners of the Convention, 16 February 1793, *AAT*, B² 29.

68. War Minister to Dumouriez, 19 February 1793, *AAT*, B¹★ 107.

69. Beurnonville to Custine, 19 February 1793, *AN*, W 99.

70. Ibid.

71. F. de Custine to Custine, 20 February 1793, *AN*, W 101.

72. F. de Custine to Custine, 23 February 1793, in ibid.

73. *Mémoires du général Custine*, 2:235–40.

74. Custine to President, National Convention, 1 April 1793, *AN*, W 99.

75. Louis-Philippe, *Mémoires*, 2:323.

76. Ibid., 2:275.

77. See this document, *AN*, W 101.

78. Contained in a packet of draft speeches, evidently intended for the Convention, in ibid.

79. Herlaut, "Négociations," pp. 517–18.

80. Lebrun to Custine, 5 April 1793, *AN*, W 99.

81. Notably, Herlaut, "Négociations," and *Querelle*; and Mathiez, "Etudes sur la Terreur," pp. 305–29.

82. Robespierre, *Oeuvres*, 8:47f.

83. Beauharnais to Custine, 25 June 1793, *AN*, W 101.

84. Cited by Kerr, *Reign of Terror*, p. 54. On 12 December 1792, at the Jacobins, Robespierre defended both Dumouriez and Custine: see Aulard, *Jacobins*, 4:574.

85. Marat, *Le Publiciste de la République française*, no. 161, 5 April 1793.

86. Police report, 8 April 1793, *AN*, AF^{IV} 1470/16. See the other documents in this liasse; also AF^{II} 451, no. 351/6; F^{1c} III, Seine, 27; and C 355/1868.

87. *Mémoires du général Custine*, 2:244–45.

88. Reproduced in Furet and Richet, *Révolution française*, p. 273.

89. Foreign Minister to Custine, 5 and 6 April 1793, *AN*, W 99. For the Convention's refusal of Custine's resignation, see *AAT*, GD/1264, 1ère série/694.

90. Custine to President, National Convention, 9 April 1793, *AN*, W 99. The Representative of the Armies of the Rhine and the Moselle exonerated Custine, 6 April 1793, in ibid.

91. Ibid.

92. Custine to Committee of Public Safety, 9 April 1793, in ibid.

93. Marat, *Le Publiciste de la République française*, no. 162, 6 April 1793.

94. Custine to President, National Convention, 12 April 1793, *AN*, W 99.

95. Quoted from *Dictionnaire de Biographie Française* (Paris, 1961), vol. 6.

96. Quoted in Bertaud, *Valmy*, p. 205.

97. See Campardon, *Tribunal révolutionnaire*, 1:6–7.

98. See Buchez and Roux, eds., *Histoire parlementaire*, 29:324–26.

99. Custine to President, National Convention, 22 April 1793, *AN*, W 102.

100. Committee of Public Safety to Custine, 29 April 1793, *AN*, W 99.

101. Not totally a precedent: Philippe-Egalité and Sillery had not been tried, but had lost their mandates in early April in the wake of the Dumouriez defection.

Chapter 8

1. A police report of 8 May notes that "Dampierre and Custine arouse violent suspicions." *AN*, AF^{IV} 1470/6.

2. Gay de Vernon, *Mémoire*, p. 171.

3. Representatives of the Army of the North to Committee of Public Safety, 11 May 1793, *AN*, W 99.

4. *Arrêté* of the National Convention, 13 May 1793, *AAT*, GD/1264, 1ère série/851.

5. Representatives of the Army of the Ardennes to National Convention, 10 May 1793, *AN*, W 99.

6. Representatives of the Army of the Rhine to Committee of Public Safety, 15 May 1793, in ibid.

7. Foucart and Finot, *Défense nationale*, 1:579–80.

8. The same day a functionary with the Army of the Rhine wrote: "Custine is

neither a general nor a patriot; rather he is a professional imbecile and a traitor." Gâteau to Bouchotte, 23 May 1793, *AN*, W 99.

9. *AN*, AF^{II} 244/2091.

10. Buchez and Roux, *Histoire parlementaire*, 29:266.

11. Custine to Brunswick, 5 May 1793, *AN*, W 99.

12. Custine to President, National Convention, in ibid.

13. See Buchez and Roux, *Histoire parlementaire*, 29:267, for testimony of Maribon-Montaut.

14. Custine to Houchard, 30 May 1793, *AN*, W 101.

15. Foucart and Finot, *Défense nationale*, 1:580.

16. Order of 29 May 1793, *AAT*, B^{1}★ 104.

17. Custine to Committee of Public Safety, 4 June 1793, *AN*, W 99.

18. Foucart and Finot, *Défense nationale*, 1:597, 600.

19. See ibid., p. 586; and Order of the Day of the Armies of the North and the Ardennes, 5–6 June 1793, *AN*, W 102.

20. Custine to Committee of Public Safety, 5 June 1793, *AAT*, B^{1} 13.

21. Custine to O'Moran, 5 June 1793, *AN*, W 102.

22. Custine to Tourville, 6 June 1793, in ibid.

23. Custine to Committee of Public Safety, 6 June 1793, in ibid.

24. Custine to Minister of War, 6 June 1793, in ibid.

25. Custine to Minister of War, 6 June 1793, *AAT*, B^{1} 13.

26. Custine to Committee of Public Safety, 13 June 1793, *AN*, W 102.

27. Ibid., 8 June 1793, in ibid.; and to Bouchotte, 9 June 1793, *AAT*, B^{1} 13.

28. "Mesures générales prises par le citoyen Bouchotte, Ministre de la Guerre, depuis son entrée au Ministère: du 15 avril au 30 juin 1793," in ibid.

29. Representatives of the Army of the North to Committee of Public Safety, 28 May 1793, *AN*, W 102.

30. Gay de Vernon, *Mémoire*, p. 177.

31. Representatives of the Army of the North to Committee of Public Safety, 9 June 1793, *AN*, W 99. Still, a week later, Custine was scarcely happy with the organization of the army; cf. Custine to Representatives of the Army of the North, *AN*, D § 364/617.

32. Chérin to Committee of Public Safety, 12 August 1793, *AN*, W 102.

33. Custine to Committee of Public Safety, 11 June 1793, *AN*, W 99.

34. Buchez and Roux, *Histoire parlementaire*, 29:259.

35. On 10 July 1793, Custine's chief subordinate General Leveneur reported to the Committee of Public Safety that the army had sworn an oath to the Constitution "with enthusiasm." *AAT*, B^{1} 14.

36. Saint-Just, "Essai de Constitution, 23 juin 1793," in *Oeuvres choisies*, p. 123.

37. See Gay de Vernon, *Mémoire*, p. 147.

38. *Père Duchesne*, no. 275, pp. 7–8.

39. "Custine," in Maurin, *Galerie historique*, 2:90.

40. Buchez and Roux, *Histoire parlementaire*, 29:314.

41. Custine to Minister of War, 20 May 1793, *AN*, W 102.

42. Celliez and Varin to Bouchotte, 5 June 1793, *AAT*, B^{1} 13.

43. Marat, *Le Publiciste de la République française*, no. 213, 11 June 1793.

44. Jacobins, meeting of 21 July 1793, cited in *Journal de la Montagne*, no. 53, 24 July 1793.

45. Herlaut, *Querelle*, p. 23.

46. A list of these names can be found in Biré, *Défenseurs*, p. 8n.

47. Report, 12 June 1793, *AAT*, B² 29.

48. Ibid., passim.

49. Ibid.

50. Ibid. I have corrected or conformed the spelling of names in some cases.

51. Celliez and Varin to Bouchotte, 24 and 25 July 1793, *AAT*, B¹ 14.

52. *Le Publiciste de la République française*, no. 206, 31 May 1793; no. 213, 11 June.

53. *Père Duchesne*, no. 251, p. 5.

54. *Journal de la Montagne*, no. 25, 26 June 1793.

55. Ibid., no. 37, 8 July 1793.

56. Celliez and Varin to Bouchotte, 17 and 20 June 1793, *AAT*, B¹ 13.

57. Minister of Foreign Affairs to Minister of War, 1 July 1793, *AAT*, B¹ 14.

58. Celliez to Varin, 2 July 1793, *AN*, W 99.

59. Celliez to Bouchotte, 4 July 1793, *AAT*, B¹ 14.

60. Herlaut, *Querelle*, p. 27.

61. *Le Publiciste de la République française*, no. 235, 6 July 1793; *Père Duchesne*, no. 257, p. 5.

62. *Père Duchesne*, no. 262, p. 6.

63. [Roux], *Le Publiciste de la République française, par l'ombre de Marat*, no. 248, 27 July 1793.

64. See Herlaut, *Querelle*, p. 9; also Foucart and Finot, *Défense nationale*, 1:611.

65. Custine to Minister of War, 6 June 1793, *AAT*, B¹ 13.

66. Ibid. and *AAT*, B² 29.

67. Minister of War to Committee of Public Safety, 14 June 1793, *AAT*, B² 29.

68. Bouchotte to Custine, in ibid.

69. *AAT*, B¹ 13.

70. See his correspondence of 17 July 1793, *AAT*, B¹ 14.

71. *AAT*, B¹ 13. Custine was then inspecting Lille and consulting with La Marlière. See also Herlaut, *Querelle*, p. 16.

72. Favart to Custine, 25 June 1793, *AN*, W 99. Also, Buchez and Roux, *Histoire parlementaire*, 29:325–26.

73. Lavalette to Vincent, dates cited, *AAT*, B¹ 13, B¹ 14.

74. La Marlière, 27 June 1793, *AN*, W 100. This archive has a large bundle of La Marlière papers.

75. At least in the trial documentation of the "Parquet" sources, chiefly W 100.

76. Undated, *AAT*, B² 29.

77. Custine to Committee of Public Safety, 3 July 1793, *AN*, W 99.

78. See their complaint of 13 July 1793 to the parent society, *AAT*, B¹ 14.

79. Lavalette to Bouchotte, 17 July 1793, *AAT*, B² 29.

80. Bouchotte to La Marlière, 20 July 1793, in ibid.

81. *AAT*, B¹ 14.

82. Proclamation of the Representatives of the People to the Army of the North, 23 July 1793, in ibid.

83. Aulard, *Jacobins*, 5:311; also, *Journal de la Montagne*, no. 56, 27 July 1793.

84. Custine to Bouchotte, 2 June 1793, *AAT*, B¹ 13.

85. Custine to Committee of Public Safety, 13 June 1793, *AN*, W 99.

86. See Beauharnais to Custine, 14 June 1793, *AN*, W 101. It is true that Custine had described Beauharnais as an "esprit sage, actif et intelligent" in requesting him in replacement of Desprez-Crassier on 30 April 1793. To Committee of Public Safety, *AN*, W 99.

87. Beauharnais to Committee of Public Safety, 16 June 1793, *AN*, W 101.

88. Ruamps to Montaut, 16 June 1793, *AN*, W 102.

89. See Custine to Committee of Public Safety, 2 June 1793, in ibid.; and Custine to same, 30 June 1793, *AN*, W 101.

90. Custine to Committee of Public Safety, 1 July and 7 July 1793, *AN*, W 102.

91. See *AAT*, B¹ 13.

92. See Custine on the subject, 27 May 1793, to President, National Convention, *AN*, W 99.

93. Wimpffen to Custine, 6 July 1793, *AN*, W 99.

94. Custine to Wimpffen, 15 July 1793, in ibid.

95. Custine to Citizens of the General Assembly [*sic*] . . . in Caen, 19 July 1793, in ibid.

96. Custine to Citizens of the Popular Society of Bordeaux, 14 July 1793, in ibid.

97. Custine to President, National Convention, 19 July 1793, in ibid.

98. See Herlaut, *Querelle*, p. 19.

99. Order of the Committee of Public Safety, 5 July 1793, *AN*, W 101.

100. Custine to Representatives of the People of the Committee of Public Safety, 16 July 1793, in ibid.

101. See note 97, above.

102. *Le Publiciste de la République française*, no. 230, 1 July 1793.

103. "Une pièce suivie des observations."

104. *Père Duchesne*, no. 259, p. 4.

105. Bouchotte to Custine, 12 July 1793, *AAT*, GD/1264, 1ère série.

106. Custine to Bouchotte, 16 July 1793, *AAT*, B¹ 14.

107. F. de Custine to Custine, 13 July 1793, *AN*, W 306/380.

108. Gay de Vernon, *Mémoire*, pp. 208–9.

109. Ibid., p. 209.

110. Herlaut, *Querelle*, pp. 35–36. At his trial, Custine was attacked by Charles, *ci-devant* Prince of Hesse converted to a republican commissioner of war, for his negligence of the Jacobin Club during his July return. The accused replied cautiously: "I think that the Jacobin Club has rendered great services to the common good (*chose publique*) . . . but I also know that foreign courts have supported emissaries in its midst, concealed by the false façade of patriotism." Buchez and Roux, *Histoire parlementaire*, 29:286.

111. Custine to Committee of Public Safety, 22 July 1793, *AN*, W 102.

112. Administrators of Arras to Committee of General Security, 25 July 1793, *AN*, W 99.

113. Celliez to Hébert, 19 July 1793; and to Bouchotte, 22 July 1793, *AAT*, B¹ 14.

114. Celliez and Varin to Bouchotte, 24 July 1793, in ibid.

115. See "Déclaration du Citoyen Vincent," p. 47.

116. See Gay de Vernon, *Mémoire*, p. 212.

117. For example, Militant Frenchmen of the Army of the North and the Ardennes to . . . the Committees of Public Safety and General Security, 18 July 1793; First Mayenne Batallion, 22 July 1793; First Ille-et-Vilaine Battalion, 26 July, 1793. *AN*, W 102.

118. Custine to President, Committee of Public Safety, 26 and 31 July 1793, *AN*, W 99.

119. Cited from Custine trial dossier, *AN*, W 280.

120. Ibid.

121. See ibid.; also Buchez and Roux, *Histoire parlementaire*, 29:254–61.

122. See "Procès-Verbal de Séance du Tribunal: Déclaration des Témoins," Vincent's abbreviated statement; and Buchez and Roux, *Histoire parlementaire*, 29:324–25.

123. Aulard, *Jacobins*, 5:369.

124. Ibid.

125. *Journal de la Montagne*, no. 79, 20 August 1793.

126. See ibid., no. 87, 28 August 1793.

127. On 26 July 1793, Desbrulys anxiously tried to convince the Committee of Public Safety that Custine had issued no objectionable passwords. *AAT*, B¹★ 104. The Condorcet reference is specifically to the "Girondin" constitution draft prepared by that unfortunate legislator.

128. Buchez and Roux, *Histoire parlementaire*, 29:289–90.

129. Ibid., p. 255.

130. Ibid., p. 335.

131. *Journal de la Montagne*, no. 68, 8 August 1793.

132. Buchez and Roux, *Histoire parlementaire*, 29:335.

133. Ibid., p. 337.

134. Aulard, *Jacobins*, 5:386.

135. Buchez and Roux, *Histoire parlementaire*, 29:337.

136. Ibid.

137. *AN*, W 285/127.

138. Sanson, *Mémoires*, 4:161.

139. Ibid., 4:162.

140. Cf. Royer, at the Jacobins, 30 August 1793. Aulard, *Jacobins*, 5:383–84.

141. See Hébert's remarks at the Jacobins, 13 November 1793 (23 Brumaire, an II), in ibid., 5:511f.

142. Robespierre, at the Jacobins, 9 December 1793 (19 Frimaire, an II), in ibid., 5:549–50.

Chapter 9

1. The merit of the Tocqueville-Cochin-Furet view of the etiology of the French Revolution (guarded from the excesses of a Burke, a Barruel, or a Taine in his extreme pages) is that it is a serious analysis of the movement of the ideas and values *within* parts of society that have been traditionally pitted *against* one another in simplistic socioeconomic interpretations.

2. Bénichou, *Sacre de l'écrivain*.

3. Cf. Delisle de Sales, *Vie littéraire et politique*, p. 13; Nourrisson, *Trois révolutionnaires*, p. 335.

4. For example, "L'amour entra,/ Il y plaça/ Ses traits et sa flamme légère./ De ces yeux-là/ L'amour blessa/ Tous ceux que sa flamme attire." Cited in Nourrisson, *Trois révolutionnaires*, p. 336.

5. See Favre, *Mort dans la littérature*, 1:75–76.

6. "Eloge de M. de La Caille," in Bailly, *Eloges*, p. 128.

7. Arago, *Biographie*, p. 5.

8. Ibid., p. 164.

9. Nourrisson, *Trois révolutionnaires*, p. 333.

10. Hahn, "Quelques nouveaux documents," pp. 339–40.

11. Arago, *Biographie*, p. 11.

12. See Delisle de Sales, *Vie littéraire et politique*, p. 21.

13. See, in general, Kelly, "History of the New Hero," pp. 3–24.

14. Marius Septet, "Le serment du Jeu de Paume et la déclaration du 23 juin," *Revue des questions historiques* 49 (April 1891): 512; quoted by Brucker, *Bailly*, p. 2.

15. Bailly, "Eloge de Charles V," *Eloges*, p. 11.

16. Bailly, *Mémoires*, 2:232.

17. Bailly, "Eloge de Corneille," *Eloges*, p. 39.

18. Ibid., p. 50.

19. Bailly, *Astronomie moderne*, 1:141–42.

20. Bailly, "Elogé de Corneille," *Eloges*, p. 40.

21. Empiricism was somewhat double-edged on the subject of history: it endorsed the genetic method of understanding, but distrusted reported, as opposed to experienced, events—especially when the reports seemed to contravene common sense, right reason, or the laws of nature.

22. Cassirer, *Philosophy of the Enlightenment*, p. 199.

23. See Meinecke, *Historism*, pp. 24–29; and Reill, *German Enlightenment*, pp. 6–7, 31–32, 38–39. Reill plays down Leibniz's role which Meinecke had brought forward.

24. Bailly, "Eloge de Leibniz," *Eloges*, p. 130.

25. Ibid., p. 134.

26. Rousseau, "Discourse on Inequality," *Political Writings*, 1:141.

27. Bailly, "Eloge de Leibniz," in *Eloges*, p. 140.

28. Ehrard, *L'idée de nature*, p. 389.

29. Arago, *Biographie*, p. 23.

30. Mérard de Saint-Just, *Eloge historique*, pp. 186–87.

31. Condorcet, *Eloges des académiciens*, 4:414.

32. Delisle de Sales, *Vie littéraire et politique*, p. 38.

33. Lafayette, *Mémoires*, 2:302.

34. Delisle de Sales, *Vie littéraire et politique*, p. 38.

35. Ibid., p. 25; Grosclaude, *Malesherbes*, p. 17; and De l'Isle de Sales [*sic*], *Malesherbes*, pp. 76–78.

36. Delisle de Sales, *Vie littéraire et politique*, p. 37.

37. Hahn, "Quelques nouveaux documents," p. 345.

38. Delisle de Sales, *Vie littéraire et politique*, p. 24.

39. Ibid., p. 25.

40. Lafayette, *Mémoires*, 2:300.

41. Bailly, *Lettres sur l'Atlantide*, 11th letter, p. 21.

42. Daniel Roche, "Encyclopédistes et académiciens," in Furet et al., *Livre et société*, 2, esp. pp. 81–86. To this distinction made by Roche it is necessary to add a third category—at least by 1770: the lumpen-intelligentsia or "Grub Street" writers. See esp. Robert Darnton, "The High Enlightenment and the Low-Life of Literature in Pre-Revolutionary France," in Johnson, *French Society*, pp. 53–87.

43. Article "Académie," *Encyclopédie*, 1:52a.

44. Hahn, *Anatomy*, p. 1.

45. See Hautecoeur, *Pourquoi les académies*, p. 3.

46. Hahn, *Anatomy*, p. 3.

47. Ibid., p. 9.

48. Fontenelle, *Histoire de l'Académie*, 1:xxviii.

49. Lavoisier, "Fragments de l'Eloge de Colbert," *Oeuvres*, 6:124.

50. Condorcet, speech of 6 June 1782 to the Académie des Sciences, in *Oeuvres*, 1:416–25, passim.

51. Baker, "Science, elitism, and liberalism," pp. 129–65.

52. Hahn, *Anatomy*, p. 70.

53. Ibid., p. 170.

54. Baker, "Science, elitism, and liberalism," pp. 136–37, 149–50, 164.

55. Groethuysen, *Philosophie*, p. 42.

56. Bailly, *Mémoires*, 1:45.

57. Ibid., 2:73.

58. Bailly, *Astronomie moderne*, 1:v. Bailly was of course not alone in his presumption of unequal mental endowments. Turgot had declared that "nature, distributing her gifts unequally, has given to certain minds an abundance of talents which she has refused to others." "A Philosophical Review of the Successive Advances of the Human Mind," in *Turgot on Progress*, p. 43.

59. Ibid., 1:v–vi.

60. Ibid., 1:viii.

61. Ibid., 1:ix.

62. See d'Alembert, *Preliminary Discourse*, p. 26.

63. Bailly, *Astronomie moderne*, 1:xi.

64. Ibid., 1:xii–xiii.

65. Ibid., 1:xvi.

66. Ibid., 1:62.

67. See Hahn, *Anatomy*, p. 151f.

68. Bailly, *Mémoires*, 1:64–65.

69. Ibid., 1:66.

70. See Bailly, *Astronomie moderne*, 1:155–56, 256.

71. Ibid., 3:316.

72. Bailly, *Lettres sur l'origine des sciences*, Voltaire to Bailly, 9 February 1776, p. 14.

73. Ibid. Voltaire to Bailly, 19 January 1776, p. 6.

74. Ibid. Voltaire to Bailly, 9 February 1776, pp. 12–13.

75. Ibid. Bailly to Voltaire, 10 August 1776, p. 15.

76. Ibid., p. 17.

77. Ibid., pp. 185f, 205.

78. Fontenelle, *De l'origine des fables*, pp. 16–17.

79. Delisle de Sales, *Vie littéraire et politique*, p. 30, citing Bailly, *Essai sur les fables et leur histoire*.

80. Smith, *Jean-Sylvain Bailly*, p. 427.

81. Ibid., pp. 427, 466.

82. Le Bihan, *Francs-Maçons parisiens*, gives no record of him.

83. Nourrisson, *Trois révolutionnaires*, p. 343.

84. Voltaire, *Correspondance générale* 94 (April 1776):47.

85. Buffon, "Epoques de la Nature," in Piveteau, *Buffon: corpus général*, pp. 188–89.

86. See Darnton, *Mesmerism*.

87. Ibid., pp. 38, 117. See also Bailly, *Lettres sur l'Atlantide*, p. 14.

88. *Rapport des commissaires chargés par le Roi de l'examen du magnétisme animal*, pp. 3–5.

89. Ibid., p. 17.

90. Ibid., p. 18.

91. Ibid., p. 25.

92. Ibid., p. 42.

93. Ibid., p. 62.

94. See Tenon, *Mémoires sur les hôpitaux*. On the hospital report, see Monin, *L'état de Paris en 1789*, pp. 247–51.

95. Bloch, *L'assistance*, p. 336.

96. See Arago, *Biographie*, pp. 77–78.

97. Bailly, *Mémoires*, 1:4.

98. Ibid., 1:7.

Chapter 10

1. Delisle de Sales, *Vie littéraire et politique*, p. 42.

2. Bailly, *Mémoires*, 1:3.

3. Fernand-Laurent, *Bailly, premier maire*, p. 114.

4. Bailly, *Mémoires*, 1:17.

5. Ibid., 1:8–9.

6. "Avis au Tiers Etat de la Ville de Paris" and "Liste des Amis du Peuple," excerpted in Chassin, *Elections et cahiers*, 2:310–13.

7. Bailly, *Mémoires*, 1:10.

8. However, it is equally plausible to think that the delay was caused by the great changes in the political physiognomy of the capital since its last election of estates in 1614.

9. For details, see Chassin, *Elections et cahiers*, 2:319–31.

10. Bailly, *Mémoires*, 1:11.

11. Ibid., 1:12. This is obviously not the Marxian dichotomy of "bourgeois" and "citizens."

12. Ibid., 1:14.

13. Chassin, *Elections et cahiers*, 2:306.

14. Bailly, *Mémoires*, 1:15.

15. Delisle de Sales, *Vie littéraire et politique*, p. 55.

16. Bailly, *Mémoires*, 1:23–25.

17. Ibid., 1:26–27.

18. Ibid., 1:75–77.

19. Ibid., 1:77.

20. Ibid., 1:42.

21. Ibid., 1:46–47.

22. Ibid., 1:44, 46.

23. Ibid., 1:59.

24. Ibid., 1:58; and Fernand-Laurent, *Bailly*, pp. 170–71.

25. Ibid., 1:70.

26. See Chassin, *Elections et cahiers*, 2:325.

27. Bailly, *Mémoires*, 1:64–66.

28. P. Quenard, "Tableau historique de la Révolution," cited in Chassin, *Elections et cahiers*, 2:313.

29. Ibid., 2:314.

30. Bailly, *Mémoires*, 1:113.

31. Ibid., 1:132.

32. Text by Target, on motion of Mounier.

33. Bailly, *Mémoires*, 1:242.

34. Ibid., 1:272.

35. Ibid., 2:90.

36. Ibid., 1:90.

37. Ibid., 1:219.

38. Ibid., 1:242.

39. Lafayette, *Mémoires*, 2:300–301.

40. Barère, *Mémoires*, 1:245–46.

41. Bailly, *Mémoires*, 2:73.

42. Ibid., 2:74.

43. Ibid., 2:227.

44. Ibid., 2:166.

45. *AN*, C★ I¹, "Procès-verbal—séances et délibérations de l'Assemblée générale des électeurs de Paris: 26 avril–30 juillet 1789," pp. 296–97.

46. Bailly, *Mémoires*, 2:193.

47. Ibid., 2:196.

48. Ibid., 2:203.

49. *AN*, C 134, "Extrait des déclarations de l'Assemblée générale de MM. les électeurs de Paris du 19 juillet 1789."

50. Ibid. See the registers of the districts; and for the delegations and compliments from other communities, dossier 11.

51. Bailly, *Mémoires*, 2:231.

52. Bailly, "Discours au roi."

53. Bailly, *Mémoires*, 1:278.

54. Ibid., 2:46.

55. Ibid., 3:17.

56. Ibid., 2:64–65.

57. Ibid., 2:379.

58. Ibid., 1:330–31.

59. Ibid., 2:92.

60. Ibid., 2:201.

61. Ibid., 1:326.

62. Ibid., 2:339.

63. Ibid., 3:101.

64. Ibid., 3:71; also 3:5.

65. Ibid.

66. *Le Patriote français*, 10 May 1792.

67. *Mémoires de Brissot, Bibliographie des mémoires*, 32:418–19.

68. *Révolutions de France et de Brabant* 1, no. 6, December 1789, p. 256.

69. Bailly, *Mémoires*, 2:228.

70. Robiquet, *Personnel municipal*, pp. 33–34.

71. Brucker, *Bailly*, p. 39.

72. Ibid., p. 34.

73. Ibid., p. 21.

74. Ibid., p. 23.

75. Bailly's principal opponent was Danton, who received 1460 votes. Needless to say, most Parisians were still disenfranchised.

76. See Robiquet, *Personnel municipal*, pp. 185–89, 191–95.

77. "Lettre de M. Bailly, Maire de Paris, à MM. des Districts" (30 August 1789), pp. 5, 7–8.

78. Bailly, *Mémoires*, 2:284.

79. Ibid., 2:318.

80. Lafayette, *Mémoires*, 2:301.

81. Bailly, *Mémoires*, 2:328.

82. Lafayette, *Mémoires*, 2:301.

83. Quoted by Robiquet, *Personnel municipal*, p. 465.

84. Bardin, "M. Bailly, Maire de Paris, traité sans égard et comme il le mérite," pp. 5, 8.

85. Aulard, "Bailly et l'affaire," p. 290.

86. Bailly, *Mémoires*, 2:340.

87. Bailly, "Lettre de M. le Maire à la Section de Gravilliers," p. 3.

88. See Brucker, *Bailly*, p. 72.

89. Robiquet, "Correspondance avec Necker," pp. 256–79. Originals in *BN*, fonds français 11,696, 1er régistre. See also Buchez and Roux, *Histoire parlementaire*, 4:172–95.

90. Robiquet, "Correspondance avec Necker," p. 261.

91. Bailly, *Mémoires*, 3:226–27; and see entry of 10 January 1790, *AN*, AF^{II} 48/375.

92. See Bailly-Lafayette correspondence, *BN*, fonds français, 11,697 (esp. 10 January 1790, 2 February 1790, 4 March 1790, 8 June 1790, 4 April 1791).

93. Ibid.

94. Ibid.

95. "Lettre à M. Bailly, maire de Paris, par un de ses disciples," p. 64. The following quote is from "Confession générale du très-haut et très-puissant seigneur," p. 5.

96. *AN*, F^7 3688^1.

97. Ibid.

98. Marat, *Ami du Peuple*, no. 163, 25 May 1790.

99. Martel, in *Orateur du Peuple* 2, no. 63, pp. 501–2.

100. See Bailly to Lajard about Marat, *AN*, AF^{II} 48/376.

101. *Ami du Peuple*, no. 327, 1 January 1791.

102. Ibid., no. 357, 31 January 1791; see also nos. 325, 404, 439.

103. Ibid., no. 479, 26 May 1791. These papers having "as their only design to incite crimes and to overthrow the constitution" were a constant thorn in Bailly's side. See his *Mémoires*, 3:15.

Chapter 11

1. *J.-S. Bailly à ses concitoyens*, pp. 8–9.

2. Ibid., pp. 23–25, 26–27.

3. For background, see Lacroix, *Actes de la Commune*, 5:371–98.

4. See Braesch, "Pétitions," 142:192–93. Robert, a leader of the Cordeliers, had collected his views in *Avantages de la fuite de Louis XVI*. Bonneville skirted the issue somewhat by demanding a "gouvernement national." Cf. *Bouche de Fer*, no. 82, 4 July 1791, p. 6.

5. Furet and Richet, *Révolution française*, p. 184.

6. Cf. the remarks by Rudé, *Crowd*, p. 87, about the emphatic influence of the petit bourgeois leaders on the *menu peuple*.

7. These principles are well summarized in "Adresse à la Nation" (ms. in the handwriting of Chaumette), *Orateur du Peuple* 7, no. 5, pp. 35–37: ". . . I say: it is

not up to a tribunal to judge the king, it is up to the people . . . his is judged by public opinion. The king is a traitor; he is found wanting as the leading public servant." Chaumette also urged the people: "Gather in primary assemblies." *Révolutions de France* 9, no. 105, 9–16 July 1791. Robespierre declared: "The impunity of the crime is the violation and overthrow of the public order. If the criminal is an important public functionary, it is far more dangerous not to punish his assaults. . . . How can it be that one cites the laws to place a man above them so that he can violate them?" *Ancien Moniteur* 9, no. 196, 15 July 1791, p. 125.

8. *Ami du Peuple*, 18 December 1790.

9. Fournier, *Mémoires secrets*, p. 46. Fournier also advised his fellow clubists "to seize [arms and ammunition], to rouse the nation and put it at the height of its military capacities" (p. 47).

10. See Brucker, *Bailly*, p. 112.

11. Mathiez claims, in an assertion that would extenuate the action of the Paris Municipal Council in declaring martial law, that they were motivated by the strictures of the Assembly. Mathiez, *Club des Cordeliers*, p. 138.

12. *Orateur du Peuple* 6, no. 46, p. 373.

13. See Reinhard, *Chute*, pp. 141–46; and Braesch, "Pétitions," 142:17.

14. Morris, *Diary of the French Revolution*, letter to Robert Morris, 16 July 1791, 2:220.

15. Vovelle, *Chute de la monarchie*, p. 166.

16. Petition of 14 July 1791, *AN*, C 75/729. This petition, according to Braesch, was a product of the Cordeliers, drafted by Robert, with the aid of Peyre, Vachard, and Dunouy.

17. Reinhard, *Chute*, p. 146.

18. *Révolutions de Paris* 9, no. 106, 17–23 July 1791, p.61.

19. Blanc, *Histoire de la Révolution*, 5:501.

20. See Fréron, *Orateur du Peuple* 7, no. 7, p. 56: "Aren't the National Guardsmen your brothers, friends, relatives, and fellow citizens?"

21. *Révolutions de Paris* 9, no. 106, pp. 61–62. Braesch, "Pétitions," p. 188, puts forward the claim that the article was written by Robert. His evidence is not convincing, and the point is not of great importance here.

22. See Reinhard, *Chute*, p. 145. And cf. Bailly's testimony to the National Assembly, *Ancien Moniteur* 9, no. 200, 19 July 1791, p. 163.

23. *AN*, C 75/729.

24. Ibid., "Municipalité de Paris. Par le maire et ses officiers municipaux. Extrait du régistre des délibérations du corps municipal. Procès-verbaux des 17 et 18 juillet 1791. . . ." For documentation that seems to betray this fear of foreign agitators, see the papers of the Paris Comité des Recherches in *AN*, D XXIX[b] 33/347; and for the debate of 16 July, see Buchez and Roux, *Histoire parlementaire*, 11:91.

25. Bailly, *Mémoires*, 3:5, 71.

26. Rudé, *Crowd*, p. 89; Reinhard, *Chute*, p. 146.

27. *AN*, C 75/729, "Municipalité de Paris . . . Procès-verbaux des 17 et 18 juillet 1791," pp. 5–6. On examination of Lacroix, *Actes de la Commune*, it is

difficult to assign any special importance to the choice of Le Roulx, Hardy, and Regnault as commissioners.

28. Ibid., p. 4.
29. Treilhard to Bailly, 17 July 1791, *AN*, W 294/235.
30. Aulard, "Bailly et l'affaire," p. 292.
31. *AN*, C 74/726.
32. Ibid.
33. *AN*, W 294/235.
34. *J.-S. Bailly à ses concitoyens*, p. 18.
35. Ibid., p. 34.
36. The essence of this description is drawn from Reinhard, *Chute*, pp. 148–51.
37. *AN*, C 75/729.
38. Ibid. The terse notice in the *Moniteur*, session of 17 July, 9:152, is the following: "M★★★. News is going around that just now two good citizens have fallen victims to their zeal. They were at the Champ de la Fédération, and told the gathered people that they ought to carry out the law. No sooner had they said this than they were hanged. (An indignant feeling burst forth.)"
39. *AN*, W 294/235.
40. Ibid.
41. Testimony of Fauvet, captain of chasseurs, 17 July 1791, in ibid.
42. See Mathiez, *Club des Cordeliers*, p. 143.
43. Fournier was one of the delegation who accompanied the commissioners back to the Place de la Grève. He recounts his own confrontation with Bailly and the words of the latter: "*We are betrayed and compromised; we must resort to martial law*." *Mémoires secrets*, p. 50. Fournier managed to return to the Cordeliers and thence to the Champ de Mars before the shooting began (p. 52).
44. Delisle de Sales, *Vie littéraire et politique*, p. 56. The reference is to Bailly's performance in the fledgling Constituent Assembly.
45. Quoted in Reinhard, *Chute*, p. 150.
46. *Révolutions de Paris* 9, no. 106, p. 64.
47. Ibid., pp. 64–65.
48. Ibid., p. 65.
49. *AN*, C 75/729, "Municipalité de Paris . . . Procès-verbaux des 17 et 18 juillet 1791," pp. 10–11.
50. Ibid., pp. 11–12.
51. *Ancien Moniteur* 9, no. 200, 19 July 1791, p. 164.
52. *Ami du Peuple*, no. 524, 20 July 1791.
53. *Révolutions de Paris* 9, no. 106, p. 73.
54. Fournier, *Mémoires secrets*, p. 52.
55. For Bailly's account—"public order was totally destroyed, the country was in danger"—see *AN*, C 74/726, dated 18 July 1791. The present is cited from *AN*, C 75/729, "Municipalité de Paris . . . Procès-verbaux des 17 et 18 juillet 1791," p. 15.
56. See documents of the public prosecutor of the sixth arondissement, in ibid.
57. *Ami du Peuple*, no. 524, 20 July 1791.

58. *Orateur du Peuple* 7, no. 13, p. 103.

59. Ibid., 7, no. 11, p. 86.

60. Ibid., 7, no. 23, p. 180.

61. *AN*, W 294/235. Regarding the Feuillant repression, see Aulard, "Républicains et les démocrates," esp. 485–92. All this was not without pathos: cf. *Journal du Club des Cordeliers* 9 (Paris, 1791), p. 82, "Variétés," 2 August 1791: "The people of Paris are not yet ripe for liberty. That word, always on our lips but not deeply anchored in our hearts, is a misfortune attached to the human fate of loving oneself too well and not knowing how to sacrifice particular interests to the general interest." Cited by Mathiez, *Club des Cordeliers*, p. 158.

62. See Buchez and Roux, *Histoire parlementaire*, 11:126–27.

63. *Orateur du Peuple* 7, no. 52, p. 409.

64. Arago, *Biographie*, p. 141f. Also, Buchez and Roux, *Histoire parlementaire*, 29:366.

65. *J.-S. Bailly à ses concitoyens*, p. 22.

66. *Révolutions de Paris* 9, no. 106, p. 68.

67. Aulard, *Jacobins*, 3:207.

68. Arago, *Biographie*, p. 123.

Chapter 12

1. *Orateur du Peuple* 7, no. 15, p. 116.

2. In June 1792, a friend, fearing for Bailly's life, offered to help him flee to America, but the astronomer refused. See Mérard de Saint-Just, *Eloge historique de Bailly*, p. 137.

3. See Gillispie, "Jacobin Philosophy of Science," p. 257.

4. Brissot, *De la vérité*, pp. 165–66.

5. See Bailly's letter of 9 December 1792, *AN*, C 243/C II 304. Already, on 25 October 1792, Renaudin, at the Jacobin Club, had demanded Bailly's head.

6. See the question of Citizen St.-Félix, *AN*, W 294/235. This is apparently the same St.-Félix who had threatened to assassinate Lafayette, at the Cordeliers Club on the morning of 17 July 1791. See *AN*, D XXIX[b] 33/347.

7. *AN*, W 294/235, declaration at Melun, 9 July 1793.

8. For documents, see *AN*, F[7] 4854/6.

9. Buchez and Roux, *Histoire parlementaire*, 29:352.

10. *AN*, W 294/235.

11. Buchez and Roux, *Histoire parlementaire*, 29:365.

12. Ibid. "I only received the orders of the Assembly . . . the President of the Department made the major speech": of course La Rochefoucauld could no longer describe his part; he had been stoned to death by a mob at Gisors on 14 August 1792.

13. Ibid., p. 366.

14. *AN*, W 294/235.

15. "Procès de Jean-Sylvain Bailly" (1793), p. 23.

16. Ibid.
17. *Bailly à ses concitoyens*, p. 31.
18. "Jugement rendu qui condamne Jean-Sylvain Bailly," p. 2. See also *AN*, W 294/235.
19. Ibid., p. 3.
20. Ibid., p. 4.
21. Sanson, *Mémoires*, 4:319.
22. Ibid., 4:320.
23. Morellet, *Mémoires*, 2:437.
24. Sanson, *Mémoires*, 4:325.
25. Ibid., 4:329.
26. Mérard de Saint-Just, *Eloge historique de Bailly*, p. 142.
27. Sanson, *Mémoires*, 4:333.
28. *Révolutions de Paris*, no. 215, 23–30 Brumaire, an II, pp. 222–23.
29. Hill, "Commentary on Papers of Gillispie and Williams," p. 315.
30. Thibaudeau, *Mémoires*, 1:71.
31. Gillispie, "Jacobin Philosophy of Science," p. 279.
32. Darnton, "High Enlightenment and Low-Life," pp. 84–85.
33. Gillispie, "Jacobin Philosophy of Science," p. 264.
34. Marat, *Correspondance*, pp. 28, 38.
35. *Ami du Peuple*, no. 194, 17 August 1790.
36. Marat, *Charlatans modernes*, p. 7.
37. Ibid., p. 10.
38. Hahn, *Anatomy*, p. 157.
39. *Ami du Peuple*, no. 163, 25 May 1790.
40. Chamfort, *Oeuvres principales*, p. 128.
41. See Julien Teppe, *Chamfort*, pp. 56–57.
42. Chamfort, *Des académies*. For a rebuttal, see Suard, "De l'Académie française et de M. Chamfort," in *Mélanges de littérature*, 3:67: "une satyre . . . un relevé très-malin de ridicule."
43. Chamfort, *Des académies*, p. 10.
44. Ibid., p. 14.
45. Ibid., p. 28.
46. Ibid., pp. 16–17.
47. Ibid., p. 30.
48. Ibid., pp. 36–37.
49. Ibid., p. 39.
50. (Anon.), "Séance extraordinaire et secrète," pp. 55f.
51. Kors, *D'Holbach's Coterie*, pp. 264, 281.
52. Hahn, *Anatomy*, pp. 224–25.
53. *Ami du Peuple*, 7 July 1792.
54. Cited by Fayet, *Révolution et science*, p. 21.
55. McKie, *Lavoisier*, pp. 78–80.
56. Lavoisier, *Oeuvres*, 6:403–63.
57. Lavoisier, "Sur la convocation des Etats-Généraux," *Oeuvres*, 6:328.

58. Ibid., p. 320.
59. Lavoisier, "Instructions données par la noblesse du Bailliage de Blois à ses députés aux Etats-Généraux (1789)," *Oeuvres*, 6:335.
60. Ibid., 6:336, 339, 343, 357–58.
61. Quoted by Velluz, *Vie de Lavoisier*, p. 146.
62. Quoted in McKie, *Lavoisier*, pp. 352–53.
63. Quoted in Grimaux, *Lavoisier*, p. 201. At exactly the same time, Bailly was complaining to Lafayette, with regard to the "democracy," of "more and more seditious pamphlets published every day." Bailly to Lafayette, 10 January 1790, *BN*, fonds français, 11,697.
64. Grimaux, *Lavoisier*, pp. 201–2.
65. *Ami du Peuple*, no. 353, 27 January 1791.
66. Cited in Grimaux, *Lavoisier*, p. 207.
67. McKie, *Lavoisier*, p. 358.
68. Ibid., p. 363.
69. Pouchet, *Sciences pendant la terreur*, p. 6.
70. *Archives Parlementaires*, 70:522.
71. Ibid., pp. 523–24.
72. Hahn, "Problem," p. 40.
73. McKie, *Lavoisier*, p. 378.
74. Kors, *D'Holbach's Coterie*, p. 287.
75. See Kafker, "Encyclopédistes et la Terreur," pp. 284–95.
76. Morellet, *Mémoires*, 2:449.
77. Mercier, *Nouveau Paris*, 2:36.

Chapter 13

1. His family name was Lamoignon: to distinguish himself from illustrious relatives, our subject appended the name of his property in the Orléanais, acquired by the family in 1719, and he generally passed under that name.
2. He often joked about having been born on the date of the execution of the famous criminal Cartouche, little knowing that he would meet a similar end. See Jean-Baptiste Dubois, *Notice historique*, p. 4n. Dubois was Malesherbes's admiring servant.
3. See Martainville, *Vie de Malesherbes*, p. 55: ". . . he was prodigiously educated: he knew by heart all the classical authors, ancient and modern: Horace, Virgil, Ovid, among the Latin writers: Corneille, Racine, La Fontaine, Molière, and Voltaire among the French. . . ." Also, see the inventory of his extensive library: *BN*, fonds français, 20,844; and *Catalogue des livres de la bibliothèque de feu Chrétien Guillaume Lamoignon-Malesherbes*:7413 items.
4. See Grosclaude, *Malesherbes: témoin et interprète*, pp. 5–6.
5. Malesherbes, *Pensées et maximes*, no. 4, pp. 38–39.
6. See ibid., no. 3, p. 38.
7. Malesherbes, *Mémoires sur la Librairie et sur la presse*, p. 97.

8. Letter to d'Alembert, 1779, quoted in Grosclaude, *Malesherbes*, p. 161.

9. Cf. Malesherbes, *Pensées et maximes*, no. 120, p. 86: "As soon as a prince says: *my will shall be the solitary law of my kingdom*, that prince can count nothing but enemies"; and Grosclaude, *Malesherbes*, quoting him in 1774: "There is no king who hasn't a fondness for despotism." The profound royalism of Malesherbes will receive later demonstration.

10. "Mémoire sur les personnes et les familles auxquelles on donne en France le nom de prince," *Archives Tocqueville*, L. 147, cited in Grosclaude, *Malesherbes*, p. 697.

11. "Réponse au Comte de Sarsfield," 28 November 1766, in Grosclaude, *Nouveaux documents*, pp. 42f.

12. Cf. *Pensées et maximes*, no. 69, p. 63: "The people is all too ready to delude itself; it too often confuses trouble and impatience with love of liberty; but it only wishes a change of masters. . . ."

13. See especially Grosclaude, *Rousseau et Malesherbes*.

14. Cf. Malesherbes, *Pensées et maximes*, no. 65, p. 61: "Feeling is more persuasive than reason: our accomplice is more powerful than our judge."

15. See Boissy d'Anglas, *Essai*, 2:114; cf. Martainville, *Vie de Malesherbes*, p. 193: "He often said that he was angry at not having traveled before becoming a minister, for one must know men in order to govern them."

16. "Lettre à M. de Sarsfield" (1777), *Arch. Rosanbo*, carton 20, dossier 4, cited in Grosclaude, *Malesherbes*, p. 13.

17. Malesherbes to Moultou, 17 March 1791, in Grosclaude, *Rousseau et Malesherbes*, p. 324.

18. Cf. the remark of the Abbé de Véri: "no one is more eloquent or open on the subject of his own feelings." Cited in Grosclaude, *Malesherbes*, p. 324.

19. Malesherbes, *Pensées et maximes*, no. 10, p. 41.

20. See Grosclaude, *Malesherbes*, pp. 390n, 392.

21. The story is told by numerous biographers; see ibid., p. 747. This reference to a Roman image may cause the reader to wonder why my exposition of Jacobinism *per differentiam* has made little or nothing of the theme of "classical republicanism" or "civic humanism" in these events. "Classical republicanism" is indeed involved in the recovery of politics and in the imagery and vocabulary of 1789 and after; it also has a lineage. Keith M. Baker is presently working in this area (for an indication of its thrust, see his "French Political Thought at the Accession of Louis XVI," esp. pp. 298–302). In a direct treatment of Jacobinism it would be negligent to avoid this issue. However, for my present purposes (just as for Furet's *Penser la Révolution française*), "classical republicanism" would introduce disproportions and confusions. Even that *locus classicus* of consensualist thought, Sieyès's *Qu'est-ce que le Tiers Etat?*, relies solely on Germanic imagery.

22. Malesherbes, *Pensées et maximes*, no. 31, p. 48.

23. Molleville, *Mémoires secrets* 3:21; Tocqueville, *Episodes*, p. 10.

24. Grosclaude, *Malesherbes*, pp. 25–26. Another famous ancestor was Malesherbes's great-uncle, Nicolas Lamoignon de Bâville (1648–1724), who, as *intendant* of Languedoc, waged the Camisard Wars against the Protestants. In two

memoirs written to d'Alembert as background for his academic "Eloge de Fléchier," Malesherbes defended the actions of his kinsman as moderate and conforming to orders. See Grosclaude, *Malesherbes*, esp. pp. 426–41. One may speculate, however, that Malesherbes's labors for the Protestants were in part stimulated by a familial sense of redressing injustice.

25. Ibid., pp. 27–28.

26. Martainville, *Vie de Malesherbes*, p. 15.

27. "Réflexions morales," *Arch. Rosanbo*, carton 4, dossier 2, cited in Grosclaude, *Malesherbes*, p. 29. Lamoignon called himself Blancmesnil after one of his properties.

28. Ibid., p. 30.

29. See ibid., pp. 27, 33; and J. Furet, "Malesherbes," p. 6.

30. For Chateaubriand's remarks on Malesherbes, see *Mémoires d'Outre-tombe*, 1:144–45.

31. "Lettre exhortatoire de M. de Lamoignon à M. de Malesherbes son fils," 16 April 1737. *Arch. Rosanbo*, carton 4, dossier 5, cited in Grosclaude, *Malesherbes*, pp. 45ff.

32. Ibid., p. 45.

33. Ibid., pp. 46–47, 51.

34. Ibid., p. 46.

35. Ibid., p. 48.

36. Ibid., p. 49.

37. Ibid., p. 47.

38. Ibid., p. 53.

39. Ibid., pp. 52–53.

40. Malesherbes, *Pensées et maximes*, no. 161, p. 109.

41. Ibid., no. 58, p. 58.

42. Malesherbes was supervised by the Jesuits between the ages of six and sixteen; Voltaire had also attended Louis-le-Grand.

43. Grosclaude, *Malesherbes*, pp. 55–60; and Furet, "Malesherbes," p. 2.

44. Grosclaude, *Malesherbes*, p. 60.

45. Letter to Morellet (draft), February 1758, *BN*, fonds français, 22,191, fos. 148ff.

46. See Egret, *Louis XV*, pp. 117, 120ff

47. See Delisle de Sales, *Malesherbes*, pp. 145–46.

48. Rousseau to Malesherbes, 17 January 1771, in Grosclaude, *Rousseau et Malesherbes*, p. 64.

49. Ibid., pp. 65–66.

50. Malesherbes, *Pensées et maximes*, no. 50, p. 56.

51. Henri-Robert, *Malesherbes*, pp. 134–35.

52. Dubois, *Notice historique*, p. 40.

53. See Grosclaude, *Malesherbes*, pp. 464ff.

54. Young, *Travels in France*, p. 71.

55. Dubois, *Notice historique*, pp. 62–63; Delisle de Sales, *Malesherbes*, pp. 65ff; Martainville, *Vie de Malesherbes*, pp. 33, 110.

56. Act of the Municipalité de Malesherbes, 11 Germinal, an II, *AN*, W 376/851.

57. Delisle de Sales, *Malesherbes*, p. 76.

58. On the Montgolfiers, see Manceron, *Hommes de la liberté*, 3:244–53.

59. *Discours prononcé dans l'Académie françoise*, p. 5.

60. Malesherbes, *Mémoires sur la Librairie et sur la presse*, pp. 54, 91–92, 272.

61. Malesherbes, "Mémoire sur les lois qui ont exclu les protestants des places et de quelques professions" (1787), *Arch. Rosanbo*, carton 17², cited in Grosclaude, *Malesherbes*, p. 601.

62. Malesherbes, *Observations sur Buffon et Daubenton*, 1:8, 216.

63. Ibid., 1:23.

64. Ibid., 2:8–9.

65. See Delisle de Sales, *Malesherbes*, p. 73.

66. See Grosclaude, *Malesherbes*, pp. 499ff.

67. Ibid., pp. 701–2.

68. For these events, see Flammermont, *Chancelier Maupeou*, pp. 1–18; and see *AN*, O¹ 280.

69. Grosclaude, *Malesherbes*, p. 278.

70. "Eclaircissements de Malesherbes," *Arch. Rosanbo*, carton 9, dossier 4, cited in ibid., pp. 278–80.

71. *BN*, nouv. acq., 20,507, cited in ibid., p. 99: "A just man whose moral authority was acknowledged to be as unyielding as the law itself, outstanding in a constancy that the mutability of human life could manage neither to corrupt nor to shatter. . . ."

72. *BN*, fonds français, 22,191, folio 148.

73. Malesherbes, *Pensées et maximes*, no. 61, p. 60.

74. Cf. Martainville, *Vie de Malesherbes*, p. 66.

75. Malesherbes, *Mémoires sur la Librairie et sur la presse*, p. 306.

76. Malesherbes, "Troisième mémoire sur la Librairie," cited in Grosclaude, *Malesherbes*, p. 166.

77. Cour des Aides, remonstrances of 23 June 1761, *AN*, Z¹ A 186.

78. Malesherbes, *Pensées et maximes*, no. 94, p. 73.

79. Malesherbes, To the Abbé Morellet, February 1758, *BN*, fonds français, 22,190, fos. 148ff.

80. See, for example, Jean-Louis and Maria Flandrin, "La circulation du livre," in Furet et al., *Livre et société*, 2:58ff.

81. Shaw, *Problems and Policies*, p. 97.

82. See Furet, "Malesherbes," p. 3.

83. Grosclaude, *Malesherbes*, p. 79.

84. Malesherbes, *Mémoires sur la Librairie et sur la presse*, p. 73.

85. See Grosclaude, *Malesherbes*, pp. 106–13, 120–25.

86. Malesherbes, *Mémoires sur la Librairie et sur la presse*, p. 92.

87. Letter to Cardinal de Bernis (1758), *BN*, fonds français, 22,191, fos. 6ff.

88. Ibid., folio 68.

89. To d'Alembert, 23 January 1758, ibid., fos. 143ff.

90. Malesherbes to Rousseau, 25 December 1761, in Rousseau, *Correspondance générale*, 7:11.

91. See Grosclaude, *Malesherbes*, pp. 158–59; and, in general, Delafarge, *L'affaire de l'abbé Morellet*.

92. To Sartine, *BN*, fonds français, 22,191.

93. *BN*, fonds français, 22,131. The comparison is with the unrestricted press in England.

94. Malesherbes, *Mémoires sur la Librairie et sur la presse*, pp. 76–77.

95. Malesherbes, *Pensées et maximes*, no. 105, p. 78.

96. Grosclaude, *Malesherbes*, p. 104–5.

97. Ibid., p. 109.

98. See Malesherbes to Diderot, 11 July 1754, *BN*, nouv acq., 3345, folio, cited in ibid., p. 114.

99. Pope Clement XIII condemned the *Encyclopédie* on 3 September 1759.

100. See Grosclaude, *Malesherbes*, pp. 134–35.

101. D'Alembert to Voltaire, 28 June 1758, *BN*, nouv. acq., 3395, folio 150, cited in ibid., p. 113.

102. See ibid., pp. 187ff.

103. Voltaire to d'Alembert, 27 February 1761, in Voltaire, *Correspondance générale*, 45:184.

104. Grosclaude, *Malesherbes*, p. 203.

105. See Rousseau, "Quatre lettres à M. le Président Malesherbes," in *Oeuvres complètes*, "third letter," 1:1142.

106. Cited in Henri-Robert, *Malesherbes*, p. 89.

107. Martainville, *Vie de Malesherbes*, p. 66.

108. Abbé de Véri, *Journal*, 1:128.

Chapter 14

1. See Egret, *Louis XV*, pp. 9–17, passim.

2. Ibid., pp. 11, 15.

3. Bluche, *Magistrats du Parlement de Paris*, pp. 91–92, 111–15.

4. Egret, *Louis XV*, p. 13 and n.

5. Ibid., pp. 9–10.

6. Ibid., p. 15n.

7. Ibid., p. 9.

8. "Oriental despotism" as a category in French political polemic goes back at least as far as the Huguenot exile controversialists; cf. the anonymous *Soupirs de la France esclave qui aspire après la liberté* (1689). It was undoubtedly reinforced by Montesquieu's *Lettres persanes* (1721). The best treatment of this subject is Orest Ranum, "Personality and Politics," pp. 606–27. Nicolas-Antoine Boulanger's *Recherches sur l'origine du despotisme oriental* was posthumously published in 1761; it develops the theory that the origins of religion and despotism could be found in

the response of early civilizations to the cataclysms of nature—a question rather far from Malesherbes's orbit of interest.

9. Malesherbes, *Pensées et maximes*, no. 100, p. 76.

10. For background, see Taveneaux, *Jansénisme*, passim.

11. See Egret, *Louis XV*, pp. 19ff; and Taveneaux, *Jansénisme*, pp. 185ff. A thorough treatment of the subject is furnished in Van Kley, *Jansenists and the Expulsion*, esp. pp. 23–29, 229ff, where the author speaks of "a political rhetoric that advanced into territory where Jansenism or parlementary Gallicanism had separately feared to tread."

12. "Lit de justice pour l'enregistrement de deux déclarations sur les affaires ecclésiastiques," 13 December 1756, in Flammermont, *Remontrances*, 2:151.

13. Taveneaux, *Jansénisme*, p. 204, citing Pierre Barral, *Manuel des souverains* (1754), pp. 138–40.

14. Nicolas le Gros, *Du renversement des libertés de l'Eglise gallicane dans l'affaire de la constitution Unigenitus* (1717), 1:344, in Taveneaux, *Jansénisme*, pp. 208, 212.

15. Cardinal de Bernis, *Mémoires*, 2:103–4, cited in Egret, *Louis XV*, p. 89.

16. [Le Paige], *Lettres historiques*, fourth letter, 1:153.

17. "Remontrances sur le traitement subi par les Parlements de Rouen et de Bordeaux," Flammermont, *Remontrances*, 2:138.

18. "Séance royale dite de la flagellation," 3 March 1766, in ibid., 2:566.

19. Albert Soboul, *Précis d'histoire de la Révolution*, p. 70.

20. Egret, *Louis XV*, pp. 16–17.

21. Turgot, *Oeuvres et documents*, 1:435.

22. Dakin, *Turgot and the Ancien Régime*, p. 140.

23. The date 1355 is questioned by Dupont-Ferrier, *Origines et premier siècle*, p. 269. This author sees it as forming slowly between 1370 and 1390.

24. Lefebvre de la Ballande, *Traité général des droits d'aides* (Paris, 1770), p. 259, cited in Egret, "Premier président," p. 97.

25. Egret, "Premier président," p. 99.

26. Recognition and praise in a systematic argument for the kingdom's merchants goes back at least as far as Montchrétien's *Traicté de l'économie politique* of 1615, 2:137–38.

27. Cour des Aides, remonstrances of 7 July 1756, *AN*, Z[1] A 185. As for the phrase "sum of real wealth," see Allison, *Lamoignon de Malesherbes*, who labels Malesherbes a "physiocrat idealist" (p. 74).

28. Malesherbes, *Pensées et maximes*, no. 176, p. 121.

29. Cour des Aides, remonstrances of 21 November 1759, *AN*, Z[1] A 185.

30. "Réponse du Roi du 18 août 1768," *AN*, Z[1] A 188.

31. Cour des Aides, remonstrances of 9 July 1768, ibid.

32. Malesherbes to Madame Douet, 24 June 1772, in Grosclaude, *Nouveaux documents*, p. 209.

33. Cited in Egret, *Louis XV*, p. 102.

34. Malesherbes to Rousseau, 25 December 1761, in Grosclaude, *Nouveaux documents*, p. 35.

35. Cited in Grosclaude, *Malesherbes*, p. 293n.

36. Cour des Aides, remonstrances of 17 November 1759, *AN*, Z^1 A 185.

37. Cour des Aides, remonstrances of 9 February 1770, *AN*, Z^1 A 188.

38. Malesherbes, *Pensées et maximes*, no. 141, p. 97.

39. Cour des Aides, remonstrances of 9 February 1770, *AN*, Z^1 A 188.

40. Malesherbes, *Pensées et maximes*, no. 121, p. 87. The French notion of "checks" is traceable to the "three bridles" of Claude de Seyssel's anti-Machiavellian work of the sixteenth century, where they were listed as *religion*, *justice*, and *police* (in the wide sense). See Keohane, *Philosophy and the State*, pp. 36–38.

41. Cour des Aides, remonstrances of 2 September 1768, *AN*, Z^1 A 188.

42. "Itératives remontrances, arrétés et représentations," 2 February 1766, in Flammermont, *Remontrances*, 2:535.

43. Cour des Aides, remonstrances of 23 July 1763, *AN*, Z^1 A 186. Malesherbes was not first: the Parlement of Rouen had done this on 10 May 1760. See Egret, *Louis XV*, p. 127n.

44. Cour des Aides, remonstrances of 2 September 1768, *AN*, Z^1 A 188.

45. See Egret, "Premier président," p. 117.

46. Cour des Aides, remonstrances of 18 February 1771 (reply to edict of December 1770), *AN*, Z^1 A l88.

47. For details, see Egret, "Premier président," pp. 111–12; also Grosclaude, *Malesherbes*, pp. 227–34.

48. Cour des Aides, remonstrances of 14 August 1770, *AN*, Z^1 A l88.

49. Ibid.

50. Most of the following is from Egret's *Louis XV*, pp. 158–79.

51. Brittany, a *pays d'état*, had both a parlement and estates. It is with the parlement that d'Aiguillon had his quarrel.

52. In French legal definition, a Cour des Pairs was the Parlement of Paris with the peers of the realm added.

53. "Discours du chancelier," in Flammermont, *Remontrances*, 3:129.

54. For text, see Flammermont, *Chancelier Maupeou*, p. 104.

55. Ibid., p. 117.

56. Cour des Aides, remonstrances of 31 August 1770, *AN*, Z^1 188.

57. For the disgrace of Choiseul, see Flammermont, *Chancelier Maupeou*, pp. 139–206.

58. Ibid., pp. 1–2.

59. De Manières, cited in ibid., p. 31.

60. Ibid., p. 43.

61. See Dakin, *Turgot and the Ancien Régime*, pp. 155–56.

62. See Egret, *Louis XV*, p. 222.

63. Notably in 1754, when it had to recall the Parlement of Paris from exile and, to a lesser extent, in the Breton crisis.

64. See Flammermont, *Chancelier Maupeou*, pp. 50–51.

65. Cited in ibid., p. 141.

66. Ibid., pp. 236–37.

67. See Kelly, "Conceptual Sources of the Terror," pp. 18–36.

68. Cour des Aides, remonstrances of 14 September 1756, *AN*, Z¹ A 185.

69. Malesherbes, *Pensées et maximes*, no. 139, p. 96.

70. Cour des Aides, remonstrances of 18 February 1771, *AN*, Z¹ A 188.

71. Ibid.

72. Ibid. This reference to the Estates-General has been alluded to above, n. 43. However, the Abbé de Véri records that both Malesherbes and Turgot argued against the expedient when it was mooted in the Royal Council in 1776. See Abbé de Véri, *Journal*, 2:8.

73. See Grosclaude, *Malesherbes*, p. 239.

74. See Egret, *Louis XV*, pp. 195–96.

75. Cour des Aides, *AN*, Z¹ A 188.

76. *AN*, O¹ 353.

77. *AN*, O¹ 595/20.

78. *AN*, O¹ 353/50.

79. *AN*, O¹ 353/66.

80. *AN*, Z¹ A 188.

81. Voltaire, *Réponse aux remontrances de la Cour des Aides par un membre des nouveaux Conseils souverains* (1771), in *Oeuvres complètes*, 28:385–88.

82. *AN*, O¹ 353.

83. Dakin, *Turgot and the Ancien Régime*, p. 140.

84. Ibid., pp. 144–45; and Grosclaude, *Malesherbes*, pp. 206–7.

85. See Egret, *Louis XV*, pp. 224–25.

86. See, in general, Grosclaude, *Malesherbes*, pp. 255ff.

87. For example, Félix Nogaret, "Epître à Monsieur Lamoignon de Malesherbes," cited in ibid., p. 328: "Champion of the law's domain,/ Soul of feeling, fruitful brain,/ Humanity's protector, thou./ May gentle grace forever reign/ On thy just and peaceful brow." My translation.

88. Grosclaude, *Malesherbes*, pp. 291–305.

89. To Turgot, 5 August 1774, cited in ibid., p. 296.

90. 4 August 1774, ibid.

91. To Turgot, 21 August 1774, ibid., p. 300.

92. *Arch. Rosanbo*, carton 10, dossier 4, cited in ibid., p. 301. It is a strong plea for legal professionalism (hereditary).

93. Ibid.

94. Abbé de Véri, *Journal*, 2:145ff.

95. Dakin, *Turgot and the Ancien Régime*, pp. 145–46.

96. Cour des Aides, "Discours-séance de la rentrée," 21 November 1774, *AN*, Z¹ A 189.

97. Ibid., 27 November 1774.

98. Cour des Aides, remonstrances of 6 May 1775, ibid.

99. Grosclaude, *Malesherbes*, p. 324.

100. See Grosclaude, *Malesherbes*, pp. 316–23.

101. Abbé de Véri, *Journal*, 1:373–74.

102. Grosclaude, *Malesherbes*, pp. 330–54, passim.

103. See Malesherbes to Madame Douet, 20 June 1776, in ibid., p. 393; also p. 447. For full details on Turgot, see Faure, *La disgrâce de Turgot*.

Chapter 15

1. The "constitutionalist" tradition of French political thought was truncated by the emigration of Protestants after 1685; it survived during the eighteenth century mainly through the parlementary remonstrances, fugitive texts of legal theory, and the great focal point, Montesquieu's *De l'esprit des lois*. Keohane has much to say about the wellsprings of French constitutionalism in *Philosophy and the State*.

2. Malesherbes, *Pensées et maximes*, no. 3, p. 38.

3. *Arch. Rosanbo*, carton 8, dossier 1, cited in Grosclaude, *Malesherbes*, p. 756.

4. This may be related not only to Malesherbes's perception of the actual evolution of French government but also to theories of *legal despotism* (cf. Mercier de la Rivière's *Ordre naturel*) coming into vogue in his time. Moreover, Malesherbes had a relative notion of despotism: "The idea of despotism or of absolute power that people have had in different times and in different territories is not the same." Cour des Aides, remonstrances of 6 May 1775, AN, Z^1 A 189.

5. Montesquieu, *De l'esprit des lois*, 8:6.

6. Cour des Aides, remonstrances of 13 November 1759, AN, Z^1 A 185.

7. Ibid., remonstrances of 9 July 1768, AN, Z^1 A 188.

8. Flammermont, *Remontrances*, "Remontrances sur les actes de violence commis contre les différentes classes de Parlements," 26 December 1763, 2:416.

9. "Seconde mémoire," *Arch. Rosanbo*, carton 10, dossier 4, cited in Grosclaude, *Malesherbes*, p. 301.

10. Cour des Aides, remonstrances of 14 September 1756, AN, Z^1 A 185.

11. Ibid., remonstrances of 9 July 1768, AN, Z^1 A 188.

12. Montesquieu, *Lettres persanes*, lxiv.

13. Cour des Aides, AN, Z^1 A 188.

14. Malesherbes, *Pensées et maximes*, no. 147, p. 102; cf. no. 112, p. 82.

15. Cour des Aides, AN, Z^1 A 189.

16. Malesherbes, *Pensées et maximes*, no. 94, p. 73.

17. "Troisième mémoire," *Arch. Rosanbo*, carton 10, dossier 4, cited in Grosclaude, *Malesherbes*, pp. 301–2.

18. Montesquieu, *De l'esprit des lois*, 11:2–4; 12:2–3. See Malesherbes's "Mémoire sur les avocats (1774)," *Arch. Rosanbo*, carton 10, dossiers 1–2, cited in Grosclaude, *Malesherbes*, pp. 303–4; also Boissy d'Anglas, *Essai*, 1:300.

19. To d'Alembert (1779), *Arch. Tocqueville*, L. 119, cited in Grosclaude, *Malesherbes*, p. 161.

20. Montesquieu, *De l'esprit des lois*, 2:5.

21. Ibid., 5:9, 12.

22. Malesherbes to Comte de Sarsfield, 28 November 1766, in Grosclaude, *Nouveaux documents*, p. 55.

23. *Arch. Rosanbo*, carton 18, dossier 4, cited in Grosclaude, *Malesherbes*, p. 656.

24. Ibid., p. 662.

25. See Rousseau, *Emile, ou de l'éducation*, pp. 279–80.

26. Rousseau, "Quatre lettres à Malesherbes," *Oeuvres complètes*, 1:1145.

27. Yet, on the complexity of the subject, see Shklar, *Men and Citizens*, pp. 127ff.

28. "Mémoire sur les personnes et les familles," *Arch. Tocqueville*, L. 147, cited in Grosclaude, *Malesherbes*, p. 697.

29. "Mémoire sur la Librairie fait du temps de l'exil" (1773?), *Arch. Rosanbo*, carton 7, dossier 1, cited in ibid., p. 289.

30. Huë, *Dernières années*, p. 419; Delisle de Sales, *Malesherbes*, pp. 266–67.

31. Malesherbes, "Lettre à Sarsfield," p. 42.

32. Ibid., pp. 42–44.

33. Ibid., p. 45.

34. Ibid., p. 47.

35. Ibid., p. 49.

36. Hume, "Of Refinement in the Arts," in *Political Essays*, p. 123.

37. Rousseau, *Oeuvres complètes*, 3:8–9, 206.

38. Turgot, "On Universal History," *Turgot on Progress*, pp. 103–4.

39. Article "Luxe," *Encyclopédie*, 9:771a.

40. Malesherbes, "Lettre à Sarsfield," p. 50.

41. Ibid., pp. 50–51.

42. Ibid., p. 52.

43. Ibid., p. 53.

44. Ibid.

45. Ibid., p. 54.

46. Cf. Grosclaude, *Malesherbes*, p. 443.

47. Ibid., pp. 444ff.

48. Baudot, *Notes historiques*, p. 157.

49. See Schelle, *Du Pont de Nemours*, pp. 97, 129.

50. Turgot, *Oeuvres et documents*, to Dupont, 25 March 1774, 3:662.

51. See Grosclaude, *Malesherbes*, pp. 390–93; and Dakin, *Turgot and the Ancien Régime*, pp. 247, 249, 259–63.

52. Turgot, *Oeuvres et documents*, 1:435.

53. "Fragments sur les Parlements," 15 November 1768, in ibid., 3:30.

54. Article "Fondations," *Encyclopédie*, 7:74a.

55. Cf. Grosclaude, *Malesherbes*, pp. 418–23, 584–87.

56. Malesherbes, *Pensées et maximes*, no. 166, p. 174.

57. See Egret, "Premier président," pp. 100–107.

58. Cour des Aides, remonstrances of 9 July 1768, AN, Z^1 A 188.

59. Most specifically in the Monnerat case. Ironically, Malesherbes had married into a family of tax farmers.

60. "Mémoire sur les occupations de la noblesse en temps de paix," *Arch. Tocqueville*, L. 147, cited in Grosclaude, *Malesherbes*, p. 693.

61. See Manceron, *Hommes de la liberté*, 1:205–9.

62. Grosclaude, *Malesherbes*, p. 336.

63. "Mémoire sur la réformation de la Maison du Roi," *Arch. Rosanbo*, carton 11, dossier 5, cited in ibid., pp. 337–40.

64. "Mémoire sur la nécessité de diminuer les dépenses," *Arch. Rosanbo*, carton 18, dossier 2, cited in ibid., pp. 652–53.

65. Letter to Turgot, September 1774, *Arch. Rosanbo*, carton 10, dossier 2, in ibid., p. 300.

66. See Abbé Morellet, *Mémoires*, 1:157.

67. "Mémoire sur l'exécution des jugements portant condamnation corporelle," (1773), *Arch. Rosanbo*, carton 9, dossier 4, cited in Grosclaude, *Malesherbes*, p. 283; cf. pp. 353–54.

68. "Mémoire sur les ordres du roi," *Arch. Rosanbo*, carton 12, dossiers 1–2, in ibid., p. 330. Cf. Delisle de Sales, *Malesherbes*, pp. 41–44.

69. Cour des Aides, remonstrances of 14 August 1770, *AN*, Z^1 A 188.

70. See Grosclaude, *Malesherbes*, p. 334.

71. "Mémoire sur les ordres du roi," ibid., p. 409.

72. Necker's reforms of 13 February 1780 regarding taxation, as well as the edict of 12 July 1778 creating a provincial assembly in Berry, were clearly inspired by Malesherbes's remonstrances. See Grosclaude, *Malesherbes*, p. 324; Egret, "Premier président," p. 117.

73. *Mémoires sur le mariage des protestants*, second memoir (1786), p. 62.

74. It was surely Malesherbes's own ideal to see religion disestablished, not "constitutionalized."

75. See Grosclaude, *Malesherbes*, p. 423. The early manuscript is in the Tocqueville archives.

76. Ibid.

77. "Note secrette sur le second mémoire," *Arch. Rosanbo*, carton 17^2, cited in Grosclaude, *Malesherbes*, p. 601.

78. *Mémoires sur la Librairie et sur la presse*, p. 73.

79. Published with the *Mémoires sur la Librairie* in 1809. In developing his arguments for the freedom of the press, Malesherbes again resorts to his favored historical method of presentation, citing in full detail the cases of the *Encyclopédie* and Helvétius's *De l'esprit*.

80. Malesherbes, *Mémoires sur la Librairie et sur la presse*, p. 344.

81. Ibid., pp. 344–45.

82. Ibid., p. 345.

83. Ibid., pp. 273, 430.

84. "Mémoire sur les études de la jeunesse et sur l'Université," *Arch. Rosanbo*, carton 14, dossier 4, cited in Grosclaude, *Malesherbes*, p. 453.

85. Ibid., p. 455.

86. Ibid., pp. 456–59.

87. Ibid., p. 457.

88. Ibid., p. 459.

89. *Arch. Rosanbo*, carton 7, dossier 3, cited in Grosclaude, *Malesherbes*, pp. 693–94.

90. "Motifs de la demande que j'ai faite au Roi au mois de juin 1788," *Arch. Rosanbo*, carton 18, dossier 5, cited in ibid., p. 654.

91. Ibid., p. 655.

92. "Situation présente," *Arch. Rosanbo*, carton 18, dossier 4, in ibid., p. 656.

93. Ibid., p. 660.

94. Ibid., p. 661.

95. Ibid., p. 658.

96. Ibid., p. 661.

97. Sainte-Beuve, "Monsieur de Malesherbes," 2:536.

Chapter 16

1. See Boissy d'Anglas, *Essai*, 2:87–88.

2. Martainville, *Vie de Malesherbes*, p. 214.

3. Carré, *Fin des parlements*, p. 131.

4. See Dubois, *Notice historique*, p. 27; Martainville, *Vie de Malesherbes*, p. 215.

5. Carré, *Fin des parlements*, p. 57.

6. Ibid., pp. 136–38.

7. Letter quoted in full in Mortimer-Ternaux, *Histoire de la Terreur*, 1:notes, 301–2.

8. Carré, *Fin des parlements*, pp. 185ff.

9. Malesherbes to Rolland, 26 July 1790, *AN*, W 351/713.

10. Burke's *Reflections* were published in November 1790; they defended the French parlements and condemned the new system of justice, but there is no evidence that Malesherbes was affected in the slightest by Burke.

11. *Père Duchesne*, "Ribote de Jeanbart et du Père Duchesne en réjouissance de la destruction du Parlement et du Châtelet," unnumbered, 8 September 1790.

12. Carré, *Fin des parlements*, p. 241; Shennan, *Parlement of Paris*, p. 323.

13. See Seligman, *Justice en France*, 1:339–43.

14. Carré, *Fin des parlements*, p. 247.

15. Quoted in Mortimer-Ternaux, *Histoire de la Terreur*, 1:302.

16. Malesherbes to Boissy d'Anglas, 22 November 1790, "third letter," quoted in Boissy d'Anglas, *Essai*, 2:211–23.

17. Bertrand de Molleville, *Mémoires secrets*, 3:21–29.

18. For extensive documentation of the king's trial and surrounding events, see Soboul, *Procès*. Also, Walzer's commentary in *Regicide and Revolution*, esp. pp. 54–68.

19. See "Acte énonciatif des crimes de Louis, dernier Roi des Français," which contains thirty-five heads of accusation (misnumbered forty), *AN*, C 241/ C II 285. This document formed the basis for the interrogation.

20. Cf. Soboul, *Procès*, pp. 113–20.

21. *AN*, C 243/C II 305.

22. Ibid.

23. *AN*, C 186/ C II 127, 129.

24. Huë, *Dernières années*, pp. 420–21. This and the following anecdote from Huë were allegedly related by Malesherbes during his imprisonment in 1794.

25. A fugitive king-to-be who sought temporary refuge in Switzerland was Louis-Philippe.

26. Huë, *Dernières années*, p. 418.

27. Another source has it that Malesherbes visited the king twice each day: in the morning unaccompanied, and, between five and nine in the evening, with the other lawyers. See Grosclaude, *Malesherbes*, p. 708.

28. Alissan de Chazet, *Mémoires, souvenirs*, 3:15–16, 22.

29. "Pièce: Commune de Paris. Rapport de Dorat-Cubières au Conseil de la Commune, le 21 décembre, an premier," in Beaucourt, *Captivité et derniers moments*, 2:208. See also Goret, *Mon témoignage*, p. 31. Malesherbes's cousin, Lamoignon, the Garde des Sceaux, had taken his own life after dismissal from office.

30. Hyde de Neuville, *Mémoires et souvenirs*, 1:32; also Morellet, *Mémoires*, 2:363.

31. See *Convention nationale. Défense de Louis* . . .

32. *AN*, C 182/C II 89.

33. Huë, *Dernières années*, p. 417.

34. See Sydenham, *Girondins*.

35. For a detailed examination, see Conte, *Sire, ils ont voté la mort*. See also Soboul, *Procès*, pp. 217–20.

36. Hyde de Neuville, *Mémoires*, 1:40.

37. The same confusion arises with regard to the appeal to the nation. What was to be appealed? The verdict or the sentence?

38. Hyde de Neuville, *Mémoires*, 1:42.

39. Beaucourt, *Captivité*, 2:332.

40. Huë, *Dernières années*, p. 430.

41. See Grosclaude, *Malesherbes*, p. 716.

42. Lacretelle, *Histoire de la Révolution*, 5:407.

43. The text of the letter of 10 March 1793 sent to the Comte de Provence is contained in Tocqueville, *Episodes*, pp. 37–38.

44. See Grosclaude, *Malesherbes*, p. 721.

45. Tocqueville, *Episodes*, p. 16.

46. Ibid., pp. 17–18.

47. For this and the following, see "Rapport du comité de la surveillance de la section de Bondy . . . ," *AN*, W 349/703 bis.

48. Ibid.

49. Ibid.

50. Tocqueville, *Episodes*, pp. 20–21.

51. See Carré, *Fin des parlements*, pp. 279ff.

52. *AN*, W 349/703 bis.

53. Malesherbes is evidently referring to Saint-Just's report to the Convention of 11 Germinal, an II (31 March 1794). There, however, the orator links the Orleanist plot to Dumouriez, the Girondins, and their accomplices.

54. *AN*, W 349/703 bis.

55. See Grosclaude, *Malesherbes*, pp. 742–43.

56. There are touching notes from the family attached to the copy forwarded to Rosanbo.

57. Of course d'Orléans was now dead.

58. "Dossier Lepeletier-Rosambeau [*sic*]," *AN*, F⁷ 4774¹⁸.

59. Ibid.

60. *AN*, W 349/703 bis.

61. *AN*, W 351/713.

62. Ibid.

63. Ibid.

64. Ibid.

65. Quoted in Martainville, *Vie de Malesherbes*, p. 274.

66. Tocqueville, *Episodes*, pp. 28–29.

67. For Rosanbo's reception in the Loge de la Persévérance, see *AN*, W 349/703 bis.

68. See *AN*, W 363/878 and W 376/851.

Chapter 17

1. Cf. Greer, *Incidence of the Terror*. Many of Greer's particular conclusions have been criticized, for example in Louie, "The Incidence of the Terror," pp. 379–89, but these gross figures may be considered roughly reliable.

2. See article "Corps," *Encyclopédie*, 4:266b.

3. Saint-Just, "Institutions républicaines et pensées diverses," in *Oeuvres choisies*, p. 308.

4. Rousseau, "Fragments," in *Political Writings*, 1:312.

5. See Roland Mousnier, "The Fronde," in Forster and Greene, *Preconditions of Revolution*, pp. 137–41.

6. Bluche, *Vie quotidienne*, p. 27; see also Kelly, "Duelling," pp. 236–54.

7. See article "Général," *Encyclopédie*, 7:550b–51b.

8. M. Thomas, *Eloge de Saxe*, p. 30.

9. Special provisions for "honorary" privileges favoring the nobility were made in many of the academies, complementing the regular members and correspondents. See Roche, "Encyclopédistes et académiciens," in Furet et al., *Livre et société*, p. 81; and Hahn, *Anatomy*, pp. 76ff.

10. See Bacourt, *Correspondance entre Mirabeau et La Marck*, 1:213.

11. Cobb, *Reactions to the French Revolution*, p. 117.

12. *Père Duchesne* (undated, but an early number), pp. 6–8.

13. See "Manifeste très pressant et très essentiel," cited in A. Découflé, "Aristocratie française," p. 6.

14. Saint-Just, "Rapport du 26 Germinal, an II," in *Oeuvres choisies*, p. 262.

15. Score-settling, whether personal or collective, was certainly important to the scope and virulence of the Terror. But there was a more abstract moral exaltation effectively communicated from the tribune of the Jacobin Club. As Cobb writes of Nicolas Guénot, whose major moment was the arrest of André Chénier on 17 Ventôse, an II (7 March 1794): "He enjoyed the Terror, had reached the high spot of his career at 40, was in it for what he could get out of it, and had the further satisfaction no doubt of feeling that the enemies of the Republic were also his own. . . . He was undoubtedly partly motivated by considerations of vengeance; but, in view of his subsequent career, there is not a reason to doubt his sincerity as a terrorist." *Reactions to the French Revolution*, p. 84.

16. Starobinski, *Trois fureurs: essais*, pp. 160–161.

Bibliography

General Guides

Almanach National. Paris, 1792–94.

Almanach Royal. Versailles and Paris, 1787–91.

Archives parlementaires de 1787 à 1860, 1ère série. Paris, 1867–1914.

Aulard, F.-A., ed. *La société des Jacobins*. 6 vols. Paris, 1889–97.

Brette, Armand, ed. *Les constituants: liste des députés et des suppléants élus à l'Assemblée constituante de 1789*. Paris, 1897.

Buchez, B.-J., and Roux, P.-C., eds. *Histoire parlementaire de la Révolution française*. 40 vols. Paris, 1834–38.

Caron, Pierre. *Manuel pratique pour l'étude de la Révolution française*. Paris, 1947.

Chassin, Charles-Louis, ed. *Les élections et les cahiers de Paris en 1789*. 4 vols. Paris, 1888.

Cioranescu, André. *Bibliographie de la littérature française du XVIIIe siècle*. 3 vols. Paris, 1969.

Lacroix, Sigismond, ed. *Actes de la Commune de Paris pendant la Révolution, 2ème série*. Paris, 1907.

Monin, H. *L'état de Paris en 1789: études et documents sur l'ancien régime à Paris*. Paris, 1889.

Nouvelle Biographie Générale. Reprint. Copenhagen, 1965.

Procès-verbal de l'Assemblée nationale. Paris and Versailles, 1789–91.

Réimpression de l'Ancien Moniteur, mai 1789–novembre 1799. 32 vols. Paris, 1863–70.

Roberts, J. M.; Cobb, R. C.; and Hardman, John, eds. *French Revolution Documents*. 2 vols. Oxford, 1971–73.

Thompson, J. M. *French Revolution Documents, 1789–1794*. Oxford, 1948.

Tourneux, Maurice. *Bibliographie de l'histoire de Paris pendant la Révolution française*. 5 vols. Paris, 1890.

Tuetey, Alexandre, ed. *Répertoire générale des sources manuscrits de l'histoire de Paris pendant la Révolution française*. 11 vols. Paris, 1890–1914.

Walter, Gérard, ed. *Catalogue des journaux révolutionnaires, 1789–1799*. 6 vols. Paris, 1943.

Contemporary Periodicals

Les Actes des apôtres.
L'Ami du Peuple.
Bouche de Fer.
Gazette national.
Le Journal de la Montagne.

Mercure français.
L'Orateur du Peuple.
Le Patriote français.
Le Père Duchesne.
Le Publiciste de la République française.
Le Publiciste de la République française, par l'ombre de Marat.
Les Révolutions de France et de Brabant.
Les Révolutions de Paris.
Le Vieux Cordelier.

Journals

Annales E.S.C.
Annales historiques de la Révolution française.
Diderot Studies.
Dix-huitième Siècle.
French Historical Studies.
Past and Present.
Révolution française.
Studies in Burke and His Time.
Studies on Voltaire and the Eighteenth Century.

Philippe d'Orléans

ARCHIVES

Bibliothèque de l'Institut de France. Cartons 2048–51.
Bibliothèque Nationale, manuscripts: fonds français 12,760; nouvelles acquisitions 2772, 22,257, 23,617.
Archives Nationales: AF^{II} 48, AF^{IV} 1470, B^1 15, BB^{30} 24, BB^{30} 163, BB^{37} 163, C 45, C 150, C 184, C 190, C 251, C 252, C 273, C 280, C 281, C 285, D III 235, F^7 4385, F^7 4389, R^4 283, W 285, W 294, W 524, Y 10598.

PRINTED SOURCES

Works by Philippe d'Orléans

D'Orléans, Louis-Philippe-Joseph, Duc. *Correspondance de Louis-Philippe-Joseph d'Orléans avec Louis XVI, la Reine, Montmorin, Liancourt, Biron, Lafayette.* . . . Paris, 1800.
———. "Exposé de la conduite de M. le duc d'Orléans dans la Révolution de France. Rédigé par lui-même à Londres." [London, 1790].

———. "Instructions données par S.A.S. Monseigneur le duc d'Orléans à ses représentans aux bailliages." N.p., 1789.

———. "Lettre de Louis-Philippe-Joseph Egalité, ci-devant d'Orléans, envoyée hier à Paris. . . ." N.p., [1793].

———. "L.-P.-J. Egalité à ses concitoyens." Paris, 16 January 1793.

———. "L.-P.-Joseph Egalité au citoyen Milcent." Paris, 22 February 1793.

———. "Mémoire justificatif pour Louis-Philippe d'Orléans, écrit et publié par lui-même, en réponse à la procédure du Châtelet." N.p., [1790].

———. *Traité philosophique, théologique et politique de la loi du divorce*. Paris, 1789.

Works about Philippe d'Orléans

Alissan de Chazet, *Vie politique de Louis-Philippe-Joseph d'Orléans-Egalité* (Paris, 1832).

[Anon.]. "A moi, Laclos, un mot." N.p., [1790?].

———. "A moi, Philippe, un mot." N.p., [1790?].

———. "A toi-même, Laclos." N.p., [1790?].

———. "Adieu de Louis-Philippe-Joseph, duc d'Orléans, à la ville de Paris et à ses habitans" N.p., [1789].

———. "Adresse d'un aide de camp de la Garde Nationale à ses concitoyens, concernant l'arrivée de Louis-Philippe d'Orléans." [Paris, 1790].

———. "L'ami des Français, suivi d'un précis succinct sur la conspiration du duc d'Or. . . . s." [Paris, 1790?].

———. "L'assassinat de la Famille Royale: plan présenté à Mgr. le duc d'Orléans par le Marquis de ★★★, trouvé sous le portail du Louvre, près le jardin de l'Infante." N.p., n.d.

———. "Au régicide d'Orléans." [Paris, 1791].

———. "Avis aux bons patriotes sur le retour certain de Monsieur le duc d'Orléans. . . . [Paris, 1790].

———. "La cabale d'Orléans ressuscitée et dévoilée." N.p., [1790?].

———. "Ce que c'est que l'histoire du Châtelet d'après les intéressés." N.p., [1790].

———. "Le citoyen vengé." [Paris, 1789].

———. "Compte rendu au conseil de M. d'Orléans, par M. Laclos sur la position actuelle des affaires." [Paris, 1790].

———. "Contrat d'union du duc d'Orléans avec ses créanciers." Paris, [1791].

———. "Copie de la lettre de M. le marquis Ducrest à Mgr. le duc d'Orléans." [Paris, 1788].

———. "Les crimes de Louis-Philippe d'Orléans." [Paris, 1790].

———. "Détail de l'arrivée de M. d'Orléans à Paris." [Paris, 1790].

———. "Discours de M. Louis-Philippe-Joseph Capet, ci-devant Duc d'Orléans, prononcé par lui-même à l'Assemblée Nationale." Paris, 11 July 1790.

———. "Eclaircissemens sur la prétendue mission du duc d'Orléans." N.p., [1789].

———. "L'écouteur, ou une soirée au Palais de Philippe, à Cocopolis, l'an III de la Papîrocratie." [Paris, 1791].

———. "Entrevue de Messieurs le Duc d'Orléans avec le Marquis de La Fayette." N.p., [1789].

———. "Etat de situation de M. Louis-Philippe-Joseph, prince françois, et projet d'union qu'il propose à ses créanciers." [Paris, 1791].

———. "La faction d'Orléans mieux dévoilée: lettre de M. le duc d'Orléans à M. de Laclos." London, 10 May 1790.

———. "Le grand dîner des nouveaux conjurés." [Paris, 1790].

———. "Il y a lieu à accusation contre le Duc d'Orléans et le Comte de Mirabeau." Paris, 1790.

———. "Les intrigues dévoilées, ou les trente-trois factieux dénoncés." N.p., [1791?].

———. "Intrigues secrettes de Louis-Philippe-Joseph d'Orléans, dans sa résidence actuelle en Angleterre." N.p., [1790].

———. "Journée du 6 octobre 1789: affaire complette de MM. d'Orléans et Mirabeau." Paris, 1790.

———. "Lettre à Monseigneur le duc d'Orléans." [Paris, 1789?].

———. "Lettre d'un habitant de Boulogne-sur-Mer à Monsieur le Comte de la Touche, chancelier de M. le duc d'Orléans." Boulogne, 1789.

———. "Louis d'Orléans mal conseillé: réponse au mémoire à consulter et consultation pour Louis-Philippe-Joseph d'Orléans." Paris, 1790.

———. "Louis-Philippe, duc d'Orléans, premier prince du sang, au peuple françois. Par un homme de Lettre-Patriote, citoyen du district des Petits-Augustins." Paris, 1789.

———. "L. Ph. Egalité, ci-devant Duc d'Orléans, traité comme il le mérite, dans l'affaire du scélérat Louis XVI." [Paris, 1793].

———. "Mémoire à consulter et consultation pour M. Louis-Philippe-Joseph d'Orléans." Paris, 1790.

———. "Mémoire justificatif pour Louis-Ph. d'Orléans, écrit et publié par lui-même." Paris, 1790.

———. "Mémoire ou pièces justificatives de Monsieur d'Orléans." [Paris, 1790].

———. "Motion de Monsieur le duc d'Orléans pour le soulagement du peuple." Versailles, 1789.

———. "Non, d'Orléans, tu ne régneras pas." [Paris], 1791.

———. "Observations sur la destruction de la promenade du Palais-Royal, lettre d'un Anglais établi à Paris à Milord P*** à Londres." Amsterdam, 1781.

———. "Observations sur les attentats attribués à M. le Duc d'Orléans." N.p., [1790].

———. "L'Orléanride, ou le masque rouge déchiré." N.p., [1791?].

———. "Le portefeuille de Louis-Philippe d'Orléans, trouvé dans la poche de M. La Fayette." [Paris], 1791.

———. "Réflexions sur la clause de la donation du Palais Cardinal, depuis Palais Royal, portant que ce Palais ne pourra être habité que par le Roi ou par l'Héritier présomptif de la Couronne." [Paris, 1781?].

_____. "Réfutation de l'exposé de la conduite de M. le duc d'Orléans." N.p., [1790?].

_____. "Réponse à l'exposé de la conduite de M. le duc d'Orléans." N.p., [1790].

_____. "Réponse au mémoire de Louis-Philippe-Joseph, ci-devant prince du sang et duc d'Orléans." N.p., [1790?].

_____. "Réponse aux ennemis de Mgr. le duc d'Orléans." [Paris, 1789].

_____. "Réponse aux instructions envoyées par S.A.S. Monseigneur le duc d'Orléans, à ses charges de procuration dans ses bailliages, relativement aux Etats-Généraux." N.p., 1789.

_____. "Réponse aux philippiques, ou lettre du duc d'Orléans à la nation françoise." N.p. [1790?].

_____. "Réponse de M. Delaclos à M. le duc d'Orléans, pour servir de suite à la conspiration mieux dévoilée. . . ." N.p., 17 June 1790.

_____. "Réponse de M. d'Orléans à l'opinion de M. l'abbé Maury dans l'affaire de la dot de la reine d'Espagne." Paris, 1791.

_____. "Réponse d'un honnête homme à l'exposé palliatif des torts de M. le duc d'Orléans." Paris, 1790.

_____. "Le Sieur d'Orléans tout entier." [Paris], 1791.

_____. *La vie privée du duc de Chartres, aujourd'hui duc d'Orléans, par une Société d'Amis du Prince.* [Paris, 1790].

Arbeltier, M. "Un coup d'oeil impartial sur les motifs de l'absence de Monseigneur le duc d'Orléans." [Paris, 1790].

Brienne, Comte de, and de Brienne, Etienne-Charles de Loménie. *Journal de l'Assemblée des Notables de 1787.* Edited with notes by Pierre Chevallier. Paris, 1960.

Britsch, Amadée. "L'anglomanie de Philippe-Egalité d'après sa correspondance." *Le Correspondant* 303 (1926): 280–95.

_____. "Philippe-Egalité avant la Révolution." *Revue des études historiques* 70 (1904): 337–63, 478–504.

Bruel, Alexandre. "Inventaire sommaire des titres de l'apanage d'Orléans." 2 vols., in ms. *AN*, Paris, 1881.

Caillé, A. "A propos du 21 janvier 1793: un des juges de Louis XVI." Paris, 1887.

Castelot, André. *Le prince rouge, Philippe-Egalité.* Paris, 1950.

Chabroud, Charles. *Rapport de la Procédure du Châtelet sur l'affaire des 5 et 6 octobre 1789, fait les 30 septembre et 1er octobre, à l'Assemblée Nationale, par M. Charles Chabroud.* Paris, 1790.

Chen Ta Ming. *L'organisation des Assemblées des Notables de 1787 et de 1788.* Paris, 1939.

"Compte rendu par une partie des membres de l'Assemblée Nationale, de leur opinion sur le rapport de la procédure au Châtelet. . . ." Paris, 1790.

Dard, Emile. *Un acteur caché du drame révolutionnaire: Choderlos de Laclos.* Paris, 1905.

Desmoulins, Camille. "Discours de Camille Desmoulins sur le décret du bannissement de la famille ci-devant d'Orléans." Paris, 1792.

Dominique, Pierre. *Paris enlève le roi, octobre 1789*. Paris, 1973.

Doutenville, J. "Philippe-Egalité et la faction d'Orléans." *La nouvelle revue*, 4ème série. 128 (1933): 57–68, 99–110.

Ducoin, Auguste. *Etudes révolutionnaires: Philippe d'Orléans-Egalité*. Paris, 1845.

[Ducrest, Charles, Marquis]. "Mémoire présenté au roi par S.A.S. Mgr. le duc d'Orléans." N.p., [1788].

———. "Vrais principes d'une bonne constitution." N.p., [1789?].

Elliott, Grace Dalrymple. *Sous la terreur: journal d'une amie de Philippe-Egalité*. Translated by Théodor de Wyzawa. [Paris, 1906].

Etienne and Martainville. *Vie politique de Louis-Philippe-Joseph, dernier duc d'Orléans*. Paris, 1802.

"Exposé des changemens à faire au Palais, imprimé par ordre de S.A.S. Mgr. le duc de Chartres, prince du sang." [Paris, 1781].

Gamache, Louis-François. *Récit de la translation de Louis-Philippe-Joseph, duc d'Orléans, des prisons de Marseille à la Conciergerie de Paris, en 1793*. Paris, 1827.

Girey-Dupré, J. M. "Justification de M. d'Orléans, ou réflexions d'un bon citoyen sur la conduite du Châtelet." [Paris, 1790].

Hébert, Jacques. "Philippe d'Orléans et le ci-devant Comte de Mirabeau, jugé par le Père Duchesne, sur la Procédure du Châtelet." [Paris, 1790].

Hyslop, Beatrice Fry. *L'apanage de Philippe-Egalité, duc d'Orléans, 1785–1791*. Paris, 1965.

Jaussan. "Réponse à la cabale d'Orléans . . . par un membre de ladite cabale." [Paris], 4 June 1790.

"Journée du 6 octobre 1789. Affaire complette de MM. d'Orléans et Mirabeau." Paris, 1790.

Laurentie, P.-S. *Histoire des ducs d'Orléans*. 3 vols. Paris, 1832.

Louis-Philippe. *Mémoires, 1773–1793*. 2 vols. Paris, 1973.

Louvet, J.-B. *La vérité sur la faction d'Orléans et la conspiration du 10 mars 1793*. Paris, an III.

Maricourt, A. de. *Louise-Marie-Adélaïde de Penthièvre, duchesse d'Orléans*. 2 vols. Paris, 1913–14.

[Mazain]. "La cabale d'Orléans ressuscitée et dévoilée, par un bon citoyen." [Paris, 1790?].

Monin, H. "Philippe-Egalité." *Révolution française* 20 (1891): 442–51.

[Montjoie, Félix L.-D.]. *Histoire de la conjuration de Louis-Philippe-Joseph d'Orléans*. 4 vols. Paris, 1796.

Montpensier, Duc de. *Mémoires sur son arrestation et sa captivité*. In *Bibliothèque des mémoires relatifs à l'histoire de France pendant le XVIIIe siècle*, vol. 9, edited by M. F. Barrière, Paris, 1856.

Morand, Hubert. "Philippe-Egalité et la construction du Palais-Royale." *Le Correspondant* 304 (1926): 290–93.

Mounier, J.-J. "Appel au tribunal de l'opinion publique, du rapport de M. Chabroud. . . ." Geneva, 1790.

———. "Exposé de la conduite de M. Mounier dans l'Assemblée Nationale, et de ses motifs de son retour en Dauphiné." Paris, 1789.

"Pièces justificatives du Rapport de la Procédure du Châtelet." Paris, 1790.

Procédure criminelle, instruite au Châtelet de Paris. 2 vols. Paris, 1790.

Procès-verbal de l'Assemblée des Notables tenue à Versailles, en l'année 1787. Paris, 1787.

Procès-verbal de l'Assemblée des Notables tenue à Versailles, en l'année 1788. Paris, 1789.

Publius [pseud.]. "Scandales de son Altesse sérénissime Monseigneur le duc d'Orléans." N.p., 1789.

"Remontrances du Parlement sur l'usage des lettres de cachet, l'exil de M. le duc d'Orléans, et l'enlèvement de MM. Fréteau et Sabatier, arrétés le 11 mars 1788." Paris, 1788.

Renouvin, Pierre, ed. *L'Assemblée des Notables de 1787. La conférence du 2 mars.* Paris, 1920.

Ribes, Raimond. "Grande dénonciation du duc d'Orléans et de ses complices." N.p. [1792?].

Royer, M. "Grandes nouvelles de Monseigneur le duc d'Orléans." [Paris, 1790?].

Salle, M. "Recherches de Salle, député de la Meurthe, sur les agens et les moyens de la faction d'Orléans." [Paris, 1793].

Sambat, M. "Circulaire de la Société des Amis de la Liberté et de l'Egalité . . . à leurs frères des départemens." Paris, 1792.

Scudder, E. S. *Prince of the Blood.* Leipzig, 1938.

Shennan, J. H. *Philippe, Duke of Orleans.* London, 1979.

Sillery, Charles-Alexis Brulart, Marquis de. "Discours de M. Sillery à la Société des Amis de la Constitution, sur la prétendue faction d'Orléans." Paris, 1792.

———. "Opinion de M. le Marquis de Sillery, relative à la Déclaration des Droits de l'Homme." [Paris, 1789].

Tournois, M. *Histoire de Philippe d'Orléans et du parti d'Orléans.* Paris, 1840.

Valence, Général. *Lettres du général Valence, pour servir de suite aux mémoires du général Dumouriez.* Frankfurt and Leipzig, 1794.

"Véritable intérrogatoire et véritables réponses de Louis-Philippe-Joseph Orléans." N.p., 1793.

Voidel, J.-G.-C. "Jean-Georges-Charles Voidel à ses concitoyens." Paris, 1793.

Custine

ARCHIVES

Archives de l'Armée de Terre (Vincennes): B[1] 12, B[1] 13, B[1] 14, B[1] 15, B[1]* 103, B[1]* 104, B[1]* 105, B[1]* 106, B[1]* 107, B[2] 29, B[2]* 121, GD/1264, 1ère série.

Bibliothèque Nationale, manuscripts: fonds français 22,133.

Archives Nationales: AF[II] 45, AF[II] 244, AF[II] 451, AF*[II] 286, AF*[II] 294, AF[IV] 1470, BB[3] 30, BB[3] 81A, BB[16] 703, C 260, C 264, C 266, C 355, D § 364, F[1c] III (Seine), F[7] 3688[3], F[7] 4385[1], F[7] 4402, W 99, W 100, W 101, W 102, W 280, W 285, W 306.

PRINTED SOURCES

Works by Adam-Philippe, Comte de Custine

Custine, Adam-Philippe, Comte de. "A MM. les magistrats de Francfort. Réponse du citoyen français, général en chef Custine. . . ." N.p., 23 December 1792.

———. "Apperçu rapide de la position de la France, à l'époque de la prétendue coalition des Souverains de l'Europe contre sa Constitution." Paris, 26 August 1791.

———. "Compte des différents articles de l'arrêté pris par l'Assemblée nationale dans la nuit du 4 au 5 août 1789 . . ." [Others follow: five "comptes rendus" in all.] Paris, 1789–90.

———. *Comptes rendus par M. de Custine à ses commetans*, Annexes, *Archives parlementaires, 1787–1860*. Série 32, "Table chronologique de la Constituante." Paris, 1867–1914.

———. *Déclaration des droits du citoyen français*. [Paris, 1789].

———. "Discours prononcé par M. le Comte de Custine d'Aufflance, Président, à la clôture de l'Assemblée des Trois Ordres de Lorraine, tenue en l'Hôtel de Ville de Nancy, le 25 janvier dernier." [Nancy, 1789].

———. "Lettre écrite par M. de Custine lieutenant-général, commandant à Landau et de la conquième division, à M. Levasseur, député du départment de la Meurthe." Paris, [1792].

———. "Opinion de M. de Custine . . . sur la loi présentée par le Comité de Constitution sur les Emigrans." Paris, 1791.

———. "Opinion du comte de Custine relative à la proposition faite de déclarer les biens du clergé appartenans à la nation." N.p., [1789].

———. "Plan à consulter, d'instructions et de pouvoirs à donner aux Députés de la province de Lorraine et celle des Trois-Evéchés, aux Etats-Généraux." Nancy, 1789.

———. "Rapport des commissaires de l'Assemblée nationale envoyés dans les départements du Rhin et des Vosges, fait par Custine, Chasset, Regnier de Nancy." Paris, 1791.

Works about Adam-Philippe, Comte de Custine

Acomb, Evelyn M., ed. *The Revolutionary Journal of Baron Ludwig von Closen, 1780–1783*. Chapel Hill, 1958.

[Anon.]. "Crimes et forfaits, moeurs et liaisons du général Custines depuis sa nomination au grade de général. . . ." N.p., [1793].

———. "Custine Tout Entier, ou la vérité toute nue: il en est temps." N.p., [1793].

———. *Vies et mémoires des Grands Capitaines de la France*. Vol. 2, *Custine et Dumouriez. Mémoires du général Custine . . . , précédés d'une notice sur le général Dumouriez*. Paris, 1831.

Babeau, Albert. *La vie militaire sous l'Ancien Régime*. 2 vols. Paris, 1890.

[Baraguey d'Hilliers, Général?]. *Mémoires du général Custine, rédigés par un de ses aides-de-camp*. 2 vols. Hamburg and Frankfurt, 1794.

Bertaud, J.-P. "Le recrutement et l'avancement des officiers de la Révolution." *Annales historiques de la Révolution française* 44 (November–December 1972): 513–36.

———, ed. *Valmy: la démocratie en armes*. Paris, 1970.

Beuve, O. *Glanes d'histoire révolutionnaire*. Vol. 1, *Les Troyens et l'armée du général Custine, 1793*. N.p., 1908.

Bien, D. D., "The Army in the French Enlightenment: Reform, Reaction, and Revolution." *Past and Present*, no. 85 (November 1979), pp. 68–98.

———. "La réaction aristocratique avant 1789: l'exemple de l'armée." *Annales E.S.C.*, January–February 1974, pp. 23–48; March–April 1974, pp. 505–34.

Blanchard, Claude. *Guerre d'Amérique, 1780–1783: Journal de campagne de Claude Blanchard, commissaire de guerres principal au corps auxiliaire français sous le commandement du lieutenant-général comte de Rochambeau*. 2 vols. Edited by M. La Chesnais. Paris, 1881.

Caron, Pierre. *La défense nationale de 1792 à 1795*. Paris, 1912.

Carré, Henri. *L'armée française à la fin de l'Ancien Régime*. Paris, 1908.

Chuquet, Arthur. *Les guerres de la Révolution (3ème série): L'expédition de Custine*. Paris, 1892.

Les combattants français de la guerre américaine, 1778–1783. Paris, 1903.

Corvisier, André. *L'armée française de la fin du XVIIe siècle au ministère de Choiseul*. 2 vols. Paris, 1964.

———. *Armies and Societies in Europe, 1494–1789*. Translated by A. T. Siddall. Bloomington, Ind., 1979.

"Entretien du citoyen général Custine avec Théophile Mandar, commissaire national du conseil exécutif provisoire de la République française, dans le département du Mont-Terrible." [Belfort, 1793].

Foucard, Paul, and Finot, Jules. *La défense nationale dans le Nord, de 1792 à 1802*. 2 vols. Lille, 1890–93.

Gay de Vernon, Jean-Louis-Camille. *Mémoire sur les opérations militaires des généraux en chef Custine et Houchard pendant les années 1792 et 1793*. Paris, 1844.

Hartmann, Lt.-Col. *Les officiers de l'armée royale et la Révolution*. Paris, 1910.

Herlaut, Général Auguste-Philippe. *Le colonel Bouchotte, ministre de la Guerre en l'an II*. 2 vols. Paris, 1946.

———. "Les négociations du général Custine avec l'ennemi (décembre 1792–mai 1793)." *Annales historiques de la Révolution française* 9 (1932):517–33.

———. *La querelle de Bouchotte et de Custine*. Paris, n.d.

Labarre de Raillicourt. *La noblesse militaire*. Paris, 1962.

Latreille, Albert. *L'armée et la nation à la fin de l'Ancien Régime*. Paris, 1914.

Léonard, Emile G. *L'armée et ses problèmes au XVIIIe siècle*. Paris, 1958.

Lort de Sérignan, Comte de, ed. *Le duc de Lauzun (Général Biron): Correspondance intime, 1791–1792*. Paris, 1906.

Mathiez, Albert. "Etudes sur la Terreur: le Comité de Salut Public et le complot de l'étranger." *Annales historiques de la Révolution française* 3 (1926): 305–29.

_____. "Le premier Comité de Salut Public et la guerre." *Revue historique* 158 (1928): 259–69.

Maugras, Gaston, and de Croze-Lemercier Comte P. *Delphine de Sabran, Marquise de Custine*. Paris, 1912.

Michon, Georges. *La justice militaire sous la Révolution*. Paris, 1922.

Money, J. *Souvenirs de campagne de 1792*. Paris, 1849.

"Une Pièce suivie des observations du citoyen Vincent. . . ." [Paris, 1793].

Rice, Howard C., Jr., and Brown, Anne S. K., eds. *The American Campaigns of Rochambeau's Army, 1780, 1781, 1782, 1783*. 2 vols. Providence and Princeton, 1972.

Rittweger, E. *Custine in Frankfurt und die Wiedereinnahme der Stadt durch die Deutschen, 1792*. Frankfurt, 1867.

Sorel, Albert. "La mission de Custine à Brunswick en 1792, d'après des documents inédits." *Revue historique* 1 (1876): 154–83.

Thomas, M. *Eloge de Maurice, Comte de Saxe*. Paris, 1759.

Tuetey, Louis. *Les officiers sous l'Ancient Régime*. Paris, 1908.

Vincent, François-Nicolas. "Déclaration du Citoyen Vincent . . . contre Custine; énonciative des pièces qui établissent les trahisons de ce ci-devant Général." [Paris, 1793].

Bailly

ARCHIVES

Bibliothèque Nationale, manuscripts: fonds français 11,696, 11,697, 20,705; nouvelles acquisitions 1301, 5969.

Archives Nationales: AF^{II} 48, B^1 11, C 32, C 39, C 43, C 44, C 45, C 46, C 71, C 74, C 75, C 76, C 134, C 139, C$\star$ I^1, D III, D IV 49, D IV 50, D IV 51, D XXIX^b 33, D XXIX^b 36, D XXIX^b 44, D XXXIV 5, F^7 3264, F^7 3688^1, F$\star^{11}$ 3, W 290, W 294, W 524.

PRINTED SOURCES

Works by Jean-Sylvain Bailly

Bailly, Jean-Sylvain. "L'assemblée générale de tous les Français au Champ-de-Mars, pour le pacte fédératif du 14 juillet." [Paris, 1790].

_____. "Discours au roi, prononcé par M. Bailly, doyen de la chambre des communes, le 6 juin, suivi de la réponse du roi." N.p., [1789].

_____. *Eloges*. Berlin, 1770.

_____. *Essai sur les fables et leur histoire*. 2 vols. Paris, an VII.

_____. *Histoire de l'astronomie ancienne*. 2 vols. Paris, 1781.

_____. *Histoire de l'astronomie moderne*. 2d ed. 3 vols. Paris, 1785.

_____. *J.-S. Bailly à ses concitoyens*. [Paris], 1793.

———. "Lettre adressée . . . aux soixante sections de la commune de Paris." Paris, 1790.

———. "Lettre aux représentants de la Commune, relativement à la division des sections de la capitale." [Paris, 1790].

———. "Lettre . . . aux soixante sections, sur la prohibition des jeux." Paris, 1790.

———. "Lettre de M. Bailly, Maire de Paris, à MM. des Districts." Paris, 1789.

———. "Lettre de M. le Maire à la Section de Gravilliers, sur l'affaire de la Chapelle." [Paris, 1791].

———. "Lettre des officiers municipaux de la ville de Paris au Roi." Paris, 1791.

———. "Lettre écrite par M. le Maire de Paris, à MM. les représentants de la Commune." [Paris], 1790.

———. Lettres sur l'Atlantide de Platon et sur l'ancienne histoire de l'Asie. Paris, 1804.

———. Lettres sur l'origine des sciences, et sur celle des peuples de l'Asie, adressées à M. de Voltaire par M. Bailly, et précédées de quelques lettres de M. de Voltaire à l'auteur. London and Paris, 1777.

———. Mémoires d'un témoin de la Révolution. 3 vols. Paris, 1804.

Works about Jean-Sylvain Bailly

[Anon.]. "Confession générale du très-haut et très-puissant seigneur, Messire Sylvain Bailly, roi de Paris, et de ses complices." [Paris, 1790].

———. "Les crimes de M. Bailly dévoilés." N.p., [1790].

———. "Lettre à M. Bailly, maire de Paris, par un de ses disciples." [Paris, 1791].

———. "Séance extraordinaire et secrète de l'Académie française, tenue le 30 mars 1789, à l'occasion des Etats-Généraux." N.p., [1789].

Arago, François. *Biographie de Jean-Sylvain Bailly*. Paris, 1852.

Aulard, F.-A. "Bailly et l'affaire du Champ de Mars." *Révolution française* 13 (October 1887): 289–96.

———. "Les républicains et les démocrates depuis le massacre du Champ de Mars jusqu'à la journée du 20 juin 1792." *Révolution française* 35 (December 1898): 485–539.

Baker, Keith M. "Science, elitism, and liberalism: the case of Condorcet." In *Studies on Voltaire and the Eighteenth Century* 55 (Geneva, 1967): 129–65.

Bardin. "M. Bailly, Maire de Paris, traité sans égard et comme il le mérite." [Paris, 1791].

Bauer, E. *Bailly und die ersten Tage der französischen Revolution*. Leipzig, 1847.

Bloch, Camille. *L'assistance et l'Etat en France à la veille de la Révolution*. Paris, 1901.

Bonnechose, Emile. "Mort de Bailly." Paris, [1833].

Braesch, Frédéric. "Les pétitions du Champ-de-Mars (15, 16, 17 juillet 1791)." *Revue historique* 142 (1923): 192–209; 143 (1923): 1–39, 181–97.

Brissot, Jacques-Pièrre. *De la vérité*. Paris, 1782.

Brucker, Gene A. *Jean-Sylvain Bailly: Revolutionary Mayor of Paris*. Urbana, 1950.

Brunel, Lucien. *Les philosophes et l'Académie française au XVIIIe siècle*. Paris, 1884.

Chamfort, N. S. R. *Des académies, ouvrage que M. Mirabeau devait lire à l'Assemblée nationale*. Paris, 1789.

Citoyen d'Yervale [pseud.]. *L'antiquité dévoilée par les principes de la magie naturelle, ou Théorie des anciens législateurs* . . . [Paris], an VIII.

Darnton, Robert. *Mesmerism and the End of Enlightenment in France*. Cambridge, Mass., 1968.

David, Jacques-Louis. "Discours sur la nécessité de supprimer les académies, Convention Nationale, séance du 8 août 1793." Paris, 1793.

Delisle de Sales, J.-B.-I. *Vie littéraire et politique de Bailly*. [Paris], 1809.

Dujarric de la Rivière, R., and Chabrier, Madeleine. *La vie et l'oeuvre de Lavoisier*. Paris, 1959.

Fayet, Joseph. *La Révolution française et la science, 1789–1795*. Paris, 1960.

Fernand-Laurent, Camille. *Jean-Sylvain Bailly, premier maire de Paris*. Paris, 1927.

Fling, Fred M. "The *Mémoires* of Bailly." In *University Studies of the University of Nebraska* 3 (1903): 331–53.

Gillispie, Charles Coulston. "The *Encyclopédie* and the Jacobin Philosophy of Science: A Study in Ideas and Consequences." In *Critical Problems in the History of Science*, edited by Marshall Clagett, pp. 255–89. Madison, 1959.

Grimaux, Edouard. *Lavoisier, 1743–1794*. Paris, 1899.

Hahn, Roger. *The Anatomy of a Scientific Institution: The Paris Academy of Sciences, 1663–1803*. Berkeley and London, 1971.

_____. "Fourcroy, advocate of Lavoisier." *International Archives of the History of Science* 48 (1959): 285–88.

_____. "The Problems of the French Scientific Community, 1793–1795." In *Actes: XIIe Congrès International d'Histoire des Sciences: Paris 1968*, pp. 37–40. Paris, 1971.

_____. "Quelques nouveaux documents sur Jean-Sylvain Bailly." *Revue d'histoire des sciences et leurs applications*. 8 (1955): 339–40.

Hautecoeur, Louis. *Pourquoi les académies furent-elles supprimées en 1793?* Paris 1959.

Hill, Henry Bertram. "Commentary on the Papers of Charles Coulston Gillispie and L. Pearce Williams." In *Critical Problems in the History of Science*, edited by Marshall Clagett, pp. 309–16. Madison, 1959.

"Jugement rendu par le Tribunal Criminel Révolutionnaire . . . qui condamne Jean-Sylvain Bailly, ci-devant maire de Paris, à la peine de mort. . . ." Paris, 14 Brumaire, an II.

Lacroix, Sigismond, ed. *Actes de la Commune de Paris pendant le Révolution*, série 1. 7 vols. Paris, 1894–98.

Lameth, Charles de. "Réponse de M. le Président à la Municipalité, le 18 juillet 1791." [Paris, 1791].

Lavoisier, Antoine. *Oeuvres de Lavoisier*. 6 vols. Paris, 1893.

Marat, Jean-Paul. *Les charlatans modernes, ou lettres sur le charlatanisme académique*. Paris, 1791.

Mathiez, Albert. "Le massacre et le procès du Champ de Mars." *Annales ré-
    volutionnaires* 3 (1910): 1–60.
McKie, Douglas. *Antoine Lavoisier: Scientist, Economist, Social Reformer*. New
    York, 1952.
Mérard de Saint-Just. *Eloge historique de Jean-Sylvain de Bailly, au nom de la
    République des Lettres, par une société des gens de lettres*. London, 1794.
Nourrisson, J. F. *Trois révolutionnaires: Turgot, Necker, Bailly*. Paris, 1885.
Pagès, F.-X. *Nouveaux dialogues des morts*. Paris, 1800.
Pouchet, Georges. *Les sciences pendant la terreur*. Paris, 1896.
"Procès de Jean-Sylvain Bailly." Paris, 6 nivôse, an II (1793).
*Rapport des commissaires chargés par l'Académie des Sciences à l'examen du projet d'un
    nouvel Hôtel-Dieu*. Paris, 1787.
Rapport des commissaires chargés par le Roi de l'examen du magnétisme animal. Paris,
    1784.
Robiquet, Paul. "Correspondance de Bailly avec Necker." *Révolution française* 19
    (1890): 256–79.
———. "Correspondance de Bailly et de Lafayette." *Révolution française* 19
    (1890): 52–76.
———. *Le personnel municipal de Paris pendant la Révolution: Période constitution-
    nelle*. Paris, 1890.
Smith, Edwin Burrows. *Jean-Sylvain Bailly: Astronomer, Mystic, Revolutionary,
    1736–1793*. In *Transactions of the American Philosophical Society* 44 (1954):
    425–538.
Tenon, Jacques-René. *Mémoires sur les hôpitaux de Paris . . . imprimés par ordre du
    Roi*. Paris, 1788.
Teppe, Julien. *Chamfort: sa vie, son oeuvre, sa pensée*. Paris, n.d.
Velluz, Léon. *Vie de Lavoisier*. Paris, 1966.
Vergnaud, Marguerite. "Un savant pendant la Révolution." *Cahiers internationaux
    de Sociologie* 17 (1955): 138.
———, and Duveen, Denis. "L'explication de la mort de Lavoisier." *International
    Archives of the History of Science* 9 (1956): 43–50.
Williams, L. Pearce. "The Politics of Science in the French Revolution." In
    Critical Problems in the History of Science, edited by Marshall Clagett, pp.
    291–308. Madison, 1959.

Lamoignon de Malesherbes

ARCHIVES

Bibliothèque Nationale, manuscripts: fonds français 10,619, 10,620, 10,628, 12,768,
    13,735, 20,844, 21,832, 22,080, 22,085, 22,094, 22,122, 22,128, 22,182,
    22,183, 22,191; nouvelles acquisitions 501, 1183, 3345, 3531, 4544, 6211,
    20,507.

Archives Nationales: AF^{II} 2, B^1 93, C 182, C 186, C 241, C 243, F^7 4774^{18}, F^7 5618,
   H 1639, O^1 280, O^1 353, O^1 360, O^1 361, O^1 401, O^1 402, O^1 403, O^1 405, O^1 406,
   O^1 595, W 349, W 351, W 363, W 376, Z^{1}A 184, Z^{1}A 185, Z^{1}A 186, Z^{1}A 187,
   Z^{1}A 188, Z^{1}A 189.
Tocqueville Archives (microfilm): Series 177, Mi 70–Mi 218.
Rosanbo Archives (microfilm): Series 162, Mi★.

PRINTED SOURCES

Works by Lamoignon de Malesherbes

Malesherbes, Chrétien-Guillaume de Lamoignon de. "Discours de M. de
   Lamoignon de Malesherbes, premier président de la Cour des Aides de Paris
   a M. le Comte d'Artois . . . le 12 novembre 1774." N.p., [1774].
———. *Discours prononcé dans l'Académie françoise le jeudi XVI février
   M.DCC.LXXV. à la reception de M. de Lamoignon de Malesherbes*. Paris, 1775.
———. *Mémoires sur la Librairie et sur la liberté de la presse*. Paris, 1809.
———. *Mémoires sur le mariage des protestants.*[Paris, 1785–86].
———. *Observations de Lamoignon-Malesherbes sur l'histoire naturelle générale et
   particulière de Buffon et de Daubenton*. 2 vols. Paris, 1798.
———. *Oeuvres inédites de Chrétien-Guillaume Lamoignon Malesherbes, avec un
   précis historique de sa vie, ornées de son portrait*. Paris, 1808.
[———?] *Pensées et maximes de Chrétien-Guillaume Lamoignon Malesherbes . . .
   recueillies par E. L.★★★★*. Paris, 1802.

Works about Lamoignon de Malesherbes

Allison, John M. S. *Lamoignon de Malesherbes: Defender and Reformer of the French
   Monarchy, 1721–1794*. New Haven, 1938.
D'Argenson, René-Louis, Marquis. *Journal et mémoires*. Edited by E.-J.-B.
   Rathery. 9 vols. Paris, 1859–67.
Beaucourt, Marquis de. *Captivité et dernier moments de Louis XVI*, vol. 2. *Docu-
   ments officiels*. Paris, 1892.
Bickart, R. *Les parlements et la notion de souveraineté nationale au XVIIIe siècle*. Paris,
   1933.
Bluche, François. *Les magistrats du Parlement de Paris au XVIIIe siècle, 1715–1771*.
   Paris, 1956.
Boissy d'Anglas, Comte. *Essai sur la vie, les écrits et les opinions de M. de
   Malesherbes*. 3 vols. Paris, 1819–21.
Carré, Henri. *La fin des parlements, 1788–1790*. Paris, 1912.
*Catalogue des livres de la bibliothèque de feu Chrétien Guillaume Lamoignon-
   Malesherbes*. Paris, 1797.
Conte, Arthur. *Sire, ils ont voté la mort: la condamnation de Louis XVI*. Paris, 1966.
Convention Nationale. *Défense de Louis XVI, prononcée à la barre de la Convention
   nationale, le mercredi 26 decembre 1792, l'an Ier de la République, par le citoyen
   Desèze, l'un de ses défenseurs officieux*. Paris, 1792.

Delafarge, Daniel. *L'affaire de l'abbé Morellet en 1760*. Paris, 1912.

Delisle de Sales, J.-B.-I. *Malesherbes*. Paris, 1803.

Dommanget, Jean-Philippe. *Lamoignon de Malesherbes*. Metz, 1867.

Doyle, William. "The Parlements of France and the Breakdown of the Old Regime, 1771–1788." *French Historical Studies* 6 (1970): 441–53.

Dubois, Jean-Baptiste. *Notice historique sur Chrétien-Guillaume Lamoignon-Malesherbes*. Paris, 1804.

Dupont-Ferrier, G. *Les origines et le premier siècle de la Chambre ou Cour des Aides de Paris*. Paris, 1953.

Egret, Jean. *Louis XV et l'opposition parlementaire*. Paris, 1970.

———. "Malesherbes, premier président de la Cour des Aides (1750–1775)." *Revue d'histoire moderne et contemporaine* (1956), pp. 97–119.

Flammermont, Jules. *Le chancelier Maupeou et les Parlements*. Paris, 1883.

———, ed. *Remontrances du Parlement de Paris au XVIIIᵉ siècle*. 3 vols. Paris, 1888–98.

Furet, J. "Chrétien-Guillaume de Lamoignon de Malesherbes." In *Les contemporains* pp. 1–16. Paris, 1908.

Gaillard, M. *Vie ou éloge historique de M. de Malesherbes*. Paris, 1805.

Goret, Charles. *Mon témoignage sur la détention de Louis XVI et de sa famille*. Paris, 1825.

Grosclaude, Pierre. *Jean-Jacques Rousseau et Malesherbes: documents inédits*. Paris, 1960.

———. *Malesherbes: témoin et interprète de son temps*. Paris, 1961.

———, ed. *Malesherbes et son temps (suite): nouveaux documents inédits*. Paris, 1964.

Henri-Robert. *Malesherbes*. Paris, 1927.

Huë, François. *Dernières années du règne de Louis XVI*. Paris, 1811.

Hyde de Neuville, Baron. *Mémoires et souvenirs*. 3 vols. Paris, 1888.

Jacomet, Pierre. *Vicissitudes et chutes du Parlement de Paris*. Paris, 1954.

Lanfranc de Panthon, M. *La magistrature française au XVIIIᵉ siècle: étude sur Malesherbes*. Caen, 1877.

[Le Paige, Adrien]. *Lettres historiques sur les fonctions essentielles du Parlement, sur le droit des pairs et sur les lois fondamentales du royaume*. 2 vols. [Paris], 1753–54.

Martainville, A.-A. *Vie de Chrétien-Guillaume Lamoignon Malesherbes*. Paris, 1802.

Mémoires pour servir à l'histoire du Droit public de la France en matière d'impôts, ou Recueil de ce qui s'est passé de plus intéressant à la Cour des Aides depuis 1756 jusqu'au mois de juin 1775. Brussels, 1779.

Piou, G. *Malesherbes, homme public*. Toulouse, 1857.

Sainte-Beuve, C. A. "Monsieur de Malesherbes." *Causeries de lundi* 2 (Paris, 1858): 512–38.

Shaw, E. P. *Problems and Policies of Malesherbes as Directeur de la Librairie en France, 1750–1763*. Albany, 1966.

Shennan, J. H. *The Parlement of Paris*. Ithaca, 1968.

La souveraineté nationale d'après le droit public de la France (par M. de Malesherbes). Paris, 1872.

Tocqueville, Clérel, Comte de. *Episodes de la Terreur: extraits des mémoires du Comte de Tocqueville, suivis d'une lettre inédite de M. de Malesherbes*. Compiègne, 1901.
Véri, Abbé de. *Journal*. Edited by Jehan de Witte. 2 vols. Paris, 1928.
Vian, L. *Les Lamoignon, une vieille famille de robe*. Paris, 1896.
Vignaux, Eugène. *Mémoires sur Lamoignon de Malesherbes*. Paris, 1874.

General Works

PRIMARY SOURCES

D'Alembert, Jean Le Rond. *Oeuvres complètes*. 12 vols. Paris, 1821.
_____. *Preliminary Discourse to the Encyclopedia*. Translated by R. N. Schwab. Indianapolis and New York, 1963.
Alissan de Chazet. *Mémoires, souvenirs, oeuvres et portraits*. 3 vols. Paris, 1837.
Bacourt, Adrien de, ed. *Correspondance entre le Comte de Mirabeau et le Comte de la Marck*. 3 vols. Paris, 1851.
Barère, Bertrand de. *Mémoires*. Edited by Hyppolite Carnot and David d'Angers. 3 vols. Paris, 1842–44.
Barnave, Joseph. *Oeuvres*. Edited by Bérenger de la Drôme. 4 vols. Paris, 1843.
Barruel, Augustin de. *Mémoires pour servir à l'histoire du Jacobinisme*. 4 vols. London, 1797.
Baudot, Marc-Antoine. *Notes historiques sur la Convention Nationale, le Directoire, l'Empire et l'exil des votants*. Geneva, 1974.
Billaud-Varenne, J.-N. *Les élémens du républicanisme*. Paris, 1792.
Bossuet, Jacques Bénigne. *La politique tirée des propres paroles de l'Ecriture sainte*. Edited by J. Lebrun. Geneva, 1967.
Boulainvilliers, Henri de. *Essais sur la noblesse de France*. Amsterdam, 1729.
Brissot, Jacques-Pierre. *Mémoires, 1754–1793*. 2 vols. Paris, n.d.
_____. *Mémoires de Brissot*. Edited by M. de Lescure. *Bibliographie des mémoires relatifs à l'histoire de France pendant le XVIIIe siècle*, vol. 32. Paris, 1877.
Buffon, Georges Louis Leclerc, Comte de. *Buffon: Corpus général des philosophes français*. Edited by Jean Piveteau. Paris, 1954.
Burke, Edmund. *Reflections on the Revolution in France*. Edited by Thomas H. D. Mahoney. Indianapolis and New York, 1955.
Cars, Duc des. *Mémoires*. 2 vols. Paris, 1890.
Chamfort, N. S. R. *Oeuvres principales*. Edited by F. Duloup. Paris, 1960.
Chateaubriand, François-René de. *Essai historique, politique et moral sur les révolutions anciennes et modernes*. London, 1820.
_____. *Mémoires d'Outre-tombe*. 2 vols. Paris, 1966.
Condillac, Etienne Bonnot de. *Oeuvres philosophiques*. Edited by Georges Le Roy. 3 vols. Paris, 1947–51.
Condorcet, Nicolas de Caritat, Marquis de. *Eloges des académiciens de l'Académie royale des Sciences*. 5 vols. Paris, 1799.
_____. *Oeuvres*. 12 vols. Paris, 1847.

Constant, Benjamin. *Cours de politique constitutionnelle*. Edited by H. de Laboulaye. 2 vols. Paris, 1861.

Daunou, P. C. F. *Mémoires pour servir à l'histoire de la Convention Nationale*. Edited by M. F. Barrière. Paris, 1848.

Diderot, Denis. *Correspondance générale*. Edited by Georges Roth. 16 vols. Paris, 1955–70.

———. *Oeuvres complètes*. Edited by Assézat and Tourneux. 20 vols. Paris, 1875–77.

Dumouriez, Charles-François. *Mémoires du général Dumouriez, écrits par lui-même*. 2 vols. London, 1794.

Durand-Maillane, P. Y. *Histoire de la Convention Nationale*. Edited by Berville and Barrière. Paris, 1825.

Encyclopédie, ou dictionnaire raisonné des arts, des sciences et des métiers. 17 vols. Paris, 1751–65.

Fontenelle, Bernard le Bovier de. *Histoire de l'Académie Royale des Sciences*. 2 vols. The Hague, 1740. Reprint. Brussels, 1969.

———. *De l'origine des fables*. Paris, 1932.

Fournier l'Héritier, *Mémoires secrets de Fournier l'Américain*. Edited by F.-A. Aulard. Paris, 1890.

Genlis, Madame Félicité Ducrest de. *Mémoires sur le dix-huitième siècle et la Révolution*. 6 vols. Paris, 1825.

Grimm, J. M. *Correspondance littéraire*. 17 vols. Paris, 1813.

Hegel, G. W. F. *The Phenomenology of Mind*. Translated by J. Baillie. London, 1927.

Helvétius, Claude-Adrien. *De l'esprit*. 2 vols. London, 1776.

———. *Oeuvres complètes*. 5 vols. Paris, 1795.

d'Holbach, Baron Paul Henri Thiry. *Système social, ou principes de la morale et de la politique*. London, 1774.

Hume, David. *Political Essays*. Edited by C. W. Hendel. New York, 1953.

Lafayette, Gilbert du Motier, Marquis de. *Mémoires, Correspondance et Manuscrits du général Lafayette*. 6 vols. Paris and London, 1837–38.

La Fontainerie, François de, ed. *French Liberalism and Education in the Eighteenth Century*. New York and London, 1932.

Lanjuinais, Jean-Denis. *Oeuvres*. 4 vols. Paris, 1832.

Lavater, Johann Kaspar. *Aus Lavaters Brieftasche*. Edited by G. A. Müller. Munich, 1897.

Lepeletier de Saint-Fargeau, Michel de. *Oeuvres*. Brussels, 1826.

Louvet, J.-B. *Mémoires*. Edited by F.-A. Aulard. Paris, 1889.

Mably, Gabriel Bonnot de. *Observations sur l'histoire de France*. 2 vols. Geneva, 1765.

Malherbe, François de. *Oeuvres poétiques*. Paris, 1972.

Mallet du Pan, Jacques. *Considérations sur la nature de la Révolution en France*. London, 1793.

Malouet, Pierre-Victor. *Mémoires*. 2 vols. Paris, 1868.

Marat, Jean-Paul. *Correspondance*. Edited by C. Vellay. Paris, 1908.

Mathiez, Albert, ed. *Le Club des Cordeliers pendant la crise de Varennes et le massacre du Champ de Mars*. Paris, 1910.

Maupeouana. 12 vols. Paris, 1773.

Mercier, Louis-Sébastien. *Le Nouveau Paris*. 6 vols. Brunswick, 1800.

————. *Tableau de Paris*. 12 vols. Amsterdam, 1788.

Mirabeau, Gabriel-Honoré de Riquetti, Comte de. *Des lettres de cachet et des prisons d'Etat*. 2 vols., Hambuɪg, 1782.

Molleville, Bertrand de. *Mémoires secrets pour servir à l'histoire de la dernière année de Louis XVI*. 3 vols. London, 1797.

Montchrétien, Antoine de. *Traicté de l'économie politique*. Edited by T. Funck-Brentano. 2 vols. Paris, 1889.

Montesquieu, Charles-Louis de Secondat, Baron de. *De l'esprit des lois*. Edited by Gonzague Truc. 2 vols. Paris, 1961.

————. *Lettres persanes*. Edited by G. Truc. Paris, 1946.

————. *Oeuvres*. Edited by R. Caillois. 2 vols. Paris, 1949.

Morellet, Abbé. *Mémoires sur le dix-huitième siècle et sur la Révolution*. 2 vols. Paris, 1821.

Morris, Gouverneur. *A Diary of the French Revolution*. 2 vols. Boston, 1939.

Mounier, Jacques-Joseph. *Considérations sur les gouvernemens, et principalement celui qui convient à la France*. Paris, 1789.

Necker, Jacques. *De l'administration des finances en France*. 3 vols. Paris, 1784.

————. *Sur l'administration de M. Necker*. Amsterdam, 1791.

Restif de la Bretonne, Nicolas Edme. *Les nuits de Paris, ou le spectateur nocturne*. 14 vols. London, 1788–89.

Robert, François. *Avantages de la fuite de Louis XVI et nécessité d'un nouveau gouvernement*. Paris and Lyons, 1791.

Robespierre, Maximilien. *Discours et rapports à la Convention*. Paris, 1965.

————. *Oeuvres complètes*. Vol. 5, *Lettres à ses commetans*, edited by G. Laurent. Gap, 1961. Vol. 8, *Discours*. Paris, 1954. Vol. 10, *Discours*. Paris, 1965.

Roland de la Platière, Madame. *Mémoires de Madame Roland*. Edited by C. Perroud. 2 vols. Paris, 1905.

Rousseau, Jean-Jacques. *Correspondance générale*. Edited by T. Dufour. 21 vols. Paris, 1924–32.

————. *Emile, ou de l'éducation*. Edited by F. Richard. Paris, 1960.

————. *Oeuvres complètes*. Edited by M. Raymond and B. Gagnebin. 4 vols. Paris, 1959—.

————. *Political Writings*. Edited by C. E. Vaughan. 2 vols. New York, 1962.

Saint-Just, Louis Antoine Léon de. *Oeuvres choisies*. Introduced by D. Mascolo. Paris, 1968.

Saint-Pierre, J.-H. Bernardin de. *Oeuvres complètes*. 12 vols. Paris, 1826.

Seyssel, Claude de. *La monarchie de France*. Edited by J. Poujol. Paris, 1961.

Sieyès, Emmanuel-Joseph. *Qu'est-ce que le Tiers Etat?* Edited by R. Zapperi. Geneva, 1970.

Soboul, Albert, ed. *Le procès de Louis XVI*. Paris, 1966.

Staël, Germaine de. *Considérations sur la Révolution française*. 3 vols. Paris, 1820.

Suard, J. B. A. *Mélanges de la littérature*. 5 vols. Paris, 1804.

Talleyrand, Charles-Maurice de. *Mémoires du prince de Talleyrand*. Edited by Duc de Broglie. 5 vols. Paris, 1891–92.

Thibaudeau, A. C. *Mémoires sur la Convention et le Directoire*. Edited by Berville and Barrière. Paris, 1824.

Turgot, Anne-Robert-Jacques de. *Oeuvres de Turgot et les documents le concernant*. Edited by Gustave Schelle. 5 vols. Paris, 1913–23.

———. *Turgot on Progress, Sociology and Economics*. Edited by R. L. Meek. Cambridge, 1973.

Vie politique de Jérôme Pétion. N.p., [1793?].

Voltaire, François-Marie Arouet de. *Oeuvres complètes*. Edited by Garnier. 52 vols. Paris, 1877–82.

———. *Oeuvres historiques*. Edited by R. Pomeau. Paris, 1962.

———. *Voltaire's Correspondance*. Edited by T. Besterman. 107 vols. Geneva, 1953–65.

Walzer, Michael, ed. *Regicide and Revolution: Speeches at the Trial of Louis XVI*. Cambridge, 1974.

Young, Arthur. *Travels in France*. Edited by C. Maxwell. Cambridge, 1927.

SECONDARY SOURCES

Adam, Antoine. *Du mysticisme à la révolte: les Jansénistes du XVIIIᵉ siècle*. Paris, 1968.

Althusser, Louis. *Politics and History: Montesquieu, Rousseau, Hegel and Marx*. Translated by Ben Brewster. London, 1972.

Arendt, Hannah. *On Revolution*. New York, 1963.

Aulard, F.-A. *The French Revolution: A Political History*. Translated by B. Miall. London, 1910.

———. "Patrie, patriotisme sous Louis XVI et dans les cahiers." *Révolution française* 68 (1915): 301–39.

Bachelard, Gaston. *La formation de l'esprit scientifique*. Paris, 1947.

Baehrel, René. "La haine de classe en temps d'épidémie." *Annales E.S.C.*, July–September 1952, pp. 351–60.

Baker, Keith M. *Condorcet: From Natural Philosophy to Social Mathematics*. Chicago, 1975.

———. "French Political Thought at the Accession of Louis XVI." *Journal of Modern History* 50 (June 1978): 279–303.

Barber, Elinor G. *The Bourgeoisie in Eighteenth Century France*. Princeton, 1955.

Belin, Jean. *La logique d'une idée force: l'idée d'utilité sociale et la Révolution française, 1789–1792*. Paris, 1939.

Bellanger, Claude et al. *Histoire générale de la presse française*. Vol. I, *Des origines à 1814*. Paris, 1969.

Bénichou, Paul. *Le sacre de l'écrivain, 1750–1830*. Paris, 1973.

Biré, Edmond. *Les défenseurs de Louis XVI*. Lyons, 1896.

Blanc, Louis. *Histoire de la Révolution française*. 11 vols. Paris, 1858.

Bluche, François. *La vie quotidienne de la noblesse française au XVIIIe siècle*. Paris, 1973.

Bouloiseau, Marc. *Le comité de salut public*. Paris, 1968.

_____. *La République jacobine, 10 août 1792–9 Thermidor, an II*. Paris, 1972.

Cahen, Léon. *Les querelles religieuses et parlementaires sous Louis XV*. Paris, 1913.

Calvet, Henri. *Un instrument de la Terreur à Paris: le Comité de Salut Public ou de surveillance du Département de Paris*. Paris, 1941.

Campardon, Emile. *Le tribunal révolutionnaire de Paris*. 2 vols. Paris, 1866.

Carcassonne, Elie. *Montesquieu et le problème de la constitution française au XVIIIe siècle*. Paris, 1926.

Cassirer, Ernst. *The Philosophy of the Enlightenment*. Translated by Fritz C. A. Koelln and James P. Pettegrove. Boston, 1955.

_____. *The Philosophy of Symbolic Forms*. Vol. 3, *The Phenomenology of Knowledge*, translated by Ralph Manheim. New Haven, 1952.

Castries, Duc de (René de La Croix). *Mirabeau, ou l'échec du destin*. Paris, 1960.

Cavanaugh, Gerald J. "Turgot: The Rejection of Enlightened Despotism." *French Historical Studies* 6 (Spring 1969): 31–58.

Censer, Jack Richard. *Prelude to Power: The Paris Radical Press*. Baltimore and London, 1976.

Chaunu, Pierre. *La Civilisation de l'Europe des lumières*. Paris, 1971.

_____. *La mort à Paris, 16e, 17e, 18e siècles*. Paris, 1978.

Chaussinand-Nogaret, Guy. "Aux origines de la Révolution: noblesse et bourgeoisie." *Annales E.S.C.*, March–June 1975, pp. 265–78.

Chevallier, J.-J. *Barnave, ou les deux faces de la Révolution, 1761–1793*. Paris, 1936.

Chevallier, Pierre. *Histoire de la Franc-Maçonnerie française*. Vol. 1, *La Maçonnerie, école de l'égalité, 1725–1799*. Paris, 1974.

Chèvremont, F. *Jean-Paul Marat, esprit politique*. 2 vols. Paris, 1880.

Chill, Emanuel, ed. *Power, Property, and History: Joseph Barnave's Introduction to the French Revolution and Other Writings*. New York, 1971.

Cobb, Richard. *Reactions to the French Revolution*. London, New York, Toronto, 1972.

_____. *Terreur et subsistances, 1793–1795*. Paris, 1965.

Cobban, Alfred. *Aspects of the French Revolution*. New York, 1970.

_____. "The *Parlements* of France in the Eighteenth Century." *History*, February–June 1950, pp. 16–32.

Cochin, Augustin. *La Révolution et la libre pensée: la socialisation de la pensée (1750–1789); la socialisation de la personne (1793–1794); la socialisation des biens (1793–1794)*. Paris, 1924.

_____. *Les sociétés de la pensée et la démocratie: études d'histoire révolutionnaire*. Paris, 1921.

Dakin, Douglas. *Turgot and the Ancien Régime in France*. New York, 1965.

Darin, M. V. *Bossuet, Port-Royal et la Franc-Maçonnerie*. Paris, n.d.

Daumard, A., and Furet, F. *Structures et relations sociales à Paris au XVIIIe siècle*. Paris, 1961.

Découflé, André. "L'aristocratie française devant l'opinion publique à la veille de

la Révolution (1787–1789)." In *Etudes d'histoire économique et sociale du XVIII*
siècle, edited by A. Découflé, F. Boulanger, B.-A. Pierrelle. Paris, 1966.

Derathé, Robert. *Jean-Jacques Rousseau et la science politique de son temps*. Paris, 1950.

Di Padova, Theodore A. "The Girondins and the Question of Revolutionary Government." *French Historical Studies* 9 (Spring 1976): 432–50.

Egret, Jean. *La pré-révolution française, 1787–1789*. Paris, 1962.

Ehrard, Jean. *L'idée de nature en France à l'aube des lumières*. Paris, 1970.

Faure, Edgar. *La disgrâce de Turgot*. Paris, 1961.

Favre, Robert. *La mort dans la littérature et la pensée françaises au XVIIIe siècle*. 2 vols. Lille, 1977.

———. *La mort au siècle des lumières*. Lyons, 1978.

Ford, Franklin L. *Robe and Sword: The Regrouping of the French Aristocracy after Louis XIV*. Cambridge, Mass., 1962.

Forster, Robert, and Greene, Jack P. eds. *Preconditions of Revolution in Early Modern Europe*. Baltimore and London, 1970.

Fox-Genovese, Elizabeth. *The Origins of Physiocracy*. Ithaca, 1976.

"Franc-Maçonnerie et la Révolution française." *Annales historique de la Révolution française*, numéro spécial: July–September 1969.

Fugier, André. *La Révolution française et l'Empire napoléonien. Histoire des relations internationales*, edited by Pierre Renouvin, vol. 4. Paris, 1954.

Furet, François. *Penser la Révolution française*. Paris, 1978.

———, et al. *Livre et société dans la France du XVIIIe siècle*, vol. 2. Paris and The Hague, 1970.

———, and Richet, Denis. *La Révolution française*. Paris, 1965.

Gaxotte, Pierre. *La Révolution française*. Paris, 1928.

Gay, Peter. *The Enlightenment: An Interpretation*. Vol. 1, *The Rise of Modern Paganism*. New York, 1966. Vol. 2, *The Science of Freedom*. New York, 1969.

Giscard d'Estaing, François; Fleury, Michel; Brandenburg, Alain-Erlande. *Les Rois retrouvés: Notre-Dame de Paris*. Paris, 1977.

Godechot, Jacques. *La contre-révolution, 1789–1804*. Paris, 1961.

———. *Les institutions de la France sous la Révolution et l'Empire*. Paris, 1951.

———. "Nation, patrie, nationalisme et patriotisme en France au XVIIIe siècle." *Annales historiques de la Révolution française*, no. 206 (1971), pp. 481–501.

Godfrey, J. L. *Revolutionary Justice: A Study of the Organization, Personnel, and Procedure of the Paris Tribunal, 1793–1795*. Chapel Hill, 1951.

Goetz-Bernstein, H. A. *La politique extérieure de Brissot et des Girondins*. Paris, 1912.

Goldmann, Lucien. *The Philosophy of the Enlightenment: The Christian Burgess and the Enlightenment*. Translated by Henry Maas. London, 1973.

Gottschalk, Louis. *Jean-Paul Marat: A Study in Radicalism*. Chicago, 1967.

———, and Maddox, Margaret. *Lafayette in the French Revolution Through the October Days*. Chicago, 1969.

Goubert, Pierre. *L'Ancien régime*. 2 vols. Paris, 1969.

———, and Denis, Michel, eds. *1789: Les Français ont la parole*. Paris, 1964.

Greer, Donald. *The Incidence of the Terror during the French Revolution: A Statistical Interpretation*. Cambridge, Mass., 1935.

Grimsley, Ronald. *Jean d'Alembert, 1717–1783*. Oxford, 1963.

Groethuysen, Bernard. *The Bourgeois: Catholicism vs. Capitalism in Eighteenth-Century France*. Translated by Mary Ilford. New York, Chicago, San Francisco, 1968.

————. *Philosophie de la Révolution française*. Paris, 1956.

Guéhenno, Jean. *Jean-Jacques Rousseau*. 2 vols. Paris, 1962.

Gusdorf, Georges. *L'avènement des sciences humaines au siècle des lumières*. Paris, 1973.

————. *Dieu, la nature, l'homme au siècle des lumières*. Paris, 1972.

————. *Les principes de la pensée au siècle des lumières*. Paris, 1971.

Hampson, Norman. *A Social History of the French Revolution*. Toronto, 1963.

Harding, Robert R. *Anatomy of a Power Elite: The Provincial Governors of Early Modern France*. New Haven and London, 1978.

Hazard, Paul. *The European Mind, 1680–1715*. Cleveland and New York, 1963.

————. *European Thought in the Eighteenth Century: From Montesquieu to Lessing*. Cleveland and New York, 1965.

Hirschman, Albert O. *The Passions and the Interests*. Princeton, 1977.

Hubert, René. *Rousseau et l'Encyclopédie*. Paris, 1928.

————. *Les sciences sociales dans l'Encyclopédie*. Paris, 1923.

Hyslop, Beatrice Fry. *French Nationalism in 1789, According to the General Cahiers*. New York, 1934.

Jacob, Louis. *Les suspects pendant la Révolution, 1789–1794*. Paris, 1952.

Jaurès, Jean. *Histoire socialiste de la Révolution française*. 9 vols., Paris, 1904–11.

Jette, Marie Henri. *La France religieuse au XVIIIe siècle*. Paris and Tournai, 1956.

Johnson, Douglas, ed. *French Society and the Revolution*. Cambridge, 1976.

Kafker, F. A. "Les Encyclopédistes et la Terreur." *Revue d'histoire moderne et contemporaine* 14 (1967): 284–95.

Kelly, George Armstrong. "Conceptual Sources of the Terror." *Eighteenth-Century Studies* 14 (Fall 1980): 18–36.

————. "Duelling in Eighteenth-Century France: Archaeology, Rationale, Implications." *The Eighteenth Century* 21 (1980): 236–54.

————. "From Lèse-Majesté to Lèse-Nation: Treason in Eighteenth-Century France." *Journal of the History of Ideas* 42 (1981): 269–86.

————. "The History of the New Hero: Eulogy and its Sources in Eighteenth-Century France." *The Eighteenth Century* 21 (1980): 3–24.

Keohane, Nannerl O. *Philosophy and the State in France*. Princeton, 1980.

Kerr, Wilfred B. *The Reign of Terror, 1793–94*. Toronto, 1927.

Kors, Alan Charles. *D'Holbach's Coterie: An Enlightenment in Paris*. Princeton, 1976.

Krieger, Leonard. *Kings and Philosophers, 1689–1789*. New York, 1970.

Kuhn, Thomas. *The Structure of Scientific Revolutions*. 2d ed. Chicago, 1962.

Labrousse, Ernest. *La crise de l'économie française à la fin de l'Ancien Régime et au début de la Révolution*. Paris, 1944.

Lacour-Gayet, G. *La Marine militaire de la France sous le règne de Louis XVI*. Paris, 1905.

Lacretelle, Charles de. *Histoire de la Révolution française*. 5 vols. Paris, 1824–25.

Le Bihan, Alain. *Francs-Maçons parisiens du Grand Orient de France, fin du XVIIIe siècle*. Paris, 1966.

————. *Loges et chapitres de la Grande Loge et du Grand Orient de France (2e moitié du XVIIIe siècle)*, Paris, 1967.

Lefebvre, Georges. *The Coming of the French Revolution*. Translated by R. R. Palmer. Princeton, 1947.

————. *The French Revolution from 1793 to 1795*. Translated by J. H. Stewart and J. Friguglietti. London and New York, 1964.

————. *La grande peur*. Paris, 1932.

————. "La Révolution et le rationalisme." *Annales historiques de la Révolution française*, January–March 1946, pp. 4–34.

Lenôtre, Georges. *The Tribunal of the Terror*. Translated by Frederic Lees. Philadelphia and London, 1909.

Ligou, Daniel. "La Franc-Maçonnerie au XVIIIe siècle (position des problèmes et état des questions)." *L'Information historique*, May–June 1964, pp. 98–110.

Louie, Richard. "The Incidence of the Terror: A Critique of Statistical Interpretation." *French Historical Studies* 3 (Spring 1964): 379–89.

Madelin, Louis. *The French Revolution*. New York, 1923.

Manceron, Claude. *Les hommes de la liberté*. Vol. 1, *Les vingt ans du Roi*. Paris, 1972. Vol. 2, *Le vent d'Amérique*. Paris, 1974. Vol. 3, *Le bon plaisir*. Paris, 1976.

Manfred, A. Z. "La nature du pouvoir jacobin." *La Pensée*, no. 150 (1970), pp. 62–83.

Manuel, Frank. *The Eighteenth Century Confronts the Gods*. Cambridge, Mass., 1959.

Martin, Gaston. *La Franc-Maçonnerie française et la préparation de la Révolution*. Paris, 1926.

Martin, Kingsley. *French Liberal Thought in the Eighteenth Century*. New York, 1963.

Mathiez, Albert. "Les doctrines politiques des physiocrates." *Annales historiques de la Révolution française*. March–April 1936, pp. 193–203.

————. *The French Revolution*. Translated by C. A. Phillips. New York, 1962.

————. *Girondins et Montagnards*. Paris, 1921.

————. "Les philosophes et le pouvoir au milieu du XVIIIe siècle." *Annales historiques de la Révolution française*, January–February 1935, pp. 1–12.

————. *La vie chère et le mouvement social sous la Terreur*. 2 vols. Paris, 1973.

Maurin, Albert. *Galerie historique de la Révolution française*. Vol. 2. Paris, 1848.

Meinecke, Friedrich. *Historism: The Rise of a New Historical Outlook*. Translated by J. E. Anderson. London, 1972.

Merleau-Ponty, Maurice. *Humanism and Terror*. Translated by John O'Neill. Boston, 1969.

Michelet, Jules. *Histoire de la Révolution française*. 5 vols. Paris, 1889.

Mignet, F. A. *Histoire de la Révolution française*. 2 vols. Paris, 1836.

Minogue, Kenneth. *The Liberal Mind*. New York, 1968.

Mornet, Daniel. *Les origines intellectuelles de la Révolution française*. Paris, 1934.

Mortimer-Ternaux, M. *Histoire de la Terreur*. 7 vols. Paris, 1862–69.

Mousnier, Roland; Labrousse, Ernest; and Bouloiseau, Marc. *Le XVIIIe siècle, révolution intellectuelle, technique et politique, 1715–1815*. Paris, 1953.

Olivier-Martin, F. *Histoire du droit français des origines à la Révolution*. N.p., 1948.

Ollivier, Albert. *Saint-Just et la force des choses*. Paris, 1954.

Palmer, Robert R. *The Age of Democratic Revolutions*. 2 vols. Princeton, 1969.

————. *Catholics and Unbelievers in Eighteenth Century France*. Princeton, 1939.

————. *Twelve Who Ruled: The Year of Terror in the French Revolution*. Princeton, 1970.

Parker, Harold T. *The Cult of Antiquity and the French Revolution*. Chicago, 1937.

Parquez, Jacques. *La bulle Unigénitus et le Jansénisme politique*. Paris, 1936.

Plongeron, Bernard. *Conscience religieuse en Révolution*. Paris, 1969.

Proust, Jacques. *Diderot et l'Encyclopédie*. Paris, 1962.

Ranum, Orest. "Personality and Politics in the *Persian Letters*." *Political Science Quarterly* 84 (1969): 606–27.

Reill, Peter Hanns. *The German Enlightenment and the Rise of Historicism*. Berkeley, Los Angeles, and London, 1975.

Reinhard, Marcel. *La chute de la royauté*. Paris, 1969.

————. "Elite et noblesse dans la seconde moitié du XVIIIe siècle." *Revue d'histoire moderne et contemporaine* 3 (1956): 5–37.

Rémusat, Charles de. *Mémoires de ma vie*. Edited by C. H. Pouthas. 5 vols. Paris, 1958–67.

Richet, Denis. "Autour des origines idéologiques lointaines de la Révolution française: élites et despotismes." *Annales E.S.C.* 26 (1971): 255–89.

Robin, Régine. *Histoire et linguistique*. Paris, 1973.

Roblot, René. *La justice criminelle en France sous la Terreur*. Paris, 1938.

Roche, Daniel. *Le siècle des lumières en province: Académies et académiciens provinciaux, 1680–1789*. 2 vols. Paris, 1978.

Rocquain, Félix. *L'esprit révolutionnaire avant la Révolution, 1715–1789*. Paris, 1878.

Roger, Jacques. *Les sciences de la vie dans la pensée française au XVIIIe siècle*. Paris, 1971.

Roustan, Marius. *Les philosophes et la société française au XVIIIe siècle*. Lyons and Paris, 1906.

Rudé, George. *The Crowd in the French Revolution*. Oxford 1959.

————. "The Outbreak of the French Revolution." *Past and Present* 8 (1955): 28–42.

————. *Robespierre: Portrait of a Revolutionary Democrat*. New York, 1975.

Sanson, Henri. *Mémoires des Sanson: sept générations d'exécuteurs, 1688–1847*. 6 vols. Paris, 1862.

Schelle, Gustave. *Du Pont de Nemours et l'école physiocratique*. Paris, 1888.

Scott, William. *Terror and Repression in Revolutionary Marseilles*. London, 1973.

Sée, Henri. *Economic and Social Conditions in France During the Eighteenth Century*. Translated by E. H. Zeydel. New York, 1927.

Seligman, Edmond. *La Justice en France pendant la Révolution*. 2 vols. Paris, 1913.

Shackleton, Robert. "Jansenism and the Enlightenment." *Studies on Voltaire and the Eighteenth Century* 57 (1967): 1387–97.

Shklar, Judith N. *Men and Citizens*. Cambridge, 1969.

Skinner, Quentin. "Meaning and Understanding in the History of Ideas." *History and Theory* 8 (1969): 3–53.

Soboul, Albert. *La France à la veille de la Révolution*. Paris, 1966.

———. *Histoire de la Révolution française*. 2 vols. Paris, 1962.

———. *Précis d'histoire de la Révolution française*. Paris, 1962.

———. *Les sans-culottes parisiens en l'an II*. Paris, 1962.

———. *La société française dans la seconde moitié du XVIIIe siècle*. Paris, 1969.

Sorel, Albert. *L'Europe et la Révolution française*. 8 vols. Paris, 1904–11.

Starobinski, Jean. *1789: Les emblèmes de la raison*. Paris, 1973.

———. *Trois fureurs: essais*. Paris, 1973.

Sydenham, M. J. *The French Revolution*. London, 1969.

———. *The Girondins*. London, 1961.

Taine, Hyppolite. *Les origines de la France contemporaine*. 6 vols. Paris, 1876–93.

Taveneaux, René, ed. *Jansénisme et politique*. Paris, 1965.

Thiers, Adolphe. *The History of the French Revolution*. Translated by Frederick Shoberl. 5 vols. London, 1838.

Thompson, J. M. *Robespierre and the French Revolution*. New York, 1971.

Tocqueville, Alexis de. *Democracy in America*. Translated by Henry Reeve. 2 vols. New York, 1945.

———. *The Old Regime and the French Revolution*. Translated by Stuart Gilbert. New York, 1955.

Ullmann, Walter. *A History of Political Thought: The Middle Ages*. Harmondsworth, England, 1965.

Van Kley, Dale. "Church, State, and the Ideological Origins of the French Revolution: The Debate over the General Assembly of the Gallican Clergy in 1765." *Journal of Modern History* 51, 1 (1979): 629–66.

———. *The Jansenists and the Expulsion of the Jesuits from France, 1757–1765*. New Haven and London, 1975.

Vovelle, Michel. *La chute de la monarchie, 1787–1792*. Paris, 1972.

———, ed. *Mourir autrefois: attitudes collectives devant la mort aux XVIIe et XVIIIe siècles*. Paris, 1974.

———. *Religion et Révolution: la déchristianisation de l'an II*. Paris, 1976.

Wade, Ira O. *The Structure and Form of the French Enlightenment*. 2 vols. Princeton, 1977.

Wallon, Henri. *Le tribunal révolutionnaire de Paris*. 6 vols. Paris, 1880.

Walter, Gérard. *Histoire de la Terreur, 1793–1794*. Paris, 1937.

———. *Marat*. Paris, 1953.

———. "Le problème de la dictature jacobine." *Annales historiques de la Révolution française*. November–December 1931, pp. 515–29.

———. *La Révolution française vue par ses journaux*. Paris, 1948.
Welch, Oliver J. G. *Mirabeau: A Study of a Democratic Monarchist*. London, 1951.
Weulersse, Georges. *La physiocratie à la fin du règne de Louis XV*. Paris, 1959.
———. *La physiocratie sous les ministères de Turgot et de Necker*. Paris, 1950.
White, Hayden. *Metahistory: The Historical Imagination in Nineteenth-Century Europe*. Baltimore and London, 1975.
Wilson, Arthur M. *Diderot: The Testing Years, 1713–1759*. Oxford, 1957.

Index